POWERS OF PILGRIMAGE

Powers of Pilgrimage

Religion in a World of Movement

Simon Coleman

NEW YORK UNIVERSITY PRESS
New York

NEW YORK UNIVERSITY PRESS
New York
www.nyupress.org

References to Internet websites (URLs) were accurate at the time of writing. Neither the author nor New York University Press is responsible for URLs that may have expired or changed since the manuscript was prepared.

Library of Congress Cataloging-in-Publication Data
Names: Coleman, Simon, 1963– author.
Title: Powers of pilgrimage : religion in a world of movement / Simon Coleman.
Description: New York : New York University Press, [2021] |
Includes bibliographical references and index.
Identifiers: LCCN 2021009003 | ISBN 9780814717288 (hardback) |
ISBN 9781479811946 (paperback) | ISBN 9780814717295 (ebook) |
ISBN 9781479811953 (ebook other)
Subjects: LCSH: Pilgrims and pilgrimages. | Voyages and travels.
Classification: LCC BL619.P5 C654 2021 | DDC 203/.51—dc23
LC record available at https://lccn.loc.gov/2021009003

New York University Press books are printed on acid-free paper, and their binding materials are chosen for strength and durability. We strive to use environmentally responsible suppliers and materials to the greatest extent possible in publishing our books.

Manufactured in the United States of America

10 9 8 7 6 5 4 3 2 1

Also available as an ebook

To Leslie

CONTENTS

Introduction

Encounters and Approaches

Encounters

On a beautiful spring afternoon, I found myself in the grounds of Canterbury Cathedral.[1] Dusk was about to fall, and having spent all day at a nearby conference, I felt happy to wander around at my own pace, half listening to the murmured, multilingual conversations of sightseers as they rambled through the close. Eventually, I entered the building itself. I had visited the place many times before—and had even carried out fieldwork there—but the cathedral is always liable to feature something new.[2] It serves as the worldwide center of the Anglican communion but is also a famous pilgrimage site, commemorating the martyrdom of Archbishop Thomas Becket in 1170. Nowadays, it houses a multimillion-pound heritage project called the Canterbury Journey.[3]

My decision to go in was well rewarded. Joining the usual mixture of visitors—pilgrims, day-trippers, schoolchildren—I became engrossed in a temporary exhibition scattered throughout the nave of the building, like so many stations of the cross. People moved among its various parts, sometimes with reverence, always with deliberation. The objects of our attention were piles of old clothes—creased, jumbled, chaotic—placed alongside shoes worn out by overuse. Just below the ceiling, surreally, another tattered bundle of garments hovered far above the ground.

The exhibition was the work of renowned war artist Arabella Dorman, a result of her collaboration with an Anglican Diocese in gathering possessions discarded by refugees from around the world who had ended up in Lesbos and Calais.[4] Her aim was to display objects that had recently been in contact with the otherwise anonymous bodies of people fleeing to Europe for a better life. Reframed by the artist, these clothes

and shoes constituted secular relics of human travail and a deeply un-
settled European landscape, marked once more by bitter disputes over
political borders and forms of belonging. Staring at them, I recalled that
in 2015, the British prime minister David Cameron had used the word
swarm to describe refugees camped in Calais, stoking a moral panic
around the specter of unchecked human movement.[5] In doing so, he
played on anxieties that would have disastrous consequences for his own
career, contributing to the anti-Europe, pro-Brexit vote that led to his
resignation a year later.[6]

Dorman titled her work *Suspended*, and the artistic metaphor had
both temporal and territorial dimensions, depicting the refugee experience of separation from everyday life alongside the vertiginous, physical
precarity of enforced migration. Such ongoing suffering differed from
the brutal martyrdom of Archbishop Becket, the event at the center of
Canterbury's famous pilgrimage. Nonetheless, the close juxtaposition of
two forms of sacrifice, separated by nearly eight and a half centuries, did
not seem out of place.

It might seem strange to embark on a book about pilgrimage by describing a chance encounter with an exhibition taking place within a
famous Christian shrine. I have not depicted a fervent prayer, a pious
procession, or an episode of miraculous healing. Instead, I have focused
on everyday objects transfigured into politicized art. Some of the visitors who toured the exhibit probably did see themselves as pilgrims.
Most, I suspect, did not. Yet Dorman's work points directly to some
of the central concerns of this book: the continued and often growing
salience of places and tropes of pilgrimage in the contemporary world
and the complexity, ambiguity, serendipity, and frequent diffuseness of
such salience. The instances of pilgrimage described in this book include
activities at the center of sacred shrines alongside others at the periph-
eries of such spaces. We will explore what happens at sites themselves
but also the preparations for, and the aftermath of, going on pilgrimage.
This book traces both formal and informal ritual behaviors as they are
manifested in and around sacred locations, but it also argues for a much
wider understanding of pilgrimage as a religious and cultural field.[7] At
its broadest level, this book presents a new way of recognizing, describing, and analyzing the significance of pilgrimage as a human activity. In
doing so, it offers a new theoretical lexicon and framework for explor-

ing pilgrimage, while demonstrating how it should be understood not solely as going to, staying at, and leaving a sacred location but also as manifested in much more disparate times, places, scales, positionalities, and practices.

The book focuses on contemporary instances of pilgrimage. But that does not mean it ignores the significance of the past. We will note, for instance, how many religious traditions have built stories of travel into accounts of their foundation. The Israelites engaged in exodus from Egypt, wandering with Moses until they reached the Promised Land, and major Jewish festivals often incorporate dimensions of mobility.[8] The biography of the Muslim prophet Muhammad is marked by his struggle with the Quraysh for the right to conduct the pilgrimage to Mecca. The Buddha left a life of ease to become an ascetic, spending decades moving throughout the Indian subcontinent. Jesus trekked across what many now call the Holy Land, taking apostles with him—and in some narratives engaged in even more traveling, such as ending up in the pilgrimage site of Glastonbury in the southwest of England (Bowman 2008). The founders of many of today's prominent religions were associated with religiously inspired movement, even as their message encouraged a shift away from local cultic celebrations toward adopting wider ethical, social, and geographical perspectives.

Pilgrimage is particularly fascinating as a form of embodied historiography, a reconstituting of history that can be done through ritual acts and material objects as well as through words. Indeed, a place such as Canterbury provides a seductive physical and imaginative pathway to the past; the visitor is invited to recall Becket's last journey to the cathedral, the many centuries of faithful pilgrims who followed after him, and the literary heritage of Chaucer's famous fourteenth-century *Canterbury Tales*.[9] Yet it is a sociological truism that such connections with the past are rarely direct, since traditions must constantly be invented anew to retain their social and cultural power.[10]

The capacity of contemporary pilgrimage to evoke history cannot fully explain its current popularity as both practice and idea in many parts of the world. As a regular or occasional pastime, pilgrimage has arguably been one of the great cultural success stories of the past century or so, the very period when large parts of the world (focused on but not confined to Euro-America) are supposed to have been abandoning conventional patterns of religious engagement, obligation, and worship.[11] While older, well-established shrines within Catholicism such as Santiago de Compostela in Spain have experienced significant growth in visitors since the 1990s, even a recently formed site such as Medjugorje in Bosnia-Herzegovina, which initially rose to prominence after visions of the Virgin Mary were recounted by a group of young people in 1981, now attracts over a million people a year.[12] The Shikoku pilgrimage, a 1,400-kilometer-long route around a Japanese island that involves the pilgrim visiting eighty-eight Buddhist temples, has been drawing more and more people to its pathways, around two hundred thousand according to a report from 2020.[13] Indeed, the numbers now visiting some sites in the world are truly extraordinary. The Muslim Hajj—the annual pilgrimage to Mecca in Saudi Arabia—regularly attracts well over two million people from around the world, even though a quota system keeps the numbers down to (barely) manageable proportions.[14] The Hindu pilgrimage festival Kumbh Mela attracts tens of millions, making it possibly the largest number of people ever assembled—however loosely—for a common purpose. A BBC report on the 2019 festival revels in the statistics: a budget of nearly $400 million US, visitors over forty-nine days totaling more than the combined populations of Britain and Spain, and almost two hundred miles of roads laid around the festival grounds in Uttar Pradesh, northern India.[15]

While nostalgia has often played a role in reviving the image of the pilgrim, we must also look elsewhere—to contemporary manifestations of mobility, to novel varieties of religion, to creative forms of ritual construction and engagement, to shifting forms of materiality and consumption—if we are to comprehend the social, economic, cultural, technological, and religious forces behind the apparent resurgence of pilgrimage and pilgrimage-related practices. We should also question the universality of conventional Western assumptions of what religion is and where it should be located, including the notion that "genuine" pilgrimage needs to be associated with discrete, formally recognized and intensely experienced forms of religiosity. A further problem relates to scale; we might be dazzled by the size of the Kumbh Mela or surprised by the number of people apparently interested in Santiago de Compostela, yet such numbers not only conceal a multitude of motivations but also tempt us to focus on more spectacular concentrations of pilgrimage activity rather than taking into account the dispersed, fragmented quality of many pilgrimage practices.

Most significant for this book's argument is something else that Dorman's exhibition suggests: the possibility of multiple *articulations*—interrelations of varying degrees of flexibility, explicitness and force—between whatever is recognized as pilgrimage and apparently very different activities. Consider how *Suspended* highlighted and ritualized the plight of refugees whose abandoned clothes were allowed to gain a prominent place at Canterbury but whose bodies had been detained at a distant border.[16] In other words, the first reference to pilgrimage in this book does not encourage us to head toward an isolated shrine at the top of a steep mountain or to locate the spectacular meeting place of sacred rivers. Rather, it situates us in the center of a bustling city and is focused on a troubled confluence of seemingly incompatible forms of mobility, ranging from pious movement to casual tourism to forced migration. This example forces us to ask where pilgrimage ends and other forms of displacement begin, or rather, how different forms of movement may become interwoven in powerful but complex ways. While *Suspended* was based in a Christian venue, its assumed audience was not restricted to the followers of any particular religion, and it was likely to have been viewed by people of many faiths and none.

This book acknowledges the importance of self-consciously exclusive examples of pious travel. But it also suggests how we can expand our ethnographic and analytical gaze in reconsidering the salience, scope, and scale of contemporary forms of pilgrimage-related activity. It argues that we need to reflect on how pilgrimage sites, journeys, rituals, tropes, stories, and metaphors are entangled with each other and with wider aspects of people's lives, ranging from something as trivial as a stroll down the street to the magnitude of forced migration to another continent. A vital corollary of this argument is that it is important not to regard formalized or intensely focused ritual as somehow more significant or deserving of study than more diffuse or flexible practices. From this perspective, understanding why it is justifiable to analyze Dorman's exhibition through a pilgrimage frame of analysis is not a secondary question. It is just as important as observing the official liturgy that sometimes takes place around Becket's shrine, just a few meters away in the same building.

Pilgrimage, then, may be viewed as significant in part because of its deep, if not always fully acknowledged, interconnectedness with other forms of ritualized and non-ritualized activity. In practice, this observation has become increasingly prominent in writings about pilgrimage over the past couple of decades. Merely to assert the existence of connectedness does not take us very far, however. We must examine *how* and *when* links are made (or denied), and we need to develop a methodology as well as an analytical vocabulary to understand such processes and their sensitivities to social, spatial, and cultural context. This is therefore a book about pilgrimage but also an anthropological account of ritualized, materialized, narrativized forms of articulation between pilgrimage and other behaviors. Tracing varieties of articulation might involve highlighting certain connections and contexts unnoticed or not overtly expressed by participants, such as the influence of the larger political economy of mobilities within which contemporary pilgrimage practices are enacted, including the ways in which pilgrimage typically relies on the existence of an extensive infrastructure of transportation, resource provision, and governance. It might equally involve looking at strategic attempts by people to deploy a pilgrimage idiom in carrying out some other action such as a public protest, a family gathering, a revival of religious commitment—even an art exhibition, such as that of Dorman. Or again, it might entail carefully documenting the actions and attitudes of people who are endeavoring to conform to the ritual behaviors and material pathways constituting a pilgrimage route that has long been hallowed and set apart. All these behaviors come under the purview of pilgrimage, and all involve different ways in which a given "sacred journey" cannot be understood merely as a discrete, sui generis event—or even just a journey. In addition, all raise questions about how participants and observers of pilgrimage alike comprehend an activity that raises challenging analytical questions about the significance of religious, cultural, institutional, and political borders, about relations of social and spatial distance and proximity, and about shifting temporal frames in people's lives.

Given this self-consciously expansive approach, it is clear that an initial focus on Dorman's exhibition, located temporarily in Canterbury Cathedral, does not take us away from what is most important about much of contemporary pilgrimage. Rather, it poses questions about connectivity and salience that take on particular urgency under current conditions in many parts of the world where multiple mobilities exist alongside heightened mutual religious awareness. For the purposes of this book's argument, the paradoxical advantage of the dry, Latinate word *articulation* is that it does not specify in advance the precise motivation, social strength, or physical medium through which interrelations and exchanges of gesture, meaning, and value might be achieved between pilgrimage and other activities. It leaves open the degrees and qualities of agency and obligation involved among participants while permitting the possibility that connections might ramify or atrophy over time. It covers pilgrimage's connections with both movement and place without privileging one over the other or predetermining that any given direction or orientation is prior.[17] It also leaves open the question of how to define (or whether to introduce the concept of) the sacred, and it permits the possibility of cultural, societal, religious, and scalar articulations being far from smooth—even decidedly "frictional" (Tsing 2005)—in their operation. For instance, Dorman's exhibition created a powerful impact not only because of the similarities it hinted at between a martyred saint and suffering refugees but also because of the troubling incongruities entailed in juxtaposing the beauty and apparent permanence of a recognized pilgrimage site with the messy, transitory quality of enforced migration, almost forcing people who thought they had come to visit the former to acknowledge the existence of the latter.

The aim of this book is not to expand pilgrimage out of existence, to render it so vague and ubiquitous that it can no longer be discerned in any meaningful or useful way. Instead, by introducing an extended but flexible metaphor of articulation, the volume's goal is to reinforce a point made by the anthropologist of pilgrimage Michael Sallnow when he argues that the study of pilgrimage "demands that a priori assumptions concerning the relationship between religion and society be abandoned" given that "the link between ritual and secular processes should be regarded as analytically determinable in each case, rather than simply assumed" (Sallnow 1981, 179). Sallnow's point is that we cannot simply assume that pilgrimage as an ostensibly religious institution will either echo or reverse wider social structures. A much more complex interplay is likely to exist between social relations of pilgrimage and those generally classified by scholars as secular, including political, legal, and economic realms of activity. I go further in stating that while of course many human activities create links between people, institutions, and activities, contemporary forms of pilgrimage are particularly significant for the ways they make processes of separation and reconnection the object of concern in itself—intellectually, ritually, spatially, physically, emotionally.

An advantage of *articulation* as a term lies in its double meaning. Its dictionary definition refers to the formation of something, such as a sound, a gesture, or a more complex form of behavior, but also to "the action or manner of jointing or interrelating" (i.e., making a connection).[18] It encourages us to consider how an institution is constituted by internal relationships alongside links with realms beyond itself. These two types of articulation, formation and connection, operate together. We shall see how some pilgrimage practices come into being, are fundamentally or partially constituted, *through* forming associations between activities. Dorman's exhibition illustrates such creative connectivity by bringing material evidence from migrants in Lesbos and Calais into the world of prayer and pilgrims in Canterbury. She prompts visitors to engage in semi-liturgical movement as they walk between each "station" of apparently discarded clothing.[19]

The notion of articulation has a long set of resonances within studies of religion and culture in general, which we will touch on at various points in later chapters. Useful initial reflections are provided by Magnus Marsden and Kostas Retsikas (2013) in their introduction to *Articulating Islam*, where they unpick such terms as *Muslim identity* and *being Muslim* through focusing on ways in which people constantly emphasize and de-emphasize religious commitments, according to circumstance.[20] In this view, what becomes notable is not only the making of a connection in itself but also how and when such a link is made, who makes it, and what media are used. In their terms, Islam is continuously reproduced and transformed through its enmeshment with other fields of social life and becomes more of a "dynamic interface" than a "stable essence" (4).

Marsden and Retsikas's approach to religious action has the apparent disadvantage of making scholarly focus seem decidedly fuzzy. However, recognition of ambiguity and instability is often precisely the result of clear-sighted observation and analysis. Indeed, such volatility may be the very object of interest—most certainly in relation to pilgrimage—in any study that examines processes of articulation and disarticulation, connection and disconnection, assembly and disassembly, with a newly keen and exacting eye. Under some circumstances, people will attempt to separate, say, religion from politics and commerce, while at other times, such categories of action will be harder to disentangle for both the analyst and the informant. Contemporary pilgrimage itself, less a single, stable thing than a shifting, patterned cluster of practices that are often only ambiguously religious (see, e.g., Margry 2008), seems especially prone to making particular kinds of articulations across social landscapes. Not only does it typically reflect on and incorporate the movement of people between places and states of varying ritual focus and intensity, but it is also a highly mobile ritual form in itself, able to be transferred across and rearticulated within very different social and cultural circumstances and scales of operation. Despite superficial appearances, it is a notably open form of ritual, especially in its more popular guises, typically controlled only imperfectly by religious authorities, accessible to people of highly varying degrees of religious commitment and performed by broad publics (not merely specific congregations) that are themselves shifting and sometimes relatively anonymous.[21]

One example of such openness is provided by a 2016 press report in the *Japan Times* with the title "Shikoku's 'Path Less Traveled' Is Busier Than Ever."[22] The author, Takaki Tominada, observes:

Earlier this month at Ishiteji Temple—No. 51 on the route—in Matsuyama, Ehime Prefecture, foreign visitors were walking the pilgrimage route in pouring rain, wearing the customary white costumes and conical sedge hats worn by pilgrims.

Albert Kirch, 56, from Basel, Switzerland, was taking a break on a bench with his friend Mikio Nakaoka, an employee of a trading company in Osaka who is in his 60s. The two met on the pilgrimage and have been continuing their journey together ever since.

"I just like pilgrimages in general," Kirch says, explaining why he was taking part in the Shikoku Henro. He had previously completed other routes overseas, including the Camino de Santiago in Spain, a pilgrimage that attracts hundreds of thousands of people each year.

"Shikoku Henro is physically harder, but I'm enjoying the beautiful landscape and nature here," he said. "I've lost more than 10 kilograms on this pilgrimage," he says, smiling.

Notice the wide set of social, cultural, and material connections—even appropriations—contained within this short description: the foreigners dressed in traditional clothes, the pilgrimage-inspired friendship of two middle-aged men from dissimilar cultural backgrounds, the ways in which Albert Kirch's travel biography conjoins apparently disparate pilgrimage sites, Shikoku and the Camino, and does so in part through assessing their relative effects through secular criteria of evaluation—"I've lost more than 10 kilograms." In these sentiments, it is possible to discern different assumptions about landscape, physicality, spirituality, and materiality becoming mutually implicated through the shifting frame of the Shikoku pilgrimage.[23]

The article provides a vivid depiction of popular tropes of current pilgrimage activity: easy mobility, voluntary engagement in a kind of hardship, and self-conscious cosmopolitanism (all dimensions, we might note, decidedly absent from the lives of the migrants memorialized by Dorman's *Suspended*). A social scientific perspective acknowledges the significance of such tropes without seeing them as merely derivative of official or institutional practices that form the "true" pilgrimage. Shikoku as a broad cultural phenomenon is constantly being remade through articulations and rearticulations enacted here by the two pilgrims and the journalist who writes about them.

At the same time, we should not regard such loose forms of making connections—involving promiscuous links across people, sites, religions—as somehow characteristic of all contemporary practices. Ironically, the very flexibility of pilgrimage as a ritualized frame for human activity also allows it to be molded into much more rigid, targeted, and exclusive ritual guises, such as the nationalist veneration of Russian Orthodox saints described by Stella Rock (2014), where the church attempts to purify itself of the depredations of Soviet history while reconnecting itself to specific aspects of Russian memory and landscape.[24] The adaptability of pilgrimage does not mean it will always be used to encompass diversity and pluralism; its articulations may also be aimed at carving out highly demarcated boundaries of belonging. Such tightening of tradition is just as much a feat of ideological labor as more overtly creative deployments of ritual forms.

Approaches

Analysis of pilgrimage in the ways suggested here faces obvious methodological and conceptual challenges. Where to draw the line in deciding what comes under the frame of pilgrimage activity? How to observe diffuse behaviors as well as firmly delineated ritual forms? How to make comparisons across both religions and cultures? What vocabulary to use in describing such a range of activities? We will address these questions in subsequent chapters, but first it is worth saying something about language. While written from a predominantly anthropological and ethnographic standpoint, this book provides an overview of the shifting field of pilgrimage studies. It reexamines older work, showing how it relates to contemporary research and to more recent developments in pilgrimage itself. But this rereading is meant to contain theoretical challenges, in the sense that the aim is to develop a productive vocabulary for reframing conventional perspectives by highlighting pilgrimage's capacity to form connections between people, places, and practices.

The justification for my analytical lexicon will emerge throughout the course of this book and will be complemented by ethnographic illustration. Under the overall rubric of "articulation," we will explore such terms as *laterality* (complementing the more conventional anthropological term, *liminality*), *penumbra* (drawn originally from physics), *adjacency* (taken from architecture), *porosity* (derived from chemistry as well as the social sciences), *transduction* (used in a linguistic sense), *entrainment* (from geography, via physics), and *loose* and *tight spaces* (deployed in urban geography). My uses of these terms may seem mysterious at the moment, but I aim to show how they can productively complement each other in creating an expanded field of pilgrimage studies. All have spatial associations while encouraging contextually sensitive understandings of how pilgrimage is enacted. My clustering of terms drawn from different disciplinary backgrounds is an act of articulation in itself, one that is intended to illustrate something about the connective qualities of pilgrimage.

I could certainly have chosen other ways to write. Indeed, I adopted a very different approach in a previous book. In *Pilgrimage Past and Present in the World Religions* (1995), my coauthor, John Elsner, and I took a more conventional approach to the challenge of presenting pilgrimage as a comparative topic of inquiry. Most of our chapters chronicle both the history and the contemporary manifestations of pilgrimage within a given religious tradition, ranging from Judaism to Islam to Christianity to Hinduism and Buddhism. Such framing is partly subverted by smaller sections exploring such crosscutting themes as "contestation and cooperation" or "mapping the sacred," but in general, we aimed to highlight the significance of pilgrimage practices across what have conventionally been called the world religions, allowing our juxtapositions to do much of the work of suggesting common traits. This characterization of pilgrimage aspires toward a seemingly all-encompassing view of the subject, playing down analytical or disciplinary differences in creating sketches of ideological and ritual patterns within and across religions. Such an approach has its uses, not least its capacity to highlight radical variations as well as similarities among religious traditions by throwing into relief different understandings of landscape, ritual, and the sacred. On the other hand, the ideal of global encompassment that it proposes must always be a fiction. In addition, the world-religion paradigm has been heavily criticized (e.g., Masuzawa 2005; Owen 2011) for the way in which it bundles quite different sets of practices into Euro-American modes of framing and thus delimits what a religion should consist of (scriptures, clergy, fixed ritual). More generally, there is always a tension between what humans actually do and how their actions are observed and framed by academic fields, which have their own, often hidden or under-recognized, institutional and cultural imperatives.

In this book, I do not make claims of encompassment of all pilgrimage practices or themes to explore. The thrust of the argument is that such a project would falsely objectify pilgrimage as a topic of inquiry. Nor does the volume cover all the literature being produced by this impressively vibrant, increasingly interdisciplinary field of study. My aim is to convey insights into some of the most notable patterns of pilgrimage in the contemporary world but also to reflect on how scholars themselves have observed and analyzed such patterns. Instead of adopting the survey-like perspective of my 1995 book, I here respond to a challenge I posed in later work, where I argued that it was important for future studies to avoid being caught in an intellectual cul-de-sac of focusing comparisons only on other pilgrimages, or of developing theoretical perspectives reliant on emphasizing the unique, sui generis character of pilgrimage (Coleman 2002a, 363). A mature field must be able to appeal to a variety of cultural and analytical perspectives, and thankfully, studies of pilgrimage have broadened their scope over the last two or three decades. This book contributes to such a widening effect, tracing the past confinement but also the contemporary enlargement of the field. My emphasis on processes of articulation forces the analyst to look toward a wide range of activities and institutions in following the visible tracks but also the more concealed traces of pilgrimage-related activity. The intention, however, is not merely to indicate how pilgrimage connects with other behaviors and institutions. Connectivity itself is a central theme in this book. To invoke articulation is to make claims both more challenging and more precise in considering the significance of pilgrimage as a cultural phenomenon. Furthermore, scholarly intention should be not only to learn more about pilgrimage itself but also to use pilgrimage as a cultural and analytical lens to look outward, to learn more about human behavior itself (cf. Badone 2014, 13; Coleman 2002; Danely 2015; Reader 2017).

Even as I express such aims, my work remains embedded within certain personal and intellectual frames. I write as an anthropologist who has focused much of his ethnographic work on pilgrimage within English Christian contexts, most notably the Roman and Anglo-Catholic shrines at Walsingham in East Anglia and the major cathedrals at Canterbury, Durham, York (all Anglican), and Westminster (Roman Catholic). My approach is influenced by such experiences but also by learning from colleagues based in anthropology and other disciplines (most notably religious studies, sociology, geography, history) who have often looked at very different religious and cultural contexts. Monographs are often assumed to be either case studies or comparative works, but I see this book as both, and I have tried to introduce my own fieldwork in very particular ways. Rather than focusing on a single site, I have allowed my experiences of different fields to come to the fore at various points in the text. Such work is therefore presenced at specific stages of my argument, forming strategic points of reflection and comparison.

Elsewhere (Coleman 2006b), I have discussed how many social scientists, myself included, are engaged in multi-sited ethnography (Marcus 1995) while functioning as multi-sited ethnographers, formed by the ways we blend experiences from apparently very different field sites throughout our careers.[25] I have worked in the United Kingdom and in Sweden and Nigeria, and over the years, I have alternated between studying the respective worldwide expansions of pilgrimage and Pentecostalism.[26] In line with acknowledging my status as a multi-sited ethnographer, I regularly invoke rather than sideline my parallel interest in Pentecostalism in this book, deploying it to enlarge and sometimes crosscut my analytical frame.[27] At various points, I ask what happens when we juxtapose pilgrimage practices with those of Pentecostalism, and I conjoin the respective theoretical concerns of scholars who examine these seemingly disparate religious phenomena. My approach may be unusual, but it is far from arbitrary. Both Pentecostalism and pilgrimage have experienced dramatic and unexpected growth in recent decades. Both raise important questions about contemporary forms of mobility, religious experience, materiality, and understandings of scale, space, and place. Arguably, both have become religiously, ritually, and semiotically "looser" religious phenomena—often emotionally and ritually intense, but better equipped to accommodate wider constituencies of people than might have been the case a century ago.[28] At the same time, Pentecostalism and pilgrimage have often been viewed very differently as examples of globalizing religion, with Pentecostalism regarded by scholars as much more nimble and modern than pilgrimage, more able to influence other institutions and cultural practices than the seemingly more set apart, often nostalgic practice of pilgrimage (see also Coleman 2014).[29]

The work of expanding our analytical perspectives on pilgrimage must involve complicating assumptions concerning its seeming isolation. In the process, we shall see how current forms of pilgrimage and Pentecostalism produce their own ways of articulating with wider worlds, making and modifying connections that give the lie to older stereotypes of both as largely enclaved forms of religiosity. I shall begin by arguing that while contemporary Pentecostalism tends to create articulations by reaching out into religiously and culturally diverse contexts, attempting to remake those contexts in its own image (Coleman 2000; Robbins 2004), pilgrimage more often produces connections in more subtle ways, drawing people toward its practices through processes more akin to semiotic seduction and not infrequently encouraging non-religiously committed people to engage with its ritual landscapes.[30] As the book proceeds, however, the apparent disjunction between reaching out and drawing toward will be increasingly challenged. Although the temptation is to see Pentecostalism as transcending territorial limitations in contrast to the inherently place-bound practices of pilgrimage, I shall complicate this distinction, showing how our understandings of the workings of pilgrimage—and its articulations—cannot be confined to a focus on sacred shrines.[31]

Chapters

The chapters of this book are not arranged according to world religion or historical period. Instead, I adopt a thematic approach in building my argument. The main body of the book has three parts. After this introduction, the next two chapters are contained in a section I call "Frames." My aim is to cover the definitional, methodological, and conceptual ground required to conceive of pilgrimage as both ramifying practice and expansive field of study.[32] I argue against rigid characterizations of what is and is not genuine or authentic pilgrimage and contend that we must widen our horizons in recognizing physical, cultural, and intellectual terrains of pilgrimage activity. Chapters 3, 4, and 5 contribute to a section named "Tropes." Here, I reassess classic and influential landmarks in the social scientific study of pilgrimage, showing how certain of the most significant ways of characterizing the field have provided important insights yet limited our perspectives.[33] They have left certain gaps in our appreciation of its capacities to create ritual, cultural, economic, and political articulations with other institutions and activities. In other words, they have disempowered pilgrimage to varying degrees, not in its guise as locus of divine agency but in its role as social and cultural phenomenon with influence over wider dimensions of society.

The subsequent three chapters make up a section called "Articulations." They trace the contours of an expanded pilgrimage landscape operating at different scales, levels, and locations of activity and covering place, story, and movement, respectively. While reconsidering the familiar idea of a pilgrimage center, I move us increasingly away from making that center the exclusive focus of analytical attention. In chapter 6, I examine the complex and ramifying ritual penumbra that derives from and yet extends laterally beyond certain pilgrimage shrines, diffusing ritual connections into realms often ignored by scholars. While much of the focus of this chapter draws on my work in English pilgrimage sites, I contend that the argument can, with appropriate cultural adjustments, be extended to other contexts.

This decentering of the conventional scholarly focus on shrines is continued in chapter 7, where I examine another ubiquitous yet under-explored dimension of pilgrimage: the role of narratives operating both at and far away from sacred sites and pathways. Much important discussion of pilgrimage has referred to the significance of souvenirs in mediating between shrine and home (e.g., Di Giovine 2012; Kaell 2012; Higgins and Hamilton 2020). However, I turn more toward the role of storytelling, pilgrimage testimony, and other narratives in reperforming, remembering, and retranslating pilgrimage within social, physical, and virtual contexts far from shrines or other conventional locations of the sacred. Such narratives do more than represent what happened on pilgrimage; they have the capacity to rearticulate elements of the experience in novel social and spatial circumstances.

Chapter 8 takes us into another realm of pilgrimage practice that extends our understanding of the field, what I call "economies of mobility." An increased focus on varieties of walking done by pilgrims has helped scholars divert their gaze, at least part of the time, from shrines and altars. However, I consider a still wider range of pilgrimage activities relating to mobility and immobility and more broadly to political economy (see also Coleman and Eade 2018). I develop a contrast between "enclaving" and "entraining" dimensions of pilgrimage, showing how these two ideal types of practice have different implications for processes of articulation.

In a final chapter that summarizes but also extends my argument, I come back to the possibility of considering pilgrimage as a kind of interface, a dynamic means of articulation between and across different social, ideological, and cultural realms. Recognition of such connectivities restores powers to pilgrimage that have been lost in much social scientific analysis. It also links our study of pilgrimage to more general points about the partial, inchoate, and diffuse dimensions of religion more generally, dimensions that are all too often ignored as trivial or irrelevant to the central operations of social institutions and yet are closely implicated in their workings.

Each chapter of this book might be read on its own by a reader wishing to learn about a particular aspect of pilgrimage. However, taken as a whole, the book builds a picture of pilgrimage's articulations across sites, activities, and institutions. It incorporates three leitmotifs that extend across the chapters. In personal ethnographic terms, I deploy my fieldwork on Walsingham and in English cathedrals to show how my ideas have developed but also as a means of exploring similarities and differences with other pilgrimage times and places. In comparative institutional terms, I provide regular juxtapositions with the study of Pentecostalism as a reminder of ways in which anthropological sub-fields may become trapped in parochial debates while missing opportunities to make less expected connections. Finally, in theoretical terms, I frequently revisit articulation, showing how the concept allows us to think about how ritual, narrative, mobility, and political economy are both intertwined and deeply salient to an expanded understanding of pilgrimage—and even religion—as powerful social and cultural force.

PART I

Frames

1

Pilgrimage

Beyond Definition

The Virtues of Provisionality

The distinguished American anthropologist Roy Wagner once remarked, "The things we can define best are the things least worth defining" (1981, 39).[1] Wagner's sentiment is likely to infuriate scholars from academic fields dedicated to establishing the clarity and stability of foundational concepts, but it expresses well the exploratory character of much ethnographic work. Anthropology's disciplinary rigor emerges, paradoxically, from the ability to operate through permanently provisional categories of description, observation, and comparison. Such categories—including pilgrimage—are often part of common parlance, and so scholarship involves "elaborating a more developed version of what we use all the time in our everyday lives" (Parker and Stansworth 2015, 30). The resultant analytical labor occupies what anthropologist Michael Herzfeld has described as the discipline's epistemological "middle ground" (2001, xi), navigating between postmodernism and positivism but above all exploring and questioning whatever is assumed by researcher or interlocutor to be "common sense" (1).

Demarcation of key terms within the anthropology of religion has been rendered still more sensitive by Talal Asad's (1993) influential critique of universalizing definitions, on the grounds that they not only ignore the historical specificities of whatever seems religious in a given situation but also hide the power-laden discursive processes that go into their production. Thomas Tweed (2006, 33–34) argues, nonetheless, for the necessity of definitions as a way of indicating the positionality of the researcher.[2] He divides them into different types, depending on circumstance and function. For instance, a "lexical" definition reflects ordinary linguistic usage, whereas an "empirical" one offers analytical claims that can be confirmed or falsified. To illustrate the latter, Tweed cites Rodney Stark and Roger Finke's characterization of religion from their book *Acts of Faith* (2000), which consists of ninety-nine propositions and thirty-six mini-definitions, all of which are ultimately aimed at offering "proposals about what religion is and how it functions" (Tweed 2006, 34).

Although what is meant by *definition*, let alone *pilgrimage*, is far from clear, I must address these questions as I lay out the dimensions of an expanded field.[3] In doing so, I introduce two further dimensions to the notion of *definition*. The first highlights the dual significance of the word, referring both to meaning and to degree of distinctness. Pilgrimage practices do not always exist in high cultural relief. As ethnographers, we face the challenge and opportunity of observing pilgrimage as it comes in and out of ritual focus, articulating in often diffuse and subtle ways with other aspects of human behavior. The second dimension refers to my assertion that any sustainable social scientific understanding of pilgrimage is unlikely to rely on a monothetic form of classification—in other words, one governed by a single overriding idea or principle. Rather, it needs to be multifaceted, to contain room for flexible forms of articulation and disarticulation among a number of elements.

Pilgrimage cannot be regarded as a natural category, akin to an object encountered in the physical environment.[4] I am therefore unconvinced by any assertion that we might be able to edge toward a definitive definition of the topic. As the ethnologist Peter Margry notes, numerous scholarly efforts "have certainly not led to a fully crystallized academic picture of the pilgrimage phenomenon" (2008, 13). One of the reasons is that pilgrimage, whatever it is assumed to be in any given context, does not stay the same over time.[5] A further complication is that it attracts attention from many different disciplines—anthropology, archeology, geography, religious studies, sociology, theology, and so on—so that pilgrimage studies contains a considerable variety of methods, concerns, and technical languages. Interdisciplinarity may lead to impressive results, but the assumptions and languages deployed by different branches of research are sometimes simply incommensurable. For instance, the first line of the introduction to a book dedicated to the theology of pilgrimage states, "Pilgrimage is a journey to a special or holy place as a way of making an impact on one's life with the revelation of God associated with that place" (Bartholomew and Llewelyn 2003, xii). The authors make such a claim from their perspective of being both researchers and committed Christians. In contrast, scholarly disciplines such as my own have often found it difficult to find an adequate vocabulary to describe what our interlocutors may regard as the "radical realness or presence" of spiritual power (see also Orsi 2009, 220). However, it remains problematic for me as an anthropologist to subscribe to the idea that pilgrimage should fundamentally be perceived as a means of achieving revelation. I do not dismiss the potential existence of the divine; rather, I am concerned with working through the implications of a particular disciplinary perspective. Divine revelation per se does not fit easily with defining a phenomenon that I comprehend as deeply social, culturally ramifying, and inherently multifaceted.

Anthropologist Alan Morinis says of pilgrimage, "It seems the term can be put to use wherever journeying and some embodiment of an ideal intersect" (1992, 3). Like his theological counterparts, Morinis touches on twin themes of mobility and esteem. At the same time, there is a wealth of significance in the vocabulary he deploys. Rather than "revelation of God," we read of "an ideal"—a term that does not refer to the overtly religious. Nor does Morinis make any initial judgment as to the spiritual effect of the travel. His notion of embodiment implies the likely significance of materiality, without specifying the medium to be used. Finally, the phrase "it seems the term can be put to use" provides a meta-definition more than a definition, an observation on how the term is deployed by whichever constituency is influential in any given social context.[6]

Morinis's approach is not inherently more effective than that of Bartholemew and Llewelyn. The juxtaposition of the two shows how definitions are oriented toward particular audiences, containing implicit modes of address and assumptions about methodology. In other words, the act of defining a phenomenon is not merely to describe it; it is also to prescribe and proscribe certain investigative priorities.[7] I accept, for instance, that pilgrimage usually involves moving from home to a shrine and then back again.[8] Such an assumption is reasonable and helps to focus certain research aims and methods, but it also directs attention away from such issues as the administration of sites or the ongoing links between different shrines across regions or continents.[9] Alan Morinis and Ross Crumrine agree that at the level of the individual, going on pilgrimage may imply a journey undertaken to a sacred shrine for religious purposes (1991, 2). However, they add that other levels of analysis, which go beyond marked forms of travel, must be acknowledged. For instance, from an institutional perspective, pilgrimage comprises "a wide variety of actors, places, behaviors, times, and specialists" (ibid.), an extensive and diffuse set of practices, some of which may be enacted far from obvious sites of activity.

The classificatory politics of defining pilgrimage are not confined to scholars. Evgenia Mesaritou and I (2018, 180) have traced the ideologically loaded, discursive work that goes into assigning, adopting, and rejecting pilgrim and tourist roles in contexts where the former label implies seriousness of purpose and the latter mere superficiality.[10] An excellent example is provided by the shrine of Padre Pio, a Franciscan friar and stigmatic who died in 1968 but whose crypt in San Giovanni Rotondo, in the Italian region of Apulia, remains a popular object of devotion. Much debate has surrounded the development of the site and what some see as its excessive commercialization. Anthropologist Michael Di Giovine (2013, 2016) discusses how local friars have addressed such issues by attempting to transform tourists into pilgrims, for instance by funneling visitors through the officially sanctioned spatial, temporal, and behavioral organization of the shrine. He recounts incidents where tourism is referenced by spiritual directors or travelers to reprimand others perceived to be engaging in practices they consider antithetical to ascetic Christian spirituality, such as complaining about the quality of food. The frequently uttered phrase "This is pilgrimage, not tourism" disciplines less pious visitors but also makes a claim to define the fundamental nature of the journey. Through asserting the commonsensical obviousness of a distinction between roles, it reinforces a particular ethical understanding of the situation (cf. Di Giovine 2013, 85), illustrating what Bowman (2014, 155) calls "the struggle for the power to give and enact the meaning of what a pilgrimage is."

In some places, such struggles have become more salient as the moral power to define an act *as* pilgrimage has been removed from the monopoly of clerical authorities. For instance, in his exploration of "pluralist" definitions of the term, Helmut Eberhart (2015, 122) recounts the story of Brigitte Ederer, a politician of the Social Democratic Party of Austria. In June 1994, when Austrians were voting on whether to enter the European Union, Ederer promised to go on a walking pilgrimage from Vienna to the Roman Catholic shrine of Mariazall (sixty-five miles away) if the electorate supported the proposal to join. After a positive vote, she duly fulfilled her vow. In one sense, the event challenged a Christian definition of the journey; after all, Ederer represented a secular party. Nonetheless, "the formal framework conditions for a traditional pilgrimage seem to have been in place—namely the promise and making good on this promise by walking to a famous pilgrimage shrine and visiting the church there" (Eberhart 2015, 122). In this latter connotation—acknowledging the cultural salience of engaging in a slow, semi-sacrificial progress to a renowned site—Ederer reaffirmed the ethical authority of pilgrimage as a framework for action, even as she claimed the authority to appropriate its significance. In this way, reenactment became a form of redefinition.

An example of a larger-scale political annexation and reframing of a pilgrimage landscape is provided by Nimrod Luz and Noga Collins-Kreiner's (2015) tracing of trajectories of Jewish pilgrimage in Israel. If the Holy Land has been politicized for thousands of years, the role of pilgrimage "has become more complicated with the creation of the Israeli nation-state" in the years after the Second World War (135). Since 1948, a growing connection has been evident between Zionism and pilgrimage, focused on Jewish collective identity based around Eretz Israel (the land of Israel; 141). In an effort to construct monuments to national collective memory, the state has promoted archeological sites such as Masada, a mountain in the Judean desert where Jewish rebels resisted the Roman army for three years in the first century CE (ibid.). Also significant is the location in Jerusalem of Yad Vashem, the World Holocaust Remembrance Center, next to Mount Herzel, the national burial site of fallen soldiers (142). These shrines are not avowedly religious; they point more obviously to nationalist and secular ideals. Other locations have rather different connotations, such as the Wailing Wall, a relic of the former Jewish temple destroyed by the Romans and now a contested site of prayer,[11] or saints' shrines said to have been discovered in development towns, reflecting the residence patterns of Jewish immigrants arriving primarily from Muslim North Africa (140).[12] What all these sites have in common is their embodied articulation of the complex and volatile politics of space in Israel-Palestine, associated with divisions not only between Jewish and Muslim Palestinian populations but also between Orthodox and more secular Jews and increasingly involving migrants from different parts of the Jewish diaspora. They demonstrate the growing profile and salience of pilgrimage in the country as a means of staking claims—to govern, to pray, to reside. In encouraging citizens and other visitors to regard such sites as places of pilgrimage, they naturalize deeply ideologically loaded definitions of what is implied by the term.

Pilgrimage Parochialities

The twin challenges of establishing both the meaning of pilgrimage and the scope of pilgrimage studies have been complicated by linguistic issues that embody their own politics. I refer in particular to the hegemony of the use of English in Euro-American scholarship. John Eade and Dionigi Albera, anthropologists based in England and France, respectively, note that "the singular Anglophone term—pilgrimage—clearly operates as a catchall type term that serves to translate a multiplicity of meanings and nuances in other religious traditions" (2017, 6).[13] Translations can, however, be treacherous. The use of a seemingly neutral, generic English gloss becomes less innocent in the light of the range of meanings and terms that exist in such places as India, China, and Japan, all of which create distinctions among various forms of religious mobility (ibid.). The most common word for a pilgrimage site in India—the Sanskrit term *tirtha*—generally refers to the idea of a ford as both a place and a movement, but Morinis provides further referents for the term, noting that it "can be applied to the shrine at the end of a sacred journey, but as well to a devoted wife, a spiritual preceptor, one's parents, and virtues such as truth and honesty" (1992, 3).[14] Ann Gold points out that the Sanskrit term *yātrā*, which is often juxtaposed with *tirtha*, refers to wandering but is also associated with death (1988, 59). Marcus Bingenheimer states that abstract nouns such as *religion* or *pilgrimage* do not easily map on to categories deployed in literary Chinese and finds that the closest equivalents are *chaoshan* (literally, to have an audience with a mountain) and *jinxiang* (to offer incense) (2017, 18). Ian Reader (2005) refers to numerous terms available in Japanese to refer to what might be understood as pilgrimage, observing that the ideograms used to write *henro* indicate the idea of a "linking route" (9), while the word may also refer to participants in the journey (32).[15] Even within the Abrahamic faiths, classifications of pilgrimage can look very different from Euro-American, often implicitly Christian, assumptions. The Hebrew term *aliyah* literally means "ascent" but can also imply pilgrimage to a shrine, return from the diaspora to live in Israel, the passage of a saint to heaven, and people being called to bless the Torah in synagogue (Dubisch 1995, 46; Sered 1992, 19–20).

Linguistic distinctions made within religious traditions often point to specific hierarchies of ritual value. Most famously, within Islam, the Hajj cannot simply be assimilated to a notion of visiting a sacred site or shrine; its obligatory character and fixed timing within the Muslim calendar distinguish it from the *umra*, or visit to Mecca at other times of the year (Peters 1994, xxi). The Muslim world is also characterized by numerous visits (*ziyarat*) to other sites, including saints' tombs, that often do not enjoy official approval and yet represent popular parts of the religious landscape.[16] Albertus Laksana is one of many scholars who contrast such practices to "canonical pilgrimage to Mecca" (2014, 11ff). He traces debates within the Muslim world over whether they constitute dangerous innovations without sanction in the Qur'an and sunna (traditional Muslim law). At the same time, Laksana does not dispute the importance or interest of these activities. He argues that "the ziyara tradition is a complex practice with many layers of meaning and significance" and one where the pilgrim hopes to become blessed through proximity to saints (who are regarded as friends of God) without being accused of engaging in polytheism (*shirk*) (13).

Less often remarked on are significant distinctions evident within Christianity. While the assumed Protestant mistrust of pilgrimage has become a cliché, relatively little attention has been paid to differences between Catholic and Orthodox understandings of how to approach sacred sites.[17] Both branches of Christianity contain strong supporters of pilgrimage, but what is meant by the practice varies. In his account of pilgrimage to the famous monasteries on the holy mountain of Athos in northeastern Greece, René Gothóni (1991, 293) points out that the Greek term for pilgrim, *proskinitis*, has the connotation of falling down to do obeisance. This concept links most clearly with ritual veneration of relics, kissing of icons, making confession, and meeting spiritual fathers rather than the emphasis on long-distance travel evident in many contemporary Roman Catholic accounts of pilgrimage. As Dubisch notes of Greek Orthodox practices, a person may have traveled a considerable way to perform such acts in a shrine, "or . . . may simply have gone around the corner to a village church" (1995, 75).

Dee Dyas and John Jenkins (2020) emphasize that Christian pilgrimage has never been a monolithic concept but rather represents a mosaic of sometimes conflicting ideas, historically indebted not only to the Hebrew Bible and New Testament but also to practices taken from Greek and Roman polytheistic religion, the development of cults of saints, and the creation of a Christian Holy Land by a newly converted Roman emperor, Constantine (ca. 272–337), and his mother, Helena. The resultant devotional practices have tended to promote pilgrimage as an expression of a restless Christian subjectivity while showing considerable capacity for reconfiguration across different periods and cultural contexts. Two models have actually emphasized stability of location: interior pilgrimage (cultivating the pursuit of God within the soul through monasticism, anchoritism, meditation, and mysticism) and moral pilgrimage (focusing on daily obedience to God as part of one's ultimate spiritual passage to the heavenly Jerusalem). Place pilgrimage, which scholars nowadays associate more readily with the practice, entails physical travel to holy places to express devotion and seek forgiveness, healing, or other material benefits. However, as historians, Dyas and Jenkins note that for the medieval Christian pilgrim, the journey to and from the shrine was necessary but usually secondary in spiritual terms to the journey through the shrine. They see parallels here with the Hajj, where there is no compulsion to walk and meditate on the way, given that the pilgrimage proper starts on arrival at the holy site.

Language differences have also contributed to the creation of separate intellectual genealogies within national traditions of pilgrimage studies. Here again, Eade and Albera (2017, 1–2) have made important observations in their discussion of how Anglophone scholars have often been oblivious to research published in other languages, creating a lack of awareness that has both prevented theoretical cross-fertilization and concentrated much interest on Roman Catholic pilgrimages within Western Europe and America. Reinforcing this point, Ian Reader criticizes "the hegemonic position held by the Anglophone and Christian-centric field" and traces the problematic effect of this very hegemony on his own regional specialization in Japan (2017, 181).[18] A common Christian and contemporary Western understanding of pilgrimage is that it is a marginal activity, excluded (or shielded) from more mundane institutions. Reader counters that from the perspective of Japanese scholars, it is "a practice very much central to the functioning of established traditions and institutions, and at the core of the Japanese religious world" (182). He refers to the prominent scholar Shinno Toshikazu, who has consistently argued that pilgrimage is a founding feature of Japanese religion. Reader's own work illustrates the ways in which a non-Western, non-Christian conceptualization of pilgrimage can be converted into significant comparative approaches. For instance, his observation (2017, 184) that Japanese pilgrimage scholarship has often focused on "the influences of economics and changing economic flows in historical and contemporary terms on pilgrimage practices and development" has clearly informed his book *Pilgrimage in the Marketplace* (Reader 2013).[19]

A complex challenge to the seemingly default prominence in certain circles of Christian, Euro-American assumptions is provided by Makhan Jha, an Indian anthropologist and historian of religion, who in 1991 edited *Social Anthropology of Pilgrimage*, published in New Delhi. The book contains valuable essays, but it is also notable for its geographical and institutional focus; of the twenty chapters provided, sixteen deal broadly with India, while the remaining contributions cover Catholicism in Costa Rica, Greek Orthodox practices on Mount Athos, syncretic rituals in Latin America, and the history of Mormon pilgrimage in the United States.[20] The latter pieces are written by scholars located in Europe or North America, whereas the majority, though not all, of the contributions on India are written by scholars based in the subcontinent. It might therefore seem that Jha's book presents a refutation of Euro-American orthodoxies and assumptions of dominance, and this impression is reinforced by some of his blunt language at the beginning of the book. Criticizing "romantic sloppiness passing as analysis" that "stands in need of sober correction" (1991, 26), Jha directs much of his intellectual ire toward two scholars whom we shall discuss in detail in chapter 3: "Edith Turner and . . . Victor Turner writing about Roman Catholic pilgrimage in which they were involved seemed to imply that their analysis applied to pilgrims in general. It doesn't" (ibid.). Going further back into the history of Western scholarship, he adds, "In the analysis of Indian pilgrimage, Durkheim no longer remains canonical. His axiomatic sacred-profane dichotomy is quite counter-productive for the understanding of Hindu pilgrimage" (20).

Jha's message is significant. A long tradition of writing on religion as set-apart realm of belief and ritual is put in its parochial place. Even so, a distinctly Euro-American orientation permeates his analytical framework. His first paragraph contains references to Habermas, Gadamer, Geertz, Jung, and Eliade, as well as an acceptance that Victor Turner should be regarded as "a key reference figure in pilgrimage studies" (1991, 19). Reader highlights a similar issue when he refers to the fact that Western-centric, Anglophone studies tend to provide the foil or "contrasting field against which other studies are framed," so that even Japanese scholars, "if they make use of non-Japanese studies and examples at all, invariably use Anglophone and Christian-centric examples and studies, and pay little attention to other linguistic traditions" (2017, 183).

An equally ambiguous epistemological position is adopted by Abdellah Hammoudi in his celebrated *A Season in Mecca* (2005). Hammoudi is a mobile scholar and citizen—an anthropologist born in Morocco, educated at the Sorbonne, and a faculty member at Princeton University. The book expresses his simultaneous distance from, and attempt to seek connections with, a number of discursive worlds as he goes on a pilgrimage while unsure of his relationship to his faith. The resultant text is more memoir than ethnography and one that reflects on the limitations of scholarly expression. Writing of his attempts to characterize Muslim forms of life after his experience of the Hajj, Hammoudi observes, "It was difficult to articulate and classify this in the language of anthropology. Synoptic tables, where hitherto implicit links . . . became clearly visible, proved fruitless" (274). At the same time, Hammoudi often feels alienated from the way the pilgrimage is organized by Muslim authorities and from certain rituals such as the mass slaughter of sheep. The result is a text that wrestles with translation, not only in linguistic terms but also as Hammoudi uses his eloquent (and, he would likely accept, highly privileged) voice to address both Muslims and non-Muslims, complicating academic and religious stereotypes of piety.

Concerns over the parochialities of academic representation are not unique to pilgrimage studies. Nonetheless, they illustrate the significant role of underlying political, economic, and cultural factors in influencing both the practice and the study of religious travel (cf. Asad 1993; see also Barna 2015). A good historical illustration of this point is provided by Toni Huber's (2008, 251–52) tracing of the role of monumental archeology as a feature of British colonialism in India in the nineteenth century. Such excavations literally brought a certain ideologically loaded vision of the religion to light, according to which newly discovered Buddhist holy shrines could be interpreted as contributing to an image of Buddhism as world religion. In turn, some South Asian Buddhists of the early twentieth century began to refer to India in English as their Holy Land, adopting and universalizing a European Christian discourse concerning sacred landscape (38).

A contemporary example of how political economy directs academic attention is the increased prominence of pilgrimage as an activity and object of study in Eastern Europe after the collapse of communist regimes in the late 1980s and early 1990s. Eade and Katić (2014, 1) point out that such dramatic events have prompted questions concerning relationships between politics, sacralized movement, and placemaking that have emerged from a specific region of Europe but can be applied elsewhere on the continent. However, if Eastern Europe has gained a new profile in social scientific studies within and beyond the region (thereby also laying the ground for studies of Eastern Orthodox pilgrimage to challenge Roman Catholic hegemonies), strikingly little attention has been paid to sub-Saharan Africa.[21] Andrea Saayman et al. (2014) lament the lack of comparative work available to inform their study of one of the largest pilgrimages in the world—that of the annual Easter weekend meeting of the Zion Christian Church in the Limpopo Province of South Africa, attended by a million or so people (though see also Müller 2011).[22] More forcefully, Shirley du Plooy blames "the classic or traditional pilgrimage lens [that] invokes Western European and North American, Christian and particularly Catholic pilgrimages" for scholarly neglect of African cases (2017, 138). Her point is that this lens "disallows many types of journeys because they do not fit these classic/traditional conceptions of pilgrimages" (ibid.). Indeed, we may have to adjust our understandings of such concepts as "trail" and "movement" if we are even to *recognize* what is going on in many southern African contexts.[23]

Du Plooy's critique of continued stereotypes of Africa includes mention of Surinder Bhardwaj and Gisbert Rinschede's (1998, 11) comment that "Christian pilgrimage centers are virtually absent in Black Africa probably because the veneer of Christianity is thin and the influence of its own nature religions still profound" (Du Plooy 2017, 124; quoted in Müller 2011, 10). This remark reveals a conspicuous lack of awareness of the long and profound history of Christianity across the continent. It also highlights a striking contrast between the research profiles of African pilgrimage and African Pentecostalism respectively within the anthropology of Christianity. The former may have gained relatively little attention, but the latter has been one of the key driving forces in a dynamic new field, where it is seen as one of the most prominent examples of the growing significance of Christian influence within the contemporary world (e.g., Meyer 2004; Robbins 2004).[24]

A further factor in the success of Pentecostalism as a high-profile topic has been its relevance to theoretical debates far beyond Christianity. Questions relating to globalization (Coleman 2000), the reenchantment of modernity (Meyer and Pels 2003), cultural rupture (Robbins 2007), and so on have all been explored through ethnographic accounts of burgeoning Pentecostal and charismatic movements, prompted by these movements' often frenetic mobility, challenges to secular worldviews, and unabashed attempts to appropriate local cosmologies. Such questions have formed recognizable talking points that have conferred identity and shape to the anthropology of Christianity without giving the impression of a field's becoming static or unable to generate new areas of discussion (e.g., Robbins 2014). In comparison, pilgrimage studies have until recently seemed self-referential and inward looking. Quite apart from the limitations of Anglophone work, Ian Reader (2015, 24) remarks of Japanese publications on pilgrimage that they have tended to focus on issues relating to national identity, without developing overarching analytical paradigms. Helmut Eberhart (2015, 118) notes that even as German-speaking scholars have become more interested in the resurgence of pilgrimage over the past thirty years, their interpretations have been cramped by being dominated by "compensation" models of religion, which have associated participation with the need to cope with the disorientating effects of rapid urbanization. One reason for such lack of dynamic vision could be the absence of cross-fertilization among national traditions of scholarship. Searching for examples where the crossing of boundaries *has* had productive results we might think of Reader's interest in the market emerging out of his inhabiting both Euro-American and Japanese conversations about pilgrimage, and his use of insights from one to reflect on the other.

So far, then, I have highlighted a number of mutually reinforcing parochialities as they have affected pilgrimage studies. These tendencies refer to complexities of definition but have also contributed to an implicit politics of attention and inattention, raising questions as to how a full range of pilgrimage and pilgrimage-related practices is to be recognized and observed and how different academic traditions might be enabled to speak to each other. Given that the array of analytical challenges is both considerable and ethically sensitive, our responses should be energetic but also nuanced.[25] Focusing once more on the question of language illustrates the complexities of the task. The irony of the widespread use of English is that it has glossed over definitional differences but has also—especially in more recent decades—enabled increased amounts of dialogue across national scholarly borders (Albera and Eade 2015, 14; Reader 2017). The siloed character of scholarly approaches has become recognized as a problem precisely because of greater mutual awareness on the part of researchers spread across the globe, even though it is important to remain acutely conscious of the numerous inequalities involved in the production of such contacts. Summarizing the current situation, Luz and Collins-Kreiner state that "dedifferentiation . . . appears to have penetrated the study of pilgrimage through multidisciplinary collaboration. Sometimes the disciplinary cross-currents have grown so strong that it is difficult to distinguish the contribution of one discipline from the others" (2015, 143; cf. Collins-Kreiner 2010). Indeed, it would be problematic to assume that the ultimate analytical aim of any study should always be one that is maximally universalizing and cartographic in relation to some form of consensual pilgrimage studies agenda. This approach would lead to a newly problematic form of parochiality, given that a mature subfield must benefit—however incongruously—from retaining and even encouraging a variety of contending and incommensurable approaches. There are broader epistemological and methodological stakes at play here. The anthropologist Kirsten Hastrup (2013) emphasizes the importance of remaining aware of the scale of attention being deployed at any given moment in asking questions of the social world.[26] Her remark resonates with my references to the politics of both attention and definition. Hastrup writes, "Fieldwork itself is a work that selects and follows particular connections between people, places and other agents" (157).[27] If this is a salient observation for ethnographers of single places or institutions, it takes on even more importance in the study of pilgrimage, constituted by the formal or informal, literal or metaphorical, making and tracing of links between people, journeys, locations, and narratives.

In fact, there might sometimes be good analytical reasons why a particular debate over pilgrimage *should* be confined to specific disciplinary or regional concerns. I think, for instance, of N. Ross Crumrine and Alan Morinis's volume *Pilgrimage in Latin America* (1991), where restricting the focus to an (admittedly huge) geographical region eases the possibility for interdisciplinary perspectives to speak to each other, while also allowing authors to address what the editors see as distinctive research problems relating to the merging of European Catholicism with Indigenous pre-Columbian religious thought, as well as the mutual influence of African religious systems, Hinduism and Protestantism (4). More recently, Nimrod Luz (2020) has laid out the emerging dimensions of Islamic pilgrimage studies in line with political and economic developments that give this subfield its own integrity. Luz observes that although Islam originated in the Middle East among Arabic populations, subscribers to the faith have diversified both ethnically and geographically. Islam has become a key player in religious landscapes of the Middle East, North Africa, and large parts of Asia and the South Pacific, while increasing numbers of Muslims have settled in European countries as well as North and South America (Esposito, 2004). In line with Laksana's (2014) work, quoted above, scholars have had to respond to the fact that most instances of Muslim pilgrimage do not involve the Hajj or the *umra* (pilgrimage) to Mecca and do not always take these official rituals as their templates (see also Surinder 1998).[28] Furthermore, patterns of practice are clearly shaped by ongoing internal divisions. Shi'a followers accept the importance of Mecca but cherish numerous places relating to the family of the Prophet, so that Karbala, Najaf, Mashad, and other locations in Iran and Iraq are considered almost as significant. The complexities of a ramifying pilgrimage tradition are also revealed by the many *mazars* (tombs, or shrines) visited by Muslim Uighurs in Xinjiang, China, who combine Islamic and shamanic practices.[29] On the other hand, the reformist, Salafiyya movement within Sunni Islam campaigns against sainthood in promoting a return to what it regards as an original, pure Islam. Crosscutting these theological divisions are moves toward the heritagization of pilgrimage sites, as governments attempt to develop tourism around the increased mobility of Muslim populations across large parts of the world. In highlighting these issues, Luz indicated the specificities of the contemporary Muslim pilgrimage landscape without precluding other ways to think through the data. To assert the value of the strategic, provisional parochialization of certain debates within pilgrimage studies is not to challenge the right of the field as a whole to exist; rather, it fosters the flexibilities and internal tensions the field needs to thrive. Luz, as well as Crumrine and Morinis, illuminate certain features of the pilgrimage landscape to render them—however temporarily—in sharper definition.

At the same time, contributors to the discussion need not always make pilgrimage per se the highlighted object of analysis. Jill Dubisch presciently notes that "no study of pilgrimage can ever be just about a particular pilgrimage 'site'" (1995, 7), and I would add that on occasion we learn much by making pilgrimage a partial, peripheral, aspect of a larger study. Shifting pilgrimage to the background of our attention can be productive if it encourages us to consider the wider contexts in which it operates, to which it contributes, and out of which it is formed.[30] Some of my work on English cathedrals (Coleman 2018a) incorporates observations of the diffuse, ambiguous role of pilgrimage shrines within the larger thematic frame of the formation of urban publics (cf. Pritchard 2015). Such work indicates how pilgrimage may come in and out of definition in people's experiences of travel, sometimes gaining resonance precisely because its ritual outlines are not clearly articulated.[31] Perceptions of figure and ground come into play as travelers switch very quickly in their degree of focus on a given object, image, or activity in defining the significance of a social event or situation. Anthropologists Eric Hirsch and Michael O'Hanlon (1995) also examine how a given physical and cultural landscape alternates between states of foreground actuality and background potentiality as it moves in and out of social awareness. In a complex space such as a cathedral, consciousness of the pilgrimage dimension of the building is constantly in dialogue with awareness of it as social meeting place, tourist venue, heritage site, and so on.

Recognition of the ambiguities of scale, definition, and scope of pilgrimage makes our scholarly lives harder, but that is not a valid reason to avoid the challenges that it presents. We must be prepared to create productive and experimental negotiations between more cartographic and more parochial formations of the field. One approach might be to develop bold comparisons across regions that explicitly do *not* take into account Euro-American regional concerns. This strategy has already been explored for the study of Pentecostalism in André Corten and Ruth Marshall-Fratani's (2001) edited volume *Between Babel and Pentecost*, which compares Pentecostal phenomena across Latin America and Africa and avoids Euro-American scholarly mediation as much as possible. Their book is published in English but draws on scholars from non-Anglophone environments. A similar approach could be taken by juxtaposing, say, South Asian with Latin American manifestations of pilgrimage, taking into account not only pilgrimage practices but also the respective regional scholarly fields constructed around such activities.

My approach in this book responds to the problem of Christian, Euro-American hegemony in a different but complementary way; one that draws on my own expertise. Rather than bypassing such dominance by looking elsewhere, I reexamine, denaturalize, and literally re-form it. A key part of my strategy is to reflect on my experiences as an ethnographer both of pilgrimage in England and of Pentecostalism in Sweden and Nigeria. My methods are threefold: investigating the intellectual origins of Anglophone studies of European pilgrimage, critically juxtaposing them with examples of pilgrimage drawn from elsewhere, and reframing them through theoretical perspectives often derived from discussions that have little to do with pilgrimage. In the next section, however, I extend my examination by flipping perspective once more, asking, What happens when we look at how scholars and others have used pilgrimage as a means to describe other parts of our world? In other words, I examine pilgrimage less as the object of definitional practices and more as a building block in the representation of the social and cultural world.

Looking through, as well as at, Pilgrimage

A thoughtful discussion of the scholarly dilemmas involved in defining religious phenomena is provided by Thomas Tweed (2006), who writes as both ethnographer and historian.[32] Tweed suggests that religions are fundamentally about "crossing and dwelling" and "confluences of organic-cultural flows" (54).[33] In turn, theories of religion are not static positions but "itineraries" (7), "propelled by concepts and tropes that follow lines of argument and narration" (9), resulting in "purposeful wandering" (11). Anybody reading these words can hardly fail to notice how metaphors of mobility, spatiality, and orientation permeate Tweed's language. While his text is about religion in general, Tweed situates himself physically and figuratively in the midst of his fieldwork on Cuban Catholic migrants and pilgrims in Miami. In other words, he attempts to look not only *at* pilgrimage but also *through* it to argue that it provides insights into broader religious manifestations.

Tweed's approach resonates with the earlier work of two prominent analysts who have argued for the power of pilgrimage not only as a subject in its own right but also as a metaphorical means of comprehending wider dimensions of contemporary society. In an influential book called *Routes: Travel and Translation in the Late Twentieth Century* (1997), American professor of humanities James Clifford reflects on how culture increasingly makes its home in motion in a world that does not stand still but is characterized by movement through airports, markets, migrations, and so on. Under such circumstances, says Clifford, pilgrimage is of considerable use as a comparative term in ethnographic writing, since despite its sacred associations, it includes a broad range of experiences and is less class- and gender-based than the notion of travel. The second author is Zygmunt Bauman, a sociologist originally from Poland who lived in England for many years. Writing a year before Clifford, Bauman argues that new forms of nomadism are replacing old forms of sedentarism. For him, the modern world has given the metaphorical figure of the pilgrim new prominence as it comes to signify a restless seeker for identity—a search that defines contemporary life (1996, 19ff.). As Michael Stausberg (2011, 28–29) notes, Bauman also tends to contrast the meaning-making project of the pilgrim in modernity to the more play-

does pilgrimage lose it significance in our Modern world of globalization & travel?

ful metaphors that sometimes seem more appropriate to postmodernity: the unattached stroller, vagabond, tourist, and player.

What these authors have in common with Tweed is the conviction that pilgrimage is not merely an activity worthy of being studied but also a category that is good to think with (and through) because it captures a central feature of what William Cavanaugh (2008) calls the links between "mobility and identity in a global age." Another way of putting the point is that, far from being anachronistic, interest in pilgrimage as category as well as activity makes sense (even apparent common sense) given that varieties of movement, whether voluntary or involuntary, have become a marked theme of modern life for many people. As I have suggested, the cultural assumptions behind common sense should always be interrogated, just as we need to understand that the full scope of pilgrimage extends beyond movement or even the combination of crossing and dwelling that Tweed emphasizes. My main point, though, is that the deployment of pilgrimage as a productive discursive category by these theorists of contemporary hypermobility has an intriguing counterpart in the work of commentators on an earlier phase of the modern world.

Émile Durkheim, one of the Western writers criticized by Jha earlier in this chapter, is known as a foundational scholar of social order and associated ritual, and indeed of the social sciences in general, but much of the thrust of his *Elementary Forms* (1961 [1912]) comes from his striking portrayal of the dialectic between everyday dispersal and periodic reunion that characterizes the totemic religion of Indigenous Australians.[34] Drawing on Spencer and Gillen's ethnography of the Arunta tribe of central Australia, Durkheim explores the significance of the Intichiuma cult—a feast whose exact timing is dependent on the season:

> There are two sharply separated seasons in Australia: one is dry and lasts for a long time; the other is rainy and is, on the contrary, very short and frequently irregular. As soon as the rains arrive, vegetation springs up from the ground as though by enchantment and animals multiply. . . . It is just at the moment when the good seasons seems to be close at hand that the *Intichiuma* is celebrated. (1961, 367)

The rite provides the occasion for an intense religious celebration, involving both sacrifice and a communion-like in-gathering of normally scattered members of the group. Durkheim rarely explicitly mentions pilgrimage in the *Elementary Forms* (see Fedele and Isnart 2015, 175), yet the rhythm and the shape of the Intichiuma embody a basic model of mobility, in-gathering, and idealization.[35]

Just a year later, one of Durkheim's most famous students, Robert Hertz, produced an essay on the pilgrimage practices surrounding a saint in the Italian Alps, replacing a focus on the distant Australian landscape for one concentrated on rural Europe.[36] Hertz's piece emphasizes the power of St. Besse—soldier, bishop, shepherd—to bring together diverse constituencies of people linking Catholicism with older, tellurian forms of faith, focused on a simple chapel overlooking a remote valley.[37] Combining ethnography with ethnohistory, Hertz documents people's movements up to the shrine and their ritual processions as they do the rounds of the sacred mount, carrying a statue of the saint, who is dressed as a Roman soldier and holds a palm of martyrdom in his hand. He concludes, "St. Besse must have had an extraordinary power of attraction and cohesion to hold in check the centrifugal forces that were tending to break up the little community of his worshippers" (2017, 38).

Hertz's focus is on a little-known community far from urban centers, but he asks fundamental questions about the creation of conflict and cohesion in a heterogeneous society—questions that resonated with the era's emergent sociological interests in nationalism, industrial expansion, and cultural and ideological pluralism. The direction of Hertz's approach initially appears very different from that of Clifford and Bauman, given that its focus on community contrasts with their interests in chronic mobility; yet in both cases, we see theorists deploying pilgrimage—with its combined dimensions of movement, search for ideals, and ability to conjoin seemingly separated spatial and ethical spheres—as an intellectual foundation out of which to construct a wider sociology and anthropology, ranging from depiction of the underpinnings of solidarity to what Bauman (2000) famously called "liquid modernity."

Another famous turn-of-the-twentieth-century work of northern European scholarship deployed pilgrimage as a guiding frame for a broader comparative argument about human society. Toward the end of the Victorian era, textual scholar James Frazer published the first two volumes of *The Golden Bough* (1890), an opus that eventually stretched to well over a million words. The work became enormously popular—quite an achievement for an erudite text whose aim, it seemed, was to explain a long-forgotten murder case from classical Roman times: the ritual assassination of the priests who successively guarded the pagan shrine at Nemi, situated a little way outside of Rome. Yet on reflection, perhaps the success of Frazer's book was not so surprising. There was something alluring about the way it enlisted readers into exploring the rituals and mythologies of peoples around the world and simultaneously into a consideration of the history of human rationality and irrationality. At the end of the epic work, Frazer offered a memorable metaphor of movement coming to a halt: "Our long voyage of discovery is over and our bark has dropped her weary sails in port at last. Once more we take the road to Nemi" (Frazer 1951, 827). It now becomes clear that Frazer—a proto-anthropologist, though not a fieldworker—has been taking readers on a journey that is closely akin to a pilgrimage. We have departed from and returned to the same spot, having explored realms beyond the everyday. Whereas a pilgrim might seek religious revelation, however, Frazer's task has been to move us toward secular enlightenment and away from what he saw as irrational superstition, such as that represented at pagan Nemi—and also, he implies, in Christianity.[38]

Frazer's account would soon be superseded by works written by people who personally undertook journeys that he could only describe or imagine. Unlike much of the work of Durkheim, the British scholar's vision of human society has not stood the test of social scientific time, though some of his ideas concerning magic and the harvesting of ideas from a wide variety of cultures continue to inspire modern Pagan practitioners (see Luhrmann 1989, 167). Frazer's views on totemism were also rejected by Durkheim. However, both writers showed how an implicit pilgrimage model could be central to the foundation of their respective visions, one that emphasized the enduring power of ritual in Durkheim's case and that expressed suspicion of it in Frazer's case. But if Durkheim's theoretical and methodological position was triumphant in the battle to define much social science in the subsequent decades, it also posed a problem for scholars of pilgrimage. He implied that it was vital to delve into specific contexts to understand both the logic and the landscape of a people's way of life. Frazer the textual scholar had flitted between cultures of the world, paying little heed to the details of immediate environments, yet for a later, fieldworking version of anthropology, pilgrimage presented the problem of how to demarcate and explore an inherently expansive field that might stretch across disparate spaces and distinct communities.

This was a challenge that Hertz the ethnographer would never fully be able to address, for he died in military action during the First World War.[39] Nor did his work release a flood of studies focused on contemporary pilgrimage practices, though important writing did appear in subsequent decades. In 1936, the Hungarian ethnologist Sándor Bálint described the pilgrimage made by the people of Szeged to Máriaradna, emphasizing the significance of material culture alongside influences on economic and cultural traditions (Bálint 1936). Gábor Barna (2015, 97) notes that these themes were only taken up again by scholars in the second half of the twentieth century. Anna Niedźwiedź (2015, 78) refers to Stefan Czarnowski, a cultural historian and sociologist of Poland who had been a student of Marcel Mauss.[40] Just before his death, Czarnowski penned a highly influential article on the religious culture of Polish villagers, which presented pilgrimage as an important dimension of the religious culture of peasants: "In spiritual elevation during services and processes, then in unreserved participation in joy, in dance and drunkenness, in walking from stall to stall, the individual somehow becomes immersed in the community" (Czarnowski 1938, 158).[41] As Niedźwiedź points out, this description of unbridled fellowship anticipates later anthropological debate over the concept of *communitas*, developed by the Turners and discussed in chapter 3. It also comes close to what Durkheim had famously understood to be the "collective effervescence" produced by shared rituals, and Niedźwiedź observes (79) that Czarnowski appreciated the identity-building dimension of pilgrimage and its ability to create organic bonds between individual villagers and wider collectivities, including the nation. In these latter observations, Czarnowski anticipated an important paper by the American anthropologist Eric Wolf on the Virgin of Guadalupe as a Mexican national symbol (1958). To a great extent, Wolf's argument elaborated on the Durkheimian and Hertzean (and arguably Czarnowskian) paradigm of focusing on the socially integrative power of ritualized journeying to a central, shared image or icon. However, he soon moved on to other things, and generally speaking, the field did not reignite, at least in Euro-American scholarly debates, until the work of the Turners in the 1970s.[42]

Once revived, the study of pilgrimage would resonate with new developments in social scientific methods and interests, not only the varied mobilities discussed by Clifford and Bauman (cf. Huang 2107, 285) but also interest in post-secular forms of spirituality (e.g., Nilsson and Tesfahuney 2016), and in due course "multi-sited ethnography"—based on the assertion that researchers could achieve sufficient ethnographic depth while tracking between spatially separated sites (Coleman and von Hellerman 2011; Marcus 1995).[43] Nonetheless, the fundamental question remained within pilgrimage studies, particularly in its ethnographic guises: precisely *where* and *how* to focus one's attention? This is the problem I continue to address in the next chapter, where I move toward a working definition.

2

Constructing the Field

More Than Shrines

Scales of Attention

Spread out over space and time, frequently characterized by intermittent bursts of energy followed by periods of seeming quiescence, pilgrimages pose numerous challenges to ethnographers as to where to focus their gaze. Robert Hertz's (2017) solution in the early part of the twentieth century was to concentrate largely on ritual activities carried out in the environs of a single shrine. Much later, as pilgrimage became a more popular object of study toward the end of the century, researchers began to recognize the limitations of traditional methods of fieldwork. In-depth understanding of a single locale remained valuable but also began to seem myopic in the face of an increasingly interconnected world, alongside a growing appreciation of the complexities of pilgrimage organization and participation.[1]

Some of the problems of situating contemporary fieldwork are expressed by Hillary Kaell in her account of American Christian pilgrimages to the Holy Land. She refers not only to the proliferating cultural associations connected with sacred travel but also to the need to situate journeys within broad temporal, social, and biographical contexts:

> Underlying my approach is the recognition that the experience of pilgrimage extends before and after the trip itself. It is embedded in pilgrims' everyday lives. This book's orientation therefore differs from most other work on modern pilgrimage; it is the first in-depth study of contemporary American Holy Land pilgrimage and, more broadly, the first major study of Christian pilgrimage that tracks how participants prepare for the trip and remember it upon return. (2014, 3)

[handwritten: preparation & recollection as vital components of the pilgrim experience]

43

Shrines
vs
ppl
themselves

While Hertz assumed that his field of study was constituted by the role played by a shrine in the religious, social, and economic life of a region, Kaell's interest is directed more at the experiences of individual pilgrims. Rather than assuming that her main center of ethnographic attention should be a single shrine, Kaell emphasizes the salience of numerous, often mutually distant, locales, including ones that are decidedly mundane. Achieving ethnographic depth is undoubtedly made harder as a consequence of such a diffuse and multi-sited approach, but the analytical payoff is clear. The Holy Land experience chronicled by Kaell becomes "fully embedded in longer trajectories; as a stage in an individual's life course; as a part of cultural, theological, and political trends; and as an aspect of ongoing relationships at home" (27).[2]

In advocating for an expanded field, Kaell might also have mentioned Jill Dubisch's *In a Different Place* (1995). This book describes pilgrimage to the Church of the Madonna of the Annunciation on the Aegean island of Tinos, emphasizing connections between wider context and Christian shrine. Admittedly, there are cogent reasons why the two texts seem to occupy different corners of the pilgrimage studies field. Dubisch is dealing with Greek Orthodox rather than Roman Catholic and Protestant interlocutors. Her account of the church and associated pilgrimages forms part of a longer research engagement with Tinos and one that has dealt with questions relating to migration, gender, and Mediterraneanist questions of honor and shame (e.g., Dubisch 1972). While Dubisch focuses largely on the physically bounded space of an island, this strategy enables her to present an enlarged vision of pilgrimage, locating it within a more extensive ethnographic and analytical framework than is common in many studies (Dubisch 1995, 7). Her effort to render pilgrimage boundaries fuzzy and permeable provides important ethnographic insights into ways in which the shrine is articulated with island, regional, and national culture. The pilgrimage complex emerges as rewarding to study precisely because it *cannot* readily be defined—in either the dictionary sense of having a clear denotational meaning or the ethnographic sense of retaining sharp distinctness from other customs and practices.

In Kaell's and Dubisch's work, we see two excellent studies that wrestle with questions of figure and ground in establishing pilgrimage as their object of research. Dubisch memorably presents her site not as a bounded space but as

a web—at its center the object of devotion, but with strands spun outward both by the pilgrims and by other forces (such as the media, the
church, and national politics). . . . Thus the site is permanent through
the presence of its physical center, which provides a magnet to pilgrims,
but impermanent and constantly fluctuating in its personnel, as well as
mutable in the accumulation of its history and the meanings assigned to
it over time. (1995, 38)

Dubisch's depiction of pilgrimage as a reticulate and shifting accumulation of acts and practices parallels another rich ethnography of
pilgrimage, Ann Gold's (1988) *Fruitful Journeys*. Gold examines the
varieties of pilgrimage carried out by Hindu inhabitants of a village in
Rajasthan. She notes that while pilgrims' journeys are usually round
trips, Hindu pilgrimage has most commonly been studied from the
perspective of the journey's destination—"the temple town, the lake, or
mountain shrine—with little attention to its closure or return lap" (1).
By contrast, she bases herself in a village "whose residents are much else
before they are pilgrims and for much more of the time than they are
pilgrims" (2). She therefore anticipates Kaell's methodology for studying Christian pilgrims by quite some years, but again in the context of a
different set of academic debates and ones rooted in study of Hinduism
rather than Christianity. She observes that her "initial decision to study
pilgrimage from a village rather than a crossing place was founded on
the conviction that pilgrims must be understood first as householders.
Transformations of their persons or life aims in the pilgrimage process
would only be intelligible from that foundation" (34).[3]

Just as Dubisch uses pilgrimage to reflect on broader questions of
reflexivity, ethnographic writing, and feminist approaches in anthropology, so Gold explores wider issues—in her case relating to the com-
memoration of the dead in rural life in India. Both approaches enable
us to observe the significance and effects of pilgrimage from a variety
of epistemological and ethnographic perspectives. Gold also expands
our ethnographic horizons by showing how pilgrimage is diffused at
numerous scales in the lives of villagers; small shrines dedicated to local
deities are found near water tanks, in village streets, in pasturelands, and
so on, attracting greater or lesser degrees of attention, their reputations
for effectiveness rising and falling over time. While trips to local shrines

are integrated into normal existence—perhaps squeezed into the gaps in a day's work—the *yātrā* to a more distant, major shrine at the Ganges River at Hardwar or the temple of Jagannath Puri is more readily connected with high ethical aspirations, such as achievement of merit (*puṇya*), the removal of sins, or even final release (*moksha*).

Gold's work combines in-depth ethnography with an appreciation of how villagers' lives are oriented toward a differentiated landscape of sacralized places. Elsewhere, I and others (Bajc, Coleman, and Eade 2007, 325–26; cf. Bajc 2006) have referred to how smaller or newer shrines in a pilgrimage system may echo the characteristics of a better-known destination, so that they become akin to fractals both mirroring and diffusing from a major shrine, while sometimes becoming centers in their own right.[4] Such work uses complexity theory to indicate how pilgrimage locations catalyze further patterns of both concentration and diffusion of worship. Pioneering work on the theme of the relationships between sites has come, perhaps tellingly, not from a conventional ethnographer but from a cultural geographer, Surinder Bhardwaj. In *Hindu Places of Pilgrimage in India* (1973; see also, e.g., Feldhaus 2003), Bhardwaj presents a typology of sites, assessing the possibility that "higher-level" shrines might have a greater proportion of religiously more mobile pilgrims than "lower-level" ones. While he is dealing with assumptions concerning space, hierarchy, and merit that emerge from a Hindu, Indian context, his depiction of ranking measured in terms of catchment area has attracted comparisons with pilgrimage patterns elsewhere.[5] Ian Reader (2005), for instance, reports that pilgrims to the sacred island of Shikoku come from every part of the country and even overseas, making it a national pilgrimage in contrast to more modest sites in Japan (25–26).[6]

In later work, Bhardwaj (1991) expands his understanding of the spatial and scalar scope of pilgrimage. He emphasizes the heightened importance of pilgrimage landscapes for Hindus who have settled in the United States. Not only do most Hindu homes in America maintain a small family altar for favorite deities, saints, and deceased elders (81), but identity is anchored at larger and more visible levels in diasporic space through the building of temples and establishment of shrines. Like Thomas Tweed's (1997) study of Cuban migrants in Florida, Bhardwaj's work shows that such sites may bridge new and old senses and spaces of belonging. For instance, the fact that Pittsburgh contains a confluence of rivers has allowed it to be interpreted as equivalent to the Ganges, resulting in a "remarkable transformation of the Steel City to a sacred centre" (1990, 93). *is it the sites that transform the*

Bhardwaj is keenly aware that no pilgrimage landscape remains fixed. *pilgrims* He asserts (1999) that growth and change (including, we might add, de-*of the* cline) are encoded within the pilgrimage process. In an obvious exam-*pilgrims* ple, Sikhs and Hindus shared many sites in India before their political *who* polarization made such intermingling of streams less sustainable. At the *transform* time of Bhardwaj's writing in the late 1990s, the number of Hindu pil-*the* grims to the famous Sikh Golden Temple of Amritsar had become barely *sites?* a trickle.[7] He concludes that a pilgrimage system should be understood as a living entity sustained by movement of travelers, akin to a human body kept alive through the constant circulation of blood. His use of a fluid metaphor is reminiscent of Tweed's (2006) notion of religion as "flow," or even Bauman's (1996) "liquid modernity," but for him, it leads to a discussion of how chaos theory may also be applied to pilgrimage sites and the ways in which they attract visitors. In other words, he invokes a branch of mathematics developed to understand dynamic systems by showing that behind apparent surface randomness, underlying patterns may indeed be discerned, even if such patterns are much more unpredictable than the repetitive workings of a closed system of mechanical operations.[8]

Bhardwaj's broadly ranging approach is clearly appropriate to his interest in finding regularities of movement within larger pilgrimage systems.[9] More ethnographic work has also attempted to explore the implications of tracking relationships across fields of dynamically though diffusely interlinked shrines.[10] In their introduction to a special issue devoted to the topic, Marc Loustau and Kate DeConinck criticize "singularism" in pilgrimage studies, by which they mean the tendency for some researchers to focus on individual shrines, sites, or routes, reflecting "the lingering effects of anthropology's long standing preference for place over movement and circulation" (2019, 14).[11] Admittedly, neglect of "what it means, for both individuals and communities, to encounter different pilgrimage sites over time" is not a criticism that can be leveled at Gold's assiduous tracking of the pilgrimage careers of the villagers she studies (ibid.). However, Loustau and DeConinck are examining jour-

neys made under very different circumstances to those that characterize Gold's text. They focus largely on Euro-American Catholic contexts,
highlighting cases where hierarchical relationships among sites are unclear, and emphasize that their interest lies in examining how pilgrims
"juxtapose multiple pilgrimage sites in and through culturally, socially,
and institutionally mediated stories, memories, objects, and spaces" (13).
They observe that the habit of visiting multiple shrines is growing in
popularity around the world, fostered by particular networks and institutions such as the European Marian Network, which facilitates collaboration among Catholic pilgrimage sites, involving the movements of
millions of people per year.

Loustau and DeConinck focus on Catholics, but they present a
broadly applicable way to de-parochialize pilgrimage studies by showing how travelers are often acutely aware of the salience to their lives of
multiple religious landscapes.[12] They deploy a useful framing metaphor
to describe what happens when connections between apparently separate sites and experiences are constructed through journeys, objects,
narratives, or memories: the palimpsest. This term refers to a document
produced when its original writing is removed to create space for later
inscription, but leaving traces of the earlier text.[13] It therefore provides a
means to reflect on ways in which sites, stories, histories, and materialities become intertwined. For instance, DeConinck (2019) presents an intimate portrait of an American Catholic woman who conveys the statue
of an angel to different sites of traumatic remembrance, facilitating
"trans-situational bonding" (131) in the process of creating biographical,
cultural, and spiritual meaning out of emblematic situations of tragedy.

If the idea of the palimpsest blurs the spatial, spiritual, and temporal
boundaries of the single site, it illustrates what Loustau and DeConinck
see as the dialogical construction of human experience that emerges
from "the interplay of subject and objects, the singular and the multiple,
and individuals and communities" (2019, 9). In contrast to the Frazerian
top-down model of *The Golden Bough* (1890), where the writer swoops
in and out of cultures and case studies, they acknowledge the considerable ritual, semiotic, and emotional labor that goes into the creation of
biographical, material, and imaginative bonds between pilgrimage sites
by pilgrims. Their approach reminds me of my own work on pilgrimage and cathedrals in England. While a colleague on the project, Tiina

Sepp, was carrying out fieldwork at Canterbury in 2014, she talked to a middle-aged man called Michael. At first glance, Michael, a committed Methodist, seemed like an unlikely source of information about pilgrimage. Yet when he heard about our project, he was eager to recount his experiences. Originally from Yorkshire, in the north of England, he now lived in the south of the country but often holidayed in Wales. What was striking about Michael's conversation was that each of these places featured in his list of the pilgrimage sites that were most important to him:

> St. David's [in Wales] is very close to the wild wilderness, you know, cliff tops, sea, which is a strong thing for me. In York, it's where I come from, Yorkshire's where I come from, it represents the strengths of the hillsides, you know, the history. And Canterbury clearly is the center of our Protestant faith. So those three places are . . . maybe I'll feel it elsewhere, I don't know, but those are my three . . . like a magnet.

Narrative, nature, memory, and meaning-making combine in Michael's words as he weaves together three shrines in giving an account of pilgrimages that punctuate his life. The places form a division of spiritual and spatial labor that encompasses a peripheral wildness (St. David's), a powerful sense of home (York), and an acknowledgment of an ecclesiastical center (Canterbury). Landscape also takes on a kind of unifying agency, associated with notions of strength in both Wales and Yorkshire. Above all, Michael's comments provide a powerful warning against the dangers of singularism in the study of pilgrimage; for Michael as pilgrim, the features of his spiritual landscape are multiple, operative at different scales, and ineluctably interlinked.

If work on pilgrimage lends itself to multi-sited approaches, the examples I have explored indicate the different directions an ethnographic perspective might take. Kaell provides an example of how focus on activities at a sacred site should be augmented by tracking how the religious center relates to the domestic, everyday life of the pilgrim, though this task is enormously complicated by the fact that visitors to a shrine may come from multiple parts of a region, nation, or world. An alternative strategy is provided by Dubisch's blurring of the boundaries between a shrine and its immediate context—an approach that takes into account the fact that some visitors may come from far away, while others may regard the shrine as part of their home environment. Another methodological ploy is evident in Gold's decision to make a single village the foundation of her fieldwork but then to follow pilgrims from their homes as they make journeys of very different lengths and degrees of commitment out into a ramifying landscape of shrines. The perspective might shift again when adopting a more cartographic view, as suggested by Bhardwaj, who surveys wider systems of shrines and movements between them. Finally, Loustau and DeConinck combine an ethnographic methodology with an attempt to track ways in which pilgrims create and imagine links between sites, lending a further dimension of complexity to the pilgrimage field of study.[14] None of these approaches on its own can fully cover the full potential of the pilgrimage field that expands beyond the classic model of moving to and from a sacred center, but taken together, they provide a powerful array of options.

Between Definition and Articulation

By tracing numerous theoretical and methodological pathways into pilgrimage studies over the past two chapters, I have conveyed the difficulties but also the possibilities entailed in constructing a working definition of pilgrimage that is sustainable across disciplines, religions, and regions. At a highly generic level, I have explored cases involving movement in relation to a place that represents an ideal, an aspiration, and/or a divine presence of some sort.[15] In line with the monothetic approach that I mentioned at the beginning of chapter 1, these elements might be presented as necessary and sufficient in order to classify a given activity as pilgrimage. Yet this classification would not take into account key indices such as length and frequency of travel or degree of commitment of participants. It is not sufficiently nuanced to deal with the fact that everyday attendance at a church, mosque, or temple also involves movement to a place that is valued. The problem of definition is compounded by the fact that no single feature of pilgrimage separates it from other forms of religious behavior. Ritual, travel, inspiration from scriptures or charismatic figures, use of relics, circumambulation, healing through divine intervention, belief in the miraculous, and so on could all be combined with each other in various ways without constituting what we might regard as pilgrimage.

how to distinguish pilgrimage from ___ without losing the acknowledged complexity of the subject

A pragmatic response to these challenges is to say that for the purposes of constructing a field flexible enough to encourage comparative conversations, we should abandon any attempt to produce a monothetic definition.[16] Rather, we should deploy what the anthropologist Rodney Needham (1975), drawing on Wittgenstein's concept of "family resemblances," has called "polythetic classification" (see also Coleman and Hackett 2015, 12). In this view, a given class of object or activity is defined through a number of features; but while any single example will contain some of those features, it need not contain all. Individual members of the class will therefore vary in their similarities to each other.[17] From a polythetic perspective salient characteristics of pilgrimage include, though are not confined to, sacralized space, solemn vows, foundational and other narratives (oral or written), marked movement of people and material culture, connections between institutions and activities, the possibility of transformation, and mediating institutions associated with any of the other elements.[18]

Such a polythetic approach is helpful for my purposes, though it leaves definitional dilemmas. How many characteristics must be present to gain entry into the class of pilgrimage activity? Who decides what the characteristics should be? Furthermore, how can we say that what we classify as, say, movement or narrative in one context will be sufficiently similar to what we observe elsewhere? These questions are important, but they also beg the basic ethnographic question that I raised at the beginning of chapter 1. Both fieldwork and the work of cross-cultural comparison are constituted through classifications that are inherently provisional and dialogical. Analysis is rendered still more complex when dealing with a multifaceted and contested institution. Would we therefore be justified in claiming that a field constructed around such a slippery topic is incapable of sustaining coherent scholarly discussion? I propose three responses to this question.

First, it is reasonable to suggest that pilgrimage as an ethnographic or theoretical object of study does not always need to be clearly demarcated to provide viable, fruitful areas of investigation.[19] Questions drawn from elsewhere may usefully be applied to situations that involve, but do not need to establish the precise boundaries of, pilgrimages and shrines. For instance, *Medusa's Hair* (1981), by Gananath Obeyesekere, is a bold exploration of psychoanalysis and symbolism that happens to deploy an ethnographic account of Hindu and Buddhist pilgrimage practices in Kataragama.[20] Pilgrimage also provides excellent contexts through which to examine questions of healing and responses to human suffering, where an exact definition of pilgrimage itself is arguably of secondary importance (e.g., Dubisch and Winkelman 2005).[21] Another approach that uses pilgrimage as illustrative of wider processes involves work on gender relations.[22] Anna-Karina Hermkens, Willy Jansen, and Catrien Notermans's edited volume *Moved by Mary* (2009) explores both the emancipatory and the reactionary dimensions of Marian devotion, paying particular attention to women's representation in both religious and academic practice, issues also discussed extensively by Dubisch (1995), among others.[23] Finally, Premakumara de Silva (2020) locates a study of Sri Lankan pilgrimage within a wider discussion of the anthropology of youth, showing how young people negotiate and transform inherited forms of religious behavior.[24] In all these cases, pilgrimage provides a rich behavioral and institutional background for discussion of theoretical concerns that might also have been explored in other, very different, ethnographic contexts.

Second, it is nevertheless possible to assert that studies of pilgrimage have sometimes generated distinctive debates. An obvious example, explored in the next chapter, is Victor and Edith Turner's (1978) deployment of specific terms such as *communitas*, *root paradigms*, and *the liminoid* in constructing their influential template of (Christian) pilgrimage. Whether or not we judge it to be sufficient or sustainable, their approach has encouraged focus on pilgrimage per se as a marked sphere of human action, posing specific questions over the formation of human fellowship at sacred places.

A third response points more directly to the strategy I promote in this book, which negotiates a pathway between understanding pilgrimage as "mere" ethnographic background, on the one hand, and as discrete, sui generis activity, on the other. In observing pilgrimage through a lens of articulation, I take its cultural and institutional distinctiveness to be inherently flexible, negotiable, and bound to context. At the same time, I understand it to entail the making and remaking of separation and union, dislocation and relocation. Pilgrimage thus adopts the double identity of articulation; it encompasses both degrees of *distinctiveness* and varieties of internal and external *connectedness*.[25] Indeed, the focus of my analysis becomes the very ambiguity but also power of pilgrimage, its often socially, culturally, and spiritually charged capacities for disassembly and reassembly, autonomy and entrainment.

These themes will be revisited in future chapters, where my argument will be concretized and explicated through ethnographic accounts. First, however, I need to reexamine and critique the course of pilgrimage studies as it developed between the time when Hertz published his piece on St. Besse in 1913 and when Kaell produced her account of Holy Land pilgrimage in 2014. The next chapter deals with the most influential twentieth-century contribution to the study of pilgrimage within the world of Anglophone anthropology. I show how this approach opened up the field in ways that proved inspiring yet constricting, highlighting many spiritual, spatial, and social connections made by pilgrims but fatefully ignoring or neglecting others. Brilliant as it was, it paid scant attention to the full powers of pilgrimage.

PART II

Tropes

3

A Trope Made to Travel

Communitas

Forming a Field

Some concepts refuse to fade away, no matter how often they are dismissed or deconstructed. Within pilgrimage studies, the obvious candidate for such undead status is *communitas*. Even after enduring numerous criticisms, the term continues its intellectual trajectory along a pathway located somewhere between trope and cliché.[1] In her last book, Edith Turner, who developed the concept with her husband Victor Turner in the 1960s and 1970s, claimed that communitas "has to do with the sense felt by a group of people when their life together takes on full meaning" (2012, 1). Her sentiment combines description with aspiration, illustrating the attractive yet slippery dimensions of an academic idea that also represents an ethical ideal.

In this and the next two chapters, I use the category of the trope to refer to analytical motifs that circulate widely within a subfield, guiding research and discussion. Such devices are not to be condemned; rather the reverse—they emerge and retain salience because they provide rare insights, enabling resonant conversations to take form.[2] Accordingly, communitas can be seen as a trope whose influence has reflected the allure of its original conception. But it has also run the risk of stifling other perspectives because of its sheer ubiquity. The continued authoritative movement of communitas through scholarly texts illustrates what linguistic scholars call "entextualization," a process whereby a stretch of language (or, in this case, an analytical term) becomes reified and easily removable from its original context so that it can be applied elsewhere.[3] We can see this process in action as we trace the significance of communitas in the Turners' work and beyond. Its development reinforced their increasing propensities for both broad comparison and high abstraction as they shifted their focus on Africa toward wider fields of interest, combining anthropological, theological, literary, and ethical concerns.[4] The trope expressed and reinforced their passionate response to political and cultural developments in the latter half of the twentieth century, and it was taken up in the work of numerous other scholars. Yet even as the image of communitas spoke to numerous disciplines and extended its reach into discussions of many human activities, ranging from sacred travel to rock concerts, it also limited understandings of the scope, influence, and complexity of social and material articulations associated with pilgrimage.

Journey toward Ritual

The story of the emergence of *communitas* as an analytical term has been much told and retold. Some of what follows is well known, but it expands current perspectives in two ways. First, I lay out the intellectual, social, and cultural influences on the Turners, which have been documented by some scholars but often ignored within pilgrimage studies.[5] Understanding these influences helps explain how *communitas* became a term and a trope that lent itself very readily to being circulated across texts and case studies. Second, I argue that readings of the Turners' work have focused attention on some of its dimensions but ignored others, at least as they were framed in the Turners' most famous work on pilgrimage, *Image and Pilgrimage in Christian Culture* (1978).

Mathieu Deflem (1991, 2) points out that Victor Turner (1920–83), born to an electrical engineer and an actress, studied English language and literature as an undergraduate at University College, London, in the late 1930s and early 1940s. Victor and Edith Brocklesby Davis (1921–2016) were married in 1943, and Edie was to become an important contributor to work that is sometimes attributed too readily to Vic alone (Engelke 2004, 2008; Glazier 2018, 37).[6] A literary sensibility remained salient to both Turners, even as they became increasingly interested in anthropology during the early 1940s.[7] Both also retained a propensity to combine moral commitment with claiming outsiderhood. Victor remained a pacifist during the war, serving as a noncombatant bomb-disposal officer, and Edith became a founder member of the Campaign for Nuclear Disarmament in the 1950s.[8] Victor completed his PhD not in establishment Oxbridge but at the newly formed Department of Anthropology at the University of Manchester. The latter provided an intense social and intellectual forum, committed to debating questions of social justice and change, urbanization, migration, and the radical politics of a postwar, postcolonial landscape, particularly in Africa.

The founder of the Manchester Department and Victor's doctoral supervisor, Max Gluckman, was originally trained in law and encouraged what was called the extended case-study method, also termed "situational analysis," which anatomized socially complex and conflictual sets of encounters to discern wider norms and assumptions at play. Gluckman critiqued the structural functionalism of his anthropological education and emphasized the need to view argument and contradiction as "key to social order and process" (Evens and Handelman 2006, 3), combining a Durkheimian interest in stability with a Marxian interest in dialectical relations. This perspective encouraged a questioning of "the unambiguous boundedness of groups," as the anthropologist was encouraged to traced the intermeshing of different social formations—an approach that would prompt some of Gluckman's students to develop a "network vision of situated social process" (Frankenberg 2006, 210).[9]

The fieldwork that resulted in Victor's PhD was based on research among the Ndembu of Northern Rhodesia (now Zambia), published with the suggestive title *Schism and Continuity in an African Society: A Study of Ndembu Village Life* (Turner 1957). Deflem (1991, 4) observes that the book reflected some of the intellectual avenues imposed by Gluckman, who apparently advised Victor to avoid writing about Ndembu ritual until he understood their social structure (see also Engelke 2008, 281).[10] Also in line with Gluckman's emphasis, Victor considered that structure emerged in part out of relations of tension and dispute within and between villages, alongside mechanisms that could be introduced to mitigate the effects of strife. As Edith explained to the anthropologist Matthew Engelke, Victor's "version of political anthropology was local-level politics and the actual political rivalries" (Deflem 1991, 279).[11]

The most famous concept to emerge out of this early work was the idea of the social drama, the assertion that Ndembu social life was made up of successive periods of discord, rupture, and resolution, reflecting inherent contradictions in the principles underlying social life alongside ongoing efforts to seek ways to coexist (Kapferer 2006, 136). Victor retained Gluckman's concern with understanding order in a dynamic, chronic sense, as well as the tendency to think in dialectical terms of society being made up of shifting alliances and oppositions. In his chronicle of the history of the Manchester School, Richard Werbner (1984, 157) notes how a focus on the micropolitics and the ritualization of social relations led to interest in the ways groups form and reform—segmenting or coming together in crosscutting alliances (ibid.). *Schism and Continuity* thus presented rich accounts of the dilemmas and conflicts of interest facing "humanly rounded individuals" (176–77) as they balanced social order with strategic manipulation. It explored the power of symbols and language but also the push and pull of human transactions (176), while posing questions about the seemingly ineluctable character of social processes as they enveloped the life and fate of the actor.

Many of the themes that would inform the Turners' future work on pilgrimage had now been established. However, soon after Victor submitted his thesis, the couple initiated a series of intellectual and social breaches of their own, personal dramas with no easy resolution. In 1957, Victor not only renounced Marxism and his membership of the Communist Party but also, along with Edith (the daughter of an Anglican clergyman), joined the Roman Catholic Church. The following years saw them devoting their attention more closely to Ndembu ritual as a topic in its own right. Deflem (1991, 5) attributes this shift both to the theatrical influence of Victor Turner's mother and to the sheer importance of ritual to the Ndembu. Frankenberg suggests another significant motivation: its wider relevance "in their own shared similar experience in the Eucharist and in pilgrimages of his newfound and her rediscovered Catholic faith" (2006, 215). This impression is reinforced by Edith in her characterization of that time: "I suppose that for us there was something of this ritual fever in the Catholic Church" (quoted in Engelke 2008, 284). The conjoining of ethnographic field with intimate styles of worship reinforced a blurring of boundaries that would continue as their domestic and professional lives blended in a powerful combination of religious calling and intellectual commitment.

These ruptures involved significant continuities. The Turners retained their desire to support the underdog and to value popular expressions of culture. The turn to ritual reinforced their interest in heightened expressions of social life—dramas or performances where roles were openly enacted or rejected, basic principles exposed—through an understanding of the differentiated rhythms of social life. Much later, Edith Turner reflected that her husband emerged from the "process anthropology" developed in Manchester with the desire to "set out the rituals he had documented, not as structured custom, but as moment-by-moment living situations" (2012, 6). One of the further significant arguments of *The Forest of Symbols* (V. Turner 1967) was that Ndembu ritual contained so-called dominant symbols, deployed across different rituals, which evoked clusters or fans of abstract, interconnected meanings but also catalyzed arousing experiences, so that—in rather Durkheimian fashion—such rituals might become effervescent occasions when the socially "obligatory" was converted into the humanly "desirable" (30). The implication was that mind and body could work together in the consolidation of social and cultural commitment.[12]

The isolation of ritual as an object of study contributed to what would become a more general shift in the Turners' work, toward a broader comparative scale and a greater abstraction of cultural focus and conceptual apparatus. The change in emphasis occurred at a significant point of transition for the Turners, when they were about to depart to the United States for Victor to take up a professorship at Cornell University.[13] It appears that during this interlude, Victor was reading Arnold van Gennep's *Rites of Passage*, a work originally published in France in 1909 by an important contemporary and rival of Durkheim.[14] Van Gennep referred to pilgrimage, but it was not a major dimension of his writing (Fedele and Isnard 2015, 173). However, the notion of the rite of passage provided several key elements for the Turnerian view of ritual and ultimately their approach to pilgrimage: an ambitious attempt to make generalizations about rites around the world combined with an interest in popular religion, alongside an argument that showed how rituals not only operated at times of social and cultural transition and crisis but also displayed an inherently dynamic form in their very constitution (cf. Deflem 1991).[15] Although he looked to a very different intellectual genealogy from that of the Turners, van Gennep shared with them an attempt to reconcile structural and transitional dimensions of social order. He claimed that rituals marking and enacting social transformations followed a strikingly common pattern of separating initiates from society, holding them temporarily in threshold-like periods of liminality and then reintegrating them back into society as publicly acknowledged occupants of their new social status.[16]

The idea of "passage" resonated well with the Turnerian emphasis on "process." In one response to van Gennep, Victor Turner produced a now famous essay, "Betwixt and Between: The Liminal Period in *Rites de Passage*" (1964). Turner focuses on a single part of van Gennep's grammar of ritual: the period of liminality, rendered distinct from the behaviors surrounding it. Turner emphasizes that during liminality, ritual initiates are kept apart from everyday life, while many of their distinguishing features—gender, personality, status—are stripped away, rendering them equal to each other and socially nullified, even blank. During this period of transition, when they are neither one thing nor the other, initiates become particularly receptive and submissive to powerful sacred symbols and the effects of playful if temporary reversals of social order. Liminality therefore presents an alternative to the status quo, but it usually ends in people being returned, albeit transformed, to everyday structures of life and new obligations associated with their novel status.[17] What is ultimately changed is not society but the person and their role in that society.

[margin handwritten note: how do liminal moments reverse the social order?]

Liminality is presented by the Turners as most prevalent within social and ritual systems constituted by forms of stability, repetitiveness, and communal participation, which they see as characteristic of tribal as opposed to Western, industrial contexts. This distinction between industrial and non-industrial now seems anachronistic, but the basic argument is that liminality emerges out of situations of social and collective obligation (V. Turner 1974, 42) where even the breaking of rules ("anti-structure") is regulated and carefully framed and where the initiate is ultimately pitched back into a society marked by rigid normative structures and shared role expectations (Coleman 2018a).[18]

Such ideas were being developed by the Turners as they were migrating away from a British anthropological focus on social structure (as well as the strictures of the Manchester School) toward relatively freer, North American interpretations of culture and symbol (see, e.g., Geertz 1973).[19] Engelke (2008, 284) notes that the important book *The Ritual Process: Structure and Anti-structure* (V. Turner 1969), based on lectures delivered in 1966 and written while the two were at Cornell, was produced at a time when the couple—as ever combining the personal and the professional, the practical and the theoretical—were hosting ritualized anthropology seminars in their home. Academic presentations (structure) would lead to beer and informal conversations (anti-structure/liminality) followed by focused discussions (reaggregation).

At a larger scale, the 1960s saw periods of student revolt (Moore and Myerhoff 1977) and mass dropping out of hippies alongside the increased visibility of newer Pentecostal and charismatic movements. All these events contributed to a wider sense that anti-structure could be witnessed not only at the center of Ndembu ritual but also on the streets and campuses of Euro-American life. Indeed, such antinomianism might even be said to have permeated the rituals of Roman Catholicism to which the Turners were devoted, given the prominence of the controversial Vatican II reforms, instituted during the 1960s to modernize and democratize the liturgies and wider structures of the church. It seemed that "process" was in the air.

Journey toward Communitas

If the late 1950s and 1960s saw significant personal, political, and intellectual transformations for the Turners, *The Ritual Process* signaled a further development in the speed and direction of their anthropological trajectory. This is not only the book where the concept of communitas was first developed; it also represented a shift in focus from the Ndembu to a much wider, comparative, perspective. Chapter 3, called "Liminality and Communitas," begins with a summary of van Gennep and then combines summaries of African ethnography with brief glances at millenarian movements, hippies, and Benedictine monks. The next chapter, "Communitas: Model and Process," starts with reference to student seminars that Victor ran at Cornell, moves through Tolstoy, Shakespeare's *The Tempest*, the poverty of Franciscan monks, Indian *bhakti* movements, and ends with Bob Dylan. Van Gennep's liminality is abstracted still further and extended, positioned on the borders between orderly transition and wider societal change. Edith herself later described this book as marking a turning point, shifting "attention to the ways of the West" (1992, x). It helped establish a mode of academic address that appealed to anthropologists but also went beyond disciplinary boundaries.

It is in chapter 3 of *The Ritual Process* that Victor Turner argues that the character of human relationships during the liminal period "is of society as an unstructured or rudimentarily structured and relatively undifferentiated comitatus, community, or even communion of equal individuals who submit together to the general authority of the ritual elders," adding that "I prefer the Latin term 'communitas' to 'community,' to distinguish this modality of social relationship from an 'area of common living'" (1969, 96). The term was probably borrowed from a book by urban planners Percival and Paul Goodman called *Communitas: Means of Livelihood and Ways of Life* (1947), an influential and visionary text devoted to the best methods of managing the postwar city and thus very different from an anthropological depiction of the radical equality found in conditions running the full gamut from millenarian movements to tribal relations of matrilaterality.[20] Victor actually removes his version of the concept from rootedness in conventional understandings of place: "I have tried to eschew the notion that communitas has a specific territorial focus, often limited in character, which pervades many definitions" (1969, 126).

In the Turnerian view, escape from structure, territory, and "societas" did not need to result in what the seventeenth-century political scientist Thomas Hobbes had famously called a "warre of every one against every one."[21] Rather, it might be funneled more positively into "a relationship between concrete, historical, idiosyncratic individuals" (V. Turner, 131) and one where "these individuals are not segmentalized into roles and statuses but confront one another rather in the manner of Martin Buber's 'I and Thou'" (132; Buber 1923). The invocation of Buber, an Austrian-born Jewish philosopher and theologian, seems significant for what it says about the expanded intellectual and ethical landscape through which the Turners were now moving with some speed. According to Edith Turner (2012, 6), at stake was the imagining of a form of solidarity that neither celebrated the triumphalist individualism of postwar America nor recalled the ominous mass rallies of 1930s Germany.[22] For Buber and the Turners, the conjuring of a sense of I-Thou represented a spontaneous removal of mediating obstacles so that a temporary relationship of mutual flow might emerge between people, creating unbounded reciprocity and unfettered interpersonal connection—what Buber called *Zwischenmenschliche* (V. Turner 1969, 127).[23] These equalizing tendencies had both semiotic and spiritual implications; the cultural and the social baggage of everyday life could be cleared away, producing both a Christian ideal of irenic reconciliation and a countercultural celebration of authenticity. Even so, communitas was not the pure opposite of structure; over the course of social, cultural, and institutional life, the two were in a "tensional dynamic" (Vadakkiniyil 2019, 16)—conjoined and mutually defining (Turner 1969; see Higgins and Hamilton 2020, 2).[24] At one point *The Ritual Process* refers to the ways in which Christianity retains traces of "the passage quality of the religious life" (1969, 107) in the depiction of the believer as stranger to the world and/or pilgrim. Four years later, Victor published what would become a celebrated essay in *History of Religions* called "The Center out There: Pilgrim's Goal," where he refers to wider-ranging work in progress on "those pilgrimage processes, many of which have consolidated into pilgrimage systems, to be found in the major historical religions: Christianity, Islam, Judaism, Hinduism, Buddhism, Confucianism, Taoism, and Shintoism" (V. Turner 1973, 191). Laying out much of his future approach, this paper links pilgrimages with the idea of networks, suggesting that sites are notable for the ways in which they bring together multiple journeys to and from the relevant sacred location. The notion of the "center out there" claims the possibility of creating a location for religious authority separate from political or economic concentrations of power.[25] It plays on the structural peripherality of many sites—the fact that they are often reached only through arduous journeys along routes that become increasingly sacralized along the way (214)—even while asserting that they have a magnetic quality, generating a field of communications and other activities that may result in the adjacent growth of cities and other infrastructure such as markets and roads.

However, it is with the jointly published *Image and Pilgrimage* in 1978 (dedicated to the late Max Gluckman) that the Turners take the next step in developing their processual approach through providing a major study of Christian pilgrimage, one that explores sacred travel as a prime ritual activity through which communitas is cultivated. By this point, the Turners had spent a decade or so at the University of Chicago but had also carried out numerous pilgrimages in Europe and the Americas.[26] *Image and Pilgrimage* does not look at all like a conventional ethnographic monograph.[27] A preface and initial chapter signal the intellectual and methodological move that the Turners felt that they were making: "The 'extended case-method' has been temporarily set aside, the 'social drama' abandoned, in order to expound the interrelations of symbols and meanings framing and motivating pilgrim behavior in a major world religion" (Turner and Turner 1978, xxiv). We see here a rejection of some of the Manchester School approach alongside a scaling up to examine the operations of a globe-spanning religion—the "Christian culture" contained in the subtitle. The focus shifts from social context to symbolic complex; from village-bound Ndembu to mobile pilgrim; from intimate rivalries to anonymous encounters. It opens up the possibility of a dazzling comparative survey that resisted the linear assumptions of inevitable secularization that pervaded many social scientific studies of religion of the period (cf. Luz and Collins-Kreiner 2015, 145).

The enlarged scope of the perspective operates not only across space but also across time, as historical accounts and narratives are examined along with contemporary observations. Indeed, temporal considerations form part of the Turners' categorizing of four different types of pilgrimage, which include but also transcend Christianity (Turner and Turner 1978, 17–18): (1) prototypical forms, established by the founder of a historical religion or his disciples, such as Rome and Jerusalem (Christianity), Mecca (Islam), Benares and Mount Kailas (Hinduism), and Kandy (Buddhism); (2) pilgrimages displaying syncretism with earlier religious practices (including Chalma in Mexico, with its Ocuiltecan and Aztec elements); (3) pilgrimages of the European Middle Ages; (4) the post-Tridentine period of European Catholicism (referring broadly to Catholic theological responses to the Reformation), especially from the nineteenth century onward, marked by fervent personal piety, antisecularism, and elements of self-conscious medievalism.

These classifications inform some of the organization of the book, which devotes individual chapters to Mexican pilgrimages (especially Guadalupe), the ancient St. Patrick's Purgatory, originally medieval pilgrimages including Walsingham, and postindustrial Marian pilgrimage such as Lourdes. In the middle of these accounts, one chapter takes a semiotic approach to the vexed question of iconophily and iconoclasm, with special reference to Marian pilgrimage as it is manifested in Christian history and theology. Some of the tone of the writing can be discerned from the following two extracts from the chapter on St. Patrick's Purgatory in Lough Derg in Country Donegal:

> The pilgrim may now break his fast. He eats in the hostel, seated on a long bench by a plain table, his bare feet resting on the cold cement floor. He is provided with an oaten biscuit, eaten dry, or dry bread, which may, as a concession to the gourmet in all of us, be toasted! In drinks he has a choice: cold or hot water . . . flavored with salt and pepper or sweetened. (Turner and Turner 1978, 120)

> Each boatload of pilgrims contains a cross-section of human society that has a special interest. Sharp contrasts in age are frequent: two men of ninety have been known to have made the pilgrimage in recent years, while girls and boys in their very early teens are always among the crowd. . . . When the newcomer casts off his footwear it is a symbol that he is shedding at the same time all those externals that make up status and lend importance to the individual: house, family and dependents, atmosphere, daily occupation. If he is a personage in his ordinary life, he here undergoes an immense levelling and becomes just one of the crowd. (ibid., 134)

In fact, the second paragraph is not a direct observation but a quotation by the Turners from a book by Irish author Alice Curteyne (1944). It is presumably included because it exemplifies a communitas-like experience, as genders, generations, and classes are rendered temporarily irrelevant. This dimension of the pilgrimage is reinforced by the Turners' universalizing, even impersonal references in the first paragraph to "the pilgrim." Much of the focus is on pilgrimage as exceptional yet widely accessible experience, a sharp disciplining and humbling of the body in order to cultivate both the soul and a particular form of sociality. Operations of church authorities are mostly placed in the background, rendered less relevant than the actions of ordinary pilgrims praying and processing in and to extraordinary places.[28] The book celebrates a populism embodied by noble and uncomplicated forms of piety.[29]

The reader's movement across the landscape of *Image and Pilgrimage* involves a rapid if exhilarating intellectual ride through a "Christian culture" that is broad but still largely made up of major Catholic shrines of Europe and Mexico. At the same time, the book contains much more than can be encompassed by the concept of communitas (Coleman 2014). Early on, the Turners state that pilgrimage should be understood in relation to larger histories and materialities (Turner and Turner 1978, 23), and—appropriating Weberian imagery—they accept that a Protestant ethic has often been linked to capitalism, while arguing that a "'pilgrimage ethic,' with its emphasis on 'holy travel' and the benefits flowing from such travel, may have helped to create the communications networks and contractual relations that later made mercantile and industrial capitalism a viable national and international system" (234; also V. Turner 1973, 228). Pilgrimage is even presented as a permeable form of ritualized action, given that it "is more responsive to social change and popular moods than liturgical ritual, fixed by rubric" (Turner and Turner 1978, 231). One of the broadest depictions of a wider, differentiated, pilgrimage field occurs with the programmatic statement: "We insist, as anthropologists, that we must regard the pilgrimage system . . . as comprising all the interactions and transactions, formal and informal, institutionalized or improvised, sacred or profane, orthodox or eccentric, which owe their existence to the pilgrimage itself" (22). This system includes an environment of both servicing mechanisms and antagonistic agencies.[30]

Spontaneous anti-structure that creates its own interrelatedness

Yet what is curious about such a far-reaching program is that it is largely occluded by the powerful imagery of anti-structure. While the Turners agree that "pilgrimage should be regarded not merely as an ideal model but as an institution with a history" (1978, 231), they trace the promiscuous presence of communitas across time and space, linking it to biblical language and a wider conception of "flow." The statement "Pilgrimages are an expression of the communitas dimension of any society, the spontaneity of interrelatedness, the spirit which bloweth where it listeth" (32) is illustrated not only by Christian shrines but also through occasional references to other religions, such as when it is claimed that "Islam is ideally conceived as a vast communitas of cobelievers" (188).[31] Indeed, Dionigi Albera (2019b) observes that the image of the Hajj forms an ideal counterpart of the Turnerian paradigm, given its focus on large-scale, consciously set-apart in-gathering.[32] Tendencies toward liminality are also located in local-level pilgrimage shrines in Hinduism as well as in Christianity (239). Generally, idiosyncrasies of history and culture are acknowledged but erased through the depiction of forms of anti-structure that take some of their character from the structures with which they are in tension yet maintain pan-human ontological consistency through the spirit-like appearance of a communitas capable of appearing anywhere.[33]

One further dimension of the book should also be mentioned, as it illustrates further the freeing of the Turnerian depiction of anti-structure from specific social bonds or contexts. The Turners pose the question of what happens to liminality in so-called industrial societies. While they accept that it can continue to exist in certain tightly knit organizations such as Masonic orders, they argue that it tends to move toward a looser condition, which they term *the liminoid.* While resembling the liminal in its manifestation within spaces set aside from mainstream productive and political events (see also V. Turner 1974, 32), the liminoid emerges from contexts marked by cultural pluralism, an extensive division of labor, fragmentation, individualization, contractual relations, commercialization—and, above all, choice. Thus, "optation pervades the liminoid phenomenon, obligation the liminal" (43). The liminoid is devoted to play and experimentation, realized through such varied media as literature, scholarly exploration, drama, sport, and ritual. Whereas the liminal is "eu-functional" (contributing to existing social structure [52]), the liminoid has the potential to embody social critique. In this vein, while the Turners see Christian pilgrimage as sharing features with passage rites, including release from mundane structure and homogenization of status (1978, 253–54), they conclude that it is for the most part a liminoid rather than strictly liminal phenomenon, given its origins in the voluntary decision to leave home to visit a shrine. As we shall see in this and later chapters, the question of obligation remains a productive if troubling theme in the characterization of pilgrimage, within and beyond Christianity.

Journey toward Abstraction

As the Turners traced an ethnographic and spiritual movement from the intimate social dramas of the Ndembu to the great pilgrimage sites of the (mostly) Catholic world, communitas provided a key vehicle for their journey. Linguistic form and descriptive content came together in a concept that emerged from an analytical apparatus that appeared seductive, mobile, and increasingly unspecific.[34] The very interstitiality of communitas meant that it could appear in between very different forms of structure. A feature of *Image and Pilgrimage*, seemingly trivial, is that it ends with detailed appendices.[35] These additions might appear to provide the driest possible conclusions to such a vividly written text, but appendix A lays out the intellectual and linguistic apparatus required for others who wish to apply the general principles that underpin the book. Ethnography is therefore stripped away to reveal abstractions, often expressed in Latinate language.[36] Use of the latter appears to reinforce what Jacques Derrida has termed "mondialatinization," a process of ideologically loaded translation "where Latin became the language of the Church and then of modern science, perpetuating itself through the emergence of English as a global language" (Eade and Albera 2017, 7). The Turners' lexicon and grammar is much more extensive than the tripartite framework provided by van Gennep, and it is made up of numerous components, including dominant symbols, root paradigms, flow, transience (also called nomadism), marginality, liminality, the liminoid, and of course communitas. The latter is defined initially as "a relational quality of full unmediated communication, even communion, between definite and determinate identities, which arises spontaneously in all kinds of groups, situations, and circumstances" (250). In this sense, communitas is understood to be constituted through relations that do not depend for their manifestation on the presence of any particular type of social form or frame.

As a term, *communitas* contributes to the potential for its wide deployment by being almost but not quite an academic neologism, evoking but also distinct from *community* and *communion*.[37] It plays on a double register of sounding both Catholic and scholarly, and as a concept that is not used in everyday language (unlike, for instance, *belief*), it is insulated from the semantic vagaries of being deployed in everyday discourse. At the same time, it partially appropriates other terms such as *spirit* and *flow*, while having affinities with both Durkheimian *collective effervescence* (Olaveson 2001) and Weberian *charisma* (cf. Kamau 2002).[38]

More generally, communitas plays on a key ambiguity of Durkheimian sociology, as manifested throughout the twentieth century: the fact that the sacred may or may not refer to the explicitly or officially religious.[39] In discerning anti-structure within but also beyond conventional forms of worship, the Turners and their students were able to extend their analysis to take in social movements and other ways of opting out that touched on performance, the arts, popular culture, and so on (see, e.g., Moore and Myerhoff 1977). These ambiguities are contained within one of the most famous observations of the Turners, that the "tourist is half a pilgrim, if a pilgrim is half a tourist" (Turner and Turner 1978, 20). It is worth also taking into account the words immediately following, often omitted by commentators: "Even when people bury themselves in anonymous crowds on beaches, they are seeking an almost sacred, often symbolic, mode of communitas, generally unavailable to them in the structured life of the office, the shop floor, or the mine." The adverbs *almost* and *often* are highly suggestive, pointing toward the counterintuitive idea that sacrality and communitas might be found in seemingly unreligious places.

On the one hand, then, anti-structure thrives on some kind of dialectical relationship to whatever is deemed structural.[40] On the other, the retention of *almost* reveals an anxiety over too easy an equation between the assumed asceticism of pilgrimage and the hedonism implied by certain forms of tourism. The half pilgrim/half tourist formulation is thus notable in its ambivalence, distinguishing between but also conjoining pilgrimage and tourism, implying that they might be evaluated along a single criterion of assessment: the extent to which they contain the transient, transcendent quality of communitas.[41] It is notable that Edith's (2012) much later book on the topic has the subtitle "The Anthropology of Collective Joy"; the latter is an attractive sentiment, one that that can be realized on the beach as easily as in a shrine.

Communitas, despite its seeming ineffability, is broken down by the Turners into a number of variations, which begin to complicate the picture of easy and abstracted flow (see appendix A of Turner and Turner 1978, 252; also Turner 1973, 193–94). First comes the spontaneous or existential kind, "which defies deliberate cognitive and volitional construction" and is both temporary and in tension with social structure. A secondary, normative sort is said to "capture" (Turner and Turner 1978, 252) communitas within institutional forms, ethical precepts, and rules. The third variation is called ideological, involving "the formulation of

1. relies on the existing structure to which it returns
2. within structure
3. reimagining structure

remembered attributes of the communitas experience in the form of a utopian blueprint for the reform of society" (ibid.).

This list has a rather Weberian flavor in the way it hints that communitas represents a charismatic experience always liable to being compromised by bureaucratic rules and institutions (Di Giovine 2011, 252; cf. Peacock 2018, ix). At the same time, it is rather non-Weberian in its value-laden, spiritual implications. The Turnerian description seems to place highest value on the most fragile manifestations of communitas—those that most clearly embody the spontaneity necessary for unmediated I-Thou relations.[42] Victor (1973) states that his preliminary survey of types of communitas indicates that the most common form in pilgrimage situations is actually "normative"—in other words, already hedged around by a degree of institutionalization (194). Nonetheless, hope is at hand: "Yet the communitas spirit is still latent in the norm and can be reanimated from time to time" (ibid.). Much later, Edith's *Communitas* celebrated the concept's "shyness and its untouchability by commercialization and institutionalization" (xii), claiming further that "communitas is most likely to turn into something else when watched. Researchers can only get a purchase on this slippery thing when they are right inside of it" (8).

In subsequently recharacterizing the Turners' depiction of communitas, it is tempting to deploy some of their own analytical vocabulary to understand its place in their intellectual trajectory. Here I recall their older notion of the dominant symbol moving across ritual contexts, containing a fan of interconnected and cognitive meanings while also being capable of provoking intense physiological experience. Similarly, communitas is not only mobile but also incorporates a range of theoretical and theological references—to the spirit, to charisma, to flow, to process, and so on—alongside the emotional and physical effects of anti-structural, threshold-like behaviors: theology combined with phenomenology. Yet while dominant symbols among the Ndembu embody culture-specific themes, including matriliny and local understandings of both fertility and maturity, communitas draws on a processual symbology assumed to apply to humanity as a whole. It seems that the Turners were attempting to create a language through which anthropological, ethical, and spiritual sensibilities might be combined, creating for themselves a liminoid discursive space within their own discipline.

Elsewhere, I have argued that the scaling up of academic perspective evident in *Image and Pilgrimage* was also highly prescient in envisioning a self-conscious anthropology of Christianity a quarter of a century or so before the subfield fully came into existence (Coleman 2014). The latter's goal to treat the religion as a coherent tradition (Robbins 2003) with a certain cultural logic (McDougall 2009, 185; Tomlinson and Engelke 2006, 19) has parallels with the earlier Turnerian depiction of a broad Christian culture.

Just as the Turners' work on Christianity anticipated later research, so it can be examined retrospectively in light of the central preoccupations of the newer subfield. In an influential overview, Fenella Cannell argues that Christianity was a "repressed" theme within anthropology over the formative period of the discipline (2006, 4). This lack of recognition reflected the need to separate the discipline from theology as a legitimate method for studying religion (14). At the same time, the very proximity of Christianity to the culture of many Western ethnographers rendered its more diffuse influences "only imperfectly perceptible" in the construction of such potentially ethnocentric categories as ritual and belief (5; cf. Asad 1993). Cannell notes that these gaps in self-awareness have increasingly been exposed over the years but are still evident. Where anthropologists have discussed Christianity, they have often taken as normative a non-materialist and ascetic stereotype of the religion, one that has tended to highlight the cultivation of forms of subjectivity and interiority that look rather Protestant, even Calvinist (20).[43] One of the reasons why such a perspective has resonated with anthropologists and others—whether or not they profess any personal faith—is that the stereotypically Protestant focus on transcendence, freedom, and individuality fits more broadly with the "supposedly destined trajectory of modernity" (39).

Cannell's arguments are complemented by Webb Keane (2006), writing in the same volume about "anxious transcendence." Keane explores links between characteristically Protestant ideas of personhood, individuality, and sincerity and broader, modern notions of authenticity and freedom where it is assumed that realization of a true and free self involves release from obligations of kinship, tradition, and regimented forms of self-expression (Keane 2006, 318). Sincerity in these terms becomes a form of transcendence, rendering the person transparent to themselves and to others, so that "I am making myself—as a private and inner self—available for you in the form of public, external expressions" (317). Keane accepts that these sentiments are idealized; indeed, our chronic anxieties as modern subjects arise precisely from our inability to ever fully abstract ourselves from material limitations and standardized means of expression. We are condemned to permanent failure in our attempts to achieve ultimate freedom and authenticity, yet we are conditioned to keep trying.

Keane and Cannell expose anthropology's anxieties about transcending its Christian inheritance, as well as the wider resonance of ideas that suggest the possibility of breaking free of binding, seemingly inauthentic obligations to tradition. They refer to underlying tensions between broadly—or at least stereotypically—Protestant and Catholic understandings of Christianity and modernity (Norget, Napolitano, and Mayblin 2018), centering around differing understandings of materiality and mediation. At the beginning of the twentieth century, such tensions informed Weber's tendency to portray Catholicism as a backward, idolatrous, magic-oriented faith (Stark 1968). Sixty years later, they also became evident in the reverberations around the Second Vatican Council, the great ecclesiastical reform taking place as the Turners were turning to the Catholic faith and which was aimed at modernizing the church and simplifying its liturgies while seeking a degree of reconciliation with Protestantism.[44]

Given these debates, it is striking that Edith noted in her preface to the paperback edition of *Image and Pilgrimage* that "I now find myself interested in tracing how the revival of the Catholic pilgrimage system paralleled the revivalist movements in Protestantism" (2011, xix). For her, both celebrated authentic and popular, rather than artificial and elite, culture. Furthermore, communitas—located across people rather than within objects, centering on spontaneity and directness, "not yet externalized and fixed in structured form" (see E. Turner 2012, 3)—addressed long-standing tensions between Protestant and Catholic attitudes toward materiality and mediation while reconciling the two.[45] Through its ideal vision of pilgrimage, Catholicism could celebrate tradition and spontaneity at the same time, and through the same act.

The developments described by Cannell and Keane reflect a Protestant-inflected intellectual agenda, whereas the Turners were ostensibly constructing a Catholic landscape of worship. Nonetheless, the latters' preoccupations came very close to some of the themes highlighted by Cannell and Keane concerning transcendence, sincerity, and personhood. The Catholicism the Turners foregrounded was not the mundane one of parish adherence and regularized worship but the one of evanescent moments of devotion achieved after exceptional effort, when ties to kinship and home could be stripped away in favor of purified, transcendent fellowship.[46] In this dual focus on the embodied experience of faith alongside the spirit-like character of communitas, the Turners were actually wrestling with tensions over the relationship between abstraction and experience that had surfaced earlier in their depiction of dominant symbols—ritual objects that might take the form of a tree among the Ndembu or be exemplified by the Virgin Mary in Catholic culture but which combined high moral principles with grosser dimensions of physicality and desire (see Turner and Turner 1978, 247), perhaps exemplifying what Edith also called "the oxymoron 'the body of the spirit'" (xxi).

There is a further dimension to this juxtaposition of transcendence and materiality. It refers to the broader theoretical and methodological abstractions and expansions of scale being attempted by the Turners, which would become a preoccupation of the later anthropology of Christianity. The central chapter of *Image and Pilgrimage*, dealing with the key historical and theological questions of tensions between iconophily and iconoclasm, is also devoted to Marian shrines and the figure of the Virgin Mary. While much of the chapter concerns Mary as intercessor, healer, and dominant symbol in various historical cases, the chapter ends on a normative note that brings together three elements: first, her power as personification of the church in its "nonlegalistic aspect, a collective mother in the order of freedom"; second, her affinity with anti-structure—"As Mary goes, so goes the Church. . . . As communitas goes, so goes the Church"; and third, the significance of Mary in pointing to a universal communitas yet one always vulnerable to being subverted by "political structure" into becoming localized, and thus "a symbol of xenophobic localism" (Turner and Turner 1978, 171). Here, the Turners are celebrating the powers of a dominant symbol in her most extensive, globalizing manifestation (intimate yet universal), and they are doing so in a text that emphasizes the benefits of transcending specific contexts through a processual anthropology that cannot be confined to the boundaries of any single ethnographic case.[47] As Yueh-po Huang puts it, the Turners strive to provide not only "a sense of unified common humanity" but also a *liberation* "from particularism and social categories." In this sense, communitas represents a spiritually infused activity unconfined by specific material form or context, even as its fellowship is oriented toward the expression of a profoundly human sociality. Thus, the trajectory of Turnerian processual anthropology proceeds by combining a number of elements that are expressible through dialectical relationships: larger-scale cultural analysis juxtaposed with smaller scale fieldwork; sacralized movement with sacred place; abstract faith with embodied commitment; egalitarianism with hierarchy; a modern concern to achieve religious purity and transcendence with respect for tradition and ritual discipline. The relationships between terms vary from near opposition to complementarity. But the overall direction is ultimately toward abstraction, and their image of pilgrimage provides an immensely powerful and exhilarating vehicle through which to embark on an ongoing journey that is at once scholarly and spiritual.

A further way to characterize the Turnerian project is to see it not only as a journey toward abstraction but also as a striving for the universal.[48] As Anna Tsing (2005, 1) points out, drawing on Gayatri Spivak (1999), there is a sense in which the universal is something that "we cannot not want"—a form of what I have been calling seduction (cf. Di Giovine and Picard 2015). Yet as Tsing's book shows, every form of universalism has its own history and inflection. In the case of the Turners, they exchange a form of emancipatory philosophy (Marxism) for another that strives toward general liberation (Christianity, expressed most notably through pilgrimage).[49] Both projects oppose structure with movement; yet if claims to articulate the universal tend to have a powerful missionary flavor, they also implicitly pose a significant question: not merely who or what is included, but also who or what is *excluded*, by the paradoxical particularities of the universal, as expressed in any given cultural and intellectual context. I therefore explore this question in the next section.

The Journey Continued

Victor died in 1983, relatively soon after the publication of *Image and Pilgrimage*, but his legacy lived on and was cultivated energetically by Edith, who for the next three and a half decades moved the processual approach further in phenomenological and psychological directions, not least through her distinctive contributions to the anthropology of consciousness (e.g., E. Turner 1993). There is no doubt that "the theory has proven to be foundational in the social scientific study of pilgrimage and, later, (secular) tourism" (Di Giovine 2011, 247). Arguably, it helped pave the way for studies examining the embodied quality of pilgrimage experience (e.g., Klungel 2009). Researchers also readily found parallels beyond studies of Christianity or Christian contexts. Kiran Shinde (2011, 337) notes, for instance, that "debates about possibilities of communitas are also found in many scholarly works on Indian pilgrimages (e.g., Gold 1988; Morinis 1984)."[50] Even a scholar who would become synonymous with powerful opposition to the model, Michael Sallnow, acknowledged that it "proved widely influential in the . . . upsurge of interest in the phenomenon amongst social anthropologists" (1981, 163), in part because it provided a way of discussing ritual that was not tied to particular political, ethnic, or social boundaries (also Werbner 1977, ix).

With influence came critique. A much cited response from Erik Cohen (1992) focuses skepticism on the Turnerian imagery of a center divorced from sociopolitical concerns and does so from the perspective of an ethnographer of Thai Buddhist shrines.[51] Cohen (35) points out that the model tends to generalize from Catholic examples, in other words, cases where the separation between religious and political domains is institutionalized (see also Reader 2005). Other cultural and religious situations, such as "Eastern and particularly the Indian, religions—Brahmanism, Hinduism, Buddhism" (Cohen 1992, 35), do not demarcate such spheres in a similar fashion.[52] Moreover, certain prominent Christian pilgrimage centers, including Rome (not highlighted in *Image and Pilgrimage*), can hardly be called remote and "out there" in the Turnerian sense (36).[53] A further problem is the Turners' rather deterministic assumption that larger centers will automatically be more inclusive than local shrines. Cohen prefers to think of shrines in terms of the greater or lesser degrees of formality required of pilgrims.

One of the most incisive commentaries on the Turnerian legacy comes from Donald Weber (1995), who traces the shifting reception of the work within American cultural studies. Weber refers to the initial excitement roused by paradigms of ritual process and communitas in the 1970s, followed by a questioning of the model some two decades later. From the perspective of cultural studies scholars of the 1980s and 1990s, the rite of passage framework over-emphasized consensus and ordered resolution of social contradictions (530). The apparent teleology of the model rendered it apolitical, unable to provide theoretical and ethnographic space for figures in American society—such as many migrants, for instance—who "unlike ritual liminars . . . have no cultural assurance of a final stable resolution of their ambiguity" (ibid.). Ironically, a Turnernian model of "social leveling and attendant cultural bonding" became regarded as expressing a position of privilege in its emphasis on forms of ritual reincorporation that overlooked identity politics and disputed boundaries (ibid.). Weber concludes (following Rosaldo 1990) that social dramas come to express structure more than process, communitas over contingency, and shared culture over political contestation. For these reasons (527), the model of the liminal has become replaced in American cultural theory by a more flexible notion of the border, which permits much more ambiguity over the stakes and outcomes of social engagements.[54]

Works concerned more directly with the political and economic dimensions of pilgrimage have adapted the Turnerian framework in ways that make it more ethnographically and historically nuanced. In her work on a global Sufi cult originating in Pakistan, Pnina Werbner (2003, 17) notes that the relationship between a political and a sacred center is likely to shift over time, rendering it historically contingent.[55] Moreover, moments of "experienced communitas" during annual rituals are themselves the product of "complex logistical planning, a highly discipline division of labour, constant vigilance on the part of the organisers," resulting in what she calls "counter-structure" rather than anti-structure (18).

Many authors agree that the Turnerian framework of flow and fellowship is stimulating but, ironically, too rigid to apply to all pilgrimages.[56] Ellen Badone and Sharon Roseman remark, "While communitas may be one element of the pilgrimage experience, this social and emotional quality cannot be assumed to exist in all pilgrimages; nor can the concept be used as a master key to unlock the meaning and significance of pilgrimage for all participants in every cross-cultural setting" (2004, 4).[57] Their point is reinforced by a perceptive observation from Alan Morinis, who argues that the encompassing character of the rite of passage framework distorts our appreciation of the complexity and diversity of the phenomenon (1984, 257–60; 1992, 8).[58] In other words, we can see the Turnerian model riding on the coattails of van Gennep's seemingly ubiquitous motif, yet such widespread applicability becomes a trap, concealing other fruitful perspectives. Redescribed through the analytical vocabulary I present in this book, the idea of the rite of passage provides a powerful sense of the *internal* articulations between different elements of ritual but is far less effective in detailing how such ritual then articulates with *wider* institutional realms. In a complementary critique, Susan Naquin and Chün-fang Yü (1992, 7) state that the communitas model not only places too much analytical attention on pilgrims' experience per se (22; see also Jha 1990, 24), it also draws attention away from the Turners' insights on "the dialectical relationship of peripherality and centrality of the pilgrimage centres" as well as "the dynamics of growth and decline of the pilgrimage phenomena" (7).[59] The very search for universalism and commonality encourages scholars to look exclusively for similarities among examples, and yet: "We have found . . . that it may be time to reconsider the chaos of pilgrimage and to listen again to the cacophony" (ibid.).[60]

Restoring the chaos and cacophony entails challenging assumptions concerning rigid behavioral dichotomies between the sacred and profane. In her study of Greek Orthodox pilgrimage, Dubisch (1995, 95) prefers to see communitas as a relative rather than absolute condition and as a latent potential rather than the defining feature of the journey. Reader (2005) points out that the existence of permanent pilgrims around Shikoku, who are engaged in travel on an ongoing basis, challenges binary divides between home and shrine (see also Shultz 2009, 42; cf. Yamba 1995).[61] In his condemnation of what he sees as the inherently Roman Catholic view of the Turners, Makhan Jha cites an observation from the renowned Hindu pilgrimage site of Varanasi (Kashi), when he watches a pilgrim taking the "holiest of all possible baths at a Ghat" while holding a radio to his ear in order to monitor a cricket match taking place in Calcutta. Jha adds, "Neither the anthropologist nor any of the other pilgrims thought this improper—only the tour guide from the Clarks Hotel haranguing a group of American tourists in a boat did" (1990, 20).

It might be countered that the Turners' theory emerged out of, and was primarily directed toward, a broad conception of Christian culture. Yet despite their occasional nods toward some non-Catholic examples, such as charismatic forms of worship, the Turners paid little attention to Orthodox Christianity with its specific views of personhood, community, authority, and materiality (see, e.g., Hann and Goltz 2010, 13). As a result, their "Christian culture" became geographically expansive but theologically and culturally constricted. For example, Elizabeth Oram's (2002) analysis of Coptic pilgrimage to the Monastery of St. Antony in the Eastern Egyptian Desert refers briefly to the liminal quality of monasteries. However, she is much more concerned with demonstrating the integration of the monastery and shrine into an ecclesiastical and social landscape where monks become guides and mentors as well as ascetics. Indeed, they inhabit an institution that has moved from being an isolated desert outpost into becoming a modernized center of mass pilgrimage, accessible to urban populations. Catholic self-mortification plays little part in Oram's analysis, even when pilgrims climb the steep path to visit St. Antony's cave (also Coleman 2019).

Most devastatingly, the passionate promotion of communitas has invited equal and opposite ethnographic responses emphasizing the fomenting of structure through sacred travel. Barely three years after the publication of *Image and Pilgrimage*, Donald Messerschmidt and Jyoti Sharma reported that during their fieldwork in the Nepal Himalayas, "we sought evidence to support or refute Turner's concept of anti-structure or communitas" (1981, 572). Their conclusions are worth quoting at length:

> The few instances of assistance, humane gestures of help and comfort between strangers thrown together on an arduous mountain trek under treacherous monsoon conditions, were no different from those observed on a crowded cross-country bus two weeks later and did not stand out as behavior unique to pilgrimage. In short, the pilgrims fully supported the structural status quo, taking care to abide by the standard rules of avoidance and austerity to maintain individual and caste purity. . . . Our

data, then, refute the communitas hypothesis; this pilgrimage is fundamentally and unequivocally a structure-affirming occasion. We now posit an alternative to Turner's hypothesis: that pilgrimage serves to highlight and reinforce the principal themes idiosyncratic to a religious system. Communitas seems a reasonable expectation of Christian pilgrimage, reinforcing Christianity's stress on 'brotherly love' and equalitarian social relationships, while structure-affirming behavior . . . seems a more reasonable expectation of pilgrimages within the hierarchical system of Hinduism, a system which rewards social division.

Such a view strongly opposes the idea that the special fellowship described and almost prescribed by the Turners is universal across religions.

Even within Catholic Christianity, communitas has often appeared hard to locate in a form that the Turners would have recognized. A little over a decade after the publication of *Image and Pilgrimage*, an edited volume emerged whose subtitle referred to the emergent field of "The Anthropology of Christian Pilgrimage" (Eade and Sallnow 1991). In this text, the central image of fellowship was replaced by one of chronic conflict. Eade and Sallnow's book will be discussed in the next chapter, but for now it is worth noting the irony: a Turnerian model of social relations originally inspired by Gluckman's emphasis on situational analysis and contradiction eventually became challenged by a new model whose central trope was precisely that of contestation.

By 2008, Peter Margry had concluded of the Turners' work that "the theory has been falsified over and over again on the basis of ethnographic case studies" (2008, 21). Yet what interests me about Margry's statement is not so much the assertion that communitas has been found wanting as his observation that it has *repeatedly* been discovered to be inadequate.[62] Sustained falsification in the natural sciences tends to mean that a theory soon drops from attention.[63] What is intriguing about communitas is its capacity to withstand recurring intellectual assassination. It has been "disproved" again and again; but scholars of pilgrimage are continually provoked into searching for its existence.[64]

It is likely that an important part of the explanation for communitas's continued animation within pilgrimage studies lies in its qualities as an entextualizable concept, and its capacity to move across contexts in simplified, self-contained, and relatively coherent form.[65] Arguably, its autonomous character is reinforced by *Image and Pilgrimage*'s tendency to present journeys as extraordinary, goal-centered, one-off events rather than being entangled in complex and lasting ways with everyday life (Reader 2005, 249–50).[66] Furthermore, communitas offers a seductive semiotics whereby the researcher is enticed to search for its presence or absence, to index a given site or situation in relation to the degree of authentic communitas found.[67] Indeed, the concept seems actively to invite such inquiry in determining what is most significant about any given system of pilgrimage. Even Messerschmidt and Sharma's stern refutation of its applicability for Hinduism provides a case in point. They do not find any communitas, but much of their project is nonetheless framed by the attempt to assess the relative generosity and equality—or otherwise—of relations among pilgrims.[68]

Subsequent research that has been snared into searching for communitas does not challenge the ontology of the concept so much as decide whether it does or does not apply in the case under consideration. Indeed, its very ineffability may encourage researchers to locate its traces. A case in point is Sean Slavin's account of his walk to Santiago de Compostela: "While I do not claim to have observed instances of communitas amongst pilgrims to Santiago, they did create common ground with each other by sticking to simple conversations about present events. They would commonly talk about the landscape, the day's events, the history and myths of the route and, sometimes, deeper issues of theology and philosophy" (2003, 12). Or again, as part of Jonathan and Sukanya Miles-Watson's insightful observations on pilgrimage in the Himalayas: "Communitas is not entirely absent from Indian pilgrimage. After their ritual bath at the Manimahesh dal the pilgrims establish a bond or *mitri* with a fellow traveller by anointing their foreheads with a symbolic tilak or sign from the waters of the lake" (Miles-Watson and Miles-Watson 2011, 328). Or, once more, in John Sherry Jr. and Robert V. Kozinets's exploration of the New Age Burning Man ceremony in Nevada, where they describe a sacred building: "The Temple is a personal labor of love, designed and largely executed by a people's artist. It is widely viewed as the single most heartfelt gift given to the entire community . . . It convenes community in the heart of community, and harnesses communitas in the service of mindfulness or soulfulness" (2007, 132). Or in a final example, taken from an historical study of Chinese pilgrimages to Mount Tai, where speculation about the mountain's presence is built into interpretation of the past: "Communitas within any particular pilgrimage society would probably have been strong, given the members' common point of origin and their mutual membership in an organization that outlasted the pilgrimage" (Dott 2004, 92).[69] All these authors are writing long after *Image and Pilgrimage* came out, and all express some doubts about the widespread applicability of the concept; but it is still indexed in a way that assumes that it might somehow exist—in social contexts that range from the contemporary Nevada desert to late imperial China.

The ways in which communitas has been deployed post–*Image and Pilgrimage* reinforce its dizzying trajectory and further entextualization. Often, as in the examples just given, it is deployed in isolation from much of the rest of the analytical lexicon that constitutes Turnerian processual anthropology or the wider environment of servicing mechanisms and antagonistic agencies that the book also mentions. In addition, the variations listed by the Turners tend to be conflated into a generic state of solidarity and equality.[70] The stripping away of the subtleties of the concept often involves using the word *liminal* to describe pilgrimage behaviors, even in highly complex, voluntaristic social contexts. In practice, the attempt to distinguish the liminal from the liminoid has generally failed to strike a chord in the scholarly imagination (Coleman 2018a); Andrew Spiegel suggests that one reason for this failure is that the distinction rests on far too crude a division between "primitive" and "modern" societal types (2011, 11).[71]

Such simplification leads us to consider a further dimension of the seductive semiotics of communitas that we shall explore further in chapter 5. The concept resonates with a broader anthropological tendency to focus on situations of maximum intensity and high relief in examining religious commitment (cf. Bandak and Jørgensen 2012), a tendency that reflects a Durkheimian inheritance of emphasizing the importance of overtly marked and set-apart ritual activity but also the Manchester School's interest in crisis as revelatory of social principles. The Turnerian emphasis on anti-structure hedged around by protective behaviors continues this trend even further. What is significant about the imagery of "the center out there" is not only its depiction of a sacred realm separated from the everyday, but also the idea of the center as a framing device, encircling and amplifying ritual and symbolic commitment among those who have gathered together from far and wide.[72] Yueh-Po Huang captures the attractiveness alongside the problematic character of this depiction of sociality in describing how the Turnerian model relies on "containing several features, including fixed static communities, informants as embedded only in the local context, and all pilgrims sharing the same place and culture" (2017, 284), and in this respect, he echoes Donald Weber's (1995) worries over the consensuality implied by liminality. The model becomes an aspirational vision as "it not only provides local people with a sense of unified common humanity, but also liberates them from particularism and social categories" (Huang 2017, 284–85). Yet, as much pilgrimage research has subsequently shown, unity can turn on itself—as for instance those who go on the Hajj discover that ingathering may produce not so much solidarity as an intensified awareness of mutual difference (ibid.).[73]

Concluding Remarks: On Entextualization and Enclaving

In November 2013, a group of anthropologists including myself contributed to a special panel of the American Anthropological Association, which that year was being held in Chicago, the Turners' home town for a number of years. The panel was being held to reflect on the impact of *Image and Pilgrimage* as a recognized anthropological classic that had been published thirty-five years earlier. I knew that Edith was nervous about the occasion and the reception the book would receive, but her talk was a typically committed, passionate performance, using language that ranged between the academic and the poetic. After other people had given their presentations, she remarked that speakers and audience could scarcely fill the huge space allocated to the session. So she took control, arranging us in a large circle where everybody—ranging from young graduate students to aged professors—could ask questions and converse on an equal basis.

Perhaps even more than what was said on that occasion, Edith's spontaneous action was eloquent in its directness and generosity, converting the hierarchy of the panel into a sociality that embodied academic communitas. The circle she created was inward looking, but for a positive reason. She helped to focus attention and direct participants away from the limitations of the space and the feeling of mutual distance created, giving our conversation an intimacy and intensity rare at such anonymous conferences. Scholarly discussion was combined, as so often in Edith's life, with concrete practice.

This chapter has been appreciative but critical of the most influential trope within pilgrimage studies. In highlighting the entextualized quality of communitas, I have traced both the positive and the less positive effects the concept has had on the field. I have drawn attention to communitas's tendency—like the circle that Edith created at the American Anthropological Association—to focus on actions separated from the everyday, highlighting points of peak intensity and concentration. It has provided a model that can flow easily between fieldwork contexts yet has had the effect of maneuvering pilgrimage studies into an intellectual enclave, disarticulated from wider academic conversations and socialities to which it could contribute.[74]

An obvious point of comparison is with the study of Pentecostalism. While Edith clearly saw parallels between pilgrims and Pentecostals in the 1960s, considerable differences in the subsequent trajectories of research into these two phenomena has become evident. Over the past half century or so, increased academic interest in both pilgrimage and Pentecostalism has not only reflected the increasing mobility of populations in many parts of the world but has also brought popular expressions of religion to the fore. Nonetheless, while Pentecostalism has made its mark as a dynamic religion of the migrant to the world city or the wealthy inhabitant of the suburban megachurch, until the last couple of decades or so, pilgrimage has mostly been presented as an escape to remote and set-apart landscapes.

In gaining a high academic profile, the new Pentecostal paradigm has done much to form the current anthropology of Christianity and other scholarship, granting researchers a powerful means to discuss the globalization of religious forms—readily representing an example of a "religion made to travel" as it follows population movements across the world (Dempster, Klaus, and Petersen 2011). On the one hand, Pentecostal Christianity tends to replicate "its doctrines, organizational features, and rituals in canonical, Western form wherever it is introduced" (Robbins 2004, 118), while on the other, it seems skilled at accepting "local enchanted cosmologies only to attack them, thus profoundly altering the way they are understood" (126–27). Such Christianity can be represented as inherently mobile but also deeply engaged—no matter how controversially—in attempting to touch and transform wider contexts. In these terms, Pentecostalism is what I have called a "part culture," presenting worldviews in tension and highly strategic struggle with the values of any given host society (Coleman 2006b, 2). It exists in and through the production of borders, rather than remaining in tightly sealed enclaves.

By contrast, scholarly emphasis on the anti-structural dimensions of pilgrimage has tended to direct attention toward features that take it *away* from close connections with other centers of action and debate. If Pentecostalism is a "part" culture, pilgrimage is made to seem more like an "apart" culture (Coleman 2014); and if Pentecostalism reaches out toward society in order to convert it, the Turnerian depiction of pilgrims striving hard to arrive at the "center out there" turns attention away from all the political, economic, and cultural dimensions that go into the creation and maintenance of any pilgrimage environment.

The intellectual journeys embodied in these two popular religious forms have taken them in different directions for much of the past half century. Indeed, the somewhat inward-looking character of pilgrimage studies has also been reflected in its lack of intersection with the burgeoning anthropology of Christianity. Fortunately, however, there are signs that perspectives on pilgrimage are being taken in new directions. If Pentecostalism seeks influence through overt appropriation of culture, the powers of pilgrimage can be shown to operate through forms of cultural articulation that are not always so obvious—yet which must not be ignored. Before exploring such forms more fully, I must turn to two other tropes that have contributed to the study of pilgrimage in recent decades and ask what they too have enabled and occluded in their making of a subfield.

4

Frictional Energies

Contestation

Challenging the Paradigm

Victor and Edith Turners' wide-ranging vision of communitas and anti-structure proved ethically seductive but ethnographically unrealistic to many researchers. The old trope did not die but began to be challenged by alternative understandings of the staging of pilgrimage. During the 1980s and 1990s, the idea of contestation began to emerge as an organizing motif for depicting the dynamics of sacred shrines. This chapter begins by exploring the intellectual and cultural context of the development of an inherently conflictual image of sacred travel. It goes on to show how the communitas and contestation models gained momentum through their dialectical relationship, with their apparent mutual antagonism giving frictional energy to both positions. I also argue, however, that it is misleading to regard communitas and contestation as purely opposed tropes, given that they share significant assumptions that have continued to define but also to delimit understandings of pilgrimage (see also Coleman 2002, 2014), making some vital ethnographic and theoretical connections but bypassing others. The end of the chapter suggests ways in which both tropes might be extended and given new, more productive life through being juxtaposed with more recent work on—and beyond—pilgrimage. These concluding remarks take us back to reconsidering articulation as a framing concept.

In 1981, the anthropologist Michael Sallnow published a paper on pilgrimage in the Central Andes with the title "Communitas Reconsidered" (1981). Sallnow had carried out ethnographic fieldwork in Peru in the mid-1970s and gained his PhD at Victor Turner's old Anthropology Department in Manchester under the guidance of Richard Werbner—an

Africanist who had traveled in the opposite direction to Turner, moving from the United States to Britain, and a scholar who had helped to maintain Max Gluckman's legacy in the department.

Sallnow's paper focuses on "the sociodynamics of pilgrimage" (1981, 164), with observations derived from working in Ccamahuara, a community of peasant cultivators and pastoralists (see also Sallnow 1987, 1991). He provides a comprehensive study of networks of kinship-based and contractual forms of collaboration among informants, networks that are significant to both subsistence and ritual relationships since the two cannot easily be separated. The article sketches out a diffused landscape of parishes and chapelries, each with their own patron saint, which attract visits from dispersed constituencies of pilgrims representing differing ethnic, economic, and regional interests (1981, 168). In his later book, *Pilgrims of the Andes*, Sallnow (1987, 97) remarks that "the contemporary configurations of Christian miraculous shrines in Cusco must be understood in relation to pre-Hispanic social and political processes in the central Andes and to the spatial dimension of these processes in particular." He emphasizes that both subversive and dominant forms of power are expressed in and through material terrain: "Social relations became spatial relations, conceptualized through an energized landscape finely contoured in accordance with gross physical topography" (ibid.; see also Sallnow 1991).

Sallnow notes that gatherings of pilgrims at important annual fiestas involve devotees attending less as individuals and more as members of groups based on "home communities, neighbourhoods or parishes" (1981, 169), entailing a high degree of social obligation among those who sponsor and support such journeys. The corporate identity of a band is reinforced by the formalization and coordination of its members' movement to a given shrine, with participants bearing an icon of the relevant saint and engaging in often tense ritual exchanges with other, equivalent groups of pilgrims whom they encounter on the way.[1] For instance, once camped at a shrine, members mark out their territory with stones and compete with other bands over the quality of their costumes, dances, and music, sometimes even descending into the barely restrained violence of whipping the legs of dancers from other groups.

Sallnow's skepticism toward a Turnerian view of pilgrimage is expressed in his conclusion that "the simple dichotomy between structure and communitas cannot comprehend the complex interplay between the social relations of pilgrimage and those associated with secular activities" (1981, 179).[2] In this ethnography, the presence of a supposedly universalistic Christian cosmology is belied by the endemic competition and conflict that are not merely evident within, but are actually fostered by, regional cults of pilgrimage. Sallnow adds that the positing of any single or deterministic view of the goal of pilgrimage is likely to be "spurious," given that such travel is "a polymorphic phenomenon" (163). The multidimensional aspects of pilgrimage also tend to confound the Turnerian tendency to view structure and anti-structure in terms of a zero-sum game where more of one necessarily means less of the other (see Sallnow 1987, 9).

Sallnow's fieldsites belong to the broadly Christian culture that the Turners try to characterize, yet his methodology is very different, and this gulf helps explain why he draws such different conclusions. Whereas the Turners traveled around the world, focusing on shrines perceived as sacred centers, Sallnow followed the movements of informants from their homes to shrines and back, giving a far more detailed sense of the physical, social, and economic landscapes that they inhabited and traversed both during pilgrimage and at other points of the year—working, worshiping, walking. His approach comes much closer to that of Ann Gold (1988), whose well-rounded ethnographic study of pilgrimage in Rajasthan was discussed in chapters 1 and 2. In addition, whereas the Turners located their analysis in the context of the theopolitical and liturgical debates around Vatican II and other social movements, such matters were of little relevance to Sallnow's Andean informants. For the latter, the most salient reference groups remained kin and neighbors, while the interconnectedness between divine and the material worlds was self-evident rather than subject to anxieties over idolatry. The Turners were deeply concerned with the cultivation of personal conviction in the face of secularism, but such worries over private belief had no real purchase in the Andes, a place where social and cultural obligations produced considerably fewer opportunities for liminoid spiritual experimentation than were evident in Western pilgrimage contexts.

It is clearly easier to conclude that the motivations and socialities of pilgrims are capable of being purified into flowing I-Thou relationships if emphasis is laid on the experience of the seemingly autonomous, possibly anonymous, individual traveler.[3] This point echoes the work of Max Gluckman (1955) on Barotse law courts and his well-known contrast between "multistranded" (we might even say multi-articulated) relations where people are connected to each other in numerous ways that are difficult to tease apart, and "single-stranded" relationships where only a single point of connection is recognized. Sallnow's ethnography demonstrates how difficult it is to sustain the conditions for people within the same band to relate to each other through pared down, simplified associations when other parts of their lives are so mutually embedded through proximity, kinship, subsistence, and so on, but also given that people invest much social and economic prestige in hosting and participating in ritualized journeys.[4] Pressures to produce egalitarianism might also foment conflict in the context of the wider dynamics of relations between pilgrimage bands. Sallnow observes:

> Intragroup collectivism . . . is offset by intergroup differentiation. External opposition goes hand in hand with internal leveling, and the boundaries of the [group] seem to be drawn more tightly the farther the party ventures from its homeland. Pilgrimage contingents, regardless of provenance, stand opposed to one another as identical elements of the macrocosm . . . it is the equality of opposition rather than the equality of brotherhood. (1987, 203)

Within a few years, such observations would be placed within a wider comparative frame. When Sallnow teamed up with fellow anthropologist John Eade to produce the work that would become the key text in consolidating the trope of contestation, a fruitful form of collaboration was established that benefited from their complementary approaches.[5] Eade's biography formed an important bridge between the Turners' religious experiences and Sallnow's ethnographic observations. His engagement with pilgrimage emerged originally through personal and social rather than academic commitments (Eade 2019). Raised a Protestant but having converted to Catholicism as a young adult, he, like the Turners, had spent time in Zambia, where he participated in the congregational activities of the local church. Then, as a student at Oxford, he joined a group that began to make annual journeys to Lourdes. Eade became a *brancardier,* a volunteer helper ensuring the smooth operation of pilgrims' movements through the shrine, often guiding pilgrims through the fraught process of bathing in Lourdes's famed holy water.[6]

In common with the Turners, Eade had witnessed the events of Vatican II with a sense of anticipation, seeing their potential to break down the hierarchies and liturgical formalities of what had been a "fortress church" in Europe (Eade 2019, 2–3).[7] However, his disillusionment with the effects of the reforms combined with his growing ambivalence toward the organization of activities at Lourdes. He observed the frequent tensions between more authoritarian volunteers at the French shrine and the desires of visiting diocesan groups to tend to their sick and handicapped parishioners in their own way (5). Eade's immersion in Lourdes as a volunteer exposed him directly to the frictions involved in mediating between visitors and administrators. He observed at close quarters the continued influence of structure on the management of pilgrims as he himself became a part of shrine *infra*structure. Furthermore, rather than moving between multiple shrines around the world, he witnessed pilgrimage as an accumulation of repeated ritual actions to the same site rather than as a discrete, peak experience.[8]

A vivid sense of Eade's ambivalent stance—caught between the demands of the church and the desires of pilgrims—emerges in the following beautifully observed passage, describing the role of the brancardier in the intense and intimate space of the baths:[9]

> The organizers' attempts to create an atmosphere of tranquil prayerfulness and reflection in the baths are invariably compromised. Frequently, there is much humour and teasing. Helpers will jolly sick pilgrims along, while sick pilgrims, in turn, will joke about their infirmities. The problems of wet socks, shoes that will not fit on again, or the weight of an infirm person can all be the subjects of light-hearted exchanges. . . . When a cubicle is not occupied, brancardiers are frequently tempted to joke amongst themselves about the national differences between them, their social backgrounds, their experiences of Lourdes, and so on. (Eade 1991, 62–63)

This short extract tells us much about the complexities of relationship, affect, and perspective, told from the point of view of the pilgrim/volunteer. The shrine administration's injunction to create a solemn tone is soon forgotten in a situation that involves potentially tense negotiations between brancardiers and bathers as the pressure to hurry visitors along combines with the sheer physical awkwardness of interactions. In contrast to the fragile, evanescent quality of spontaneous communitas, we see the implicitly urgent—decidedly normative—temporality of bureaucracy, which must process a given number of pilgrims per day. Eade shows how the behavioral frames of the space may change rather quickly, as brancardiers move from dealing with bathers to addressing each other, not through engaging in, say, meditative prayer, but by highlighting the humor of cultural differences evident at the shrine.

In reflecting on the sometimes ludicrous rather than ludic dimensions of Eade's experience, we might contrast his memories of damp socks with the Turners' depiction of the pious pilgrim at Lough Derg, bare feet resting on a cold floor as an expression of sacrificial devotion (1978, 120). Eade's detail takes us away from the official core of ritual engagement to say something revealing (so to speak) about the management of bathing. The fumbling behaviors and sudden switches in tone that he recounts are no less a part of pilgrimage than the dimensions emphasized by the Turners, and they indicate a highly complex mixture of emotions, motivations, and socialities.

Eade's personal experiences of going to Lourdes contrasted with Sallnow's scholarly approach to the field. The famous Northern European shrine also presented a very different side of Catholicism to that evident in the Andes. Yet the pair's standpoints converged in two related respects: acknowledgment of the chronically conflictual character of much pilgrimage activity, and recognition of inherent pluralities of perspective within and across religious communities. In later observations, Eade (2019) referred to his long-standing research on competing constructions of community among Bangladeshi settlers in London as a formative dimension of his understanding of relations at shrines. To be sure, Gluckman and Turner had also been passionately interested in the crises, conflicts, and contradictions permeating tribal and other lives, but they had wrestled far more than Sallnow and Eade with the legacy of structural functionalism in postwar anthropology and with the temptation to understand institutions as contributing toward reproducing social institutions (Evens and Handelman 2006, 1). After all, the title of Victor Turner's (1957) early book famously counterbalanced "schism" with "continuity." By the 1990s, however, there were fewer impulses to present ritual as leading toward restoration of social order. As Eade has noted, disaffection with communitas emerged as "structuralist models were being abandoned under the impact of post-structuralist and post-modernist critiques" but also against the background of continued decolonization, the collapse of communism, transnational migration, and the overall "failure of Western grand narratives to explain this changing world" (2011, 387).

A New Trope Emerges

Deconstructionist understandings of pilgrimage led Eade and Sallnow to organize an interdisciplinary conference, which later became an edited volume: *Contesting the Sacred: The Anthropology of Christian Pilgrimage* (Eade and Sallnow 1991). Whereas the Turners had worked very closely as a pair to produce their vision of communitas, the analytical motif that permeated *Contesting the Sacred* was explored by a variety of writers, ranging from Eade and Sallnow's influential introduction through contributions by anthropologists working on scattered sites (Lourdes, San Giovanni Rotondo, Jerusalem, Sri Lanka, and the Andes) and deploying different scales and methodologies. Nonetheless, all the pieces were informed by ethnographic observations of the same religion, and for the most part all focused on spectacular locations of pilgrimage activity.

The Turners had largely removed explicit references to Marxism in their analysis of pilgrimage, but Eade and Sallnow's approach brought both Marx and, more implicitly, the post-structuralist writer Michel Foucault (Eade 1991, 75) into their theoretical purview as they pointed to the likelihood of inherently contradictory interests emerging not only between pilgrims and clergy, but also among pilgrims themselves.[10] The all-encompassing character of great pilgrimage sites was now regarded as "constituted not by a unification of discourses but rather by the capacity of a cult to entertain and respond to a plurality" (15). Under such circumstances, universalism was regarded by authors as an ideologically loaded aspiration (see also Tsing 2005), masking inequalities of power among pilgrims and between clergy and lay people. In one of the most frequently quoted passages from the introduction, pilgrimage was depicted as "an arena for competing religious and secular discourses, for both the official co-optation and non-official recovery of religious meanings, for conflict between orthodoxies, sects, and confessional groups, for drives towards consensus and communitas, and for counter-movements towards separateness and division" (Eade and Sallnow 1991, 2). Eade and Sallnow argued that "the sacred centre . . . in this perspective, appears as a vessel into which pilgrims devoutly pour their hopes, prayers, and aspirations" (15).[11] If the center retains agency in this latter image, it comes from the fetishizing tendency of visiting groups to invest the shrine with an energy that, in sociological terms, actually comes from the pilgrims themselves.[12]

Eade and Sallnow's deconstructionist perspective retains the sense of a shrine as a host for multiple interfaces among varied constituencies. Such interfaces encourage the consolidation of preexisting boundaries of identity, rather than challenging them.[13] Communitas is not removed from the pilgrimage arena but is transformed from being a unique ideal into becoming just one strategically deployed discourse among many others. Most emphasis is placed on the presence of disjunctions and incompatibilities that are not resolved, and may even be amplified, as they jostle within the intensely experienced space and time of pilgrimage.[14] Often, the shrine becomes a site of heightened visibility of the self alongside surveillance of ideological and ritual Others. Furthermore, the latter are now perceived as potential competitors for the sacred capital that is assumed to dispense blessings and legitimacy to its supplicants and/or administrators.

A side effect of the contestation approach is to expand the ethnographic field from the limited Turnerian focus on lay travelers. The task of the observer is to document the divergent ideological and institutional interests conveyed to the sacred center but also to follow the likely attempts to manage (or mask) such diversity on the part of shrine authorities. It therefore becomes necessary to trace conflicts expressed across a broadened religious environment that includes pilgrims, volunteers, church authorities, and—in the case of Christopher McKevitt's (1991) contribution to the volume—those living in the immediate vicinity of a shrine. Generally, also, the contributors to Contesting the Sacred write in a different tone from that of the Turners, avoiding Image and Pilgrimage's more phenomenological attempts to convey the intensity of "authentic" religious engagement.[15] The Turners had, of course, combined an emphasis on religious experience with the construction of a more abstract theoretical lexicon meant to lay out the components of a processual anthropology. Contestation is a more diffusely conceived concept in the sense that it is not arranged into an overarching theoretical schema. Instead, chapters of Eade and Sallnow's volume contain a variety of suggestive illustrations of how competing discourses might be housed within sacred space. For instance, the direct articulations of differences between "sacrificial" and "miracle" discourses of the body at Lourdes described by Andrea Dahlberg (1991) are complemented by Glenn Bowman's (1991) emphasis on parallel, but not always overlapping, forms of Christian religious orientation toward and within the Holy Land. On the whole, however, the ethnographic complexity caught by individual contributors is played down in the volume's more general depiction of contestation, which does not provide an extensive analytical vocabulary to characterize variations in contestatory behavior.

More systematic exploration of contestation as an analytical concept might have involved positing the possibility of an array of stances, each with particular social and ritual consequences. For instance, overt competition for the same symbolic resource is distinct from discrepant or incommensurate interpretation of a sacred figure or space. Or again, direct liturgical and ideological collisions with others are not the same as simple avoidance or lack of mutual awareness. Adopting Gluckman's vocabulary (1954), it becomes feasible to distinguish between ritualized rebellion, where pilgrims protest against a given regime of shrine governance, and more far-reaching revolution, where the aim is to remake the very constitution of the sacred, as occurred at the time of the Protestant Reformation in Europe. From another perspective, it is possible to interpret power relations exercised at shrines in terms of Michel de Certeau's (1984) well-known discussion of the operation of "strategies"— institutional attempts to gain influence—and more opportunistic, ad hoc "tactics" of ordinary people (see, e.g., Mesaritou 2009). Drawing on a later theoretical vocabulary, it may also be productive to see religious clashes as involving different understandings and evaluations of the materialities and meanings that go into the production of religious practice, what Keane (e.g., 2003) calls the "semiotic ideologies" that vary across social, cultural, and historical contexts.

This diversity of approaches takes us in different analytical directions while illuminating the continued potential of a contestation approach to pilgrimage. Each might build on Eade and Sallnow's central contention that what is distinctive about pilgrimage is its capacity to afford a meeting point for varieties of religious perspective and practice to become juxtaposed. As an activity that marks out exits and entrances, departures and gatherings, competition but also co-presence in and across different social and cultural domains, pilgrimage provides an ideal opportunity to explore entanglements and misrecognitions that occur between differing conceptions of language, religious objects, and ritual action. In doing so, it appears to take scholars in a profoundly different direction to the communitas paradigm; but the next section shows that a wholesale separation of the two approaches would be highly misleading.

Hidden Articulations

John Eade has wryly remarked that *Contesting the Sacred* promoted opposition to the starker categorical divisions made by the Turners yet ended up producing another analytical binary (2011, 387). The development of a model that revealed the presence of an apparently equal and opposite form of sociality to communitas—conflict rather than harmony, competition rather than collaboration, amplification of difference rather than sweeping away of everyday statuses and identities—still reflected the influence of the old trope, if only by producing its mirror image.

Nonetheless, we should not see these tropes purely as opposites, for they exhibit significant parallels. Both depend on the idea that important pilgrimage sites attract diverse constituencies (Bowman 2014, 154; Coleman 2002), even if this capacity to encompass diversity is read in very different ways. Despite contestation's emphasis on the retention of everyday identity, both deploy an imagery of blankness in discussing how ideological pluralities are dealt with at shrines. While the Turners refer to ways in which I-Thou relations remove obstacles to unguarded human exchanges, Eade and Sallnow's "empty vessel" image suggests the possibility of a site offering no resistance to the numerous religio-political positions articulated within its boundaries.[16] The effect of such stripping away is to grant both tropes free rein in framing what is perceived to be most essential to a given site, rather than encouraging the researcher to foreground messier, more ambivalent forms of social and material negotiation.

Most significantly, both approaches focus attention on shrines, even though they hint at the sociological possibilities inherent in looking elsewhere.[17] The Turnerian invocation of a wider pilgrimage field has a counterpart in Eade and Sallnow's argument that constituents bring their ideologies from numerous home locations. Eade and Sallnow fragment the center; they bring it from "out there" to somewhere much closer to everyday life; they show how it may be bent out of shape. Yet ultimately, they retain it as a primary ethnographic and theoretical orientation in the sense of assuming that both pilgrims' and scholars' gazes should be directed at the most obvious points of (inter)action.[18]

The consequences of this focus on arenas of ritual concentration become clearer if viewed through the comparative lens of the anthropology of Pentecostalism. One of the most powerful theoretical tropes in describing the effects of Pentecostal movements around the world in recent years has also invoked imagery of conflict. It has referred to the prevalence of "rupture," claiming that Pentecostal Christianity globalizes by accepting the reality of, yet pitting itself against, already existing spiritual forces (Casanova 2001, 437–38; Robbins 2004). The ready appropriation of local idioms for engaging with supernatural powers promotes cultural and social transformation precisely because it acknowledges and addresses homegrown traditions, obligations, and cosmological categories (Robbins 2004, 129). Pentecostalism engages powerfully and unapologetically with the culture of others in order to change that culture.

At first sight, the Pentecostal trope of rupture looks quite similar to that of pilgrimage as contestation. Both emphasize the likelihood of fractious relations with others who are also striving for hegemony in religious and wider cultural relations. Yet the gulf between the two emerges on closer inspection of their societal implications. Pentecostal rupture involves targeted articulation with competing forms of language, materiality, and divinity alongside attempts to have long-lasting effects in wider spheres of society. The trope of pilgrimage as contestation confines the immediate scope of its operations and articulations to competition with others inside a *delimited* zone—the time and space of the shrine. In this sense, contestation echoes the tendency of communitas to isolate the field from other ethnographic and theoretical concerns.

There is another, curious, way in which the work of the Turners and that of Eade and Sallnow share a similar fate, related to the respective trajectories of their arguments. Communitas and liminality suppressed other dimensions of the Turnerian argument. Similarly, the model of contestation has taken attention away from another, more positive and substantive suggestion made by Eade and Sallnow: their proposal that pilgrimage might usefully be thought of as containing coordinates of person, place, and text (Eade and Sallnow 1991, 9). In later work, Eade neatly links the components of this pilgrimage grammar to contestation by suggesting that "Lourdes remains a place in which conflicting understandings of person, place, and text are acted out on a very public stage" (2000, xxiii). Nonetheless, the triad of mutually articulated elements has proven much less influential than the idea of contestation.[19] Eade and Sallnow do not develop the suggestion in much detail, and their proposal immediately raises questions about what other components might go into the pilgrimage mix, but the idea itself would benefit from more scrutiny.[20]

From the 1990s, the motif of contestation became widespread within studies of pilgrimage. Considerable parallels are evident with Alan Morinis's and N. Ross Crumrine's arguments that "at major pilgrimage places, we see socially intersecting communities, each with their own relationship to the shrine center" (1991, 7) and that "both sociologically and theologically, the sacred place has a power which secular groups seek to tap and channel for their own temporal purposes" (8). Leslie Nthoi (2006), in his major study of the southern African Mwali cult, pitched himself not only against communitas as a governing idea but also against the assumption that a single, overriding theoretical narrative about pilgrimage could usefully be produced.[21] However, it gradually became common for both tropes to be addressed in the same analytical frame. Di Giovine's (2011, 248) overview of pilgrimage literature observes that Eade and Sallnow's agenda "was met warmly," helping to propel pilgrimage studies beyond anthropology as well as "its traditional religious focus" while remaining "a canonical text for those researching pilgrimage and religious tourism, particularly in the Western, Christian tradition."[22] It is nonetheless significant that he is making this point in the introduction to a special issue dedicated to examining the continued influence of communitas, which contains pieces that often juxtapose both models rather than dismissing one in favor of the other.[23]

Communitas and contestation can clearly coexist and even engage each other in positive ways. Di Giovine argues, "Just as it is in the ideological interest of religious authorities to embrace and promote normative communitas, it also seems to be in the interest of site managers to foster a feeling of commonality when interacting at a destination" (2011, 249).[24] From an administrative perspective, the strategic invocation of communitas might pacify unruly pilgrims, given its emphasis on unity and mutual acceptance, and the Turners acknowledged that normative communitas had the capacity to be a conservative force.[25] There is a parallel here with Andrea Dahlberg's (1991) argument in *Contesting the Sacred* that sacrificial discourse at a shrine sanctifies suffering and acquiescence to both fate and church, whereas miraculous discourse takes pilgrims into realms of religious charisma that might threaten the powers of established clergy.

If conjoined, communitas and contestation have the capacity to create a new, hybrid trope, expressive of the complexity of perspectives evident within any given shrine (e.g., Porth 2005). One of the more interesting attempts to address this possibility is provided by another pair of authors, the married couple Jonathan Miles-Watson and Sukanya Miles-Watson, writing in Di Giovine's special issue on communitas and looking beyond Christianity. The inspiration for their paper comes when they find themselves telling a neighbor in Shimla the story of their pilgrimage to the Manimahesh area (abode of the deity Shiva) in the north of the Indian state of Himachal Pradesh (Miles-Watson and Miles-Watson 2011, 319). Whereas the Turners merged their experiences of pilgrimage sites into a single voice, the Miles-Watsons self-consciously separate their perspectives, illustrating ways in which "issues of conflict and communitas can be folded into the experience of the reality of both physical and narrated pilgrimage landscapes" (ibid.). The result is an account that alternates viewpoints, skillfully laying out shifts in stance, orientation, and sociality, all linked to sensory engagement with movement and terrain. The reader learns of numerous points on the pilgrimage when not only the narrators but travelers in general might come together and when they might feel separated, as issues of gender, caste, and class gain and lose salience. The Miles-Watsons also trace the changing physical affordances of the pilgrimage landscape, seeing "the Manimahesh Yatra [as] a polyrhythmic composition of processes, where the human and the non-human, the animate and the inanimate, the physical and the mythic are joined through the act of walking" (331).

In this analysis, neither contestation nor communitas wins out over the other, given the constantly varying points of view and experience entailed in journeying through the socio-spatial environment. Both tropes are manifested and mediated through local categories of understanding and perception, as stories told on the trail direct pilgrims' attention collectively toward certain features of their surroundings (Miles-Watson and Miles-Watson 2011, 323), even as the Himalayan landscape is also personified and encountered in disparate ways, ranging from "exotic seductress" to "faithful companion" (322). A similar blend of commonality and difference becomes evident in the ways in which travelers seek *darshan* from the mountain, gazing upon it and having it gaze upon them in return: some view in ocularcentric fashion, while others incorporate looking into a more "completely embodied experience of the mountain, which includes experiences of (and with) human and non-human, terrestrial and Divine beings" (330).[26] As we saw with Michael's experience of the blending of cathedrals with cliff tops, sea, and hillsides in chapter 2, physical engagement with agentive landscapes can be key to the performative effects of pilgrimage, even if degrees of receptivity to such effects will vary according to both individual personality and cultural disposition.

Beyond Anthropology

Both the possibilities and the limitations of a contestation approach are evident. The framework highlights certain dimensions of pilgrimage experience and organization but remains underdetermined in its theoretical specification and ethnographic range. The impression that contestation reflects its intellectual and cultural zeitgeist (as anti-structure did in the preceding generation) is reinforced by work from geographers who cover similar themes but do not draw on Eade and Sallnow (1991). Noga Collins-Kreiner et al. (2013) survey various sites of pilgrimage in Israel, including the Mormon Church in Jerusalem, the Baha'i Shrine and Gardens in Haifa, and the Church of Annunciation and Shihab-a-Din Mosque in Nazareth. They search for indications of conflict and focus on events of "transgression" when (182) "people criticise something they judge as deviant in order to strengthen their own ideological position." Their conclusion is that both location and scale are key factors in identifying the likelihood of transgressive events, though their characterization of spatiality includes but also goes beyond the ritual center, referring both to the placing of a site within a given city and to the location of that city within the wider Israeli national context. For instance: "A mosque in Nazarath would not have provoked the opposition of the city's Christian[s] and the entire Christian world had it been planned for one of the city's Muslim's neighbourhoods and not immediately adjacent to the centre of the ancient holy Christian city" (196).

As Collins-Kreiner et al. admit, Israel is highly likely to produce numerous instances of tension, but the geographer of religion Daniel Olsen (2008, 172) refers to a much wider disciplinary tradition of studying the spatial politics of inclusion, exclusion, and surveillance regarding what is perceived by informants to be "in" and "out of" place (e.g., Cresswell 1996; Edensor 2000; Sibley 1995; Trudeau 2006).[27] What Olsen calls the "situationalist perspective" (see Tilley 2006) accepts that space is likely to be "inherently and continuously contested, being constantly negotiated and re-produced through re-interpretation by various social groups" (Olsen 2008, 172). The temporal dimension also seems key, given that cooperation and conflict depend on seasonal, diurnal, and other time-related circumstances. Ultimately, however, Olsen finds the imagery of contestation to be limiting. In his case study of Temple Square in Salt Lake City, he points out many examples of what might initially be seen as prime opportunities for contestation (2008, 173–74), including ways in which Mormon Church representatives view the square as a religious site, as opposed to government tourist officials who perceive it as a heritage tourism venue. However, Olsen notes that many of the stakeholders interested in tourism in the square are also members of the Church of Latter-day Saints (175). His observation reminds us of the complexities of interest, allegiance, and motivation entailed in multistranded relationships, but not highlighted in Eade and Sallnow's description of their model. More generally, Olsen sees matters of spatial hierarchy as mediating relations of cooperation and competition, so that "at certain scales, stakeholders may be amenable to cooperation, while at other scales cooperation may not be as easy to achieve" (177; see Swyngedouw [2004]). The job of the analyst is to recognize the presence and the frequent interweaving of forms of both contestation and collaboration.[28] In the rest of this chapter, I show how both tropes might be further conjoined and adapted in ways that enhance our understanding of their potentialities while bringing pilgrimage literature into dialogue with wider theoretical concerns. I begin by returning to the idea of the transcendent, set apart, "center out there."

Taking a Different Turn(er)? Rethinking Transcendence

Two years after *Contesting the Sacred* came out, an article on Taiwanese Buddhist pilgrimage was published by the American anthropologist Steven Sangren (1993; see also Sangren 1987). The piece reports on a remarkable phenomenon in which four to five million people (roughly 20 percent of the island's population) travel to Pei-kang, an urban township famous for housing an important temple of the goddess Ma Tsu.[29] The journeys, marking the birthday of the goddess on the twenty-third day of the third lunar month, are organized by temples located around the country. People bring images of the goddess to the temple in Pei-kang in the hope of gaining divine efficacy through contact with a nationally revered shrine.

Sangren addresses Victor Turner's work in his analysis of the Ma Tsu pilgrimage, and though he does not appear to be aware of Eade and Sallnow, his conclusions extend their perspective. He agrees with Turner that a significant dimension of pilgrimage is its capacity to transcend local social structure. In this sense, he reinforces the imagery of an influential center "out there." However, in contrast to the Turnerian emphasis on unstructured communitas, Sangren's characterization of the workings of transcendence shifts attention back to the operation of local social structures. For his argument, he finds inspiration in a short piece by the anthropologist Terence Turner (1977), which had reformulated van Gennep's model by emphasizing the dynamic relationship between ritual and its social context (59).[30]

Ma Tsu is viewed by Taiwanese pilgrims as a source of vital and socially productive power that is accessed away from home, so that "representatives of the community must travel outside [their local contexts] to acquire or restore it" (Sangren 1993, 573). As a result, the annual pilgrimage becomes "a ritual process that both constructs or produces society and is premised on an alienated representation of the nature of society's (and, not incidentally, individuals') own productive power—alienated because the producer or 'subject' misrecognizes its own role as such" (565). In other words, humans create their communities—but they convince themselves that they need the gods to do so. Sangren shares Eade and Sallnow's interest in the fetishization of divine power at sacred shrines. However, while the contestation model focuses its analytical and ethnographic attention on the shrine center, Sangren presents a broader ethnographic vision; the significance of the high-status temple is viewed in relation to local contexts and vice versa (cf. Huang 2017, 284).

Almost exactly contemporaneous with both *Contesting the Sacred* and the Ma Tsu paper, anthropologist Maurice Bloch's *Prey into Hunter* (1991) offers another reanalysis of "passage" models of ritual, drawing on Bloch's long-standing interests in power, legitimacy, and mystification. He proposes that while participants in the midst of a rite subject themselves to the demanding and even violent power of the divine, once the event is over, they feel empowered to engage in a spiritually legitimized conquest of the world to which they return (Bloch 1991, 5–6; see also Coleman 2005). It is true, says Bloch, that engaging in a ritual is likely to prevent participants from comprehending the true extent of their human agency; they are "mystified," in Marxist terms. However, participation invests them with a sacralized authority that may be exercised beyond the time and space of ritual action.

While the Turnerian perspective focuses on the middle, liminal phase of the rite of passage, Bloch is particularly interested in the *final* stage, the reincorporation of initiates back into society. In this sense, he reinforces Sangren's attention on the ways in which pilgrims actively engage with institutions once they reach home. Sangren (1993) does not use Bloch's distinctive language of violent social efficacy, but he does suggest that the Pei-kang Ma Tsu "pilgrimages constitute a ritual of pan-Taiwaneseness," drawing on core symbols that powerfully promote "the linked production of selves, communities, and wider collectivities" (576). Applying this extended spatial and cultural perspective to Eade and Sallnow's contestation model, we gain an explanation for why some pilgrims might be so assiduous in visiting shrines. Travelers gain access to transcendent sources of self-legitimation obtained at ritual centers. But the full significance of such centers can only be understood by taking into account their effects on, and recall within, the regular life of the community—a dimension of analysis missing from the contestation model.

The work of Sangren and Bloch encourages us to understand pilgrimage through the interplay and mutual articulations of sacred shrines with domestic contexts. Such articulations exist even when shrines appear to be set apart from the world, since it is often their apparent isolation that lends certain sites the spiritual prestige, power, and capital that can be redeployed at home. Pilgrimage behavior typically looks very different from that of the mundane world, yet it maintains intimate social and cultural connections with daily life.

Signs and Subtleties of Difference

Sangren and Bloch extend their interests in the working of power beyond pilgrimage centers but have relatively little to say about another of the central features of Eade and Sallnow's model: the amplification of competing perspectives within sacralized space. Other work has converted the model's stark association of ideological diversity with contestation into analyses that provide more subtle explorations of the complex, situational dimensions of identification and accommodation evident among those present at sacred sites. As Jennifer Porter has noted, negotiations of meaning may create not conflict but a "dialogic center" (2004, 173), while Katherine Rousseau (2016, 7–9) adapts the model in her characterization of contestation not as antagonistic or discordant but as potentially "polyphonic," bringing together the views of a range of stakeholders and participants.

Dionigi Albera (2012) provides an equally nuanced view of plurality in his analysis of the behavior of Muslim pilgrims at Marian shrines around the Mediterranean, places he calls "ambiguous sanctuaries," deploying a term coined by the English antiquarian and historian Frederick Hasluck to describe places claimed by two or more religions (10; Hasluck 1929; see also Hobart and Zarcone 2017). Albera sees such contexts as providing a "testimony to the complex imbrications between conflict and sharing, between monolithic religious identities and the hybridity of practices" (19), indicating the capacity of chronic mutual accommodation to prevail over seemingly fixed doctrinal boundaries.

As he points out, devotion for the Virgin Mary is located within Islamic as well as Christian tradition. Indeed, she is the only female figure designated by name (as opposed to role) in the Qur'an. If she is a Turnerian dominant symbol, then, she can claim scriptural justification for her ability to provide a bridge between adherents of different faiths.

Ideological overlap is one thing. Embodied choreography of sharing is another. This latter theme is developed by Glenn Bowman, whose contribution to *Contesting the Sacred* had already marked his interest in parallel ritual engagements with sacred space. Drawing on the work of the architectural scholar Michael Sorkin (1999), Bowman explores a distinction between more modernist organizations of space where people and vehicles are channeled into "nonintersecting pathways" and more traditional settings "in which flow is impeded by repeated intersection and the necessary and mutually aware sharing of place" (2016, 258).[31] Bowman's concern with the presence or absence of physical intersections has parallels with my discussion of the ambiguities in the original formulation of contestation, including the considerable differences between direct confrontation on one hand and broader coexistence on the other. A concept developed by Sorkin that Bowman finds particularly productive is that of "giving ground," involving recognition of "the right of the Other to be in the same place as oneself as well as committing to the rites of negotiating her presence" (260). Such deference and flexibility of response are the products of "the multitude of identities at play in any individual's experience of everyday life" (261) so that various dispositions and "identity articulations" may be brought to the fore at different times (see also Goffman 1959). It is both subtler than an image of pure opposition and more sociologically plausible than the assertion of an unmediated I-Thou encounter between liminars.

Bowman's general position is intriguingly close to Gluckman's discussion of the multistranded relations that bring people together, and it has implications for emphasizing the shifting frames of intensity, identification, and focus during pilgrimage (cf. Bandak 2012; Marsden and Retsikas 2013). However, his overall argument is aimed less at his anthropological colleagues and more at the assumptions of political scientists (e.g., Hassner 2009; Hayden 2002; Huntingdon 1993, 1996).[32] In the introduction to an edited volume on sharing shrines subtitled "The Politics and Pragmatics of Inter-communal Relations around Holy Places," he opposes "a wide range of popular and academic identitarian discourses contending that . . . cultural identities are essential, exclusivist, and therefore inherently antagonistic to those of others" (Bowman 2012, 1). Bowman does not wish to counter representations of conflict with "bourgeois cosmopolitan pleas for pluralism" (ibid.). Rather, he aims to use ethnographic methods to complicate simplistic assumptions of the indivisibility of identity that fail to acknowledge its emergent, contingent properties. Drawing on his work on Muslim-Christian co-usage of shrines in Palestine (e.g., 1993), he calls for "attention to the minutiae of engagements, avoidances, mimickings, avowals, and disavowals through which members of interacting communities manage the presence of the others" (4).[33]

As Bowman notes (2012, 6), two of the chapters in his collection—Anna Bigelow's (2012) on Muslim shrines in post-partition Punjab, and Maria Couroucli's (2012) on mixed Christian and Muslim practices in Anatolia—document occasions on which contemporary shrines provide opportunities for nostalgic forms of sharing between groups. Communities that are now largely separated but were historically interwoven use the material affordances of shrines to recall previous form of spatial and cultural sharing. It is not necessary to invoke the extremes of communitas to appreciate the ways in which, as Bowman puts it, "an image of a remembered community is reconstituted and embodied in practices around . . . shrines" (6). The social relations being managed under such circumstances appear to be the reverse of those discussed in Sallnow's ethnography (1987). If the (near-impossible) challenge for Sallnow's journeying pilgrims is to downplay the complications of quotidian life, the challenge revealed in the case studies from the Punjab and Anatolia is to use the spatiotemporal opportunities provided by shrines to reconstruct memories of having successfully coexisted on a daily basis.

The complexities of the ways in which shared shrines provide flexible spaces for fluid and indirect intersections of identity and history have been captured by Iuliia Buyskykh (2019) in her account of Orthodox and Greek Catholic pilgrims, now resident in Ukraine, who "return" to a Roman Catholic shrine based just over the border in Poland. Kalwaria Pacławska is a village in the south-eastern part of the country which houses a shrine that Buyskykh's relatives had regularly visited in the years before World War II, before they were expelled from the area.

Nowadays, most local inhabitants and Polish pilgrims remain unaware of their Ukrainian visitors, who are careful to manage their identity as guests (Buyskykh, 85). Ukrainians disperse throughout the shrine cathedral and carry out the same ritual gestures as others, genuflecting and bending one knee to the ground upon entering the space. They even go to Roman Catholic priests for confession. At the same time, engagement with the formal liturgies of the shrine provides opportunities to express minor yet meaningful differences in behavior: covering heads with kerchiefs and scarfs, as done in home churches; making the sign of the cross in the Byzantine form (three fingers, right to left); and possibly even praying in their own language. In common with Bowman, Buyskykh finds that theories based on assumptions of antagonism are too blunt to grasp the accommodations occurring at and around the site. Rather, Ukrainians add subtle layers of significance to the sacred space, establishing their presence yet not asserting primacy of ownership. Their engagements resemble de Certeau's tactics mentioned earlier—enacting a complex, sometimes concealed, form of contestation.

Articulation and the Productivities of Friction

Communitas and contestation work efficiently as tropes because they simplify understandings of social interfaces. Taken to their logical extremes, they present researchers with human interactions that are single-stranded and easy to present in high relief. The seemingly abrasive relationship between the two tropes has proved productive to both, and they can be made to coexist within the same study. However, communitas and contestation also focus too much attention on shrines themselves. By contrast, the works of Sangren, Bloch, and Terence Turner show how ritual centers create external connections and effects beyond their more obvious behavioral and spatial limits. Another problem with the two tropes is that they downplay the significance of more ambivalent, hesitant, and even inconsistent associations within sacred sites. Conversely, Albera, Bowman, and Buyskykh explore the nuances and contingencies of interactions among different groups of pilgrims as they occupy the same or contiguous spaces.

In the final part of this chapter, I bring such themes of relationality and connectedness into dialogue with further discussion of the notion of articulation. So far, I have argued that this idea resonates well with how pilgrimage promotes ritually and ideologically marked forms of separation and reconnection, displacement and re-emplacement—between homes and shrines, pilgrims and clergy, human and divine figures, and so on. Invoking articulation offers the possibility of imagining multiscalar fields of pilgrimage that include but go beyond specific sites of heightened activity. Following Marsden and Retsikas (2013), it can also be used to present religious action as both reproduced and transformed through entanglements with other features of social life. Indeed, these authors' appreciation of the instability and multiplicity of social and cultural formations comes in part from Deleuze and Guattari's (1980) assemblage theory, an approach that acknowledges "the labour of assembling and re-assembling sociomaterial practices that are diffuse, tangled and contingent" (Anderson and Macfarlane 2011, 124–25). Interestingly, such themes are also clearly discernible—albeit expressed very differently—in the works of Gluckman, the Turners, and Eade and Sallnow, all of whom are interested in the fragility of cultural institutions, factors underlying social alliances and schisms, and the autonomy or otherwise of religious action (cf. Latour 1993, 2005).

Talk of entanglement, diffusion, and contingency can be stimulating yet remain frustratingly unspecific, and in the third section of this book, I explore in detail what pilgrimage articulations might look like in practice. A further question relates to whether the creation of social and cultural formations is deliberately carried out. Marsden and Retsikas state that articulation is "not necessarily the result of the conscious and intentional effort of actors or of the skills and habits they have acquired and cultivated" (2013, 14), and they contrast it with a process they call "systematicity," which refers to the efforts required strategically to invoke or conceal religious identifications in the course of everyday life (2).

My own approach to articulation differs somewhat. I prefer to avoid a rigid separation between the conscious or unconscious making of connections, since in many cases, the motivations of actors—individually or institutionally—is likely to be opaque or multifaceted. While I appreciate Marsden and Retsikas's focus on the micropolitics of everyday interaction, I also emphasize the workings of politics at larger scales, relating to broad questions of economy, governance, and cultural hegemony, even in the creation and maintenance of systems of pilgrimage.

To do so, I introduce another prominent theorist of articulation, whose work overlaps with the cultural and intellectual worlds of the writers I have so far mentioned yet turns more explicitly to questions of power at different scales of analysis. Marsden and Retsikas do not mention this scholar, but his work is deeply relevant to theirs.

Stuart Hall was a sociologist and cultural theorist, born and brought up in Jamaica before he moved to the United Kingdom. He was appointed head of Birmingham University's Centre for Contemporary Cultural Studies, a research unit founded in the mid-1960s, which under his direction became a world-leading institute for the scholarly study of popular culture (Morley and Chen 1996). Like Victor and Edith Turner, Hall felt himself to be an outsider to many of the academic worlds he addressed. His sense of displaced identity came from direct experience of being a black migrant coming to study and work in postwar Britain. He was certainly aware of the Turners, and he quoted Victor's writing on symbols and ritual in an analysis of the revolutionary potential of American hippies (Hall 1969), a piece that illustrates what Donald Weber calls "the powerful fascination and attraction of the counterculture for contemporary academic 'outsiders'" (1995, 534). Hall shared the Turnerian sense of the scholarly life as social calling, yet his plural conception of cultural studies was very different from the unified vision of Christian culture that inspired the later work of Victor and Edith. Unlike the Turners, he remained committed to a sophisticated Marxism, rooted in his observation of the ethnically diverse urban communities that had come to populate post- (or perhaps neo-)colonial Britain—very similar to the populations studied by John Eade before the latter turned to studying pilgrimage.[34] Articulation became a central motif within Hall's work, reinforcing his dedication to understanding complex social structures as made of elements related "as much through their differences as through their similarities" (Slack 1996, 116). In a well-known interview, Hall explained his liking for the concept:

In England, the term has a nice double meaning because 'articulate' means to utter, to speak forth, to be articulate. It carries that sense of language-ing, of expressing, etc. But we also speak of an 'articulated' lorry (truck): a lorry where the front (cab) and back (trailer) can, but need not necessarily, be connected to one another. The two parts are connected to each other, but through a specific linkage, that can be broken. An articulation is thus the form of the connection that *can* make a unity of two different elements, under certain conditions. It is a linkage which is not necessary, determined, absolute and essential for all time. You have to ask, under what circumstances *can* a connection be forged or made? (Quoted in Grossberg 1986, 53)

As John Clarke observes, this quotation illustrates how Hall's understanding of articulation entails showing how "giving voice" and "connecting"—invoking and linking—are co-constitutive (2015, 277). Difference and similarity are now conjoined rather than perceived as mutually incompatible. Without replicating assemblage theory, Hall provides powerful imagery for any attempt to grasp how a phenomenon such as pilgrimage might be conceptualized as an array of elements rather than a fixed practice, while being linked to wider social forces "to which it can, under certain historical conditions . . . be connected" (Grossberg 1996, 141; see also Boivin 2017). This view of cultural formation is designed to avoid the strict determinism of certain Marxist positions but also to oppose the free-floating assumptions of postmodernism, given the continuing significance of relations of dominance and subordination. Also important is Hall's assumption that understanding articulation involves taking account of the workings of *attention*—giving due regard "to what connections are . . . being forged, to what threads are being forgotten and to what apparently natural and normal alignments of things are coming apart" (Clarke 2015, 284). This commentary provides a more general characterization of what in chapter 1 I called the politics of attention, which I applied to the question of how certain pilgrimage practices are overlooked not just by practitioners, but also by scholars.

Both the Turners and Eade and Sallnow wished to understand how pilgrimage involved the contingencies of making connections. However, they tended to funnel—and polarize—scholarly attention in ways that pushed analysis toward teleological conclusions concerning the presence or absence of communitas and contestation.[35] A stress on articulation encourages greater recognition of uncertainty of outcome in any given (pilgrimage) context while emphasizing the need to acknowledge the politics of human interactions at different scales. In this respect, it points to another, related, term that also takes into account the entangled and confusing character of much activity that occurs across ideological boundaries. Anna Tsing's book *Friction*, subtitled an "ethnography of global connection" (2005), deals with culture clashes and environmental politics in Indonesia. She notes that her approach "follows in the legacy of Stuart Hall's and James Clifford's 1997 revitalization of Antonio Gramsci's notion of 'articulation'" (2012, 2). Tsing describes how the resistances produced through zones of awkward engagement between diverse constituencies (scientists, entrepreneurs, village elders, and so on) may result in creative outcomes, though clearly ones where deep inequalities remain. In other words, the articulation of difference between separate bodies in motion is capable of forming more than mere conflict. It may also produce unpredictable and often transient interactions that generate new activities and expressions of identity.

In the language of pilgrimage studies, friction refers to a form of articulation that avoids focusing exclusively on occlusion of difference (communitas) or the tendency to highlight it (contestation). It can also be redeployed to form an expanded vision of the field. The latter half of this chapter has shown how the seemingly jarring relationship between communitas and contestation is actually one where a variety of resonances and connections should be discerned, so that what might seem like incommensurable models of pilgrimage can be adapted and even conjoined in certain respects. Thinking through models of articulation and associated friction makes it easier to avoid some of the many binaries associated with theorizing about pilgrimage, since assumptions concerning either total assimilation or pure opposition can be avoided. This perspective also corresponds well with the work of Albera, Bowman, and Buyskykh dedicated to showing how populations whose interests and ideologies seem opposed may find numerous and subtle forms of accommodation. Indeed, much of the finest ethnographic work occurs in those spaces where articulations of difference are understood to operate with and through numerous degrees of intensity varying across time and social situation. Pilgrimage systems may form different manifestations of center, periphery, and home to those evident in the rain forests described by Tsing, but they undoubtedly have the capacity to encourage bumpy articulations across spaces and scales of encounter, splicing together populations and forms of behavior that seem very disparate, such as the niceties of religious ritual and the wider political economy of migration.

This chapter has traced a journey not only across authors but also across concepts. It has moved from communitas to contestation, thence to assemblage and articulation, and finally alighting on friction. Admittedly, an analytical lexicon that highlights such terms falls into Derrida's trap of "mondialatinization," mentioned in the previous chapter, where Latinate language all too easily becomes the language of abstraction and theorizing. It is therefore important to try to use theoretical metaphors as knowingly as possible (Tweed 2006), retaining awareness of their implicit orientations. I shall pursue other articulations and frictions in future chapters. Next, however, I focus on a third and final trope that has helped to form the field of pilgrimage studies. I examine this newer trope's emergence and its effects and demonstrate how it does—and does not—connect with the models of sacralized travel examined so far.

5

The Center Cannot Hold

Camino

Things fall apart; the center cannot hold;
Mere anarchy is loosed upon the world
—W. B. Yeats, *The Second Coming* (1919)

W. B. Yeats was a poet beloved by Victor and Edith, but these lines conjure up sterile anarchy rather than any Turnerian aspiration toward anti-structure as source of creativity.[1] The poet's anxious sense that "the center cannot hold" offers a resonant portrayal of the way notions of sacralized centrality—whether sustained by communitas or by contestation—have ultimately proved unsustainable in the study of pilgrimage. Particularly since the turn of the twenty-first century, another trope has emerged based on a very different metaphor to the Turners' or even Eade and Sallnow's emphasis on bounded arenas of ritual action. The orientation is less on the center and more on the path, a term associated most readily with the *Camino*, the ancient pilgrimage routes leading across Europe toward the Cathedral of Santiago de Compostela in northern Spain.[2] The idea of the Camino has increasingly taken on popular and scholarly significance beyond any specific region or even religion, and while it moves away from notions of an organizing center, it highlights social relations that are far from anarchic. In examining the popularity of this third trope, we continue our trajectory away from conceptualizations of pilgrimage that place almost exclusive ethnographic attention on shrines and move further toward the exploration of other fields, other connections.[3]

On the Road

In 2010, soon after I moved from England to Canada, I spotted an advertisement for a lecture taking place in a church situated on the edge of the

University of Toronto campus. The invited speaker, a Canadian lawyer called Julie Kirkpatrick, was due to talk about her book *The Camino Letters* (2010), which was based on her experience of walking the Camino to Santiago de Compostela with her daughter. I decided to attend, and to my surprise, I found a hall that was standing room only, so that I had to listen while perched on a crowded pew at the back. A year later, I bumped into a friend and colleague from another department. We chatted about summer plans and he told me that he intended to follow one of the paths to Santiago de Compostela to enjoy some "slow walking" together with one of his children. Later still, I went with my wife to a movie theater situated a few blocks from the university. Among the trailers advertising future shows, one was called *Walking the Camino: Six Days to Santiago*.

After a while, I stopped being surprised that the Camino had such a presence thousands of miles away in Toronto. As George Greenia states: "Over the past century, it has become arguably the iconic pilgrimage in Western culture" (2016, x).[4] The Camino has become a popular cultural meme, and in the following, I want to understand how it has achieved such a status but also to ask what the consequences of its prevalence might be for the academic study of pilgrimage.

First, however, some more context. The salience of both communitas and contestation as theoretical frames continued into the new millennium, and second editions of both *Image and Pilgrimage* and *Contesting the Sacred* were published.[5] In a new introduction to the latter, John Eade observed the continued tendency to avoid "recourse to the universalist claims of structural models" (2000, xiii). The implication was that his and Sallnow's target had not been merely communitas but also the very notion of universalism.[6] As Eade recognized (xiv–xv), the deconstructionist tendencies of their volume both reflected and reinforced intellectual trends associated with the pluralization of pilgrimage studies, taking in new influences from feminism in ethnographic practice (e.g., Dubisch 1995) and a shift among anthropologists toward making Europe an object of study.[7] A broadening out of perspectives was also evident in another important text mentioned by Eade, Ian Reader and Tony Walter's edited *Pilgrimage in Popular Culture* (1993), which explored the ambiguous boundary between the officially religious and the broadly sacred, arguing that visits to such places as Elvis Presley's home at Graceland or Liverpool F. C.'s soccer stadium in England constituted sanctified travel.

Deborah Ross (2011), a theologian and author of the new preface to the second edition of *Image and Pilgrimage*, echoed Eade in stating that pilgrimage now had to be understood as existing within "a shifting religious, social and economic world" (xlii). Key questions revolved around the changing character of obligation. The Turners had tended to present liminality as appropriate to tribal situations where ritual participants were required by society to go through certain rites of passage, whereas the liminoid was a more appropriate descriptor for ritual in societies where a plurality of options was evident. For Ross:

> The liminal-liminoid distinction anticipated the present religious mood in parts of Europe, and it parallels the culture of obligation vs culture of consumption difference. The term liminal seems to have had more currency than the term liminoid, both within academic work and general parlance. Given changing religious practices, the concept of the liminoid may gain increasing relevance. (Ross 2011, xlii)

Ross links themes of optation, consumption, and secularization to contemporary searches for identity. She invokes the French sociologist Danièle Hervieu-Léger's (2000) ideal-typical distinction between two emergent patterns of faith in modern Europe, which also revolve around questions of choice: one referring to individuals who follow a self-defined spiritual path and the other involving those who take more predetermined, traditional routes to salvation. Such debates have also been central to recent academic discussions of Santiago de Compostela, a pilgrimage complex mentioned only briefly by the Turners, which has taken on a much higher profile since they were writing in the 1970s.

The *Camino de Santiago*, or Way of St. James, refers to the pilgrimage routes dispersed across Europe and leading to the Cathedral at Santiago de Compostela in Spain. The presence in the shrine of the remains of the Apostle St. James was ratified by a twelfth-century illuminated manuscript called the *Codex Calixtinus*.[8] The codex contained advice to pilgrims and records of miracles, including a story of how the saint appeared in a dream to Charlemagne (747?–814 CE), encouraging the emperor to free his tomb from Muslim control and thus lending the site a key role in the Reconquista, or Christian "liberation" of the Iberian Peninsula. The saint acquired the name Matamoros, Moor-slayer, and Charlemagne became known as the first pilgrim (Lois-González 2013, 11). Such political efficacy was juxtaposed with the possibility of gaining personal forms of healing and redemption from the saint, including forgiveness of sins.

Compostela lay largely dormant except for a brief flourishing during the time of the Counter-Reformation in the late sixteenth and early seventeenth centuries. It was given renewed attention by the Spanish government after the Second World War as part of a promotion of National Catholicism (Chemin 2016, 28). Franco allied himself with Santiago Matamoros in a bid to cement his image as a savior of Spain (Frey 1998, 238). The apostle was made into the patron saint of the country and presented as a symbol of Catholic revival within a secularizing West. At the same time, pilgrimage to the saint's grave came to symbolize the desire to unify the countries of a continent that had been ravaged by war, and plans were laid to restore the material heritage of the routes (Cazauz 2011, 356; see also Frey 1998, 239). Pilgrims began to make journeys to the site by car, and the first Friends Association, *Los Amigos del Camino de Santiago*, was formed in 1959 (Frey 1998, 242).

By the 1960s and into the 1970s, Santiago de Compostela and the Camino occupied an ambiguous position within Spain and beyond. After Vatican II, Franco's elaborate ceremonialism and nationalism seemed anachronistic to more liberal elements of the priesthood. In the face of growing numbers of tourists, the church also found itself working hard to maintain the image of a pilgrimage primarily oriented toward meditation, mortification, and piety (Frey 1998, 243). After Franco died in 1975, governmental support for the revival ceased for a time (Cazaux 2011, 357). Yet it was precisely this temporary reduction of centralized governmental control that permitted a significant shift in both identity and orientation for the pilgrimage, leading to its reanimation in a new guise. By the 1980s, difficult economic circumstances in the country prompted a search for alternative forms of income to heavy industry or beach tourism, and at the same time, Spain entered the European Union.[9] Under such circumstances, the pilgrimage appeared to offer a historical legacy that could embrace the whole of the continent. A fresh revival was prompted by European Council and Council of Europe cultural programs, with the help of UNESCO and the Catholic Church, as the Camino became the first European Cultural Itinerary in 1987, an appellation marking its claim to be a foundational institution for modern Europe (Chemin 2016; Coleman 2015a). More money became available for the restoration of pathways and the development of hostelries for pilgrims (Cazaux 2011, 357). In 1993, Camino Francés, a route running from the Pyrenees to the City of Santiago de Compostela, gained World Heritage status.

Peter Margry notes that whereas before the middle of the twentieth century, the cathedral was the primary pilgrimage destination, this orientation has now been reversed so that "the sense of a spiritual journey has become the rationale" (2008, 24). He terms this shift a move toward a form of "transit pilgrimage" that lacks a clear middle or end—or at least renders specific temporal and spatial markers far less relevant than the cultivation of movement and an experience of freedom in ritual (ibid.). Rubén Lois-González writes that this "Jacobean phenomenon [has] enjoyed a new golden age, this time with more open and diverse referents" (2013, 13). The image of St. James as warrior has been converted into St. James the cultural icon, promoted by touristic, scholarly, and political organizations that associate the pilgrimage with leading European writers, ranging from Dante to Goethe to Joyce.

While the Way of St. James (or "the Way" as it is sometimes known in an Anglicized version of the pilgrimage, which also omits immediate reference to the saint) has existed for more than 1,200 years, it is "currently experiencing one of its most dynamic moments in its history" (Lois-González 2013, 8), with around three hundred thousand people arriving at the shrine per year having made the effort to travel at least one hundred kilometers on foot or two hundred kilometers if they have come on bicycle or horseback. Nowadays, those who travel "are a representative sample of early twenty-first century society" (ibid.), though with a slight majority of males and a tendency either to be younger (twenty to thirty-nine) or more mature adults (fifty or over), a demographic that may express the popularity of the Camino as a way to mark transitions into fresh stages in life, ranging from adulthood to retirement (17). While most pilgrims come from Spain (around 70 percent), the majority of the rest are from Western Europe and the Americas (Lois-González 2013, 17; Slavin 2003, 4). The walkers and cyclists are predominantly white and middle-class (Frey 1998, 7).

For Lois-González, the Camino is "one of the few outstanding examples of patrimonialization of an international itinerary in Europe" (2013, 16) and one that now constitutes a plural space celebrating multireligiosity and multiculturalism. If geographers such as Noga Collins-Kreiner et al. (2013) and Daniel Olsen (2008) underscore the significance of multiple levels of spatial identification with sacred sites (see chapter 4; Massey 1993), the Camino provides a prime example of the power inherent in flexibility of scales of association. It can readily be claimed by a number of different interest groups. Stakeholders range from Galician nationalists to representatives of other, semiautonomous regions in Europe through which the routes pass, to other pilgrimage sites and cathedrals that perceive themselves as linked to the Camino. The phenomenon therefore offers the potential for a highly diffuse set of connections to be constructed, which encompass large parts of the continent. These interests overlap with growth in roots and heritage tourism (Basu 2004; Bowman and Sepp 2019, 78). Gomes, Losada, and Pereiro call those who make the journey "touripilgrims" on the grounds that post-secular pilgrimages to Compostela are constantly in dialogue with "religion, spirituality, materiality, sociability and tourism" (2019, 32).

The establishment of this reticulate landscape of mass movement has revived a supposedly medieval model of journeying while resonating with what Bowman and Sepp call "the rediscovery and reappraisal of pilgrimage as multivalent contemporary praxis attractive to a great range of people, including northern Europeans in whose countries pilgrimage was abolished by the Reformation and those without religious or spiritual affiliation" (2019, 74). What participants often see as a harkening back to a pre-Reformation past is more a reflection of a current religio-political landscape where the theological and semiotic stakes of Protestant-Catholic conflicts have been dampened down as clergy perceive the need to keep all ritual doors open: "The Church hesitates to impose strict limits on the pilgrimage because it is precisely the Camino's openness that can bring more into the fold" (Frey 1998, 127).[10] In this context, even quite broad theological distinctions may simply bypass the awareness of many of those who happily travel along the Camino but lack any affiliation with parishes at home. For Greenia:

The revival of the Camino de Santiago in the late 20th century seems insistent on not requiring denominational credentials of any sort, so everyone is welcome, from 'industrial-strength Catholics' . . . to mainline Christians of every tradition, to bearers of aromas, crystals, and grudges against their former churches. (2016, x–xi)

Other ambiguously sanctified spaces in Europe and America that are also experiencing high levels of popularity include cathedrals (Coleman and Bowman 2019) and multifaith prayer rooms, which "have become the most distinctive form of recent religious construction" (Woodhead 2012, 1) in a Britain where churches are also increasingly being turned into commercial spaces, temples and mosques. Parallels are also evident with "alternative" pilgrimages to French Catholic shrines dedicated to Saint Mary Magdalene, as described by Anna Fedele (2013), among whose interlocutors "there was certainly a recurring reference to the importance of being true to oneself, following one's inner voice, and not giving away one's authority to external institutions or entities" (17).[11]

All these examples involve "spaces of emergent encounter and shifting intersectionalities not only among different religious ideologies but also between what are conventionally seen as sacred and secular domains" (Coleman and Bowman 2019, 3). On the Camino, a diverse and literally moving landscape of participation is created, where it is claimed that the "essential ritual acts" no longer "occur within the bounded sacred space of the shrine" (Frey 1998, 7). Frey notes that many of her informants actually found themselves alienated by reaching their ostensible goal, since the cathedral offers a liturgical structure that appears unfamiliar and even authoritarian to the uninitiated. Arrival may mark precisely the point when people drop their self-perception as pilgrims and engage in self-consciously touristic activities of consumption, such as purchasing souvenirs, visiting monuments, or staying in hotels (166–67).

Alongside the overall emphasis on diversity and emergence, the most obvious forms of contestation produced by the contemporary Camino revolve around a particular form of symbolic capital associated with current Western assumptions about what constitutes authentic travel. Samuel Sánchez y Sánchez and Annie Hesp (2016, 3) note that in the 1960s, pilgrimage to Santiago de Compostela implied reaching the site by any means possible, most likely car, bus, or train. However, what Frey calls "the polemics of movement" (1998, 17) refer to ethical judgments frequently made nowadays over modes of transport—not by clergy, but by trekkers. In this view, "Even if one is religiously motivated, pilgrim status is reserved for those who get to Santiago by foot and pedal" (18). The idea is that if communitas is to be found anywhere, it will be located not in church but en route among the slow travelers, through acts of mutual generosity among strangers or possibly in forms of fellowship developed at rest-stops (92–94). Margry (2008) highlights judgments made by scholars and walkers of different kinds of visitor. The so-called real pilgrims (18) come via the Camino without motorized transport and are eligible for being granted a pilgrimage certificate by the church. They are thereby distinguished from the four to five million other people who visit Compostela every year.[12]

In summary, the Camino offers a very different model of pilgrimage from that presented by the Turners or by Eade and Sallnow. The primary orientation of many participants is toward the path at least as much as toward any architectural and ecclesiastical center. The *infra*structure of the path, with its rustic roads, hostels, and signage, forms the material basis for a postmodern, spiritual-but-not-religious *anti*-structure that encourages movement toward a cathedral and yet shies away from overt adherence to Christian culture or any fixed institutional status. Frey adds, "Unlike many pilgrims to Marian shrines, those who walk and cycle to Santiago often are not motivated by the pains of the suffering body but by the pains of the suffering soul" (1998, 45; see also Davidson 2014, 177). In this respect also such walkers and cyclists differ from their medieval counterparts; the slow journey is not the means to the end but the end itself, especially in a world where hypermobility has become accessible within other "walks" of life (cf. Zapponi 2011).[13]

In contrast to the celebration of idealized fellowship within communitas, or even contestation's frequent highlighting of clashes between the ideological interests of corporate groups, the Camino appears to embody a trend away from pilgrimage as collective practice into more self-consciously individualized realms of experience. Frey observes, "When pilgrims speak of the Camino as a spiritual journey there is no shared definition, but it is generally related to this idea of the uncontained, nonstructural, personalized, individual, and direct relationship one has to ultimate reality" (1998, 31). Her characterization shares the

Turners' interest in developing a processual approach to ritualized engagement but orients the non-structural toward still more idiosyncratic, hyper-liminoid realms, emphasizing "creative personal alternatives" and "privatized, DIY religion" (33) that resonate with scholarly depictions of New Age practices (Heelas 1996). In Glenn Bowman's (2016) terms, the Camino constitutes a landscape somewhere between space and place, and one where nonintersecting social pathways are possible to negotiate.

A stress on individualization has affinities with phenomenological approaches that delve into the embodied experiences of the researcher as reflexive, lone pilgrim (Slavin 2003, 5; see also Doi 2011), as well as what Sean Slavin sees as the tendency on the Camino to "walk alone, physically distant from other pilgrims or, alternatively, with other people in silence" (2003, 12). Such walking permits the development of personalized orientations and rhythms in a way that could never be achieved in a procession or in shared public transport. In keeping with this dual emphasis on both pathways and the personal, Mats Nilsson and Mekonnen Tesfahuney regard pilgrimage practices on the Camino as emblematic of a post-secular move away from "the rituals, practices and traditions of churches and religious communities" in favor of "a kind of spiritual plurality, which focuses on the individual, private, faith and practice" (2016, 21).[14] In their view, such plurality does not necessarily lead to contestation but more often to the coexistence of diversity, reflecting the assumption that categories of identification are unlikely to remain fixed.[15]

The freedoms afforded by chronic "becoming"—as well as the authenticity associated with self-expression liberated from official ritual forms—provide variations on "anxious transcendence," which Webb Keane (2006) has connected with contemporary desires to abstract the self from material limitations and standardized means of expression.[16] An intriguing exchange invoking these themes occurs in a debate between pilgrims that Frey recounts from her fieldwork (1998). While a retired Spanish man in his sixties feels unable to separate his spirituality from his religion and so needs to participate in church rituals for true fulfillment, a young Spanish woman asserts instead that "'I don't need intermediaries. I just sat back, closed my eyes, and began to pray'" (31). Frey reports that despite their evident differences, both are arguing from an ostensibly Catholic perspective. However, the analysis can be taken a step further. What is revealed is not only a generational clash but also a debate about the status of mediation as a means of achieving fulfillment. Nonetheless, while it might seem that the younger pilgrim is describing a situation where limitations of locality can literally be blocked out, her retreat into the self remains deeply embodied; she closes her eyes, "sits back" in order to pray, and does so in the context of an effortful journey along the path.

Desires for transcendence therefore seem to take a particularly interesting form in the Camino, which offers freedom from certain forms of constraint yet also gives prominence to physical exertion alongside embeddedness in, and articulation with, landscape and nature. An important dimension of the acceptability of the Camino to many post-secular pilgrims lies in the fact that it reconciles materiality and physicality with process and becoming;[17] the body is grounded and yet traveling, and so landscape is kept in motion—a markedly *slow* motion—which only comes to a stop at the cathedral itself.[18] The problematic status of Compostela as marking the "cessation of movement" (Frey 1998, 164) is overcome by pilgrims who choose to travel beyond the city, rejecting its off-putting combination of priests and tourists in order to finish their journeys at Finisterre, a coastal zone to the west that offers a landscape where the land blends into the sea and which reaches beyond Europe while also representing the medieval end of the earth, a literally "edgy" place much more easily translatable into authentic transcendence for many travelers (cf. Herrero and Roseman 2015).[19]

Journey to Exemplarity

The Camino has attracted and been marketed to many visitors, but it has also acted as an exemplar, encouraging the translation of a model of spiritually flexible, heritage-oriented, slowed-down mobility to other pilgrimage environments.[20] There is nothing unusual about pilgrimage sites appropriating symbolic resources from each other; the real interest lies in tracing what is considered valuable enough to be borrowed. In this respect, the Camino model contains a striking juxtaposition. Its diffusion embodies the widespread and easy mobility of a cultural form, yet the core practice that it is exporting consists of the self-conscious cultivation of painstaking, mindful, and effortful forms of movement.[21] A paradigm of movement explicitly grounded in place and landscape thus becomes transferable to other places and other landscapes. Its wide-spread resonance indicates how ease of travel increases the numbers of those who are able to reach sacred sites while simultaneously making them desirous of slowing down their progress toward such places.

The model's powers of replication are evident in Bowman and Sepp's (2019) tracing of the multiscalar motif of the Camino across a highly diffuse landscape of European Christianity. They note that "the Camino has become regarded increasingly as a 'prototypical' pilgrimage, particularly by those previously largely unfamiliar with pilgrimage, and copied in contexts far from Spain" (74). What Bowman and Sepp call "Caminoization" combines a positive orientation toward walking with the development of a generic material culture of certification, including the use of pilgrim stamps and passports.[22] Greenia makes a similar point, noting that this model of sacred journeying requires no "denominational credentials" as a condition of entry, yet it readily awards official recognition to those making the effort to follow the pathway provided.[23]

What often spreads via the dissemination of the Camino as practice is not just the idea of people perambulating through landscapes but also a certain style of organizing such movement so that it is both discreetly guided and open to all who wish to participate. Furthermore, it is historically distinctive and yet capable of creating links with—and catalyzing—parallel pathways across Europe and beyond. Routes leading to Compostela have been developed from and through such countries as Britain, Belgium, France, Germany, Italy, Portugal, and Switzerland.[24] The pathways easily find a home in supposedly secular regions of Europe. Bowman and Sepp (2019, 81) observe, for instance, that pilgrimage has been revived in Estonia after the end of Soviet rule through the experiences of citizens who have walked the Camino and subsequently shared their experiences through a variety of media. In Scandinavia, St. Olav Ways was designated a Council of Europe Cultural Route in 2010, creating a network of connections through Denmark, Sweden, and Norway and drawing on a material culture of pilgrim passports, certification, and a distinctive logo that replicates the Spanish model (Mikaelsson 2018).

This Scandinavian example reveals something striking about European religious history as it is turned into heritage. The willingness of the Lutheran churches to reengage with a pilgrimage tradition represents at

Survival via capitalism & secular history at the expense of religious tradition

its most theological extreme a reversal of the implications of the Reformation, or at its most pragmatic a recognition that the national church is no longer able to rely on its connections with the state in order to justify its existence. Indeed, in Sweden, where Lutheranism was disestablished in 2000, pilgrimage provides a means for clergy to remain relevant to a population that is slowly moving away from automatic membership in the church, even if the new pilgrimage routes take people more toward nature and heritage than in the direction of conventional worship (Bremborg 2013; Gemzöe 2014a).

Medieval Christian pilgrimage—with its indulgences, accumulation of wealth, and worship of saints—is often perceived as a major cause of the Reformation's move toward purification and the concomitant splitting of the European church. Yet now, in adapted form, it seems capable of reanimating engagement with a broadly Protestant tradition that has lost much of its prominence in public life. Bowman and Sepp (2019) observe similar processes for Anglican England, where Caminoization is discernible in numerous ways.[25] What they see as the "emergent pilgrim culture of Canterbury Cathedral" (85) is fueled not only by the presence of St. Thomas Becket and the popularity of Chaucer's famous *Tales* but also by the enthusiasms of people who have walked the Camino—and indeed, the cathedral is recognized as a departure point for going on the journey to Spain. Some of those who wish to walk the Camino but cannot go abroad may choose to replicate it from afar (87), transposing it into a different landscape. An informant at Canterbury tells them, "For a number of years I had been vaguely thinking of walking the Camino to Compostela. A family bereavement . . . prompted me to make the much more modest walk from London to Canterbury. . . . The walk presented itself as an apt gesture of burden-carrying, and the Cathedral an apt destination for burden-relieving" (87). A notable aspect of this reflection is its assumption that the theological differences between the cathedrals at Canterbury and Santiago de Compostela are of little import; more significant is the ritual grammar that links the activity of walking with the possibility of gaining relief from emotional baggage.[26] Indeed, the provision of blessings for pilgrims arriving at, and departing from, Canterbury Cathedral has now become a service provided by a specially appointed pastor who has herself walked the Camino (88).

The Camino is a mobile ritual *form* that encourages reflexive *contemplation* of mobility alongside the desire to *enact* such mobility—a powerful trinity of elements relating to movement. These elements are readily reinterpreted within local semiotic ideologies where specific meanings of place, movement, and fellowship are expressed. For example, American Episcopalians from Pennsylvania create the "Appalachian Camino" in their local surroundings, adapting the model to a liberal Protestant sensibility that mediates between individual spirituality and collective experience.[27] The diocese's canon for congregational life and mission and instigator of the pilgrimage writes in a newsletter, "Having done other pilgrimages . . . I just know that the journey is just every bit as important, as transformative, as the destination." One of his fellow pilgrims observes that "weekly church services weren't cutting it anymore." Her sense that the pathway as metaphor and experience mitigates the dangers of spiritual stasis is echoed by the local bishop, who states that this version of the Camino fits perfectly with her "Bishop Out of the Box" program, invoking nature rather than church history as backdrop in order to act collectively and creatively. The open-ended liturgical affordances of the model are used to reinforce particular theological understandings of divine immanence and developing fellowship. As with the Swedish Lutheran example, the natural world is valued not only because (for believers) it is evidence of God's creation, but also it represents a space that is sacralized without being "churchy." The Camino as motif also encourages self-conscious exploration of the ritual space that can be created between sacred tradition and cultural heritage (Coleman 2018a). A clear example of such an intersection is provided by Carlos Steil in his description of the development of five "new pilgrimage paths" (2018, 157) across Brazil, all modeled on the Spanish Camino. He shows how such landscapes of mobility are created not by any single authority but rather by a constellation of forces—local councils, the Catholic Church, tourist agencies, universities and civil society organizations (155). These are the administrative bodies required in both continents to translate the image of a medieval pilgrimage into a "new grammar of the sacred" (ibid.) that incorporates a flexible spirituality: religious authority converted into spiritual authenticity.[28] The Brazilian emphasis, as in Europe, is on the power of walking in and for itself, both diluting the destination-oriented Roman Catholic model of territoriality and cultivating a sense that transcendence is to be found within an "existential pilgrim space, which redefines the meaning and the place of the body in the experience of the walkers" (165). Unsurprisingly, a new vocabulary is emerging in Brazil and elsewhere to describe this shift. While a pilgrim may generally be referred to as a *peregrino*, a distinction has developed between the *romeiro* who engages with the traditions of popular Catholicism and the newer figure of the *caminhante*, or walker.

Describing an example located still further from Europe, Paul Genoni states that the "Australian embrace of the Camino" has occurred even though the country has no ancient tradition of Christian pilgrimage (2016, 177). Local cultural elements that are made to contribute to the Camino Australia include Indigenous traditions of long-distance walking among nomadic Aboriginal peoples as well as a national predilection for trekking. Some transplantation into an explicitly Christian landscape is also evident; for instance, the Camino Salvado was established in 2009 to link two Benedictine monasteries situated 160 kilometers apart in the region of Perth. However, one of the most striking images from Genoni's work comes from the interaction between Australian pilgrims and the Spanish Camino at a eucalyptus grove near Compostela. He describes how Australians perceive these trees as a sign of home: the New World rerouted/rooted to the Old.[29]

The influence of the Camino as exportable infrastructure is traceable in religious traditions other than Christianity. Describing the famous circuit of Buddhist shrines on the island of Shikoku, Ian Reader (2013, 27) points to the ways in which organizers have drawn on the Spanish example in their efforts to enhance the standing and appeal of the Japanese pilgrimage. Such rebranding includes a heritagization of the journey, rendering it more accessible to a wider clientele by linking it to a diffuse sense of tradition. What Shikoku and Compostela both cultivate is not only a spatiotemporal landscape through which travelers engage the past but also a capacity to encompass multiple discourses of the sacred.[30] Unlike the "empty vessel" described by Eade and Sallnow (1991), the attraction of these pilgrimage infrastructures depends heavily on their material characteristics—the spatial affordances they provide (paths, signs, landscape) for slowing down mobility and encouraging flexible forms of sociability as well as spirituality.

The further diffusion of the spiritual and semiotic salience of the Camino's ethos of plurality and movement is illustrated powerfully by Francesco Piraino's (2018, 164) discussion of emergent pilgrimage traditions in Western European Sufism. He documents the case of a Belgian-Moroccan faqir who undertook the pilgrimage to Santiago de Compostela and who explained to Piraino that the image of the Moor-slayer and the persecution of Muslims were things of the past (thus bypassing or ignoring new forms of European Islamophobia). For the faqir, the flexible character of the Camino proved a suitable represen-tation of the Sufi notion that a single God applied to both Christians and Muslims. The potential hybridity of the pilgrimage complex is also demonstrated by the literature scholar Alison Smith (2018, 82), who sees it as providing an opportunity to cultivate the walking meditation of the Vietnamese Zen master and peace activist Thich Nhat Hahn. Smith reinterprets the traditional spirituality of the Camino but does not con-test its significance. Her aim is rather to seek "common ground" across pilgrims "of all faiths and backgrounds," based on the assumption that "mindfulness" can transcend cultural difference (ibid.).

Pilgrimage perceived in this way—as both a physical path and a cul-tural model, laying emphasis on self-directed dimensions of movement and ritual engagement—might seem opposed to a still more famous tradition of sacred travel: the Hajj, which ostensibly involves faithful adherence to the fifth pillar of Islam by heading to a specific place at a theologically fixed time of the Muslim year. Nonetheless, the juxtaposi-tion of these two forms of sanctified journeying is instructive, for the contemporary Camino and Hajj respond and adapt to similar challenges within the global pilgrimage field. Marjo Buitelaar (2018, 35) states that "until recently, performing *hajj* was predominantly conceived of as an act of obedience carried out by older Muslims to fulfil the 'last' of their religious duties in the hope of forgiveness of their sins before dying." This tradition still has considerable salience. On the other hand, Buite-laar shows that the Hajj may be reframed by younger people in terms of more flexible understandings of ritual and its relationship to the life course, associated less with formal piety and sacrifice and more with values of personal growth (cf. also Caidi 2019). Some may even reject the standard honorific of being addressed as *al-Hajji*, while particularly among Muslims based in Western Europe, the old taboo against preceding one's parents in going on the journey is breaking down: "Muslims I have spoken to over the past few years often take the view that everyone should decide for themselves when they are 'ready' to undertake the pilgrimage" (Buitelaar 2018, 35). In these shifting attitudes toward the Hajj we see once more an interesting negotiation between obligation and freedom: a willingness to go, yet a desire to do so on one's own terms, fitting the journey into a less constrained trajectory than that evident in earlier generations and thus expressing what Buitelaar calls an "individualization and privatization of religiosity" (ibid.).

At the same time, it is important to resist the temptation to read the concerns of the contemporary Camino, or even the assumptions behind its forms of replication, into cultural contexts that display superficial similarities but belong to very different pilgrimage traditions. In his summary of Hindu pilgrimage practices in India, Chris Fuller makes a number of observations that should now sound familiar. He notes the "ever-increasing numbers of pilgrims" who "set out on longer and longer journeys" (1992, 204), the influence of the mass media in informing people about shrines (ibid., 205), and the combination of better infrastructure (roads, railways, air) with the general assumption in popular Hinduism that pilgrimage on foot gains more merit than using a vehicle (ibid., 209). Fuller also indicates that replication is an integral part of Hindu conceptions of the sanctification of space. For instance, the city of Kashi (Benares) is generally regarded as the preeminent pilgrimage site in the country, but its apparently unique position is demonstrated by its qualities of being all-inclusive and available to be countlessly reproduced elsewhere (ibid., 208, drawing on Eck 1983, 41). As a consequence, numerous other versions of the city exist throughout the country, at different scales and levels of popularity. Fuller puts the point succinctly: "Because Kashi is everywhere, it can be visited everywhere" (ibid.).

Both the Camino and Kashi suggest that the mobility entailed in pilgrimage may involve translations of place alongside the movements of pilgrims. In both cases, a site's popularity prompts people's desire to reproduce it in numerous other contexts. Yet the ideological, social, and economic impulses behind these examples of replicating pilgrimage show significant differences and draw on distinct semiotic ideologies. The multiplication of Kashi is rooted in both scriptural legitimation and a widely revered cartography of shrines that encompasses the entire country.[31] At the most abstract level, these dimensions of Hindu pilgrimage point toward the possibility of a pan-Hindu unity while drawing on a multiscalar religious topography that unites microcosm and macrocosm. Pilgrimage is sometimes conceived entirely as a journey within the self, but traveling round a sacred shrine such as Kashi might also be understood as comprehending the entire universe (Fuller 1992, 209). The Camino's replication, by contrast, draws less on scriptural legitimation or a systemic conception of sacred space and more on a burgeoning transnational religious and political economy that combines expanding mobilities, a blending of heritage and spirituality, and increased mutual awareness among shrine administrators of what is going on at pilgrimage sites in other parts of the world.[32] Thus the Camino model can take us a long way, but we must avoid facile comparisons. Replication, like mobility, takes many forms.[33]

Concealments and Limitations

The Camino has become a model for other contemporary pilgrimages and an emergent trope that has become "good to think with" for scholars wishing to explore what Sánchez y Sánchez and Hesp (2018, 5) call "the global exchanges that are reshaping pilgrimage studies." It has attracted a striking amount of attention from scholars in the social sciences and humanities. The existence of a certain degree of interest is to be expected, given the large numbers of people who are attracted to the routes across Europe. However, the Camino has become a powerful academic trope not only because of what it says about contemporary pilgrimage but also because of what it tells us about many of those who study such pilgrimage. If communitas reflected the anti-structural concerns of the Turners in the 1960s and contestation expressed some of what Jean-François Lyotard (1979) famously called the "incredulity toward metanarratives" characteristic of the 1980s and beyond, the Camino displays striking affinities not only with post-secular discourse but also with certain political, cultural, and ethical assumptions among contemporary researchers.

This point is illustrated through reflecting on Nancy Frey's *Pilgrim Stories: On and off the Road to Santiago* (1998), a rich ethnography that remains the landmark in English-language work on the contemporary

Camino. Frey's intention is to explore "the road," and she makes efforts to track pilgrims once they return home. Only in her appendices, however, does she provide details of the historical and economic development of the pilgrimage as a whole, while making brief observations on the potential ways in which the church itself might "link . . . to the modern pilgrimage" (248). Here she refers to the role of parishes as well as diocesan and other Christian groups, though her emphasis is on the church's failure to acknowledge more generalized forms of spirituality expressed by many pilgrims along the route. While Frey is making an important point about the lack of acknowledgment of broadly spiritual travelers by administrative authorities, it also seems reasonable to ask about the significance of pilgrims who do not fit her focus on individualized forms of walking. In the first chapter of the book, Frey notes that "motorized coach pilgrimages organized by parishes or cultural groups represent the majority of pilgrims who go to Santiago to visit the cathedral, pray at tomb of St James, attend Mass, or present an offering at the altar" (1998, 18), though we learn very little subsequently about these travelers.[34] Nor is there much coverage of "large-scale weekend pilgrimages as community events" (21), or indeed the occasions—such as specially declared holy years—"when large numbers of organized Catholic pilgrimages" come for special indulgences granted by the church. More generally, while Frey does accept that a cult of Catholic saints is still present, especially among older Galicians (22), this phenomenon plays little part in the book. It seems that there are even ritualized means of conjoining bus and walking pilgrimages given that participants in the former may choose to walk the final few miles into the city, but the intriguing emergence of such a hybrid form is not followed up. Finally, yet another type of pilgrimage is also mentioned by Frey, though not investigated further: large groups of Spanish friends who make the pilgrimage together on vacations and who stand out in contrast to Euro-Americans who tend to go alone or with a friend or partner (37).

My interest is not in criticizing Frey, who admirably accomplishes what she set out to do. My aim is rather to emphasize that her and many others' ethnographic attention has been focused on a particular subsection of those who travel to Compostela.[35] Frey comments that for the initial months of her fieldwork she ignored part-time pilgrims, having fallen into what she calls the "authenticity trap" of her main interlocutors (1998, 134). However, even her expanded perspective largely ignores the cultural significance of regular parish or coach trips. While many of such pilgrims are primarily oriented toward formal liturgy, they still "experience" the Camino, albeit in ways that do not appear quite as authentic from the standpoint of the post-secular traveler—or perhaps quite as interesting to those who study such travelers. In the establishment of the Camino as a scholarly trope, these categories of people and pilgrimage have faded into the background in comparison with the model of the trekking pilgrim who seeks a powerful personal experience separate from church interference. This last type of pilgrim, it must also be remembered, may take pride in his or her worn-out boots but is likely to be well-heeled enough to take time off work to make the journey.

Contrast these assumptions with Ann Gold's (1988) account of long-distance pilgrimage by coach to the famous shrine center of Puri from the Rajasthani village where she did much of her fieldwork. Gold shows how the cramped, uncomfortable conditions of the vehicle gain significance in their contrast with other experiences on the pilgrimage, such as a visit to the ocean when pilgrims joyously throw themselves into the waves (ibid., 281). Her informants travel by motor vehicle but engage in forms of world renunciation quite as powerful as those evident on the Camino. In the complexity of their experience, Gold's fellow passengers teach us not to ignore the social and material affordances of motorized travel, and they show that such mechanically powered affordances belong to the embodied culture of pilgrimage quite as much as any worn-out pair of hiking boots.

These questions of authenticity recall the ideologically loaded Euro-American contrast between what sociologist of mobility John Urry (1990) has characterized as the "collective gaze" (emergent within communal events) and its "romantic" counterpart (applicable to exclusive forms of solitude). The pilgrims described by Frey and others appreciate co-presence with others on the same trail, but in general, they seem to fit the romantic slot. I have already alluded, for instance, to Slavin's (2003, 12) reference to their tendency to "walk alone" and to the focus on "individual, private, faith and practice" highlighted by Nilsson and Tesfahuney (2016, 21). Such characterizations may not tell the whole story, however. A dimension of Camino experience that deserves more attention involves journeys undertaken by travelers that fit neither the lone pilgrim nor the ecclesiastical-group category but entail the reframing of social relations associated with home within the time and space of the pilgrimage. The most obvious examples of what I mean involve relations of kinship or friendship that are transported to the Camino and reexperienced there. To be sure, Frey (1998, 37–38) refers to how pilgrims may use the Camino as a testing ground for relationships or to celebrate anniversaries and honeymoons, while "occasionally one hears the remarkable story of parents who decide to take a year off work and journey with their children" (ibid.). However, once again, this type of social engagement receives little detailed attention, nor are its potential links with more official forms of ritual discussed.

I provided two examples of what I mean by this type of sociality at the beginning of this chapter, when I referred both to my colleague wishing to take his child on the Camino, and to the lawyer Julie Kirkpatrick's description of going with her daughter. Kirkpatrick's account (2010) is particularly suggestive. At first glance, her book appears to be a prime example of a highly individualized account, where post-secular authenticity is encountered through a romanticized journey of becoming. Such elements are undeniably present in the text. But the book is also a discussion of her experiences as mother, daughter, and spouse; and it is an exploration of friendship as she incorporates twenty-six tasks, one for each day, each set by a well-wisher, including reimagining the world from the perspective of an animal or meditating on a color. These tasks resonate well with Anna Fedele's (2013) conception of alternative, creative, ritual action within pilgrimage, but my point is that they are both solitary *and* intensely social activities, which explicitly re-presence and work on relationships from home. The model of personhood Kirkpatrick celebrates through her journey looks deeply self-oriented from one perspective but is also an intensely networked one, bonding her with an array of significant others who are given ritual expression throughout the journey. The pilgrimage provides her with the means to create social and semiotic articulations between parts of her life through connecting domestic friendship and kinship with experience of embodied travel, while also mediating between obligation and freedom. Kirkpatrick reinforces relationships with distant persons (alive and dead) even as she surrounds herself with the strangers who are physically walking the Camino alongside her.

We will examine these potentially dense articulations between domestic life and pilgrimage experience in more detail in the next two chapters. For the moment, I want to reflect further on the popularity of the Camino as object of analysis, and in particular on its attractiveness—and limitations—as social scientific trope. I do so through my recurring comparative lens of Pentecostalism as field of study. In 1991, the anthropologist Susan Harding published an essay that was to prove an important touchstone in what would become the subfield dedicated to tracking the increasingly global influence of Christian fundamentalist, evangelical, and Pentecostal movements. As one of the first anthropologists to study a newly vibrant conservative Protestantism, Harding found herself subject to sharp questioning from colleagues as to her motives. The title of her piece, "Representing Fundamentalism: The Problem of the Repugnant Cultural Other," indicates the epistemological but also the *ethical* problems of writing about interlocutors who looked deeply anomalous for anthropologists of the time. These believers were often based in the home context of the scholar, possessed a powerful public voice, celebrated material success rather than self-denial and appeared committed to a rigid belief system that they wished to spread to others.[36] Such Christians did not endear themselves to liberal academic sympathies, but they eventually attracted scholarly interest, however grudging. They could no longer be ignored.

My depiction of such conservative Christianity provides an ethnographic, epistemological, and ethical mirror image of what is regularly represented as happening along the Camino in its guise as both ethnographic field and post-secular trope. Many contemporary Camino travelers are well-off, but they explicitly cultivate forms of temporary self-denial. While the physical boundaries of the Camino are relatively narrow, its ideological leeway appears to be wide—and no overt attempt is made to convert others to a single faith, unless it is that of walking rather than driving. Whereas fundamentalists, evangelicals, and Pentecostalists emphasize the world-conquering character of mission, celebrating swift movement across space (Coleman 2000), the ideal mobility of the Camino is slowed down, appreciative of nature and carrying out its work of seduction more subtly. Indeed, such slowing down permits the affordances of the landscape to gain in agency as the traveler engages closely with the striking vistas but also the physical resistances of land

that must be traversed using one's own energy. Secular scholars studying Pentecostalism are faced with the constant dilemma of how far their
own ritual participation should go during fieldwork, given the difficulties of engaging in prayer, faith healing, or glossolalia. In stark contrast,
it is no accident that the Camino is both a popular object of study and an
attractive leisure-time option for non-believing or agnostic academics.[37]
It has come to be admired as an activity not of the repugnant other, but
of the reflexive—and religiously uncommitted—self. Nonetheless, such
admiration also implies a politics of attention: a neglect of the wider pilgrimage system to which the Camino remains attached, and which has
provided much of the rationale for its continued existence.

A Trio of Tropes

My exploration of communitas, contestation, and Camino highlights
tropes that first emerged in social scientific research devoted to Anglophone, Christian-oriented contexts. All three also came to influence
debates conducted in other languages and on other religions. The
motif of the Camino in particular gained a significant profile at a time
when dialogues between scholars from different cultural and institutional backgrounds began to be opened up to a greater extent than
before. Nowadays, many of those writing about the Way contribute to
Anglophone debates while also writing from non-English-speaking
institutional bases.[38]

Thinking through tropes permits direct forms of comparison and
juxtaposition, and an intriguing set of crosscutting parallels, comple-
mentarities, and distinctions has emerged. Communitas and contestation retain the importance of a ritual center. Contestation and Camino
acknowledge the significance of a plurality of perspectives. Camino and
communitas emphasize the positive links between pilgrimage and the
co-presence of anonymous others, and both show how pilgrimage trans-
forms time, the former by slowing it down, the latter by valuing spontaneity. Even as the trope of the Camino escapes from the tyranny of
the ecclesiastical center, it creates a different form of behavioral enclave,
disconnecting shrine from journey, formal liturgy from informal experience, collectively or institutionally experienced pilgrimage from individualized journeying. Indeed, while they remain productive, all three

tropes occlude other ways of thinking about pilgrimage. None focuses much direct attention on social relations "at home."[39] None provides a systematic account of how activities related to pilgrimage articulate in complex ways with other forms of mobility that are all too evident in the contemporary world, including migration and refugeehood, though parallels and/or contrasts with tourism are acknowledged.

Given the need to transcend these limitations, I refer to the conclusions of the previous chapter, where I used Stuart Hall's work on articulation to consider how an expanded pilgrimage field might consist of elements related through differences as much as through similarities. In such a view, the work of connection and the work of creation cannot be kept apart, and both are given particular significance in an activity such as pilgrimage that is made up of disjunctions and conjunctions across time and space. In the third section of this book, I explore these articulations. I argue for the need to develop new modes of attention in the study of pilgrimage, to expand our assumptions as to where it is located, and to find new ways to characterize the ways in which it creates interfaces with other human activities. I do not claim to exhaust all these possibilities, but I undertake to advocate for their potential in extending the scope and significance of the study of pilgrimage.

PART III

Articulations

6

Pilgrimage Penumbras

From the Liminal to the Lateral

New Metaphors, New Tropes, New Directions

Pilgrimage leaves traces in locations that have often been ignored, and its practices are not as stable or distinctly defined as has sometimes been assumed. In his study of shrines, Jacob Kinnard (2014) emphasizes "the vibrant messiness of religious practice, the multivocality of religious objects, the fluid and hybrid dynamics of religious places, and the shifting and entangled identities of religious actions" (xiii; cf. Rousseau [2016, 42]). This section of the book both acknowledges and analyzes such messiness. Chapter 7 will trace the rich social lives of narratives as they reconstitute pilgrims' experiences far distant from conventional shrines, and chapter 8 will follow ways in which pilgrimage connects with multiple other landscapes of mobility. For now, however, we stay closer to shrines, shifting attention to activities often overlooked by scholars of pilgrimage: those that exist around and in relation to sacred places, constituting zones of ambiguous engagement where ties with orthodox and public styles of worship are unclear or under negotiation, and where expressions of ritualized action may take surprising forms. Examining the subtleties of such action will require a new analytical vocabulary to sketch out the dimensions of a ramifying, variegated field of study. We will see how a language of articulation that is capable of characterizing connections across difference must invoke not only enclaves and borders but also adjacencies and intersections. Particular attention will be devoted to the development of two related concepts, both deeply rooted in the spatial dimensions of pilgrimage practice. One is the notion of the penumbra, a zone of operation whose outer edges cannot be determined with any certainty. The other refers to laterality and the lateral, terms encompassing actions or attitudes that derive yet simultaneously deviate from conventional or expected orientations and stances.[1]

Both of these concepts will be developed further, but it is important to emphasize straightaway that in asserting the need to study tangential spaces and behaviors surrounding sites, I am not referring to the market activities that typically spring up in such areas. The tendency for such enterprises to develop has long been recognized by researchers, who may also invoke them to define areas of secular activity that contrast with sacred cores of pious intensity (cf. Hammoudi 2005). Rather, our focus will be on ambiguously ritualized behaviors performed in the indistinct environs of shrines. In *Image and Pilgrimage*, the Turners note:

> Near the central shrine the ingoing routes become evermore beset with way stations (lesser shrines, chapels, holy wells, and the like), and the pilgrims' progress becomes correspondingly slower as they advance. These sacred valves and resistances are designed to build up a considerable load of reverent feeling, so that the final ingress to the holiest shrine of all will be for each pilgrim a momentous matter. (1978, 23)

They paint a powerful picture of the progressive sacralization of space, and their imagery suggests that the route becomes ever more defined and deliberate, propelling the pilgrim inexorably toward the sacred center. In doing so, they capture some, but far from all, of the ritualized experiences discernible in the immediate vicinity of sites.[2] Pilgrimages also play indirect host to those less willing or able to engage in such linear spiritual progress, revealing a more complex set of social and spatial orientations and articulations than a single-minded passage toward "the holiest shrine" might suggest.

The image of the penumbra is especially useful in describing the ill-defined areas of pilgrimage-related operation around shrines (Sing 2019, 14). The term refers to "a shadowy, indefinite, or marginal area," and more specifically to the region of partial shade that is cast by an object.[3] If translated from the language of physics to that of anthropology, it suggests the presence of an undetermined zone of activity that blends and blurs with wider, everyday social, ethical, and cultural environments but whose existence depends precisely on its continued connection with a more defined and public ritual center. It does not imply a narrowly defined direction and has ambiguous dimensions—therefore suggesting a very different spatial range to the passage and boundary imagery that still pervades much writing.[4]

The anthropologist Michael Jackson has also explored the idea of the penumbra in his experimental text *The Palm at the End of the Mind: Relatedness, Religiosity, and the Real* (2009).[5] He describes himself as interested in

> those critical situations in life where we come up against the limits of lan-
> guage, limits of our strength, yet are sometimes thrown open to new ways
> of understanding our being-in-the-world, new ways of connecting with
> others. Whether such border situations are quintessentially religious, his-
> torical, biographical etc. may be beside the point for the meaning of hu-
> man experiences remains ambiguous. (ibid., xi–xii)

Jackson finds thinking about the penumbral useful because it has "con-notations of a phenomenologically indeterminate zone" (xii) between complete shadow and complete illumination, an area of uncertainty that breaks from the fully known and may "presage new possibilities of relatedness" (13). The ambiguity of the experience is compounded by the lack of clarity over agency and control in such situations. As he puts it, "To speak of the penumbral is, therefore, to invoke this hazy and indeterminate region between a world where we experience ourselves as actors and a world where we experience ourselves as acted upon" (39). Like Jackson, I link penumbras with situations of exploratory, uncer-tain articulation, where it may be difficult to separate out the religious from other dimensions of life.[6] While he refers specifically to border situations, however, I see penumbras as hosting fields of pilgrimage performance that entail still more opaque realms of activity where such boundaries may not be present or apparent.[7]

The image of the penumbra not only points to the ideological, liturgi-cal, and literal shadows cast by pilgrimage sites and rituals but also sug-gests the presence of unpredictable constituencies whose motives may be equally unclear. Global pandemics excepted, contemporary pilgrim-ages are generally more accessible—physically, economically, socially—than ever before.[8] While scholars have paid considerable attention to tourists at pilgrimage sites, they have often done so in the context of making distinctions between religious and secular actions and motives. Research has tended to ignore other categories of semi-detached visitors, even though many sites should be seen as expansive ritual and institutional complexes where the presence of marked ritual intensity also affords the possibility of a vast array of more dispersed and indistinct forms of engagement, attitude, and spectatorship.[9] The fact that these latter behaviors are often low key and inchoate does not mean that they should be overlooked.[10] In reflecting on penumbras, I therefore introduce the kind of interlocutor whom I have often encountered in my fieldwork: one who is unsure whether they should even think of themselves as on a pilgrimage or who has traveled to a shrine for reasons that may arouse unsettling sensations of both devotion and revulsion. Examining practices within penumbras highlights the movements of visitors who negotiate between centripetal and centrifugal impulses, often dealing with the ambivalent experience of wanting to be in the vicinity of a site without becoming too closely enmeshed in its publicly marked spaces and rituals. Relevant here is Anna Tsing's (2005) discussion of the formation of zones of "awkward engagement" that permit transient, faltering, yet significant encounters and interactions; such areas do not permit easy integration, but host complex expressions of "interconnection across difference" (4).

Even as it avoids the sharp borders implied by sacred centers (or internal contestations), the penumbral dimension of pilgrimage resonates with the emergence of a new mini-trope in contemporary pilgrimage literature. I have been struck by the increased use of the words *porous* and *porosity* in descriptions of the experience of visiting sacred sites.[11] Religious studies researcher Michael Agnew refers to the "translocative and transtemporal crossings which point to the porous and malleable boundaries of the pilgrimage shrine" (2019, 50). Anthropologist Carlos Steil, reflecting on the intersections between Roman Catholicism and New Age sensibilities, talks of "the porosity of the boundaries separating the experience of the sacred and the secular spheres of modern life, showing that the motivations for setting foot on these paths no longer fit pre-established frameworks of the kind locating tourist and religious experiences in separate domains" (2018, 157). The most extensive use of the term comes from Katherine Rousseau (2016) in her partly ethnographic, partly art historical study of spatial interaction and memory in Marian pilgrimage sites alongside "the varied potential for porous boundaries at pilgrimage places, where heterogeneous audiences engage with the pilgrimage environment and its interpenetrating devotional, cultural, and commercial aspects" (23). For Rousseau, the balance between porosity and boundedness differs according to the type of pilgrimage involved. She argues that the Gothic Cathedral of Chartres is relatively self-enclosed, though "devotional and commercial place interpenetrates as the cathedral houses its own shop and the city leverages the place as part of an overall urban development strategy" (76). In contrast, Medjugorje, in Herzegovina, where apparitions of the Virgin have been claimed since 1981, displays more "dramatically and spatially porous boundaries" (9) whose dynamism reflects the newness of the pilgrimage, its relative lack of recognition (and control) by church hierarchies and the complex recent history of the collapse of the Yugoslavian state. The apparitions are mobile, occurring in hillsides, chapels, the local church, even in other countries where the visionaries have traveled. Medjugorje and its surrounding landscape are permeated by signs of Marian devotion, so that the location "problematizes the notion of a spatially centered and clearly bounded site, in physical and conceptual terms" (138). These and other pilgrimage contexts described by Rousseau demonstrate the physical as well as the ideological dimensions of porosity and the ways in which sacred places should not automatically be seen as having unique and epiphanic qualities that render them remote from the world around them; rather, they are likely to be in continuous and complex negotiation with the world of the ordinary (282).[12]

By introducing the concept of laterality alongside that of penumbra, I contrast its indirectness to the linearity of the pathway. I also side-step the Turnerian (1978) rite-of-passage model, which highlights the intense experience of inhabiting the anti-structural, fragile, closely guarded, threshold-like realm of pilgrimage. As I noted in chapter 3, Victor Turner sometimes encouraged use of the term *liminoid* rather than *liminal* to encompass the voluntaristic, idiosyncratic quality of ritual behaviors in modern societies, though his distinction was not taken up very much in subsequent literature. Here, I draw a different kind of distinction, one that builds on my interests in pilgrimage as articulating rather than isolating different frames of action. Both liminality and laterality invoke spatial metaphors, but the analytical and ethnographic space they encompass is significantly different. Liminality emphasizes the power of inhabiting a realm that is part of a linear passage between two mundane states—both an "escape from" and a "not yet." Laterality has the capacity to share this subjunctive, sometimes playful quality of action but reaches or simply stumbles across divisions between supposedly set-apart and everyday action, provoking negotiations and entanglements, however inchoately or awkwardly manifested, between adjacent behavioral frames and spaces.[13] While Turnerian liminality implies intensity of immersion, laterality encompasses more varied responses by those who may be unsure whether or how to participate. For the Turners, the shift from the liminal to the liminoid hinged on the voluntaristic character of the latter, but lateral actions display not only ambivalence but also ambiguity as to the visitor's willingness, duty, or ability to engage in pilgrimage activity.

Given that laterality implies being located at one remove from ritual action while also being partially oriented toward—and sometimes inadvertently seduced by—such action, it is a state highly likely to be experienced in penumbral zones.[14] However, penumbras do not provide the only contexts where productive fieldwork on laterality is possible. Lateral engagement may take place within the center itself, characterized by being loosely articulated or aligned with conventional expressions of pilgrimage ritual. A ritual action may therefore be lateral not only because of spatial separation but also because of temporal disjunction— for instance, occurring at a time that does not coincide with the staging of conventional liturgy. In either case, it suggests a relationship with shrines that contrasts with Turnerian imagery but also with aspects of the contestation model. Eade and Sallnow's depiction of shrines as mere voids and empty vessels does not sufficiently capture the material and ritual entanglements experienced by visitors as a result of the physical affordances of shrines and their surroundings (1991, 15). My argument here is more in the spirit of de Certeau's (1984) exploration of "tactics" as forms of opportunistic response in relation to more coherent institutional terrains.[15]

In encouraging heightened recognition of the fuzzy, ritualized shapes that are discernible in both penumbras and lateral engagements, I am invoking the politics of attention I originally discussed in chapter 1. Now, however, the focus is also on the forms of recognition and practices of spectatorship evident among visitors themselves. The art historian David Morgan (2005) has emphasized the need to develop nuanced understandings of the different modalities of viewing manifested in religious and spiritual contexts. His well-known notion of the sacred gaze asks how objects or places become invested with spiritual significance and points to the social and spatial frames that go into the construction of a given form of scrutiny. The interest here is in observing how visitors engage in viewing practices in penumbras as well as at ritual centers. It becomes important to ask whether it is possible to distinguish between gazes and more casual glances, but also between direct and sideways (lateral) looks as the complexities of visitors' own positionalities and points of view come into play. We must also add another dimension to such inquiries into looking—that of being viewed by anonymous or significant others: not merely seeing, but being seen, in and around sites, in places of performative obscurity as well as of overt display.

To substantiate these claims through ethnography, I draw on my observations during fieldwork at Walsingham and at a number of cathedrals that contain shrines (Canterbury, Durham, York, and Westminster).[16] These places form part of an interconnected landscape of national Christian pilgrimage and are deeply rooted in English religious practices, but I shall eventually turn to comparative questions about whether and how laterality and penumbras might be discernible in other, very different, religious and ethnographic contexts.

Walsingham: Direct Gazes and Sideways Looks

The contemporary Christian landscape in England is a fragmented one, characterized by deep secularization alongside specific sites of revival. Neo-Pentecostal congregations attract particularly energetic believers, often reflecting the aspirations of West African and Latin American migrants who regard Britain as a new mission field (Coleman and Maier 2013). Many such Christians congregate in warehouse-like spaces that combine affordability with capacity to expand. Equally striking are the new multifaith centers, described by Linda Woodhead as "the most distinctive form of recent religious construction" in modern Britain, catering for varieties of performance (2012, 1).[17] The ritual commitment suggested by these venues contrasts with that implied by sociologist

Grace Davie's (2007a, 127) influential notion of "vicarious religion," which she defines as "religion performed by an active minority but on behalf of a much larger number"—including ritual carried out in sight of benignly disposed but behaviorally distanced publics. Indeed, in a later piece, she uses a familiar metaphor in reflecting on her wider purpose: "How do we understand the religious penumbra of modern European societies and how should we describe this sociologically?" (Davie 2010, 262).

Compared with neo-Pentecostal missions and multifaith centers, the pilgrimage site of Walsingham looks anachronistic: located in the far reaches of rural, predominantly white, north Norfolk, scattered around a village full of quaint houses and picturesque ruins.[18] Yet such appearances are deceptive. Walsingham was voted "the nation's favourite spiritual site" in a BBC poll from 2003.[19] In a country where weekly attendances at Church of England parish churches are meager, dipping to below 2 percent of the population in 2016, Walsingham represents a remarkable place of human assembly, gathering diverse publics in the vicinity of Christian practices.[20] One recent estimate puts the number of official pilgrims at around one hundred thousand a year, but three or four times that number visit annually.[21] The popularity of Walsingham also points to a wider trend in English and more broadly Northern European Christianity, that of paying visits to ancient and prominent sites of worship, although not necessarily for overtly religious reasons.

In their chapter on Walsingham in *Image and Pilgrimage* (1978, 175–202 passim), Victor and Edith Turner concentrate on the pre-Reformation shrine. They report that networks of medieval roads culminated at the Slipper Chapel, a fourteenth-century building located a little way from the village and "the point from which the final ritualized approach . . . was made" (182). Indeed, the word *slipper* may derive etymologically from *slype*, meaning "covered passage" or "way through," thus providing "a perfect metaphor for pilgrimage liminality" (ibid.). The Turners say remarkably little about the modern village other than noting that when they visited in the summer of 1971, it gave the appearance of being "once more a thriving place of pilgrimage" (175). Toward the beginning of the book, they do speculate that perhaps Canterbury, "center of the ecclesiastical structure" (ibid.), might, like Walsingham and ancient Glastonbury, experience "a revival of its traditional pilgrimage" (ibid.), though they deem major shifts in church-state relations as well as between Anglicans and Roman Catholics to be necessary

> before tourists could shed their current guise and present themselves as pilgrims; but the fact that both Roman Catholics and Anglo-Catholics have reinstated Walsingham and Glastonbury as pilgrim centers (and even timidly participate in joint processions on occasions at Walsingham) may be a straw in the ecumenical wind. (Turner and Turner 1978, 20)

It seems that the Turners, writing in the 1970s, can sense the possibility of these traditional sites becoming popular destinations but are operating with the twin assumptions that tourism must cede definitively to pilgrimage and that the ethnographic gaze should be fixed on centrally located symbols of faith. Let us contrast their account with one offered to me by someone who has scrutinized the contemporary pilgrimage in a rather different way:

> England's Nazareth is a place where pilgrimage has been happening ever since 1061 with a short gap of 400 years which we've now got over. . . . I think the sacramental ministry is crucial, I think first and foremost the reminder of baptism . . . it's about reconciliation, aspiration, all of those things . . . and that's what the well is all about. Obviously the Eucharist is central in terms of people participating in a meal and therefore sense of belonging, that they were in sort of the presence of heaven. The ministry of the confessional is very important, obviously it's changed over the years, it's not quite the sort of functional encounter that it was, but it's widened and I think may be more useful to a wider variety of people, because it does have this kind of exchange feel about it. It's dangerously close to counselling, but we're very aware that it never becomes counselling in all ways. . . . And then I think perhaps most of all there's the sense in which Walsingham is like a huge icon, it's like, almost like a theme park, a Christian theme park, in which we set out . . . the wares, and then allow people to make of it what they will, and I think there's something about that which is very therapeutic, that they'll make the stations of the cross, they'll just come and sit in the shrine and sit in the gardens, they'll go and light candles, they'll sit in the Holy House and just look at the image, they'll go for a walk up to the parish church, they go and visit the

orthodox chapel or they'll go and buy things in the shops to take home. All of that I think is very, very significant, because it's the best kind of spiritual direction which actually allows a pilgrim to find his or her own way in what, you know, God offers, and it's the movement of the spirit directing the soul, and I think we just sort of make available, you know, these resources and people use them as . . . they're best able.

This is a long quotation but a revealing one. It comes from an interview I carried out in the 1990s with Father Martin Warner, at that time administrator of the Anglican shrine at Walsingham.[22] In contrast to the Turners, I was particularly interested in the contemporary significance of the Anglican shrine in the context of English Christianity—though as Father Warner's responses revealed, the past could never quite be ignored. His reference to "England's Nazareth" can be traced to a fifteenth-century ballad about Walsingham according to which, in 1061, a local aristocratic woman called Richeldis had a dream that she was transported to the Holy Land by the Virgin Mary. There, Mary told her to build in the Norfolk countryside an exact copy of Jesus's childhood home. As an origin myth, this story provides a superbly concise weaving together of multiple religio-political strands of Christian history. It links Norfolk to a biblical landscape, it brings into existence an English site of worship just prior to the Norman invasion of 1066, and it commemorates the Annunciation and Incarnation through the faithful actions of a single woman. In turn, Father Martin's ironic reference to "a short gap of 400 years which we've now got over" refers to the depredations of the Reformation. Walsingham was largely destroyed as a pilgrimage site during the sixteenth century before being restored by both Roman and Anglo-Catholics some four centuries later.[23] Nowadays, the village is marked not only by ruins but also by a proliferation of semi-restored sacred spots. The modern Anglican shrine and grounds were originally constructed in the 1930s under the guidance of an energetic priest and have been considerably developed in subsequent decades, while the Slipper Chapel and associated shrine complex are run by Roman Catholics, who first acquired the site in 1894.[24] The weight of Anglican ritual movement is pitched toward the north, while Roman Catholic processions often start from the middle of the village but then have to move in a southern direction down a road called the holy mile, so that they conclude at the Slipper Chapel. Meanwhile, in the center of the village, behind a wall and gate, lie a ruined priory window and blank expanse of grass, owned by neither party but established archeologically in the 1960s as the true location of the original shrine. This area's symbolic under-determination provides the ultimate in accommodating space for temporary and serial occupation by Anglican and Roman Catholic processions that come at different highpoints in the church calendar.

The potential for Walsingham to provide tightly orchestrated "passages" to the sacred core of the pilgrim's choice—Anglican or Roman Catholic—is aided by tours that regularly convey pilgrims into the center of the village. While relatively few people nowadays trek, Camino-like, to Walsingham, buses provide enclaved spaces of travel for parishes or other religious fellowships situated around the country (cf. Feldman 2002). In Turnerian terms, they enable commuting as communitas, and their enclosure effect is reinforced as a given parish comes to Walsingham at the same time each year, stays up to a week in dedicated pilgrimage accommodation, and even brings its own priest. One Anglican woman from the north of England who had been involved in organizing her parish's annual journeys to the village for decades told me toward the end of her pilgrimage, "Tonight was the first time I've been down the High Street all week."[25] Her remark takes on more significance once it is realized that the High Street is situated just two hundred meters from the Anglican shrine. Her loyalties to one part of the village, and thus to one version of pilgrimage, were clear.

On the other hand, Father Martin's description of Walsingham shifts from a centripetal focus on the Anglican shrine to documenting an ever more ramifying set of activities occurring in other directions and spatial frames: sitting in the gardens, going to the parish church, visiting the many gift shops in the High Street, even looking at the Orthodox Chapel in the adjoining village. His list provides a centrifugal set of semi-ritualized activities, which he sees as providing the "best kind of spiritual direction" on the grounds that it allows pilgrims considerable latitude in establishing connections while visiting a holy place. He worries about certain secular temptations, such as the dangers of reverting to mere counseling, and thus he proposes a characteristically Anglo-Catholic balancing of the sacramental with the immanent—the Eucharist with, say, sitting on a bench—one that frames much of Walsingham as somewhere between icon and theme park.

When I spoke to him, Father Martin occupied the center of Anglican liturgical space at Walsingham. Yet he also demonstrated considerable awareness of the penumbral and lateral opportunities offered by the landscape surrounding him, and he certainly acknowledged the positive virtues of making ritualized connections between apparently different yet adjacent behavioral frames. His observations informed a book that he published just a year after my initial interview with him. The jacket notes of *Walsingham: An Ever-Circling Year* (Warner 1996), a slim but lavishly illustrated volume of eighty-eight pages, state that his aim is to produce "an invaluable companion for pilgrim and tourist." The text acts as both local guide and devotional tract and does not differentiate between pilgrim and tourist; both are treated as the same kind of traveler—what the foreword of the book, written by the then administrator of Walsingham's Roman Catholic shrine, calls "pilgrim-visitors" (Williams 1996, x). As we shall see, Father Martin does sometimes wish to distinguish between pilgrims and tourists, yet he is also prepared to countenance—even to encourage—a complex articulation between the two, mediated by acts of looking and overlooking.[26] "Walsingham," he states in the first line of the book's introduction, "is about vision" (Warner 1996, xvii). When I first read these words, I thought he was referring to the original hierophanic apparition granted to Richeldis, but in fact, there is no mention of that in the entire text. Rather, he explains that he is focusing attention on Mary's vision of her vocation as mother of Christ, a more metaphorical gaze and a more biblical one, resonating with the story of the Annunciation and the Archangel Gabriel's appearance before the Virgin (xvii). The actual scenes provided by Father Martin's book draw the reader's attention down some apparently different pathways; the village shrines but also the Norfolk countryside are revealed through photographs commissioned to complement the text. Liturgy and landscape, passages and penumbras, are juxtaposed and conjoined. Moreover, the sights and sites presented are not meant to be experienced through vicarious viewing alone; the book is an invitation to both prayer and pilgrimage, offered not only to the experienced Christian but also to a much wider potential constituency. Although he is the administrator of a famous Christian shrine at the time of writing his book, Father Martin demonstrates sufficient spiritual—and semiotic—awareness to understand that for contemporary constituencies, landscape can do much of the work that church buildings cannot. In this sense, his strategy parallels some of what we have seen for the Camino as well as Methodist pilgrims such as Michael (whom we met in chapter 2), where movement to and within what is perceived to be the natural world can create powerful experiences of commitment, even as the precise object of such commitment may remain vague. Some boundaries do remain relevant to Father Martin's presentation of Walsingham as ritual complex. When I asked whether he could tell the difference between pilgrims and visitors to his shrine, he responded:

> I mean it's not clear cut always, not clear cut. I think I can sometimes tell people who are definitely not pilgrims. . . . There's a group of . . . people, who have no sense of the numinous or a place with boundaries. It's very odd, I mean this kind of came home to me earlier on in the summer when I was sitting in the shrine . . . and . . . one of Father Andrew's cats sort of caught my eye, and it walked through the sanctuary, and the nave altar wasn't there at the time, it was just the ropes all round, and it just walked right through, and I thought, "What's that cat doing?" and I thought, "Why has the cat crossed those boundaries and not gone round in the way that everybody else does?". . . . I said, because the cat doesn't see the boundaries. And I suddenly thought, "Oh yes, that's what it is about these people, these poor folk who come into this place, they don't know the boundaries.". . . . But actually there are lots of boundaries which are unmarked, physically, but which are marked mentally, emotionally, in the minds of people who know.

In other words, the shrine is a place of densely packed yet hidden borders that delineate the most sacred parts of the church, while remaining permeable to curious cats and hapless humans.

Father Martin's observations are subtle but point to wider trends. The village and its surrounding paths and country roads provide efficient affordances for the viewing of others, not only in sacred shrines but also in streets, fields, and lanes. The religiously inscribed character of Walsingham makes it a place of constant ritual abutment and adjacency. There are events when viewing is positively encouraged, such as major processions through the village, occasions when national press (and protesting evangelicals) are present and anticipated. However, viewing and being viewed is often more of a serendipitous affair—casual visitors intrigued by the sight of pilgrims in intense prayer or perhaps catching a glimpse of a group carrying a statue as it disappears down the holy mile. A feature of major pilgrimage sites such as Walsingham is their combination of mutual anonymity and high emotion, public exposure and private engagement. But the place also affords much more ambiguous viewings, when one cannot be quite sure whether a person is on pilgrimage or simply out for a stroll.

The ways in which Walsingham provides the possibility of stumbling over ambiguous encounters are significant enough to become a frequent subject of narratives of the faithful. Here, an older, devoted Roman Catholic woman tells me of her observation of an incident in the Slipper Chapel:[27]

> This particular young [woman with her parents] . . . was wearing very high heels, a tight skirt and . . . jewelry, and they walked in and had their cameras. . . . And they were drawn towards the front of the church . . . and they sat and they were looking round and taking photographs. . . . And then they came to the altar and . . . this girl . . . was fascinated . . . she'd been chatting away, and she went right up to . . . the altar and said, "Doesn't that look lovely, it must be special, you know." And then she went down on her knees as if she realized it was some . . . [trails off].

Here, two gazes are conjoined, though they point in different directions. The older woman focuses on the outward signs of tourism—the jewelry, the chatter, the photos and distracted looking—before describing the young visitor's apparent realization that what she sees is "special" and worthy of a very different form of embodied response. Continuing Father Martin's metaphor, the visitor appears to move from a feline indifference to boundaries toward an inchoate respect for sacred space. The kindling of her devotional disposition is roused not during a service but at a time when clergy and congregation are absent. This incident is not penumbral, since it takes place right at the center of Catholic devotion, but it is certainly lateral.

Such visual reframings are common in my own fieldwork observations, as I have watched perceptive if inexperienced visitors approach sacred spaces and, as they look around and realize where they are, improvise an appropriate etiquette of deference. These are visitors who *do* sense that boundaries exist around certain spaces, even if they may not be sure of what their response should be. Voices are lowered; children hushed; heads bowed; possibly even signs of the cross made with brief hand movements. These ritual rearticulations recall anthropologist Alfred Gell's (1996, 27) discussion of the artwork as akin to a trap that deduces the dispositions of its victims.[28] Gell talks of how such a trap initially communicates the absence of its creator but then acts as a proxy and agent for the creator's intentionality (26), ideally resulting in capture and containment of its quarry (37). Similarly, the power of an empty chapel may lie in the way it tempts the visitor to tumble into the seductive snare of a resonant ritual center. Much of the time, no priest is present to scrutinize what happens, so altars lie apparently passive, accessible to all who come. Both the Roman Catholic and the Anglican shrines provide numerous opportunities to progress from spectatorship into abbreviated forms of ritualized action and focus—lighting candles, mumbling prayers, sprinkling oneself or others with holy water—elements of what Albera (2019a) calls a common ritual syntax that can easily cross denominational boundaries, or be performed by those with little or no faith. Without fully knowing what they are doing or why, the visitor may be drawn in.

Throughout the less formally ritualized landscape surrounding the shrines—the penumbral one where movements and orientations are scattered and diffuse—articulations with formalized or repetitive ritual are loosened further. As Father Martin has realized, Walsingham's layout permits movements away from the village, not back in the direction of home but into a sideways space of ambiguous engagement and diminished surveillance. The surrounding Norfolk countryside provides a denominationally neutral context where movements away from ritual density prove highly productive and where linear liturgical alignments are readily converted into lateral moves. One example is the regular Roman Catholic Tamil pilgrimage that includes the Slipper Chapel but then extends out to the nearby coast, even incorporating Hindu visitors.[29] Other cases are less institutionalized and much less public. One younger Roman Catholic woman described to me a pilgrimage carried out by members of a theological college.[30] Rather than heading for the Slipper Chapel, the students enacted stations of the cross across several miles of country lanes, and they did so without initially revealing to some of their fellow travelers when they had arrived at a given station. The woman talked of the extraordinary effectiveness of the following incident:

> The man . . . playing the part of Jesus . . . only had shirt sleeves and . . . and he fell over in the mud . . . and . . . got up and just said . . . angrily . . . "Oh, I've had enough of this, I'm not going on, I'm just really cold and wet." And . . . one of the students who'd just been standing in the crowd of us . . . just walked out . . . and took off his coat and gave it to [the man playing Jesus] . . . and suddenly we all realized that this was Simon of Cyrene taking the cross.

This event retains a trace of ritual formality even as it merges biblical and Norfolk landscapes in ways anticipated but not prescribed by the images in Father Martin's Walsingham guidebook—but perhaps hinted at by Richeldis's original bringing of the Holy Land to Norfolk. Participants occupy a performative space where the liminality of any formal pilgrimage shrine is *itself* sidestepped. What results is a creative articulation between devotional and everyday life that collapses temporal, ethical, and behavioral boundaries between the two. Visiting improvised stations of the cross combines with collective rambling and common experience of chilly English weather, which leaves the body itself open to both performative surprises and the vagaries of the elements. The lateral quality of the experience is enhanced in the account by a revelatory bridging of everyday irritation and biblical resonance, whose power comes from the fact that interpretive work is needed to recognize the concealed ritualization in play as a spectator steps into the "scene" and adopts a leading role. If Father Martin notes that "the best kind of spiritual direction" is one that allows pilgrims to discover their own way, this is an occasion not of individual but of more collective discovery and engagement. At the same time, the specificity of the event goes beyond mere repetition of ritual forms, indexing *that* day, and *that* group, as having special significance.

The pilgrimage landscape we are exploring here incorporates liminal passages and shrine centers, but it also expands into lateral movements and penumbral stances, conjoining these different frames of action. Despite its venerable qualities, Walsingham emerges as being well capable of incorporating contemporary forms of ritual creativity. It lacks the aggressive qualities of neo-Pentecostal reaching out into the world, and while it incorporates ideological diversity, it does so less overtly than a multifaith center. However, its quaint and often understated character contributes to its qualities as a seductive penumbra, with its pathways and ruins inviting movement across the porous boundaries between formal liturgy and evocative landscape, religion and nature. Walsingham is a pilgrimage complex boasting two ritual cores—Anglican and Roman Catholic—but it also offers a mixture of material frames that enable lateral forms of ritualization, staged in performative contexts that vary in terms of formality, visibility, and intensity and which diffuse out into the wider environment. As such, it affords possibilities for ambiguous and ambivalent experiences of engagement with pilgrimage that are not discernible by ethnographic approaches focused on formal centers and flowing paths.

This depiction of Walsingham and its environs highlights the significance of the physical affordances of pilgrimage landscapes, the ways in which altars, hedges, roads, ruins, and so on, contribute to but do not determine the embodied engagements of travelers across heterogenous locations. Parallels are evident with more-than-representational approaches in human geography. For instance, in describing the Irish shrines of Our Lady's Island and Croagh Patrick, Richard Scriven and Eoin O'Mahony (2020) emphasize that the landscapes hosting such performances are not mere backgrounds to action, but "porous arenas at the meeting of history, belief, activity and practicality" (10; see also Maddrell and Scriven 2016). Similarly, Veronica Della Dora's (2016) influential notion of infrasecular geographies presents sacralized settings as "dynamic palimpsests whose layers move simultaneously at different speeds and scales" (21).[31] As with the notion of the penumbra, the emphasis is on complexity, the interaction of place with performance, the fluidity of boundaries not only between past and present, but also between "sanctity and secularity" (Scriven and O'Mahony 2020, 3).

English Cathedrals: From the Lateral to the Loose

Walsingham forms a distinctive part of the contemporary spiritual landscape in England, but many of the religious, cultural, and economic trends that animate it are evident elsewhere. An obvious point of comparison is provided by cathedrals, which have attracted relatively little attention among anthropologists or sociologists of religion.[32] The forms of religious and ritual engagement they foster have seemed less significant than missionizing Pentecostal movements or indeed revivalist forms of Islam, but like Walsingham, they are dynamic and contemporary spaces of ritual encounter. Since the 1990s, cathedrals have seen a remarkable recovery in attendance since periods of postwar indifference (Curtis 2016), attracting regular worshippers but also "more transient communities of pilgrims and tourists" (Davie 2012, 486), including many who report that they come from other religious traditions or have no faith at all. According to an Anglican-commissioned report carried out in 2012, over a quarter (27 percent) of England's adult population, roughly 11.3 million people, said they had been to a Church of England cathedral within the previous twelve months.[33]

In common with Walsingham, these institutions have shifted since the Second World War from relative liturgical exclusivity toward adopting a much more welcoming stance. Unlike the shrine in Norfolk, however, cathedrals where I have conducted research—Canterbury, Durham, York, and Westminster—are definitively urban.[34] They combine pilgrimage activities with a multistranded range of functions as seats of bishops, congregations, administrative centers, land owners, concert halls, locations of art exhibitions, and important tourist venues, and Judith Muskett (2016) aptly characterizes such buildings as containing both sacred space and common ground. The complex character of cathedrals as hosts for pilgrimage is illustrated in an interview with a lay member of Durham Cathedral's administrative office, carried out by my co-fieldworker Tiina Sepp, exploring whether that member of staff has ever considered her workplace to be a place of pilgrimage. The response is telling in its ambiguity:[35]

Honestly, prior to being in this job I wouldn't have done, I don't think. . . . Obviously I recognized it as a Church and as a spiritual and religious place, but I guess in my head pilgrimage probably was quite a historical thing, not really something that people do necessarily in the same way now. Or if they do it, it's one of the big famous ones like Santiago de Compostela, or perhaps something that you even associate with, well—or Lourdes or somewhere like that—but also something you maybe associate with other faiths, so with Islam, visiting Mecca and things. . . . And I guess there isn't a particular—you don't see people obviously making pilgrimage in the way that you might do at some other places. . . . But now that I'm here I'm probably seeing it a bit differently. Partly because I'm learning a bit more about St. Cuthbert and also the relics and things. . . . And I guess it depends on what you define as pilgrimage, doesn't it?[36]

These remarks include an intriguing reference to the worker's coming to recognize the presence of pilgrimage in a context where it is not obvious, but where it can be detected once she learns to see things "a bit differently." As a multilayered practice, often situated uneasily between clerical and lay expectations, pilgrimage touches on many points of uncertainty for cathedrals. Anglicanism contains members of a more evangelical persuasion who regard its overt cultivation with considerable suspicion, and even for more sympathetic commentators, the juxtaposition of declining parish engagement alongside increased interest in major shrines raises unsettling questions. As the sociologist and dean of Christ Church Martyn Percy puts it:

The current boom in cathedral worship is one example of episodic belief on the rise: well-attended high quality religious services by increasing numbers, but with little evidence that this leads to an overall rise in actual Church of England membership. Indeed, what seems to flourish in modern European mainline denominational Christianity is pilgrimage, memorialisation and celebration, all of which are episodic in character, rather than intrinsically dispositional. (2013, 125)

From a more optimistic perspective, current attitudes resonate with the wider character of contemporary Anglicanism, at least in its more liberal manifestations. In reflecting on the present popularity of English cathedrals, the Anglican priest and theologian Simon Oliver suggests that "Anglicans have a particular sensitivity to the complex nature of human religiosity" (2017, 33), adding that most of them inhabit the "penumbra" of Christianity.[37]

Cathedrals, then, serve as contexts not of anti-structure but of multivalent infrastructure, playing on the porosity between spiritual engagement and cultural curiosity. Prayer might be leavened by tourism, lighting a candle combined with going to a café, attending an Evensong service justified to the self less as a commitment to faith than as an expression of appreciation of the music. Larger cathedrals incorporate elements of the popular contexts of spiritually oriented assembly I have mentioned in this chapter: the beauty and historical associations of Walsingham; the exposed capaciousness of Pentecostal warehouses; the shape-shifting quality of multifaith centers. Urban cathedrals cannot easily expand into a penumbral landscape of fields and lanes, and yet their *internal* divisions into nave, altar, crypt, saints' shrines, side chapels, and so on enable numerous behavioral frames for multiple and simultaneous activities to be juxtaposed or even conjoined. Such partitions encourage the tourist, passer-by, or undecided semi-believer to move in and out of the times and spaces of liturgy, experiencing adjacencies with conventional ritual forms. Indeed, the scale and complexity of their ritual and aesthetic infrastructures allow cathedrals to encompass but also go beyond liturgical timeframes in order to open themselves out to more flexible forms of engagement (Coleman 2018d).

As Percy's earlier comment suggests, such trends should not be read through conventional understandings of church growth. What is being offered by cathedrals, especially the larger ones, is a range of activities oriented around temporal rhythms, ritual intensities, and ideological expectations, whose co-presence is orchestrated or sometimes simply tolerated by cathedral staff. Viewed as frames for the accommodation of heterogeneous publics, cathedrals offer spaces for sometimes glancing social and ritual adjacencies, involving the close proximity of disparate behaviors—improvised prayer, flaneur-like wandering, overhearing the words of a guide—as the uninitiated position themselves alongside regular and well-practiced worshippers during a communion service or a mass, or observe a pious prayer in a side chapel.[38]

Generally, annual feast days of saints are high-profile occasions marked by more formal pilgrimages, which focus on what the Turners would have called "dominant symbols." At Durham Cathedral, for instance, a special Evensong celebrating Cuthbert is complemented by a procession to his tomb and an annual walk from the nearby town of Chester-le-Street, commemorating the final translation of the saint's body to the cathedral after the Vikings had sacked the church dedicated to him at Lindisfarne in 793. At Roman Catholic Westminster, the feast day of its priest-martyr St. John Southworth is marked by his body and reliquary being lifted from a side chapel into the middle of the nave to form a center point for solemn liturgical celebrations.[39] There are also occasions, however, when ritual behaviors of differing formality may be sutured together through more creative deployments of pilgrimage ritual. In the following example, an interlocutor at Canterbury discusses how her work involves developing strategies that can bring groups through the building while remining sensitive to their varied needs.[40] She reflects on designing a candlelit pilgrimage, held after the building is officially closed:[41]

> As we go round, I say: If you've clearly made Christian profession of faith, you might like to think about this. If you haven't, you might like to think about something which is I guess [is] less Christian language but may actually end up being the same thing, really. So we start at the back and then we literally journey. . . . And so . . . before I took a group round on my own I spent some time thinking: How does the building speak of a Christian journey of faith? How can I use the building in different places to make myself a route?

This cathedral worker acts as de facto pilgrimage leader but makes gazing at Becket's tomb—the key component of the Canterbury pilgrimage for the Turners—a small part of an ambulatory ritual oriented toward people of varying degrees of faith. A notable part in her description comes when she remarks that at one point "we go down to the Crypt and in the center of the Undercroft we stop just to be quiet. So, that's the longest place we stop, really, just to let people be still in the presence of God." This pause—in a shadowed, semi-concealed part of the building—constitutes a spatial and temporal decentering, giving priority to reflection away from the main shrine or altar. Even though it takes place within the cathedral itself, it occupies what is effectively a penumbral zone, situated at one remove both behaviorally and spatially from either the main altar or the saint's resting-place. In its partaking of proximity to but not full immersion in the liturgical focal points of the building, this activity has parallels with Arabella Dorman's *Suspended* exhibition, the display located in the nave of Canterbury Cathedral with which I began this book. Dorman's work also embodies a complex translation of pilgrimage themes, situated to the side of ritual action and yet inviting comparisons between art and liturgy in its evocations of stately movements, focused gazes, and sacrifice.

A less subtle juxtaposition—or ritual seduction—is provided by the structuring of Durham's *Open Treasure* exhibition, which provides a heritage-like history of the cathedral, the city, and the region before concluding with an exhibit on pilgrimage and a sign and passage that literally funnel the visitor back into liturgical space. As a canon at Durham who has been deeply involved with *Open Treasure* noted in an interview a little before the exhibition was finalized:[42]

> The idea has always been that it should interpret Christianity and therefore not just be a secular exhibition. . . . The . . . last time I saw the proposals there was going to be a board which says, "go back into the church" and, not exactly, worship God. . . . The people . . . yeah, they probably wouldn't realize that's what we're doing, but the idea was that somehow it should end up with encounter, hence "go back into the cathedral" or go and read a prayer or light a candle. . . . That's ultimately the aim.

As a frequent feature of Anglican cathedrals and a long-standing tradition in Roman Catholic ones, the lighting of candles provides an excellent example of Albera's (2019a) common ritual syntax. In Westminster Cathedral, candle stands are placed in chapels, often directly in front of saints and martyrs. However, the use of candles is more theologically loaded in Anglican cathedrals because of its Catholic associations. Consequently, stands may be placed in front of blank walls or columns, leaving the focus of the associated prayer ambiguous.[43] Given the function of syntax to create connections in flexible but patterned ways we might also see candles and their stands as linking liminal and lateral behaviors and spaces. At Durham, candles are lit in front of, and sometimes on, the tombs of both St. Cuthbert and St. Bede and are likely to form an important part of any official pilgrimage to such saints. However, they also act as the catalysts for impromptu performances of ritualized behavior. For instance, the following is an exchange that I observed in front of a candle stand placed in the nave of the cathedral. My fieldnotes record the following:[44]

> A father and young sons (perhaps five and six years old) come to the stand.
> OLDER BOY: "Dada, can we do that?"
>
> Father explains what to do with the candle and they light it. The boy blows his candle.
>
> FATHER: "You've blown out somebody else's." *And* "You've got to put money in, did you think about that?" *And* "You've got to write a prayer."
> YOUNGER BOY goes to the other side of the bench where I'm sitting: "I'm going to write it from over here."
> OLDER BOY: "Is it like a wish?"
>
> Younger boy shifts position so that he is kneeling on the ground, using the bench as a writing table—almost a position of prayer.
>
> OLDER BOY: "Daddy, I've done it."
> FATHER: "You're only meant to do one."
> FATHER TO THE YOUNGER BOY: "All done?"
> YOUNGER BOY: "Where should we put it?"
>
> Father looks at [the boy's] note, tells him to fold it and put it in the basket. . . .
>
> THEN THE FATHER: "Ok boys let's go."
>
> I look at one of the notes, lying open in the basket: *"To grandmother Gren"*—with a simple picture of a human figure next to it.

This incident reveals the negotiated quality of such ritual, conjoining hints of prayer with lighting a candle and writing a note to a deceased relative. It takes place in the afternoon, during a non-liturgically marked period of the day, playing out a small drama of kinship relations barely separated from the movements of wider publics passing through the space. The candle stand occupies a spot on the way to but separate from both the main altar and the elevated shrine to St. Cuthbert and thus provides an ideal staging for an activity that is serious but low key and evanescent—much more lateral than liminal or liminoid and clearly going beyond vicarious observation of clerical expertise. It would be easy to dismiss such actions as trifling—as not "truly" religious—but such a view would reveal an impoverished appreciation of the ambiguities of much religious engagement and attachment. What are revealed here are the subtleties of semiotic and affective articulations between public and private ritual, alongside the difficulties of separating out familial from spiritual obligations.

We might also use events like this interaction between father and sons to reconsider Percy's claim that such actions are episodic rather than dispositional. Percy's argument has force if we think purely in conventional institutional terms of participating in parish life. Yet viewed from a different perspective, we see children exploring how this apparently novel activity links with what they already know; "Is it like a wish?" is almost certainly a reminder of the ways in which lighting a candle in church recalls blowing out candles placed on a birthday cake. The action is therefore new but not completely alien, and its partially familiar character may form part of its seductive quality for the child who begins the engagement by eagerly asking, "Can we do that?" Such ritual engagement goes far beyond the vicarious, and it is kindled by the existence of a dispositional resonance between domestic and liturgical action.[45]

If we consider that the lighting of a candle may take place as the hum of prayers is heard coming from a side chapel, as a pilgrim brushes past having tramped from further up the coast or as a tourist pays to go up the steps to the *Open Treasure* exhibition, we can recognize the mutually constitutive powers of co-presence, adjacency, and multifunctionality in a cathedral (Coleman 2018c). Reminiscent of Walsingham, the lateral possibilities involve numerous forms of proximity to, and sometimes hesitant or deflected participation in, more official and marked forms of ritual. The formal and informal are not opposed but wrapped up in a complex ritual embrace, where liturgical order and behavioral contingency are conjoined (cf. Lambek 2013, 9, 11). Through redescribing such activities by going beyond conventional work on pilgrimage, I draw on urban spatial theory to explore the implications of the shape-shifting— and numerous articulations—that can be achieved within such a capacious context.[46]

In a book whose subject (and subtitle) is "Possibility and Diversity in Urban Life," geographers Karen Franck and Quentin Stevens (2007a, 2007b) talk of how cities are naturally composed of a great variety of place types. "Tighter," more constraining ones include office towers or libraries, where behavioral norms are relatively restrictive and surveillance is evident. In contrast, much of the public and civic realm involves expectations that are more fluid, and such "loose space" (2007b, 3) permits the chance encounter, the spontaneous event, an enjoyment of diversity and is most likely to emerge in urban contexts where access to a variety of venues combines with anonymity among strangers, variety of persons, and fluidity of meaning. Loose spaces often gain their identity and potential through their adjacent relationships with other kinds of contexts, working through porous edges that allow people to observe or even straddle thresholds, possibly allowing graduated and calibrated transitions into different realms (9).[47]

The intellectual inspirations for such a view emerge from classic theorists of the city, ranging from Georg Simmel to Richard Sennett, Erving Goffman, and Henri Lefebvre. For my purposes, Franck and Stephens's vocabulary expresses well the complexities that manifest around and within cathedrals as multiply framed and multiply claimed spaces of behavioral fragmentation, adjacency, and articulation. On a given day, a cathedral will play host to hundreds of unplanned and unpredictable sightseers of many religions or no religion before switching quite suddenly toward the tight liturgical frame required by a mass or prayer service, before accommodating a pilgrimage group whose members may range from the devout to the deeply skeptical. Cathedral space is often orchestrated to be porous but also to shift swiftly between foregrounds and backgrounds and between more or less focused and choreographed forms of behavior. A good example of this oscillatory capacity is evident at York Minister, where the milling around of visitors is interrupted on the hour by a loudspeaker that reaches into all parts of the building and asks everybody to remain still and remember that "this is a place of prayer and pilgrimage." As most people cease to talk or walk, the voice asks people to pray for causes that range from the sick to the world as a whole. After a few minutes, it lets listeners go with the words "And may you have a very memorable visit to York." Such an incident is almost anti-lateral in the sense of directing people back toward more formal liturgy, and it has precisely the character of inserting a degree of tightness into loose space. The stage management involved is far more casual than that required to set up Evensong, but unlike a formal service, it reaches into all parts of the space, reminding visitors of the regular rhythms of liturgical time and the demanding disciplines of ecclesiastical etiquette.

My description of English cathedrals looks rather different from *Image and Pilgrimage*'s aspiration for Canterbury's "traditional pilgrimage" to be revived, "with processions, candles, and religious services devoted to the martyred cleric" (Turner and Turner 1978, 20). Or rather, my point is that such practices *have* been revived, but they are surrounded and further animated by less predictable, adjacent movements of visitors whose complex modes and tonalities of engagement with ritual and spatial forms go beyond the limits of the liminal or the liminoid, and whose subtleties should not be dismissed by being placed within the catchall designation of tourism. These varied explorations of pilgrimage penumbras and lateral behavioral frames have their counterparts at Walsingham, whose public profile has grown considerably since the Turners classified it primarily as one of their "medieval pilgrimages" (175). Those who throng such sites and their environs may not always look like the most pious, committed, or knowledgeable of pilgrims, but their embodied orientations are not necessarily contesting the sacred. Nor do they particularly resemble those who toil self-consciously along the Camino, cultivating experiences of journeying rather than of arriving, though they do suggest the need for an expanded ethnographic perspective: might the cathedral at Compostela contain not merely secular walkers who feel alienated at the end of their journey, but also others who are prepared to negotiate a lateral relationship with its ritual forms?[48] Scholarly focus on the Way leaves this question unanswered.

Parish life and participation, with its weekly demands and sometimes close surveillance of behavior, may generally be on the decline in a Northern European country such as England (cf. Eade 2016). At the same time, larger cathedrals and sites such as Walsingham foster spaces where proximity and distance, obligation and self-direction, can be negotiated with much flexibility, as participation in and observation of ritual events are maintained in a delicate and sometimes tension-filled balance. Lateral and loose opportunities for semidetached engagement look more seductive to many visitors than liminal or liminoid forms of liturgy, and this point leads us back once more to consideration of questions of articulation as they are played out through ritual forms of expression. Much anthropological work—including that of the Turners—has been devoted to the question of whether and how ritual obliges its participants to follow its inherent logic and momentum, so that initial assent to participate implies involvement in tightly meshed expressions of words, bodily movements, and orientations in space. One of the classic statements of the juggernaut-like character of such engagement is provided by a figure whose work I have explored earlier, Maurice Bloch, in relation to his focus on the final stage of rites of passage and processes of reincorporation back into society (1991). Here, however, I draw on an earlier paper, "Symbols, Song, Dance and Features of Articulation" (Bloch 1974), where he examines links between enacting ritual and establishing authority among the Merina of Madagascar. Much of the articulation Bloch highlights in this piece is internally oriented. He argues that deploying a high degree of formality in both use of language and staging of ritual has the advantage of reinforcing the legitimacy of the speaker/ritual officiant because it appeals to the power of seemingly fixed precedent, using stylized and age-old phrases. The different elements of what is said and done link to and follow on from each other in seemingly inexorable ways. As Bloch famously puts it, "You cannot argue with a song" (1974, 71). However, because of the inflexibility—what Bloch (63) calls the arthritic quality—of such communication, it cannot readily respond to the specific circumstances of a given performance or set of participants, and therefore is much less precise in its meanings than everyday conversation or action would be. In adopting the "impoverished" (57) language and gestures of traditional authority and ritual an officiant gains gravitas but loses nimbleness in adapting to the demands of the moment.

Bloch's argument has been much debated and disputed but remains useful for me because it highlights a number of key questions, not only the extent to which ritual relates to the wider circumstances of its enactment but also the need to assess the strength of the internal articulations between different parts of a ritual performance. We might think of York Minster's announcement—emitted from a God-like, ubiquitous loud-speaker system—as akin to Bloch's song that brooks no disagreement, but if the framing of all cathedral behavior took on a similarly imperious tone, such spaces would soon be empty of casual visitors. In addition, the announcement can only retain its inexorability for a minute or two. My analysis of lateral and loose pilgrimage practices presents a more dynamic argument about articulation than that suggested by Bloch about the Merina, appropriate to a very different context for the staging and enacting of ritual forms. While Bloch's argument depends on the depiction of ritual that is seemingly inflexible, impermeable, insulated from context (non-porous), I am examining examples of pilgrimage that run the full gamut from highly arthritic to much more flexibly articulated in form and participation. Both formal and informal orientations to staging pilgrimage may occur during the same event, and the results may ensnare even reluctant pilgrims to move from spectatorship to action. Sometimes, the penumbra can be more powerful than the passage.

On the Generality of the Penumbral and the Lateral

Much of this chapter has focused on the culture of Christianity in the England of the late twentieth and early twenty-first centuries, a context marked by religious and ethnic pluralism, ideologies of secularism, and loosening of ties to the everyday life of institutional religion. Similarly, Davie reflects on the geographical range of "vicarious religion," which she sees as particularly well suited to European contexts where state churches have formed important roles in shaping cultural and calendrical events (Davie 2010, 263; cf. Hervieu-Léger 2000). At the same time, the existence of laterality and penumbras is not merely a result of the practices and prevailing semiotic ideologies of current manifestations of the Church of England, or indeed the English Catholic Church. As concepts, they point to a more general methodological principle of examining the performative residue of staging rituals. Depending on social, spatial, and cultural circumstances, as well as the exercise of religious authority, the rigidness of the boundaries and kinds of participation—and the sharpness of the definition of the sacred center—will vary considerably. Popular pilgrimage sites around the world tend to attract large and heterogeneous publics whose allegiance to, or knowledge of, shrine ritual cannot be guaranteed. Yet laterality as we currently observe it emerges not only from relative ignorance or alienation, since it may also reflect increased awareness of alternative ritual approaches to those recommended by traditional religious authorities.

Bloch's Merina ethnography draws an especially sharp contrast between very high formalization of ritual speech acts and everyday situations where communication operates through more creative and flexible rules of syntax.[49] I explore penumbral zones where such divisions do not apply so readily, and I argue that such zones will be discernible in other ethnographic contexts, even though their precise form and reach must depend—like any penumbra—on the semiotic and institutional character of the central core from which they are derived.[50] I am reminded here of Erik Cohen's contrast between "two polar types of pilgrimage centers, the formal and the popular" (1992, 36). In his view, serious and sublime religious activities are emphasized in some places and carried out through highly formalized action (as at St. Peter's, the Kaaba, or the Wailing Wall), while those at others are more "ludic and folksy" (36).[51] I accept the importance of thinking through the implications of how formality and informality relate to each other, though I see these modes of behavior as likely to coexist as part of the same pilgrimage event rather than being separated by site. I also assume that shrines renowned for formality and devotion may provoke lateral behaviors and penumbral spaces that are more submerged than they are at Walsingham. Robert Bianchi says of the Hajj that although he had assumed the pilgrimage would be highly ritualistic:

> In fact, the pilgrims . . . quickly learn that the only way to survive is to throw away the rule books and improvise their own coping strategies by building close-knit 'families' in which everyone looks out for everyone else so they all scrape through safe and sound. Sooner or later, nearly all Hajjis realize that the formal institutions of pilgrimage management have failed them. (2013, 11–12)

Striking as Bianchi's comments are, they cover only a specific dimension of what I see as the full range of lateral behavior, given that much of my emphasis is also on those who identify themselves as relative outsiders to official forms of religious participation. In her ethnography of pilgrims from Europe and the United States who are oriented to Mary Magdalene and inspired by neo-paganism, goddess mythology, feminism, and anthropology, Anna Fedele discusses how her informants drift in and out of engagement with the ritual forms they are presented with by leaders and guides. She understands their combination of "commitment and denial of commitment" as "a clear example" of my notion of lateral participation (2013, 160). Her observation has parallels with some of the Christian examples I have been discussing while also reflecting the particular confidence her informants seem to have in trusting their own perspectives, itself a reflection of their spiritual orientations. Such pilgrims create alternative pathways of participation to those offered by more famous pilgrimage complexes. Thus, "in activating . . . a route of pilgrimage related to Mary Magdalene and the Sacred Feminine," they link together places "complementary to the route leading to Santiago, which the pilgrims described as mainly masculine, related to a male saint and attracting mainly male pilgrims eager to test and display their capacity for physical strength and endurance" (249). Intriguingly, the Camino is viewed here not as a diversion from authority but as embodying a restrictive form of gender display. Fedele examines how the pilgrims whom she accompanies maintain a commitment to visiting Catholic shrines with parallel interests in caves, waterfalls, castles, Roman ruins, and a mental hospital (152). These actions contain elements of contestation yet incorporate the more subtle, deflecting qualities of lateral pilgrimage. Mainstream religious sites and symbols are acknowledged and used as points of orientation, but not fully embraced.

In his PhD dissertation on mountain asceticism and pilgrimage in Dewa Sanzan, a sacred mountain range in Japan, Shayne Dahl (2019) carries out fieldwork where the natural world plays in important part, albeit in a form very different from that of rural Norfolk. Dahl explores how this landscape stands in topographical contrast to the urban sprawl evident in valleys below but also in temporal distinction from aspects of capitalist modernity. Some of his focus is on the intriguing figure of Hoshinosan, an experienced *yamabushi* or mountain ascetic who leads retreats and attracts paying clients from around the country. In viewing his ethnography through the analytical categories I am proposing here,

Dahl argues that Hoshinosan adopts a hybrid approach to *shugyō* (austere training), rendering it available to those displaying greater or lesser evidence of commitment while finding "creative ways to capitalize on the penumbral space between the secular and the religious, pilgrimage and tourism, shugyō and mountaineering" (107). Such retreats "reveal constant laterality during shugyō, when participants shift back and forth between their 'modern' mode of being (even if that means time out for a cigarette or observing more than participating in ritual)" (116). These slippages allow the overall experience to be "religious and liminal" as well as "social and lateral" (210). Differently framed behaviors constantly articulate with each other during the journey. Dahl is surely correct to see penumbral space as involving a given ethics of participation, providing in his case study "both a creative and critical space between . . . Buddhist spacetime (as imagined) and the socioeconomic challenges of capitalist modernity as lived" (239). We see again how the penumbra extends links between whatever is defined as sacred and wider environments, though the forms and understandings of such penumbral articulation vary hugely according to social context and prevailing semiotic ideology. The dynamic negotiation of degrees of commitment to mountain asceticism in Japan has a faraway counterpart in the sometimes consciously orchestrated, sometimes much more serendipitous and ad hoc movements of visitors across social and material terrains in both English cathedrals and the pilgrimage site of Walsingham.

While Fedele and Dahl draw explicitly on notions of the lateral, Ann Gold's *Fruitful Journeys* (1988) belongs to a different period of anthropological writing. Earlier in this book, we examined her tracing of ways in which Rajasthani pilgrims engage in local and more distant shrines, with different motivations and practices emerging between such trips. Most relevant here is Gold's extended description of her bus journey with a mixed group of nearly seventy villagers to the famous site of Puri on the Bay of Bengal, in Eastern India. The city's temple might be expected to be the highpoint of this arduous and time-consuming expedition, but Gold observes, "No one went back to the temple on our second day in Puri for another look at the Lord Jagdish; all repaired, as if by silent consensus, to the ocean shore" (283). Going back to the shore meant rather more than simply staring at the sea, however, since "nobody performed the perfunctory ocean worship that had preceded the previous day's bathing," and instead, people enjoyed frolicking in the waves, tumbling together in the foam and sand. Gold notes that "in contrast to universal emphasis on the ocean as a prime moment of the yātrā, only a few persons interviewed mentioned the famed *darshan* of Jagdish and his companion icons with their truncated limbs as particularly profound or impressive" (284). In any contest between temple and ocean to claim the title of official icon, there could only be one winner at Puri: the shrine itself. And yet, in penumbral practice, the encounter with the churning waves did not exist separately from the rest of the visit but constituted a lateral as well as liminoid transformation of more formal experiences of ritual engagement.[52]

All these ethnographic examples occur in spaces adjacent to yet oriented toward centers of ritual action. Notions of the penumbral and the lateral provide ways to characterize ritualized behaviors through which varieties of frictional, strategic, spontaneous, and hapless engagement with sacred sites have occurred, resulting in opaque, diffused, porous, or partial articulations that may be more difficult to discern and describe than conventional forms of behavior but are no less significant. In the next chapter, I shift attention to other ways in which degrees of proximity and distance to shrines are negotiated by looking at how narratives recall, relocate, and reconstruct the image and experience of pilgrimage far from shrines themselves.

7

Telling Tales

Verbal Performances and Pilgrimage Presences

Stories on the Move

The phrase *telling tales* often has negative connotations, implying the betraying of confidences. In this chapter, however, it refers to accounts that are consequential: tales that are *telling*—precipitating effects among readers, listeners, and narrators. The focus will be on connections between pilgrimage and the recalling, recounting, and reenactment of stories, whether the latter are located in sacred scripts, virtual representations, or informal conversations and descriptions. Although the element of narrative must feature in any polythetic definition of pilgrimage, pilgrimage performed and pilgrimage described cannot readily be separated, given that tales are told before, during, and after people physically journey to and from a given shrine.[1] Indeed, the art of narrative may on occasions entirely replace the act of travel.

While the previous chapter focused on the diffusion of ritual penumbras from shrines, here we move even further away from such sacred centers. Alan Morinis remarks that assessment of the effects of pilgrimage should be focused less on dramatic transformations than on subtle understandings of how a pilgrimage endures through being interwoven into daily life and long-term understandings of personhood (1992, 179; see Frey 1998, 178). If so, narrative, with its capacity for constant iteration in different contexts (Bauman 1986), is a powerful but easily overlooked medium for extending pilgrimage presences. While much has been written about how gifts and souvenirs transport the charisma and efficacy of a site to domestic contexts (e.g., Kaufman 2005), this chapter argues for the equal or greater power of stories in the recall—but also the remaking, and the relocating—of pilgrimage experience.

Certain other kinds of tale have regularly been invoked within pilgrimage studies. Early in *Image and Pilgrimage* the Turners note:

> Pilgrimages tend to accrete rich superstructures of legend, myth, folklore, and literature. Legend may be defined as the corpus of written accounts of the marvels and miracles connected with the genesis and development of a pilgrimage system; myth, as the systematic oral tradition concerning these events; and folklore as the assemblage of unsystematized . . . tales and yarns about happenings (Turner and Turner 1978, 23).

Their characterization is useful for its observations on the varied motivations, media, and levels of formality of such tales. The storytelling they examine not only combines orality and literacy but also brings historiography together with other genres of narrating the past. In a notable but neglected section of the book, the Turners analyze accounts associated with two shrines in Mexico City—Our Lady of Guadalupe and Our Lady of the Remedies—that embody symbolic oppositions and homologies relating to Mexican history. They show how these narratives operate in mutual dialogue, forming a story cycle whose significance can be understood only when the two sites are read in relation to each other.[2]

While the Turnerian extract refers to informal discourse, a significant question for scholars of pilgrimage is whether a journey or shrine is authorized by scripture. Examining such evidence can be revealing, though it may also betray a textually oriented reflex in the study of religion, implying that sacred writings are of primary significance in legitimating ritual behaviors (cf. Kirsch 2008). Admittedly, there are times when locating pilgrimage within scriptural injunctions takes on paramount ethnographic importance. The anthropologist Abdellah Hammoudi (2005) talks of how he and his fellow pilgrims were required to engage in a ceaseless back and forth between holy writ and the spoken word before they entered Mecca. Pilgrims were prompted to ask, "'What does the Book say?'" (55–56). Such directives, ostensibly about sacred text, became disciplinary performances, working through multiple senses and media while enacting specific language ideologies. As Hammoudi puts it:

> The crowds at these training sessions wanted something specific: to register God's orders. How did one do this? The orders were "written,"

"inscribed," "prescribed" in "Scripture." So, very specifically, one had to "listen," "hear" an authoritative word about these commandments spoken by an authority, Authority itself, a powerful orthodoxy with a monopoly on the knowledge of origins. The spoken word, far from being in opposition to the written one, added to its aura, generalized it, the more so since this was after all a society founded on "Scripture." (56)

This account presents a striking image of travelers being almost soaked in scripturality (cf. Reinhardt 2014) before being permitted to approach the shrine. Text may also be literally inscribed into the pilgrimage sites of some book-based religions, as exemplified by the Mormon practice of reproducing scripture as monuments at historical sites (Mitchell 2002, 137).

As Hammoudi's example suggests, the frequent combination of powerful gatekeepers and authorized texts reveals anxieties about the pilgrimage's status as a popular activity, and one that frequently involves visions and episodes of the miraculous—evidence of unpredictable, 'untamed' dimensions of religious experience (cf. Dahlberg 1991). Existing alongside revered and canonical accounts are numerous informal reflections and responses, nowadays increasingly available on the internet, as well as stories created out of visual images and dramatic performances that extend the ways pilgrimage can be both narrated and (re-)experienced at the same time.

I analyze these different forms of narrative to develop my argument about the importance of tracing ways in which pilgrimage establishes connections between multiple and sometimes unexpected realms of experience. I ask not only what it means to be present at a pilgrimage site but also how pilgrimage might be re-presenced in realms that recall but go beyond the boundaries of conventional shrines. Drawing on his ethnography of a Zimbabwean church, but also inspired by writers ranging from Georg Hegel to Paul Ricoeur, Matthew Engelke (2007) has argued that a Christian "problem of presence" revolves around "the paradoxical understanding of God's simultaneous presence and absence" (12). His characterization of presence fits well with classic discussions of pilgrimage sites as places where memory of hierophany—the manifestation of the divine on earth—must be established and maintained. It also highlights Protestant concerns over the practice of pilgrimage. This chapter takes the concept in two further directions, which go beyond specifically Christian concerns. First, continuing observations from the previous chapter, I examine what it means to regard oneself as present on a pilgrimage when very different modes of involvement are available to visitors. Second, I explore how traces of pilgrimage activity and sensibility are recognized in sites located far away from conventional shrines or ritual centers. My problematization of presence is therefore concerned not only with how connections to the divine are cultivated, but also with how encounters with physical place and social experience may be reanimated through telling tales.

Numerous narratives have already been present in this book: in the imagery of shrines as palimpsests made up of rich layers of religious and cultural association, in the contested ideological stances adopted by different pilgrimage factions as they have wrestled over interpretations of a shrine, and in the historical and mythical tales told of the Camino. Narrative has also contributed to a theoretical attempt to characterize pilgrimage within scriptural religions. As noted in chapter 4, Eade and Sallnow's depiction of "contesting the sacred" was accompanied by a briefer observation that pilgrimage might consist of certain regular coordinates, comprising person, place, and text (Eade and Sallnow 1991, 9). The imagery of coordination is significant in the way it points to interactions between different components of equal value. At the same time, conventional use of the word *text* cannot encompass the full range of narrative behaviors comprehended by pilgrimage. In what follows, we return to these coordinates but enlarge their associations and explore their assumptions. Of particular interest is their reference—however implicitly—to an underlying structural triad of person as *mediator* between realms, place as *context* for action, and text as legitimizing *precedent*.

The next section explores how story may articulate closely with structure by sanctioning and delimiting—but also sequencing—sacred space and pilgrimage experience. Then, we follow pilgrimages as they are narrated by multiple authors at and beyond sacred shrines, articulating alternative temporal and spatial frameworks of experience.

Stories That Structure and Sanction

Important pilgrimages are described or prescribed by sacred texts perceived as foundational and generative of both imitation and blessing. For instance, the *Mahabharata* (ca. 300 BCE), a Vedic epic sacred in Hinduism, contains passages noting the religious merit to be gained from visiting numerous *tirthas,* or sacred places. It constructs a complex sacred geography that encompasses the whole of India. Surah 22 from the Qur'an focuses more on a single place, issuing a warning to those who prevent Muslims from making a pilgrimage to the Grand Mosque at Mecca but also noting (Surah 22:27), "And proclaim to the people the Hajj [pilgrimage]; they will come to you on foot and on every lean camel; they will come from every distant pass."[3] Jesus was an inveterate wanderer, even after physical death, and one of the biblical models for Christian pilgrimage comes from Luke 24:13–33, where three days after his crucifixion, Jesus meets two disciples on the road to Emmaus (Coleman and Elsner 2002b, 4)

If revered texts and other forms of devotional literature appeal to the legitimating authority of origins and history, they do so in light of political imperatives and linguistic ideologies of the present. Hans Jürgen David (2019) illustrates this point in his description of Badrinath, a temple located in the Garhwal Himalayas that is dedicated to the Hindu god Vishnu. David notes that the ideological stakes associated with the shrine have grown as the number of pilgrims has increased over the past half century or so, now encompassing around a million people a year despite the remoteness of the spot (14). In tracing narratives about the shrine circulated by local Hindu priests, David shows how such stories relocate its origins in ways that articulate with a national landscape of Hindu practice. Discounting tales that would connect the shrine either to local customs or to Buddhist activities occurring just a few kilometers north, priests highlight the significance of Adi Shankaracharya (Shankara), a saint whose hagiographies (dating from many centuries after he is assumed to have lived) describe him as visiting Badrinath. According to one pamphlet, Shankara traveled to the site from as far away as South India, where he had lived as a child. The saint was hoping to see a famous image of the four-armed Vishnu, but instead:

When Shankara arrived . . . the priest told him that the statue was no longer inside the temple. The priest further said that the statue was taken out of the temple and was hidden in the river below in fear that it might be desecrated by the Buddhists. Shankara was very disappointed at not being able to have the experience of *darśan* . . . of Badrinarayan and thus sat down to meditate. In his meditation he had a vision of Vishnu himself, who told him where and how he could find his statue. Shankaracharya went down to a place in the river that bears the name of Naradkund and retrieved the image, installing it below the temple near the hot spring. (16)

In addition:

When Shankara took the statue out of the water he saw that it was broken. Therefore he [initially] threw it back into the river. He continued this, each time retrieving other broken statues until Vishnu once again appeared in front of him, telling him that this imperfect form of himself was the one he would show to his devotees in this dark age of *kali yuga*.[4] (16)

This is a morality tale that accounts for the present dilapidated condition of the temple statue. The saint becomes involved in a rededication and purification of the site as traces of Buddhist connection from the past are acknowledged yet discarded. At the same time, the scale of influence of Badrinath is recalibrated, justifying its status as one of the Char Dham, the four major sacred sites located at the cardinal points of the Indian subcontinent.

The story also lends itself to being interpreted in terms of Eade and Sallnow's coordinates; Shankara (in dialogue with Vishnu) emerges as the "person" who acts as legitimizing agent for the "place" represented by the temple, which is remotely yet strategically located in the wider Hindu landscape. The role of "text" is more ambiguous for two reasons. First, the description is not evident in other biographical accounts of the saint, so its canonical claims are suspect. Second, it is both a single coordinate of Eade and Sallnow's triad and one that encompasses all three at once, since it prescribes how visitors are supposed to understand the intimate relationship between tale, saint, and temple.

If David provides an example of the potential for story to authorize claims to a shrine, pilgrimage narratives may also embody coercive effects through the promulgation of particular forms of ritual trajectory. Van Gennep's model, on which the Turners drew so heavily, resembles an Aristotelian drama as expressed in the latter's *Poetics*, with sequences of action involving forms of reversal and discovery but ultimately producing a dramatic whole and leading to some kind of resolution. In line with basic literary theories of narrative (Martin 1986, 81), this recurring pattern emplots a causal movement from stability, through disruption and complication, back to another point of equilibrium. Martin points out that the structure also resembles a scheme devised by the German critic Gustav Freytag, who represented a normal plot as involving a passage through exposition to conflict, to rising climax, to the denouement and resolution of the conflict.

As Martin goes on to observe (1986, 82–83), the trouble with assuming the universal applicability of this schema is that few narratives of any length or complexity display such a tightly knit unity, while modernist and post-modernist forms of writing often resist simple forms of narrative closure. I also challenge the idea that pilgrimage can be contained either ethnographically or analytically within such a narrative straitjacket. Strictly Aristotelian assumptions concerning the nature of what makes a satisfactory plot are unlikely to correspond with cross-culturally valued expressions of literary form. Nonetheless, the emphasis on enacting a sequence leading to a resolution corresponds with certain understandings of the coercive qualities of ritual. In the previous chapter, I discussed Maurice Bloch's (1974) juggernaut-like theory of ritual engagement, which describes the use of high degrees of linguistic and embodied formality to create predictable, arthritic forms of articulation between units of action. While this model is not sufficiently nuanced to apply to contemporary pilgrimage in general, it captures the ways in which certain pilgrimages are orchestrated by authoritative figures to control the narrative of a given journey, just as a narrow path physically prompts pilgrims to move in a given direction.

A striking example of the coercive qualities of sequencing is provided by the anthropologist Jackie Feldman (2002) in his analysis of visits by Jewish Israeli youth to Poland, organized by Israel's Education Ministry.[5] During these trips, students are taken to Holocaust death camps, cemeteries, the remains of former Jewish shtetls, and abandoned synagogues. They also listen to the testimonies of survivors given at sites of original suffering and are encouraged to perform ceremonies at the Warsaw Ghetto. The results are often compelling, and Feldman notes that on their return to Israel, such pilgrims are defined as "witnesses of the witnesses" (85), entrusted to pass on their experiences to classmates, friends and siblings. The trip contributes to Israeli civil religious sentiments through which individuals are provoked into strong identification with the nation as they transition into adulthood and citizenship.

Two features of these journeys are important to emphasize here. One is that the multiple narratives to which students are exposed—the fate of the Jews during the Second World War, instances of military heroism, the emergence of the modern Israeli nation—become imprinted on participants' imaginations not through words alone but also "through discursive symbolism-music and display of symbols, and sensory experiences-sights and smells" (90). What transpires is not so much a re-presencing of divinity as a remaking of the collective past, where unresolved experiences of Jewish victimhood are recalled alongside instances of powerful resistance. As narrative moves beyond mere history into personal experience, students become mutual catalysts for displays of emotion and commitment to ideals promoted by the state. Much of the power of such ritual derives from its temporal progression; Feldman observes that "the structure of each individual ceremony prescribes a sequence of redemption" (105), so that students are repeatedly taken toward points of transformative ritual closure. The past is always past, yet here, it is ritually revived before being ritually redeemed, as pilgrims encounter what Poland has to teach them but return to their own country to fulfill their historical destiny.

The second feature also emerges out of the particular challenges of the trip. Feldman emphasizes that the journey is semiotically and ideologically risky in the sense that students are being taken through a landscape where disconfirming events might be experienced, which would call into question the Israeli state's narrative of Poland's significance.[6] To counter such possibilities, travelers are formed into an "enclave," a social formation defined by Mary Douglas (1993) as one where boundaries among members are minimized but where leaving the collectivity is discouraged through the construction of barriers against what is perceived to be a threatening outside world (Feldman 2002, 90). In this context, the Israeli guard accompanying each bus acts as "the guardian of the gateways to and from Poland. . . . His highly visible physical position at the threshold of inside and outside space insures the impermeability of the environmental bubble of inside space" (ibid., 95). Although individual gestures of protest against the nationalist narrative may occasionally be made by students, "these remain individual acts of resistance, isolated alternative voices" (107).

Feldman's ethnography reveals the considerable ritualistic, ideological, and choreographic labor involved in sustaining a consistent perspective on a journey and a landscape. The Israeli state narrative is presented in a much more concentrated way than the tale of Shankara's encounter with Badrinath, given that the Hindu account must regularly compete with other versions of the temple's history and articulate with diffuse forms of ritual engagement. In contrast, Israeli students' experience is bolstered by controlled narrations and sequences of visits to sites alongside rituals that encourage active engagement.[7]

The Polish-Israeli case study provides an excellent foil for my discussion of Walsingham in the previous chapter. The lateral quality of much pilgrimage to Norfolk emerges out of very different institutional conditions: the unsupervised presence of a large constituency of spiritually undecided visitors, the provision of ritual props deployed in creative ways to disrupt conventional sequences, and the fuzzy boundaries between sacralized and non-sacralized space. Many visitors to Walsingham know little of the historical or theological background of the site and are not necessarily interested in learning them (Coleman and Elsner 1998). Such social and semiotic conditions emerge from a complicity between semidetached visitors and administrators who understand the delicate balance between exercising religious authority and remaining accessible if required. In contrast, Feldman's case study depicts a ritual process that comes close to an initiation ceremony for a generationally defined cohort of people; its rite-of-passage qualities foster the possibility of sharply delineated liminality and even communitas, with the intensity of the experience protected by institutional measures to prevent social leakage or the possibility of being exposed to alternative perspectives.

While the outcome of visits to Walsingham for visitors is difficult to predict, the Polish case comes much closer to Bloch's position in *Prey into Hunter* (1991), outlined in chapter 4, where he depicts novices who feel empowered to engage in literal or metaphorical conquest of the everyday world that they rejoin. The Israeli students are not merely entering a state of adult citizenship at the time they are traveling together through Poland; they are also, for the most part, about to enter the army to do national service. It seems ritually appropriate that their last stop involves a visit to the Warsaw Monument to the Ghetto Heroes, where they walk the symbolic Memorial Route of Jewish Martyrdom and Struggle but do so in reverse, moving from the *Umschlagplatz* (deportation square) to the monument. Feldman points out (2002, 105) that this action signifies a turn away from passive destruction and a move toward heroic revolt against oppressors, what I call a ritual rearticulation of the ritual and historical associations of the site. It constitutes a "portal of entry into the land of Israel" (ibid.). In this case, the Aristotelian sense of a resolution does seem to be satisfied, with students learning to become—and perhaps to *desire* to become—significant protagonists in the historical drama that they have been recapitulating and re-presencing. The pilgrimage moves powerfully between secular, spiritual, political, and civil registers yet retains its enclaved intensity of focus and ultimate purpose.

This youth pilgrimage illustrates the tenuous boundary between history and myth that is often negotiated during pilgrimage, as tragic elements of the Jewish past are both given deep symbolic significance and lent material facticity through being rooted in—and routed through—a selectively traversed and revealed Polish landscape. The tight fit between state narrative and ritual sequence reveals how participants may be invited not only to learn about sacralized history but also to exemplify it.

It is this question of exemplification that I wish to probe further, including its complex relationship to narratives that are already known but have not yet been fully experienced. If Feldman's piece follows Israelis as they leave Israel to trace pathways through Poland, Vida Bajc (2007) writes of pilgrims who make their way *to* the Holy Land: evangelical Christians from the United States. For travelers who have spent much of their spiritual lives absorbing scripture through reading, prayer, and sermons, the biblical landscape has long provided the focal point of their religious imaginations, being central to ideas of future redemption but also a means of experiencing the direct presence of Jesus. Framed through Eade and Sallnow's coordinates, person seems relatively clear in their journeys, embodied ultimately in the figure of Jesus; text refers to scripture.[8] Place, however, raises more troubling questions about coming into contact with divine presence. Both cultivation of a personal relationship with the Savior and intimacy with the Bible provide direct knowledge of God, but followers of reformed theology tend to regard with suspicion the idea that particular shrines are special repositories of God's grace. Furthermore, landscapes that are visibly marked by the material culture of other religions become distractions from authentic experiences of faith.[9]

Given such assumptions, uncluttered contexts provide effective catalysts for the evangelical imagination and backdrops for the transformation of static place into personally meaningful performance. Bajc describes how, guided by their pastor and with their Jewish tour guide sitting apart in the tour bus, believers reenact the biblical battle between David and Goliath in the Valley of Elah, southwest of Jerusalem (Bajc 2007, 397). Standing in the landscape, the pastor has the members of his flock take their Bibles and reflect on what they are about to perform before he rehearses the scenario with them, giving individual people the task of playing named characters from the story (398); script and scripture become mutually enmeshed, as do biblical characters and particular pilgrims.[10] Bajc describes the process of selection:

> The pastor is using his intuition and his intimate familiarity of the personalities of his parishioners to stimulate the pilgrims to relate to each other and the different roles in the script. "Now—we start with Goliath. . . . I think you would all agree the best Goliath . . . would have to be Allen," he concludes and then reflects back to the pilgrims, "don't you think?" The pilgrims nod. "Now—Goliath needs a shield-bearer, a mighty warrior who would go into battle before Goliath and would hold Goliath's shield and when you think about a mighty warrior like that I think most of you would agree that's Tilly." At this point, the pilgrims break out in loud laughter. (403–4)

This is a fun process. It is also effective. The pastor plays on group members' self-identification with the Bible alongside their intimate knowledge of each other. They are enlisted into collective engagement with a performance whose only audience—apart from the anthropologist—is themselves. Ultimately, the attempt to inhabit the storied landscape of the Bible through these performances leads to the possibility of reinforcing a still more important connection. Bajc notes:

> To have an awareness of Jesus is to experience the moments of his life. These experiences are most real and more intensive in His Land. One of the pilgrims on the tour in her mid-thirties "had this picture walking hand in hand with him, you know, a kind of a journey." One way to allow for this transubstantive connection to transpire is to imagine His life in all its details while being in His place. (400)

In a similar fashion, a woman in her early forties remarks on having strengthened her relationship with Jesus: "'I know him as a human being now, not just as a God, as my Lord, but as a man. I can know him as a friend now. He was revealed to me in my heart'" (401).

A complex sequence of translation operates in this vivid ethnography. Scriptural familiarity (acquired in the United States) is verified by seeing the Holy Land. However, a more superficial awareness of place must be transformed into experiential knowledge. The newly acquired sense of the convincing facticity and living drama of sacred text prepares the believer to become more open to Jesus as both divine and human—in other words, to restore him to presence. On the one hand, the believer learns more about Jesus by visiting the lands that he knew; on the other, his influence is not confined to any single location, given his capacity to dwell in hearts rather than shrines. Text is performed in place, but place yields ultimately to person.

The ritualized sequencing of evangelical experience in the Holy Land is not as arthritic as that evident among Israeli students in Poland: committed Protestants must be permitted to feel they have rediscovered their own relationships to biblical landscape through their efforts as performers alongside personalized devotional practices. Nonetheless, their attempts to insert themselves as faithfully as possible into biblical narrative has parallels with the young people described by Feldman, who are encouraged to see themselves as actors in the ongoing drama of the Israeli state. Both contexts demonstrate the significant roles of instructors and mediators.[11] The travelers described by Bajc are actually double-guided; they are escorted by their pastor but also by a local expert, and these two engage in a careful division of labor. It is important for the Jewish tour leader to be aware of when to occupy the foreground and when the background of pilgrims' attention so that he can provide necessary information without interfering with the spiritual challenge of interweaving scripture, landscape, and performance. Such nuanced framing contrasts with the authoritative and disciplinary training in scriptural knowledge described by Hammoudi for his experience of Hajj, or indeed the frequent *lack* of any specific guide to direct journeys around Walsingham's penumbra.[12]

In her book on visits to the Holy Land by American Christians, *Walking Where Jesus Walked* (2014), Hillary Kaell expands on evangelical believers' anxieties over fetishizing place in ways that complement Bajc's account.[13] She notes how even while addressing his flock on a boat on the Sea of Galilee, Pastor Jim reminds his flock of God's work elsewhere, in the United States. He also refers to the surrounding landscape as the equivalent to a Fifth Gospel, so that "its physical tangibility is taken as proof that the biblical narrative (and Jesus' miracle) did literally take place here and, by extension, that God's response to the pilgrims' prayers is also real" (84). Jim goes on to address a worry that the contemporary landscape has changed so much from Jesus's day that no connection with divine presence can be asserted. His rejoinder is that "this is pretty much what our Savior saw. This lake, these hills" (85); in other words, it is still possible to align oneself with Jesus's point of view—a form of embodied mimesis and relationality also captured in the image of walking with Jesus. In these terms, spectatorship is not a form of distancing but a means of spiritual self-presencing. Furthermore, the pastor directs his audience to cultivate a panoramic view, assuming mastery over the landscape while concentrating on the broad outline rather than any distracting detail.[14]

This depiction of a wide-ranging perspective on territory has its counterpart in Bajc's account. The Jewish guide who directs her group takes them to a hill where they can look at a large map and take a longer view of their surroundings:

"This face of the Valley of Elah is a traditional confrontation [spot] between the hill people and the valley people," the guide tells us, "which here would be between the Israelites or Judeans who lived in the hills and the Philistines who were down on the coastal plane." Speaking in the present tense, the guide explains that "If an enemy from the coast, more powerful internationally, succeeds in conquering this valley they are still not home. They still have another step to get up to the hill country of Judea." (407)

Present and past are linked, but not this time through the reenactment of scripture. Rather, it is filtered through the local expertise of the Jewish guide and connected with "the ongoing geopolitics of the area" (ibid.). Experiential, biblical, historical, and contemporary knowledge become mutually constitutive for believers who visit Israel not only for its heritage but also because they see the country playing a key role in current world affairs and biblical eschatology. Indeed, these questions of temporality and belonging should encourage us to reflect on the links between Bajc's and Kaell's accounts while also considering how the movements of the pilgrims they describe belong to the same geopolitical universe as those described by Feldman. The latter's interlocutors were returning to Israel as defenders of the very nation that evangelicals, in a different way, also considered to be their home.

In this section, I have mentioned just a few of the possible ways in which story can act as sanction by locating pilgrims ritually, corporeally, and narratively within well-defined and tightly articulated spaces and socialities. Clearly, such story can take numerous forms, including scriptural fragments, origin myths, powerful performances, remediations through sermons or lectures, and so on. These examples show pilgrims being encouraged to commit to dominant readings of narratives through scriptural legitimation, mediation of guides, and kindling of embodied engagement.[15] They have even been urged to become willing protagonists in the ongoing plots being enacted. Such readings translate pilgrimage sites into what the geographer of travel Derek Gregory has called "legible space," rendering them as contexts understood through specific frames of perception (1999, 115; see also Mitchell 1988, 33). Gregory develops the concept of scripting to describe the ways in which narratives stage particular places, producing "'sites' that are linked in a time-space itinerary and 'sights' that are organized into a hierarchy of cultural significance" (1999, 116). In this way, scripts produce sequences such as the ones we have seen in operation, entailing the controlled construction of visibility. In the next section, I expand our ethnographic and analytical horizons as we move to rather different versions—and articulations—of telling tales.

Loose Tales

I have examined attempts to control the production and reception of authorized narratives—in the metaphor deployed by Franck and Stevens (2007), to "tighten" and constrain the spaces, associated stories, and forms of surveillance binding visitors to shrines and other sacred areas. However, there are many circumstances under which pilgrims become tellers of tales in their own time, bringing "looser" and more serendipitous associations, articulations, and imaginations to bear on experiences at and beyond shrines. In her detailed study of narratives relating to Santiago de Compostela, Suzanne van der Beek (2018) shows how crafting of stories forms a significant part of walkers' experience of travel. Even people who do not see themselves as natural raconteurs feel a compulsion to "narrate their Camino" (32), prompted by a pilgrimage experience that requires the frequent presentation of the self to unknown others. The assumption that everyone has a story becomes institutionalized as hostels along the Camino Francés encourage guests "to introduce themselves before dinner by telling their name, nationality, and reason for being there" (33). For many pilgrims, however, the keeping of a personal diary operates away from such prompts, signaling the exceptionality of the journey and forming part of a daily routine, possibly incorporating such details as "number of footsteps taken, number of cups of coffee drunk, amount of photographs" (74). These mundane types of account(ing) take on a repetitive, even ritualistic quality, expressing personalized and voluntary attunement to what are imagined to be more collective rhythms (76).

More broadly, the diffusion of numerous types of narrative reflects the ongoing concerns of the always shifting pilgrimage population along the Camino. If we think of the authoritative stories discussed in the previous section as operating primarily through a top-down process of redistribution, these tales circulate through informal exchanges or horizontal forms of dissemination (expressed face to face, in hostel visitors' books, online, and so on), producing a meta-commentary on the running of the pilgrimage. Nancy Frey has called the Camino "a distinct space . . . similar to small-scale communities in which gossip flows freely" (1998, 235). Its numerous media of expression are conduits not only for rumors but also for useful tips, inspirational thoughts, encouragements, warnings, and so on, emerging without overt orchestration from a pilgrimage system that involves long stretches of slow, reflexive movement. It is even possible to track the emergent narrativization and mythologization of certain pilgrims or events. Van der Beek meets a pilgrim who discovers that his experience of traveling with excessive amounts of luggage has become a tale that travels independently of him. His blog post suggests that he is rather pleased:

> But what I really wanted to boast about is my very own legend that is going around on the Camino. A couple of days ago a Canadian girl came up to me to ask if I was Ben . . . >>yeah >>So you're that crazy motherfucker who walked with a 30 kilo backpack through the snow in france?!?! >>that's me. (2018, 41)

Ben claims ownership of a story that gained value through being revoiced by others: "And now the story lives on as a communal piece of Camino knowledge. And it will continue to refer to the void left by the absent author, while other pilgrims pick it up and make it a part of their own storytelling repertoire" (ibid.).[16]

This "legend" circulates through face-to-face communication and also online. From a certain perspective, internet technology offers a fundamental challenge to the authentic experience of the Camino, given that it may distract travelers from being in the moment and fully appreciating their surroundings. Frey (2017) has reflected on how some of the journey has changed since her book was published in 1998, becoming a "smart Camino" where cellphones invade the "attentional space" of pilgrims (7), encouraging them to look at screens and play computer games rather than appreciating nature.[17] However, van der Beek's example reveals forms of connectivity that are actually enabled by online technology: the swift diffusion of a story across the social and geographical space of the path as a whole, and the creation of a talking-point that leads to a face-to-face encounter between Canadian pilgrim and a mythologized Ben—"the crazy motherfucker."

The tales I describe here are subject to a much looser regime of surveillance than those evident among Bajc's interlocutors or the enclaved students described by Feldman. They are exposed to a larger and more dispersed public, but still display regularities of form and content. As van der Beek (2018, 34) observes, the longer a pilgrim spends on the Camino, the more stylized their personal stories become as a result of many recitations, while many tales are likely to be collages of personal experiences and texts heard or read somewhere else (36).

The profusion of such composite, circulatable narratives signals a shift in the relationships between coordinates of person, place, and text. The forms, genres, and modes of distribution of texts multiply in such examples and often have little to do with explicitly authorized scriptures. The salient identity of person also undergoes a transformation. Focus on the authority of a sacred figure as mediator between divine and mundane worlds shifts horizontally toward highlighting the experience of the human instigator of the narrative. An increasing proportion of pilgrimage accounts in many parts of the world have taken on autobiographical characteristics over the past century or more—a contrast to the anonymity of medieval chroniclers. Unsurprisingly, the Camino has proved to be a highly productive site of such reflexive "writes of passage" (cf. Duncan and Gregory 1999; cf. Rasch 2016).[18] Lena Gemzöe (2016, 123) observes that stories about going to Compostela have become more common in Sweden and elsewhere over the past fifteen years, just as descriptions of the pilgrimage have become more evident in guides, photo books, travel supplements, magazines, blogs, and so on. Literary works express powerful individual experiences yet follow very similar patterns. Typically, the author's inner journey is catalyzed by personal crisis. Writers are generally skeptical of established religion but take inspiration from broader spiritualities or secular genres of self-help literature. Their narratives lead not only toward inner peace but also to the process of writing itself as a form of redemption, so that "the search for an authentic self is also a search for one's voice, an author's voice" (141).[19] Indeed, such works can become decidedly intertextual, and Gemzöe provides the example of Swedish author Agneta Sjödin's book *En kvinnas resa* (A woman's journey; 2006), which refers to Paulo Coelho's famous Camino novel *The Pilgrimage* (1986), a work that concludes with its own main protagonist promising to write a book on returning home (ibid.).

Much of the expansive Camino writing industry has a Euro-American flavor, but it points to trends also discernible in other pilgrimage traditions. John Shultz (2009, 8) refers to the "deluge of first person accounts chronicling circumambulation" of the island of Shikoku that have emerged since the late 1990s.[20] In this Japanese Buddhist context, the experience tends to be framed as an epic, physically risky, and transformative adventure, often recounted by men and increasingly narrated by common people rather than priests or professional writers (15). As with the Camino, such pilgrim-authors tend to avoid referring to their experiences as conventionally religious, and once more, the transnational influence of the Spanish pilgrimage can be discerned. Shultz describes one remarkable journey carried out by a young actor called Akimoto, who states that he had been searching for an opportunity for self-dramatization and that the idea for the setting of a film came to him when he read about the Camino (148). Akimoto creates as much publicity as possible around his efforts (which eventually also appear in a book), including filming himself along the way and posting his journey online.[21] At times, the viewer is given a lens-eye view of the experience, so that the pilgrimage landscape becomes doubly mediated: both through the camera and via the (toiling) body of the narrator.[22]

The Camino and Shikoku share certain characteristics that have encouraged their frequent translation into autobiographical narrative: a large constituency of people—many of them well-educated—who do not feel especially constrained by clerical strictures; a long journey, which encourages both reflection and the extended cultivation of a semi-ascetic experience; sacred sites that are simultaneously remote and internationally known; and readerships accustomed to genres of travel writing available through multiple media, including books, films, internet sites, and blogs, and keen to engage vicariously in forms of travel that are presented as more authentic than mere tourism.

Extended Articulations

While autobiographical narratives often shift attention away from sacred figures (Eade and Sallnow's "person"), other discourses challenge assumptions concerning the appropriate "place" of pilgrimage activity. Pilgrimage may be viewed not merely as set-apart ritual but also as social imaginary—as a widely distributed set of understandings and orientations diffused throughout everyday life. The Hajj is perhaps *the* iconic example of engagement in a discrete domain of activity that is restricted in time, location, and accessibility, but the very exemplarity of this pilgrimage motivates the dispersal of its traces and effects throughout domestic and institutional realms far beyond the holy mosque and its environs. The Hajj's disseminated presence is evidenced not only in the transnational infrastructures required to ease the passage of so many Muslims annually to the site but also by its constant reinstanciation in less spectacular, often mundane, contexts far from Saudi Arabia. Carole Delaney describes the perception of the Hajj among rural Turkish Muslims:

> A particularly vivid symbol, capturing the imagination of millions of Muslims regardless of whether they have had firsthand experience of it or even of whether they are devout Muslims. In Turkish village life it looms large—as the quintessential journey and one that is recognized and legitimate. Villagers who have gone on the hajj bring back stories of their travels, and such exotic tales stand out in an environment where many have rarely even been to Ankara, the capital city, or the Mediterranean coast, let alone outside of Turkey. It occupies village activity and conversation for at least three months out of every year—the time before the pilgrims depart, the time while they are away, and the time when they return.[23] (1990, 514)

In this pre-internet example, we see the Hajj forming a potent narrative even among people who have not traveled much during their lives and how it becomes a topic of conversation as part of the seasonal rhythm of village life.[24] If we are to understand pilgrimage landscapes as made up of numerous fractals, as sites are replicated in new contexts and scales (Bajc, Coleman, and Eade 2007), then such narrative can act as one medium for the circulation and reconstitution of sacred centers.

A more recent study of the pilgrimage articulated both at and away from Mecca reveals it inhabiting an even greater range of social and semiotic forms. In calling the Hajj "an information journey," Nadia Caidi (2019, 44) examines the intersection of material, spiritual, and logistical practices incorporated into believers' everyday lives as religious subjects.

Caidi finds that for her young interlocutors, the pilgrimage recalls "nostalgic childhood stories and imagery, especially the representations of the Kaaba, omnipresent in most Muslim homes" (50).[25] Such sedimentation of memory (even for people who have not yet visited Mecca) is reinforced through recalling relatives who have performed the Hajj and who often brought back gifts of "Zamzam water (from a sacred well in the holy sites), boxes of dates, prayer mats or beads, incense, and other token items from the holy sites" (ibid.). The salient spaces of the pilgrimage are extended through reminiscences that bridge shrine and home while connecting different generations. Once people become actively involved in their own preparations to go, the process of imagining Mecca becomes even more dynamic (53). Caidi's interlocutors report becoming devoted to finding out how to do the Hajj properly, for instance through learning gender-appropriate actions and behaviors. The following remarks illustrate the combination of proximate and virtual sources typically consulted:

> On how to tie a hijab, I went to YouTube. That's where I learned how to do it. For the abaya [women's clothing], I spoke to my grandmother about it. She got the fabric for me and we got it sown. For health matters, my dad knew some things and we went to our family doctor. He helped us get prepared. My dad was my go-to source, as was my grandfather. (56)

The Hajj reverberates across relationships and institutions dispersed throughout the world (see also Buitelaar 2015, 18–19). As such, it not only contributes to the construction of religious subjectivity well before any trip is made but continues to be re-presenced in people's lives after they have come back home. Ingvild Flaskerud (2018) traces the ways in which the Hajj and other pilgrimage sites are invoked within a Shia mosque in Oslo through sharing of stories, references in weekly speeches, distribution of gifts, and so on. Narratives and other ritual behaviors associated with sacred journeys are "verbally and materially 'set in motion' as recollections and as desires for future actions, mediated in the location where Muslims live" (47). They come to figure prominently "in the lives of Muslims away from the pilgrimage sites . . . the mosque being a place in which . . . mediating pilgrimage [is] also an expression of caring for others' well-being" (52). What is being described here is not the storying of pilgrimage as mere representation of what may or may not have happened at a shrine; it is the translation of a pilgrimage sensibility into the life of the mosque and the ongoing practices, semiotic ideologies, and self-understandings of its members.[26]

A mosque provides numerous conventional cues to engage in pilgrimage imaginaries. In contrast, many returnees from the Camino encounter secular or spiritually highly diffuse contexts of reception. A similar social and linguistic infrastructure of continued presencing of the journey does not exist. The experience may be recovered through deploying and even displaying memory aids such as photos, the pilgrim's staff, the credential (i.e., the certificate indicating that the journey has taken place), diaries and so on (Frey 1998, 201). Some people form narrating communities or societies of fellow returnees (211), and van der Beek (2018, 34) comments that the thriving Dutch Society of Saint James, founded in 1986, provides an important space for personal storytelling that can revive the "Camino feeling."[27] Such reinstanciation of experience need not be seen as a purely conservative process of regaining that which has been lost. What a person shares narratively with others is likely to evolve over time. Frey notes that the narrator may come to see him or herself as a pilgrim only *through* retelling, so that "one is able to reinterpret, process the experiences, and create oneself as a pilgrim at the same time" (186). The gradual and relational re-presentation of the Camino to others has as much performative power as the original trip.

If the telling of stories is as much about gradually remolding speakers as it is about informing listeners or readers, similarly complex processes of identity construction are evident in the distribution of gifts on return from pilgrimage. Kaell (2012, 2014) traces the ways in which both Protestants and Catholics among American Holy Land pilgrims are faced with challenges of deciding how much to "show and tell" when they return. Middle-aged and older women tend to be those most involved in the purchasing and distribution of souvenirs.[28] Strategic giving—rosaries and statues for Catholics, objects with biblical quotes for Protestants—is aimed at family and especially children, and the donor has to judge carefully what to say in framing her intent. In Maussian terms, giving to others may assert a form of power, reinforcing generational hierarchy while promoting the benefits of deeper religious engagement. Thus Ella, a Catholic from Maryland, turns her offering into an attempt at mini-conversion when interacting with her grandchildren: "This is the time you really shape them by talking about it. . . . It's something that will give them a memory and spur them on in their faith" (2012, 143). In another way, however, such occasions express ambiguity over the identity of the giver. Many such women are beginning to lose parenting and economic authority over others, and thus the gift—as well as the pilgrimage itself—may reassert not only the independence of the pilgrim but also her continued role as a contributor to her family.

Kaell shows how giving blends with telling, even as she indicates how assiduously pilgrims may work to incorporate their trip into the social, spatial, and ethical relations of their home lives. It is instructive to compare this ethnography with another case study that comes from a very different cultural and religious context yet is also centrally concerned with the intermeshing of pilgrimage, gifts, and personhood. Erin Kenny (2007) bases her research in the Islamic West African city of Kankan, Guinea, a religious center whose citizens frequently journey to and from Mecca on the Hajj. Echoing Delaney (1990), Kenny establishes the salient landscape for the pilgrims whom she studies: "While most Christian notions of pilgrimage start in a certain place and 'go-forth' to another place, Muslim spatial orientations imagine both the point of origin and the act of return as central to the experience of pilgrimage" (364). Perceived in this sense, Eade and Sallnow's triad of coordinates must acknowledge not one but two places of significance: shrine *and* home. Kenny sees her interlocutors as operating in a context where personhood is more communally constructed than in the United States, so that the effects of piety routinely echo through established bonds of kinship, intergenerational obligation and moral identity (364). The returned pilgrim, acknowledged as a hajji or hajja, bestows spiritual capital on family members purely on the strength of having made the journey. They make public gifts to their imam and important friends and neighbors, while ensuring that more expensive items such as prayer rugs, elaborate clothing and *adthan* clocks (which chime at the call to prayer) go to relatives.

My juxtaposition of Kaell's and Kenny's works shows how person, place, and text are useful analytical prompts but have very different implications according to context. American returnees are less likely to come back to publicly acknowledged contexts of reception than their

Guinean counterparts. Nor can they expect that their friends and relatives will know much about the holy places that they have visited and
feel compelled to describe. At the same time, dynamics relating to identity and agency are significant in both cases if we return once more to
Bloch's (1991) image of initiates coming back, empowered, to engage and
transform the everyday world. Kaell documents a much more tentative
process than Kenney, but both authors highlight the performative effects
of the journey as they extended into other realms of activity and across
other lives.[29]

(R)e-presences

Explorations of the spatial and social rearticulations of pilgrimage away
from shrines point us to further questions concerning the role of social
media. In a remark that would initially seem to challenge the importance of having made a physical journey, Anastasia Karaflocka remarks
that "it is possible now for persons from any corner of the world to 'visit'
or perform a pilgrimage to a sacred place without stepping outside their
house" (2002, 284). Historically, such pilgrimages have, in fact, been
quite common, as domestic or other local spaces have provided proxies
of distant shrines.[30] Simulations of sacred journeys on the internet may
offer complete visual tours of sites.[31]

At the same time, there are worlds of experiential difference between
what Christopher Helland (2002) calls "religion-online," where information about a site is presented to what is assumed to be a passively
receptive audience/readership, and "online-religion," in which an active religious environment is created, permitting mutual interactions
and forms of worship *only* possible through an electronic medium.[32]
For instance, in a wide-ranging article concerning pilgrimages and
other rituals of Twelver Shia Muslims, Sabine Kalinock (2006) refers
to ways in which gender, class and ethnic identities may be concealed
on screen, defying behavioral boundaries in operation elsewhere. Similarly, Dženita Karić (2018b) traces internet use among Bosnian Muslims
located in Europe and North America, showing how platforms create
novel constellations of interaction, communication, and orientation.
For instance, striking shifts in patterns of authorship are discernible as
unprecedented numbers of female Bozniak authors publicize their pil-

grimage narratives, even if their writings "are usually shorter than those written by men and typically presented in form of an essay or series of vignettes rather than sustained travelogue" (62). Such sites also conjoin the multiple experiences of mobility salient to diasporic Muslims, celebrating both the ethnic homeland of Bosnia and the spiritual homeland of Mecca and Medina (61).[33]

Some sites create a pilgrimage presence by attempting to reproduce the on-the-spot experience of a given shrine (assuming it exists in a physical environment). Mark MacWilliams (2004, 26; see also Hill-Smith 2009, 237; MacWilliams 2002) documents the way in which an online version of Croagh Patrick in Ireland evokes the pilgrimage through video footage, complete with recordings of high winds and trudging feet. The capacity for websites to effect complex forms of transmediation is demonstrated powerfully by the short film *In the Court of the Beloved* (on Vimeo), which combines thousands of still images with ambient sounds that take the viewer along a number of different journeys, all ending in the shrine of a twelfth-century Sufi mystic called Nizamuddin Auliya. Viewers then enter "the physical space of the shrine; a unique nexus of marketplace, social space, and spiritual haven, where devotees come to offer their prayers and find a moment of reflection away from the din of Delhi traffic."[34]

The extensive efforts put into reconstituting original sites may, paradoxically, suggest that online representations can only ever be derivative of more experientially powerful, grounded experiences. However, online and offline practice can blend in powerful ways. Connie Hill-Smith refers to the "mutualising of spiritual practice between physically separate spaces" (2009, 3). An example of what she means is provided by the website My Virtual Camino, where the author/pilgrim Shemaiah Gonzalez describes how parishioners at St. James Cathedral in Seattle participate in a virtual Camino in the month leading up to the feast of the saint.[35] They pick up Camino passports after Mass before "making a commitment to the total miles we will walk each day or week," so that "each Sunday after Mass, we have our passport stamped." The resultant chain of mediations across different spaces is extensive. The Camino becomes re-presenced through rituals of parish life in the United States, as ritualized certification is granted to those who vow to engage in forms of sacralized mobility mimicking the European journey—in Gonzalez's words, as "we walk along, with our families and friends, or along community walks planned by fellow parishioners." In turn, such practices are represented on the website as examples for other parishes to follow, wherever they are.

Social media also permit dispersed constituencies to interact in real time. Hill-Smith (2009) refers to the use of Skype in some pilgrimage contexts, while the immediacy of Facebook, Twitter, and Instagram allows posts to be created quickly during a journey and for reactions from both fellow pilgrims and others to stream in almost immediately. Many internet platforms permit powerful forms of multiple address, as pilgrims send the same texts and images to fellow travelers, family and friends at home, and anonymous others simultaneously. Appealing to such dispersed constituencies may become part of the ongoing performance of the pilgrimage. Nadia Caidi, Suzan Beazley, and Laia Colomer Marquez's (2018) examination of "holy selfies" snapped during the Hajj or Umrah pilgrimage shows how such actions not only blur gender distinctions (they are taken by both males and females) but also engage a multiplicity of audiences, while defying the disapproval of Saudi authorities (8). These pictures fulfill the obligation of proving "I was/am there," demonstrating a personal presence at the Kaaba, the Masjid al-Haram (large mosque), or Mount Arafat. Posted online, they also provide narratives of spiritual journeys oriented toward both fellow Muslims and non-Muslims, projecting a positive message that takes on particular significance in a post-9/11 world (10). A sense of unbounded audience is built into pilgrimage practice itself (cf. van der Beek 2018, 162).

These observations take on particular significance in the context of major obstacles to global mobilities, such as wars and pandemics.[36] Worries over contagion seem to present a profound ontological threat to pilgrimage, removing possibilities of mass assembly, material encounter, sacralized presence, and embodied mobility. These challenges cannot be denied, but they are considerably reframed when pilgrimage is located within an expanded temporal and spatial field, extending beyond high-profile shrines and journeys into other media, other scales, in the creation of a pilgrimage sensibility. Numerous practices already present across the broad span of pilgrimage landscapes were brought into play in response to the emergence of the COVID-19 pandemic in the early part of 2020: the staging of proxy pilgrimages in "local" landscapes, the live streaming of services, the skillful management and choreography of micro-interactions at shrines themselves. In a piece called "Communion in Quarantine," Christopher Sheklian (2020) documented the reaction of Armenian Orthodox Christians to the question of how to stage Easter celebrations in 2020—a deep "problem of presence" for a "high liturgical" church committed to biblical narrative alongside a "robust sacramental life." One solution involved an internet service drawing together people located in numerous continents, oriented around an event run by a resident deacon and priest in a New York seminary. Another entailed a priest adapting traditional Antasdan Blessing of the Fields worship to social distancing by celebrating a service in a parking lot, surrounded by cars parked six feet apart. Through these practices, observes Sheklian, "piece by piece, we put the building blocks of liturgy into place" (ibid.). These Armenian Orthodox responses represent impressive adaptations to difficult circumstances, but they are not surprising. They draw on longer traditions of deploying ritualized behavior in flexible ways, stretching across the social, storied, and spatial distances that constitute much pilgrimage, which can be rendered through numerous scales and media of articulation. A pandemic may restrict certain forms of ritual mobility but catalyze others.

Narrating Presence and Distance: A Walsingham Story Cycle

This chapter has been concerned with how narrative mediates between presence and distance in pilgrimage. After an examination of stories oriented toward binding pilgrims to revered places and ritual sequences, I have followed the trajectories of tales as they have diffused away from the confines of conventional sacred landscapes, or in some cases as they been told without having a direct connection with any specific experience at a shrine. My analysis emphasizes certain themes. Stories express the pilgrim's memory of having been present on pilgrimage; but they also re-presence engagement in ways that extend the material and performative life of the journey across multiple domestic and institutional contexts. The Hajj is revived and relocated as it permeates the daily rhythms of a Turkish village, enlightens the sermons of an Imam in a Norwegian mosque, or is translated into the spiritual capital that flows through kinship, friendship, and political relations in a Guinean city.

Similarly, the Holy Land becomes a prolonged presence in the everyday life of American Christians, animating the gift from a grandmother to a child, making a scriptural reading come alive, or producing the intimate sensation of Jesus dwelling in the heart of the traveler. Pilgrimage as story, practice, and sensibility becomes both stretched and rearticulated.

In this final section, I explore ethnography that exemplifies these themes while taking appreciation of the co-constitution of pilgrimage and narrative to a further stage. I return to my fieldwork at Walsingham but also to other spaces where the Norfolk village is re-presenced through narrative and ritualized action. The case I examine entails entanglements and dialogues between tighter and looser versions of the Walsingham narrative, and it shows how narrators may sometimes desire not to overcome, but rather to establish, distance between present and past, self and shrine.

I focus on a small collection of narratives I gathered concerning a pilgrimage made annually by one extended family. At the beginning of this chapter, I noted that Victor and Edith Turner referred to the oppositions and homologies between stories associated with the Mexican shrines of Our Lady of Guadalupe and Our Lady of the Remedies. I subsequently argued for the powerful complementarity of ritualized dramas and histories enacted by young Israeli Jews in Poland and Christian evangelicals in the Holy Land. Here, I demonstrate the benefits of following a story cycle that is articulated at a much smaller scale, linked with complex tensions over kinship, belief, and obligation. I show how the social and spatial frames constructed by such stories help us reconsider the articulations among liminalities, lateralities, and penumbras.

These tales often sounded to me like born-again testimonies, though they were being voiced by people of Roman Catholic and High Anglican background. Peter Stromberg (1993) has referred to the ways in which narratives provided by evangelicals are often interpreted by listeners in referential terms, understood to be giving a more or less accurate account of things that have happened. What is often missed, he says, is that such accounts also create a ritualized speech event in the present, reconstituting the narrator's experience of conversion while incorporating the ambivalences associated with their lives as religious subjects. To some degree, such testimonies are not only about narrating a new life; they are also about negotiating unresolved distances from aspects of one's old or ongoing existence (see also Mitchell 2002, 142). There is much more to Stromberg's argument, but I have said enough to link it with my own aims: to show how my interlocutors' stories of Walsingham as place and experience are also stories of their own development as religious—and non-religious—subjects. Their accounts reveal speakers wrestling to establish both proximity to and distance from the canonical ritual and linguistic forms offered at the site. While at times they sound like testimonies, they are not purely individualistic accounts, since they are deeply embedded in complex relations of corporate belonging and obligation.

I introduce this Walsingham cycle by referring to a scene at a kitchen table in an unremarkable red brick house in the Norfolk village. I am interviewing an elderly Roman Catholic couple whom I shall call Dennis and Brenda.[37] I have been advised to talk to them by Paul, Dennis's distant cousin. Paul is a lapsed Catholic in his forties who occasionally comes to Walsingham—with considerable reluctance—when invited to take part in the impressive family pilgrimage that Dennis and Brenda put on every year. My first conversation with the couple started in the evening but stretched into the night, lasting nearly five hours and, I later realized, embodying the expansive hospitality they regularly offered visitors to Walsingham. Their stories spanned life trajectories that had drawn them toward both Walsingham and each other. Indeed, when I first met them, they were newlyweds. Dennis and his previous wife, Edna, had looked after a large family, but with their offspring having left home and retirement looming, they had known they wanted to be near Walsingham. Sadly, Dennis's plan of buying "a small cottage closer so that we could be where we originally wanted to be" was abandoned when Edna died. In the meantime, Brenda had converted to Roman Catholicism with her first husband, and after he passed away, she spent time in a convent. But she had always felt "this very strong, very, very strong message—Walsingham, Walsingham, you know, go to Walsingham." That feeling was confirmed when she came across the house in which we were now sitting. Brenda had been there only a couple of years before she and Dennis met. Dennis concludes, "To cut a long story short, we fell in love and we got married . . . and where should I come to live but in Walsingham."

Dennis and Brenda's story is deeply personal but reveals larger patterns—for instance, the fact that Walsingham regularly attracts retirees who settle there having spent many years coming as pilgrims. To finally dwell in the place is to achieve a permanent presence, removing distance between believer and shrine. Dennis and Brenda take advantage of their proximity, since they have responded to a suggestion originally made by Edna's father to institute a regular pilgrimage to the Roman Catholic shrine. When we initially spoke, Dennis had been carrying on the tradition for some eleven years, marking the Feast of Christ the King in November with a gathering of extended family that was steadily growing, reaching up to around one hundred people coming from all parts of England and comprising four generations, mostly Roman Catholic, with a few Anglicans and even a couple of Methodists. A bus would be hired to ferry many of them to the village. Everybody would then process down the holy mile (the road leading to the Roman Catholic shrine) carrying a statue of the Virgin normally kept in Dennis and Brenda's front hall and then participate in a public mass.

While it enables a regular gathering of family to be present at the Roman Catholic shrine, this pilgrimage has wider narrative resonances. As Brenda puts it, "Walsingham is, to me, an important place for unity . . . [which] unites all Christian people. . . . Lady Richeldis was told in the vision to build a Holy House of Nazareth. So that for all Christians who come here must be the center, and one day the prayer is that there'll be one shrine." She is referring here to the original site of the Holy House as the true center of the pilgrimage, and like many Roman Catholics she regrets that their current devotions are usually oriented toward a medieval chapel situated a little out of the village. However, the key point is that Walsingham has the potential to be a place of national Christian convergence, and this ambition is beginning to be realized, albeit at a small scale, by her and Dennis's efforts to unite their family with the shrine.

Paul—Dennis's cousin—and his wife, Donna, also told me their stories jointly, at their house in a city some distance from Walsingham.[38] Paul does not know Dennis well. Nor did he go on pilgrimage as a child. But he describes his London childhood as "full of church," adding, "I couldn't think of a distinction between doing things together as a family and being consciously Catholic." That worldview was fractured when

Paul lost his faith in his twenties, and he now feels decidedly ambivalent about being summoned back to be present at Dennis and Brenda's "pieties."

Donna, meanwhile, grew up in an Anglo-Catholic family in London, where church, family, and friends were united in a "very structured way, very much concerned about . . . ritual, hierarchy." She loved it, at least until she was fourteen, and she has happy memories of being taken to Walsingham by her mother as "a special kind of holiday" where it was "all very much tied in with seasons and all these sort of ritual things." However, teenage years brought rejection of Anglicanism, and nowadays she says, "You want to be quite clear that you're not part of that because you've given it up, because you've moved on." Still, she feels regret over "those sort of seasonal bits of punctuation" that she associates with faith.

For Paul and Donna, the family pilgrimage always presents a dilemma. Sometimes, when Dennis and Brenda's invitation arrives in the mail, they decide not to go. At other times, they make the trip but avoid certain activities; Paul talks of scooping up a restless child as a convenient excuse for avoiding the Rosary. Most striking are the vivid stories they told me, unprompted, of occasions when they engaged in what I am calling lateral activities, negotiating degrees of engagement, reshaping the orientation and ontology of pilgrimage and yet remaining—however tenuously—within its spatial penumbra and broader narrative and ritual frames.

Among Paul's accounts was an occasion when he arrived at Walsingham alone but chose not to join in. Instead, he placed himself to one side of the holy mile, by a disused railway track, and looked back toward the village. Standing there, he was eventually rewarded with a memorable vision:

> In the distance I saw this pilgrimage in between autumn hedgerows. . . . And my family doesn't dress up a lot, they're a sort of pretty dowdy lot, and they could have been from any era really. . . . It looked absolutely . . . magnificent, they were really processing in the pilgrimage along the lane in between the two hedgerows . . . and . . . they were my lot too, and I felt very comfortable with that, not being totally part of them but being close to them. . . . Then I walked down across the field and joined halfway, my mother was among the group and so I . . . walked with her the rest of the way.

Paul is initially dislocated from the pilgrimage, having avoided what Bloch (1974) might see as the juggernaut-like ritual sequence that requires the family to gather in the center of Walsingham before walking collectively to the Catholic shrine. His shift of stance from adjacency and vicariousness to engagement follows the realization that "this pilgrimage" is actually his family, somewhat transfigured by not being visually tied to any specific historical period. Paul's acknowledgment of "his lot" prompts him to engage in a provisional reconciliation with a procession that he knows will funnel him down to the Slipper Chapel and its formal rituals; he allows his laterality to be converted into liminality, his distance to turn into presence, as he realigns his feet, his rhythm, to the pilgrimage (Ingold and Vergunst 2008).[39] He thus allows himself to enter a ritual trap containing the liturgical devotions of his own rejected religious past. His experience contains echoes of the sequential coercion inherent in the journey of the enclaved Israeli students to Poland, or indeed of Bajc's description of the power of actively *performing* narrative within a storied landscape.[40] Anybody familiar with Pentecostal worship will also recognize the parallel with the altar call, when the person comes forward to a center of worship, as ritual engagement shifts from choice to obligation.

Paul tells of movement onto a path leading to a ritual center, mitigated by the fact that he is moving toward his mother as much as toward a pilgrimage. Donna's account, expressed as Paul sat with her, retains more of a sense of distance, albeit with an intriguing narrative twist. "It's unbelievably irritating," she begins, referring to "the 'one true religion' attitude of Catholics . . . because you want to go to an extended family event . . . and you want to take your own kids to be part of that . . . but at the same time if you're seen to do it . . . there's almost an unwritten statement that you're accepting all of that as well." Donna frustration points to the multistranded quality of the event. If Dennis and Brenda's hosting of the pilgrimage acts as a liturgical snare, it uses the seemingly non-religious bait of kinship to point toward the possibility of rekindling connections with ritual dispositions that Paul and Donna have consciously rejected, but which may lie dormant within them.

Much of the time, Donna just goes along with it all. But she also talks of adopting a more indirect, sideways approach—retaining traces of pilgrimage behavior while moving laterally into other material and relational landscapes that seem to have little to do with Walsingham yet retain subtle connections with the site. Donna had emphasized to me the link between her early faith and the power of seasonality, a force vividly expressed in her childhood memories of visiting a summery Walsingham with her mother. When I asked if she retained such ritual in her life, she did not refer back to the formal pilgrimage organized by Dennis and Brenda. Instead, she told me, "I have to fill myself with other things in order to mark the seasons":

> Fruit picking [with family] in July is always a sort of ritual I don't necessarily enjoy, but I feel, you know, bereft of something if I don't actually do it at least once, and a whole load of other things like that. . . . I find it quite an important way of marking different kinds of the year.

We might ask what connection picking fruit has with pilgrimage, but in Donna's explanation, the underlying temporal, spatial, and narrative intersections between the two emerge: the collaborative movement of the family away from the city into nature; the acknowledgment of seasonality; even the slight sense of obligation, although the decision to go on this family trip is made by Donna and Paul rather than being prompted by Dennis and Brenda. The very implicitness of the connections to formal pilgrimage is the point, indexing Donna's currently distanced stance toward her previous encounters with Walsingham itself. So again, the question of ritual entrapment and coercion is raised, but this time, Donna sidesteps its procrustean alignments through a creative form of lateralization. Notice how Paul's narrative results in his joining a demarcated pathway—a line marked out by a railway track, enclosed by hedgerows, and subject to the solemn pace of his family (cf. Ingold 2007). The affordances of this natural landscape become quite restrictive in their material implications, repaying something of Father Martin's confidence in the redemptive powers of the environs of the village. By contrast, Donna's fruit picking is far less prescriptive in the details of its physical requirements, other than the need to gather the crop. It is useful to understand her sideways move from shrine to orchard in the light of Webb Keane's (2013) discussion of "the religious work of transduction" in his consideration of how ritual relations traverse and mediate ontological difference. Transduction for Keane is not mere translation (9), since it is concerned with the shift from one semiotic modality to another, as happens, for instance, when divine words are rendered into script. My ethnographic focus is very different from Keane's, but I regard Donna as converting liturgy into something more informal yet highly significant, shifting canonical ritual form into loosely articulated family habit. She alters the ethical, ontological, and visual stakes of tradition by moving her family from a site of public religious surveillance into one of low-key anonymity. In doing so, she retains a hint of the rhythm and the "narrative arc" (Loustau 2019) of the Walsingham pilgrimage while moving a strongly Catholic ritual sensibility into a more broadly liberal, post-Protestant one. We saw how the evangelicals described by Bajc voiced their concerns over fetishizing place by emphasizing the ideal of creating a direct relationship with Jesus; Donna's more secular account echoes but also evades the tight formalities of ritual through an enactment of embodied labor, voluntarily undertaken.

To what extent, however, are Dennis and Brenda and Paul and Donna narrating a story cycle?[41] I have not gathered all the tales that could be told about their family pilgrimage; nor do I think that Paul and Donna have shared their accounts with other members of their extended family, though I am confident that they have revealed their stories to each other many times before. The significant point is that these accounts possess specific narrative features that reveal their role as testimonies, reconstituting and recalibrating personal orientations toward being present *at* Walsingham, while also being present *for* family.

Dennis and Brenda cocreate a biographical trajectory of coming ever closer to the site, reaching a state where they can claim that their domestic arrangements harmonize with their religious commitments. They have achieved a permanent presence at Walsingham, so that they no longer *perform* the landscape, they *inhabit* it. Temporary pilgrims have become permanent hosts. From that position, they work hard to create a pilgrimage that both echoes Catholic tradition and conjoins the twin demands of religious duty and family obligation. The pilgrimage to Walsingham is their gift to their extended family, whether the latter wish to accept it or not. They resemble Pentecostalists in their sense of mission, except that they work through attempting to bring others to a particular place, rather than focusing on the transnational conquering of space.

Paul and Donna's stories also begin by centering on Walsingham, but then illustrate ways of moving further from its liturgical hold—or attempting to do so. Paul's brings him back to the center, surrendering ambivalently and temporarily to conventional ritual sequence and alignment. Donna's story retains the narrative frame of a rite of passage, but the direction of the passage is now reversed, moving her and her family from the dangers of the sacred to the security of the secular as she carves out a route to a more mundane place of association. She and Paul are not only searching for degrees of distance from Walsingham's enactments of pilgrimage presence; they are also trying to unpick familial from religious commitments in negotiating the multistranded ritual trap (Gell 1996) that is being set for them, where it has been made to seem that religion and kinship cannot be separated.

Dennis and Brenda's "spiritually seductive" account is meant to move both narrators and listeners toward an appreciation of the virtues and the joys of the liminal and the centripetal in relation to the shrine. In contrast, Paul and Donna's tales of deconversion strain toward the lateral and the centrifugal. The older couple align their home and their lives with canonical narratives surrounding Walsingham, according to which the actions of a devout medieval woman built a replica of Jesus's childhood home and encouraged others to visit it. Adopting Eade and Sallnow's (1991) language, we might see the younger pair's actions as "contesting" such coercive narrative moves. Even so, such an analytical metaphor does not do full justice to their ambivalent movements and motivations, given their desire to achieve proximity to family while maintaining detachment from religion. Nor can Paul and Donna's participation easily be called liminoid; they are rather caught between distance and presence, and the result is a ritualized, awkward articulation with pilgrimage and family that feels chronically frictional (Tsing 2005): both perturbing and productive at the same time.

This troubled and partial collection of stories embodies much that we have been exploring in this chapter: the power of narrative to align pilgrims to places, sacred persons, and powerful sequences of action, but also the ability of pilgrims to distance themselves from such procrustean forces; the close entanglement of pilgrimage story with pilgrimage practice, so that the two cannot be kept apart; and the capacity of "telling tales" to convey and create pilgrimage presences beyond the confines of sacred shrines. Through Donna, we also observe the power of story to demonstrate how pilgrimage can be made to blur into other behavioral frames and rhythms that appear to have very different ontological and spiritual implications. This last theme is one that we resume in the next chapter, as we move toward examining the articulations between pilgrimage and other forms of contemporary mobility.

8

Enclaving and Entraining

Economies of Mobility

Pilgrimage Entangled

The anthropologist Pablo Alonso González (2018, 982) recounts a conversation he once had with Paco, a farmer from a Spanish village regularly visited by pilgrims making their way to Santiago de Compostela. González asks Paco whether he has ever been on the Camino and is told, "Yeah, I've walked it many times. Every day, with my sheep, up and down the road." Paco's terseness expresses the distance many locals feel from a famous pilgrimage that they perceive to be physically close but culturally remote. Whereas passing pilgrims toil along the Camino as a break from hectic schedules, for Paco, the same route constitutes a regular site of daily labor. Yet even in his sarcasm, Paco points to entanglements between two economies that coexist around the Spanish village: the agricultural and the spiritual. In doing so, he challenges the image of the path as sacred enclave by uncovering the varieties of mundane work and movement that intersect with the Camino in its guise as ancient heritage.

This chapter explores articulations between pilgrimage, mobility, and economy. It may seem obvious to bring these topics together, but they have not always been regarded as tightly conjoined. Viewed through idealized images of communitas, contemporary visits to shrines are not supposed to be sullied by commercial relations, just as popular and academic depictions of pilgrims on the move focus on exceptional moments of pious intensity—arduous slogs up mountains or solemn processions toward altars. These representations are dramatic but highly incomplete. It has become commonplace to say that other religious systems do not separate economy and politics from religion in the same way as Christianity (e.g., Cohen 1992; Reader 2015), but in practice,

Christians themselves do not necessarily adhere to such distinctions in their engagements with pilgrimage. An expanded approach to the field must also acknowledge the full range of mobilities entailed in visiting any site. Many who visit the Camino have almost certainly taken a plane to transport them to what they see as the start of their proper journey, yet discussion of the journeying that occurs before the explicit pilgrimage begins is largely absent.

There is already a well-established literature discussing relationships between pilgrimage and tourism, but much of such work has exacerbated the problem of viewing both through narrow analytical lenses.[1] Attempts to establish consistent, comparative criteria to distinguish pilgrimage from tourism risk essentializing both categories, while taking for granted the moral superiority of pure, non-commercial religion or "authentic" travel that can only be expressed through ascetic practice (cf. Badone and Roseman 2004; Cannell 2006).[2] One response to these questions of purity is to present shrines as retaining an inner core of sanctity, surrounded by commerce (e.g., Turner and Turner 1978). A more complex retort comes from Ian Reader (2015), whose work goes beyond the point of view of the traveler to take into account other interested agents, such as officials concerned with placemaking (14).[3] In criticizing the "recurrent tendency" to view manifestations of the material and the commercial as antithetical to religion (12), Reader shows how pilgrimages are often "embedded in a context of markets, consumer activity, publicity and promotion, and how they operate not just in the marketplace but through it" (8). Indeed, he notes that the close interweaving of the commercial and the sacred is recognized linguistically in Japan, given that the word *ennichi* conveys meanings related to holy days but also the idea of a market.[4]

Somewhat in line with Reader's approach, an important body of work has focused on the extensive and growing links between heritage and pilgrimage, placing attention not only on travelers but also on organizations—ranging from private corporations to national state regimes—whose job is to promote and supervise movements of visitors. Smita Yadav (2019, 2) raises the central question of whether "the potency of the sacredness of holy sites is enhanced in this era of globalizing capital," pointing to the ethical and logistical challenges of managing sacrality as both spiritual and economic asset.[5]

There is nothing new in claiming that pilgrimage sites prove profitable for their hosts (e.g., Adler 2002). The real challenge is to avoid replacing simplistic depictions of the idealized, spiritual purity of shrines with equally crude assumptions that solely economic motives are what really lie behind their operation. Reader's exploration of the expansive category of the market is an important step in this nuanced direction, though as an economic term, it does not capture all that is implied by perceiving pilgrimage as articulating with relations of production, labor, infrastructure, charity and gift exchange, all embedded within regional, national, and transnational flows of people, commodities, and capital.[6] Such processes form material underpinnings that enable or curtail different forms of mobility, including both the physical means of achieving movement and the regulatory powers of regional and national governments. In the twenty-first century, shrines and routes operate in a world of escalating exchanges and mobilities, combined with forms of economic deregulation often glossed as the neoliberal. Discernible alongside these trends are shifts in the scale and expression of mutual awareness and accountability, as governing regimes (national or clerical) react to questions posed by increasingly diverse and diffuse constituencies, ranging from formal courts of law to the rather less restrained judgments of bloggers.

A prime example of these trends is provided by the shifting landscape of Muslim pilgrimage. The neologism *hajjonomics* refers to the business of managing—and profiting from—the growth in numbers of people going to Mecca in recent decades.[7] Some commentators and planners predict that the Hajj will become central to plans to reform the basis of the Saudi Arabian economy, replacing reliance on the vagaries of oil prices with exploitation of revenue streams derived from pilgrims coming from all parts of the globe.[8] Such plans seem prudent at the level of national economy but raise contentious questions over whether it is justified to alter the fabric of the holy city of Mecca to create a more commercially oriented space. Robert Bianchi notes, "The indictment is not that Saudi Arabia has planned poorly, but that it has planned destructively by willfully despoiling an irreplaceable resource that—unlike their oil wealth—belongs not to them, but to all Muslims and to all humanity, including generations not yet born" (2013, 18). A theological layer of significance is also discernible in the Saudi attitude, given that Wahhabi clerics condemn certain behaviors—such as praying at tombs and touching holy objects—as heretical. These ethical complexities are illustrated in spectacular fashion by Saudi attempts to enforce forms of ritual discipline on pilgrims while permitting a hotel to be completed in 2011 that dwarfs the Grand Mosque and whose construction required the controversial demolition of an eighteenth-century Ottoman fortress.[9] The home page advertising the hotel in February 2020 gives a vivid flavor of what is at stake discursively, economically and theologically:

> A beacon for pilgrims in the heart of the Holy City.
> Located adjacent to the Masjid Al Haram, Makkah Clock Royal Tower, A Fairmont Hotel boasts a prime location as the closest hotel to Kaaba and yet the best for Umrah and Hajj. Standing as one of the world's tallest buildings with 76 floors, Makkah Clock Royal Tower, the focal point of the Abraj Al Bait Complex, part of the King Abdul Aziz Endowment Project, is the iconic symbol of hospitality in the Holy City. . . .
> Makkah Clock Royal Tower, A Fairmont Hotel, the architectural landmark located in the pulsating heart of the Muslim World, provides its guests with a unique opportunity to reside in elegantly furnished and superbly serviced residences with breathtaking views of Masjid Al Haram and the Holy Ka'aba.

Adopting a smoothly commercial tone, the text puts the hotel at the center of the Muslim world on the basis of its adjacency to the Kaaba, so that professional hospitality and ritual engagement are placed in direct proximity.[10] The Fairmont also makes its mark in another landscape. The tower is presented as the tallest building in Saudi Arabia (601 meters high), the fifth highest freestanding structure in the world, displaying the world's largest clock face. In effacing Ottoman history with a very different symbol of time, the construction becomes a material icon of urban development, a modernist marrying of private-sector ambition with Wahhabi governance and Saudi Arabian policies of nation building and progress.[11]

Mecca provides a high-profile illustration of the ongoing politics of placemaking that frequently surround sacred sites, as the religious, cultural and political capital associated with a famous shrine is deployed to address much wider landscapes of movement, labor and identity construction. Describing an equally politically loaded transnational field, David Geary (2018) has shown how the well-known Buddhist site of Bodh Gaya in northeast India provides a soft-power heritage resource for strengthening partnerships and creating formal bilateral aid arrangements across Asia, including collaborations with the Japanese government. These examples provide just two illustrations of shrines acting as key nodes within numerous strategic fields, and not merely those that look obviously religious.

Given what may be at stake, it is not surprising when pilgrimage "becomes subject to varied forms of control on the part of national churches, denominations, social movements, commercial enterprises, and regional and national governments, not to mention transnational organizations, such as UNESCO" (Coleman and Eade 2018, 3–4).[12] Pilgrimage's powerful links with both heritage formation and nation building must therefore be acknowledged, but the focus in this chapter is on mobility itself, on the ways in which sacralized journeys become entangled with wider fields of regulated and unregulated movement, involving the making and unmaking of borders. Included are such phenomena as migration, diaspora, and refugeehood, showing how pilgrimages encourage the mutual association of apparently very different economies and mobilities, creating fields of practice that dispel stereotypes of nostalgia or asceticism. Pilgrimage thereby becomes incorporated within a wider field of mobility studies, which "since the beginning of the new millennium . . . has shifted away from a linear conception of moving or a priori assumptions of sharp demarcations between different types of journeys" while recognizing that "mobilities interact with and are shaped by an equally diverse range of immobilities" (Amit and Salazar 2020, 1).

In light of this expanded frame, the image with which this book began of visitors viewing relics of refugees scattered around the nave of Canterbury Cathedral points to overlaps between worlds that are complexly conjoined. Such an approach to materiality and movement reinforces my recurring focus on the politics of attention and inattention. From the perspective of political economy, the very assertion of the set-apart character of sacred travel becomes a more or less conscious act of concealment. The laborious progress of the traveler who trudges along the

Camino while exercising the privilege of cosmopolitan mobility remains entangled with the shepherd tending his sheep but also with the halting trajectories of migrants, refugees, or asylum seekers who inhabit other landscapes, and who have little choice but to proceed slowly, or to come to a standstill, in their pursuit of a better life.

Pilgrimage, Mobility, and Political Economy

François Gauthier, Tuomas Martikainen, and Linda Woodhead (2013) maintain that a new form of cultural political economy has emerged in many parts of the world since the 1980s. Neoliberalization involves shifts from industrial to finance capital, and from large-scale production to consumption, global flows of people and things, dispersal of labor, and space-time compression (263–64). Such expanded market logic is often said to permeate numerous fields of social policy, from education to health care to welfare-state reform. Religion, too, becomes increasingly deregulated, transmogrifying not only into the commercial heritagization of sites but also into myriad individualized spiritualities and cults of authenticity (271; see also Taylor 1989).

There are dangers in seeing the neoliberal everywhere, taking its inevitability for granted, and permitting market metaphors to dominate social analysis. Here, the term remains useful to the extent that it highlights ongoing if uneven shifts in economies, spatial relations, and identities that inform contemporary modes of experiencing movement—as metaphor, aspiration, and embodied activity. It characterizes a period in history when the mobility of both people and capital has become a topic of acute self-consciousness and anxiety for political authorities, corporate bodies, and individuals.[13]

Some religious orientations are typically represented as adapting especially well—or at least energetically—to neoliberal conditions. Scholars have emphasized neo-Pentecostalism's spatial agility alongside its ready cultivation of close affinities between spiritual and economic aspiration; older behavioral restrictions are typically relaxed as believers search for prosperity, negotiating modern and postmodern cultural conditions while thinking of themselves as divinely empowered entrepreneurs (Bowler 2016; Coleman 2000). It has taken scholars longer to recognize ways in which pilgrimage intersects with trajectories of labor mobility and related economic processes, though exceptions exist.[14] Emanuel Marx's (2013) work on the Bedouin of Mount Sinai, originally published in 1977, revealed that most Bedouin men worked in insecure jobs and were away from their families for much of the year. In the absence of state infrastructures, regular pilgrimages throughout the Sinai region brought people together and helped "to make an alternative economy" (166).[15] Reflecting on ritualized activities in the vicinity of saints' tombs, Marx concluded that purely spiritual occasions were inconceivable, as were purely material ones (154). His point was not so much that markets emerged around shrines; it was that economy and pilgrimage could not be regarded as mutually distinct categories of behavior.

It is striking to compare Marx's conclusions with those of Carole Delaney (1990), writing about Turkish migrants over a decade later. Delaney focused on the annual trip people made home every year from parts of Europe where they had found work—a journey that formed an integral part of their lives yet appeared to be "conceptually invisible" (513) within much of the scholarly literature of the time. Delaney proposed that such semi-obligatory travel could be understood as a parallel to the Hajj (Turkish *hac*), but she also felt the need to explain why she was bringing together two terms—pilgrimage and migration—that "are not usually brought into semantic conjunction" and are generally "thought to refer to different areas of human experience and . . . to different, mutually exclusive fields of study" (ibid.).

In fact, at the very moment when Delaney was expressing such uncertainty, perspectives were emerging that expressed greater confidence over the co-location and even mixing of these categories. An edited volume published in the same year (Eickelman and Piscatori 1990a) juxtaposed pilgrimage with migration and subsumed both within the category of "Muslim travelers," while arguing for the need to recognize significant ambiguities in the meanings of journeying within Islam. Eickelman and Piscatori (1990b, 5) listed the varieties of travel (arguably) given some form of doctrinal support, ranging from the Hajj to the *hijra* (the obligation to move from countries where Islam is constrained) and occasionally even visits to local shrines (*ziyaras*) or exploration in search of knowledge (*rihla*). They added that still other forms of movement combining religious with economic motives were recognized within Islamic societies, ranging from trade to labor migration.[16]

It therefore seems no accident, despite Delaney's misgivings, that important work bringing pilgrimage into dialogue with varieties of mobility and economy should have emerged from studies of Muslim societies.[17] Social scientific writing on Christian pilgrimage in particular has generally taken longer to move toward understandings of pilgrimage as a multidimensional journey, though it has begun to catch up. Eade and Sallnow's (1991) volume helped to pave the way, despite its emphasis on shrines rather than mobility. Its long-term legacy may be its exploration of mixed motivations for Christian travel as much as its highlighting of contestation.

The apparent neoliberalization of economies in many parts of the world has been an important factor in making recognition of mobility as "both metaphor and process" (Urry 2000, 49), an increasingly constitutive dimension of social scientific description and analysis. Thomas Faist (2013, 1639–40) has explored the implicit ethical dimensions of this turn and the ways in which it suggests that movement is inherently valued, whereas fixity (including the sedentarism promoted by older models of the nation-state) comes to connote decline and disadvantage. Studies of religion have increasingly focused on varieties of mobility while acknowledging that such activity cannot be separated from other, equally fluid, spheres of action, even in the supposedly secular West. Not only have religious migrants been moving to Western, industrialized countries to take up work, but the category of religion has gained wider analytical purchase. A good example is provided by Claire Dwyer (2016) in a disciplinary overview titled "Why Does Religion Matter for Cultural Geographers?" She observes that religious topics were avoided by her colleagues in the late 1980s, yet this taboo lifted as the significance of religion in areas of public life ranging from "welfare, public space and social identity" was increasingly understood in terms of intersectionalities of social formations, power, and resistance (759). Geographers began to expand their horizons, exploring how multiple senses of the divine could be constructed through shifting assemblages of "movement, materialities and bodies" (760), often confounding (Western) sacred and secular divides.

Dwyer refers to religion as a whole, but her argument implies that pilgrimage can take on special significance given that it so obviously raises questions concerning the interlinking of place, embodied movement, and religious presence (see also Coleman and Eade 2004). Her argument reinforces the observations of James Clifford (1997) and Zygmunt Bauman (1996), discussed in chapter 1, who emphasize the usefulness of pilgrimage as analytical category in an age of heightened mobility. It also indicates ways in which studies of pilgrimage can become central to debates over religion and globalization that have more conventionally been dominated by political scientists (Singh 2013, 285).

Even so, an important irony accompanies the reemergence of pilgrimage as significant practice and object of study in mobile, post-secular contexts. The very impulses that provide pilgrimage with new salience also disrupt the analytical coordinates out of which influential models of pilgrimage have been fashioned. Delaney wrestles with this problem as she wonders how appropriate it is to bring together pilgrims and migrants, but the theoretical and methodological challenges are more fundamental. While they say little about pilgrimage, Nigel Rapport and Andrew Dawson argue in *Migrants of Identity* (1998a, 5) that previously resonant metaphors of transition and transformation lose much of their power when "cultures are not seen as separate entities that can be entered and exited." The exceptionality of the experience of moving between supposedly bounded spatial and behavioral realms (or indeed centers) is diffused when movement becomes chronic and when such realms become regarded as porous or unstable. Following John Berger (1984), Rapport and Dawson (1998b, 27) also argue that fixed notions of home are disrupted as the experience of dwelling becomes delinked from space and instead is located in routine sets of practices. Their claim speaks well to the experiences of the migrants discussed by Delaney, who negotiate between two unstable places of habitation through falling back on the ritual idiom of the Hajj as orienting metaphor. The latter seems effective not only because of its positive religious and cultural associations but also because it combines familiarity with mobility.[18] Rapport and Dawson's thesis also complicates the assertion, explored in this book through the work of Ann Gold (1988), Nancy Frey (1998), and Hilary Kaell (2014) that pilgrimage studies must take the domestic context of pilgrims' lives into account. Such an approach has helped expand the pilgrimage field by allowing home to provide a stable baseline from which to interpret the movement of the pilgrim; but homes themselves (like shrines) may be in flux.[19] This observation is acutely relevant to Delaney's interlocutors, and it applies to the lives of many of the other pilgrims explored in this chapter.[20]

Rapport and Dawson's perspective is useful, though it has limitations. Chronic movement is hardly a new phenomenon (Dubuisson and Genina 2011; Ingold 2007, 75), even if it cannot always be equated with urban cosmopolitanism. Furthermore, Rapport and Dawson sometimes overemphasize the ubiquity of the peripatetic, agentive, flexible individual (Heller 2000, 7), downplaying situations where access to movement is denied, or where resistance to it involves risky self-assertion.[21] As David Heller remarks (2000, 4), there are times when forcible eviction of a population becomes akin to imposed settlement, given that both constitute authoritarian restrictions on people's desires as to where they should live. Or, as Manuel Vásquez (2008, 179) complains in his analysis of "religion in motion," work on mobility and globalization has theorized experiences of social openness much more than those of social closure.

Migrants of Identity nonetheless emphasizes the vital point that movement remains a polythetic and heterogeneous category of experience and action (Rapport and Dawson 1998b, 23) that continues to evolve. This being so, pilgrimage must be understood not only in relation to modified categories of home, transition, and center but also through renewed appreciation of how it catalyzes, conjoins, and blends different forms and scales of mobility—secular travel with sacred procession, migration with return to sacred centers, liturgy with labor, and so on. The work that goes into the creation or occlusion of such conjunctions should be a central theme within an expanded understanding of the field. Stanley Blue (2017, 15) highlights a similar issue when he reconsiders Lefebvre's work on rhythmanalysis and asks "how exactly do connections between practices become more and less entrenched, more and less densely and complexly established?" His response is to show how activities that might in other respects be seen as "discrete spatiotemporal entities" are "linked by understandings, rules, teleoaffective structures, material arrangements, and interwoven timespaces" (5). Blue poses questions highly pertinent to the study of pilgrimage, whose status as a distinct spatiotemporal entity must coexist alongside its articulations with practices such as tourism, migration, refugeehood, and so on.[22]

My challenge is to outline diverse economies of mobility associated with pilgrimage and to demonstrate their impact on the making or denying of spatiotemporal connections and disconnections. The two stances I examine illustrate different ways in which pilgrimage establishes rhythmical practices across space and time.[23] While "enclaving" entails the work of erecting boundaries between pilgrimage and other regimes of travel, toil and governance, "entraining" reaches out explicitly into such realms in order to engage with them. Both articulate pilgrimage through managing its relationships with other fields of action, and both highlight certain kinds of connection at the expense of others. Despite their contrasts, they both position pilgrimage as a dynamic practice at the center of the creation, control, and coordination of multiple spatiotemporal sensibilities in the contemporary world.

The Pilgrim's Process: Enclaving

We have already encountered a conspicuous example of enclaving in this book. Jackie Feldman (2002) writes of how Israeli students visiting historical sites in Poland are channeled along particular spatial, temporal, and social lines.[24] A guard as well as a guide police the students, who undergo a carefully sequenced journey as they move between sites of Jewish victimhood. The ritualized enclaving described by Feldman is hardly subtle, but it may be effective in promoting identification with the Israeli state project. In its controlled orchestration, the journey of these students seems the behavioral opposite of another type of pilgrimage also occurring in Europe—that of the Camino. No sentries are called upon to protect travelers to Santiago de Compostela from the locals, and pilgrims from round the globe pride themselves on their openness to each other and to the landscape and nature. Whereas Feldman's informants spend much of their time gazing at Poland from within the confines of a bus, walkers along the Way see themselves as literally in touch with their surroundings. I want to argue, nonetheless, that even such unhurried travelers engage in enclaving activities that are highly delimiting and raise significant questions concerning citizenship, economy, and regulation of movement. While I focus on the Camino, my argument has resonances for the types of pilgrimage that it influences or echoes, where pilgrims in places as far apart as Japan and Brazil are oriented toward pathways rather than centers, generalized spiritualities rather than overt religiosities, and forms of slow movement articulated in opposition to, and yet interlinked with, experiences of hypermobility.[25]

I begin by exploring a specific trip that involves enclaving while also celebrating fluidity and freedom, and which touches on themes evident in many other narratives of travel to Compostela. In an article called "The Accidental Pilgrim," journalist Elatia Harris recounts an interview with the travel writer David Downie and his partner, the photographer Alison Harris.[26] The focus is a journey that the couple have made along the Camino to mark their respective fiftieth birthdays. David emphasizes that neither he nor Alison is a conventional Christian: "The purpose of our trek was many-fold. It wasn't a religious pilgrimage. . . . It was about rediscovery, discovery, regeneration, it was about history and linkages between past and present, between my life in France and my ties to America—and more." If the trip invokes history in both societal and biographical senses, it also uncovers other kinds of temporality:

> Put it this way—our relationship with time and place evolved. When we first set out I had this infernal talking pedometer, and I was often checking it to see how far we'd gone. I was concerned about getting to a B&B before nightfall, or finding food or water or coffee. . . . But Alison was never in a rush—she operates on Walk-About Time. After a few weeks I lost the pedometer—thank god—and then I lost my sense of time, except for following the light and darkness and the moaning of my stomach. It was one of the many wonderful transformations along the road. . . . The hardcore pilgrims have a saying. . . . In essence the first week is all about your body, the second week is about your mind, the third is when the spirit starts to free itself up. Now, as a skeptic, I can say that this little ditty irritated me no end at first. But in my case the ditty came true. In the third week something unexpected did happen. If for no other reason than this I would do a walk of this kind again, to resynchronize myself with the paradoxical timelessness of natural time. I actually feel, now, that time has no beginning and no end, that our ideas of time are mostly guesswork and a muddle.

David is describing largely the same path as that referred to by Paco, but it is not only the writer's prolixity that contrasts with the shepherd's pithiness. The journey is presented as hard work—no easy *feet*—though in its voluntary character, it bypasses the conventional labor involved in either choreographing liturgy or herding sheep. The effortful movement of the traveler catalyzes a redefined (and refined) sense of the temporal: an embodied cultivation of what—with apologies to John Bunyan (1678)—we might call the pilgrim's *process*. By the latter, I mean an embracing of change that is oriented toward personal development and acceptance of the inherent virtues of chronic self-transformation.[27] While it involves a degree of discipline, it is far from a surrender to the embodied alignments entailed in formal, arthritic (Bloch 1974), ritual participation. I first described a processual attitude toward the self in chapter 5, when I depicted the Camino and similar pilgrimages as offering resonant experiences of becoming.[28] The processual attitude is reinforced by deploying new ways in which to index personal development. For instance, as with many of the pilgrims described by Nancy Frey (1998), the evolution of David and Alison's relationship with time and place involves replacement of a mechanical, prosthetic calculation of progress (epitomized by the cursed pedometer) with a new awareness of diurnal rhythms and bodily needs. Their endeavors are productive not of prayer but of emergent experiences of connectivity that operate at different scales; resynchronization with the "timelessness of natural time" is claimed alongside new appreciation of the linkages between past and present, France and America. This being the Camino, such experiences generate more words (a different kind of work): not only Elatia Harris's article, but also a book on the journey by David (Downie 2013).

David and Alison represent prime examples of Rapport and Dawson's "migrants of identity" as they negotiate between different homes and transitions. In doing so, they demonstrate how the processual can intersect with the porous in the remaking of the traveling persona. As I noted in chapter 6, the philosopher Charles Taylor (2007) contrasts the modern, "buffered" self, separated from others, with a notion of the "porous" self that is more open to external influences, including wider cosmic forces. However, such porosity can also be experienced through encountering the sheer physicality of moving through a landscape. Even for avowedly secular pilgrims, the Camino offers the opportunity to lower barriers between passing traveler and proximate place, and this sentiment is certainly implied by David's reference to the shift in focus from body to spirit as he resynchronizes with natural temporality. His and Alison's trek along the Camino also becomes a fluid commentary on other movements that they have made throughout their lives that have generated the resources as well as the desire to take time out to go on the Camino.

David's reference to the pilgrimage's capacity to make connections between his different geographical affiliations, spanning Europe and America, has a very different tone from the homecoming journeys by Turkish workers described by Delaney. In David's eyes, the Camino offers opportunities for exploration through the idiom of the path. While he muses that he may do a walk "of this kind" again, it is far from certain that it will be back on the Camino, since he has a world of other routes to choose from. In the case of economic migrants returning home to see their family, by contrast, the Hajj provides a trusted frame of interpretation that guides them between two relatively fixed points, two types of belonging. For the former, the pilgrimage is about the journey; for the latter, it is about reaching designated places. A broadly parallel contrast is described by Tim Ingold (2007, 75) in his distinction between two modalities of travel that sketch out different lines in the landscape. "Wayfaring" describes the experience of following trails on the ground, often prompted by the footsteps of others, through active (and, we might speculate, more porous) engagement with the environment. The person becomes constituted by movement as they develop a heightened awareness of "the country that opens up along [the] path" (78). "Transport," on the other hand, is a preplanned form of navigation, often conducted in a hurry and focused on destination.

Central to the making of David's and Alison's journey as a form of wayfaring is a method of travel that requires them to take responsibility for their own movement. Alison exemplifies "walk-about time," embodying a technology of the self that has made the Camino such a resonant source of becoming for many of its travelers. Cara Anthony (2018, 1) characterizes protracted walking along the Camino as embodying "resistance" to "hypermobility" through adoption of "the least valued mode of transport in the industrialized world." While Anthony writes from a self-consciously Christian perspective that contrasts the kinetic demands of spirituality with those of secular commerce, Keith Egan (2010) invests walking the path with a broader phenomenological significance as a "trope that expresses existential issues in a bodily idiom" (107).[29] Not all the people whom Egan describes are as foot-loose as David and Alison since many are seeking relief from feelings of stagnation or depression, but they still possess the resources needed to engage in slowed-down practices of "reclaiming time" (109). In this vein, Egan draws on the writer Rebecca Solnit to present the Camino as generating opportunities for "a productive wastefulness conducive to self-becoming" (Solnit 2002, xiii; quoted in Egan 2010, 109). Elsewhere in her text, Solnit describes recreational walking as an alternative to "Si-syphean gyms" that "remove space as a coordinate of exertion" (2002, 261), and her sentiment parallels David's satisfaction at being released from his pedometer as he learns to focus not on a machine but on nature (cf. Coleman and Kohn 2007) .

In reflecting on how such commentaries relate to economies of mo-bility, we must step back briefly from pilgrimage and reflect on wider histories of pedestrianism. As the considerable success of Solnit's book *Wanderlust* (2002) indicates, traveling on foot has a rich cultural past but also a deep appeal in the present, despite or perhaps because of what An-thony sees as its lack of conventional economic value. A British counter-part to Solnit's bestseller is Robert Macfarlane's *The Old Ways: A Journey on Foot* (2012), which examines drove roads and track ways in Britain and beyond. An interest in connections between motion and reflexivity, walking and narrative—replaying old debates over links between body and mind—unites these authors.[30] Thus, Macfarlane begins his text by claiming, "This book could not have been written by sitting still. The relationship between paths, walking and the imagination is its subject, and much of its thinking was therefore done—was only possible—while on foot" (xi).

While their texts have nostalgic appeal, Solnit and Macfarlane do not shy away from the political and economic dimensions of walking. Macfarlane, for instance, describes the *sarha* of his friend Raja Sheha-deh, a Palestinian lawyer, around the hills of the Ramallah region. This Arabic term originally referred to letting cattle out to pasture (reminis-cent of Paco's words) but then became a way to describe a form of wan-dering without any fixed plan. In the context of Israel's surveillance of Palestinian territories, it was further resignified by Raja into resistance—deploying roaming as "a way of defeating the compression of space of the Occupation" (Macfarlane 2012, 213; cf. Meneley 2019; see also She-hadeh 2007).

Practices like the *sarha* demonstrate not only the performative power of walking but also the ways in which its connotations shift over time as economies of mobility change. Ingold (2004, 321) notes that for most people in Britain in periods before paved roads and public transport, walking was not a means of self-development so much as the only way to get anywhere. The few who could be classed as recreational travel-ers preferred not to walk (Wallace 1993), and in the eighteenth century, European elites often wrote about their travels as if they lacked the need to exert the lower halves of their bodies: "Skimming across the surface of the country, they would alight, here and there, to admire the view" (Ingold 2004, 322). Only in the subsequent century did walking become a prime activity for people self-consciously at leisure. Virtue combined with vigor as exploring the countryside on foot became de-fined in opposition to urban and even industrial regimes of time, work and space—ironically facilitated by technological developments in mass transport, such as the train (cf. Barush 2016; Ingold 2004, 322; Wallace, 1993, 65–66).[31]

This brief excursion into varieties of pedestrianism indicates how doing the Camino shares features with a longer history of recreational walking, one that emerges out of the development of Western leisure itself as distinct temporality and activity.[32] While following the path shares certain features with wayfaring, it differs from some of the ethno-graphic and historical examples provided by Ingold in its choice of "inef-ficient" locomotion despite the ready availability of other methods. Such deliberate wastefulness nods toward more overtly religious forms of sac-rifice, bridging religious and non-religious frames of reference. Proceed-ing on foot to Compostela—as along other pilgrimage pathways, such as the burgeoning late modern Lutheran trails in Sweden described by Anna Davidson Bremborg (2013)—offers spiritually inflected forms of becoming in spaces held adjacent to, but at one remove from, religious institutions.[33] It also mediates between tighter and looser spaces (Franck and Stephens 2007). I originally adopted these categories in chapter 6 in my descriptions of how formal liturgical frames coexist in cathedrals with less obviously focused forms of ritualized behavior. My point now is that walking the Camino involves complex negotiations between the tight and the loose. Following a path is emphatically not the same as participating in a formal procession toward an altar, and its practitioners often deny that they have a fixed endpoint. Yet it remains largely confined within the borders of a given route, demands effort from those who undertake the journey, and falls into distinct, repetitive rhythms and cadences.

Camino walkers generally aim to achieve separation from the worlds of commerce and hypermobility, deploying a "polemics of movement" (Frey 1998, 17) that pits pedestrian authenticity against motorized transport. As we saw with David and Alison, they may also claim new capacities to bond with their immediate surroundings, developing a new "somatic mode of attention" (cf. Csordas 1993; Österlund-Pötzsch 2010): David's "resynchronization" is paralleled by the way Nancy Frey's interlocutors reference a "direct relationship . . . to ultimate reality" (Frey 1998, 31). Nonetheless, I want to argue that further dimensions of enclaving are at play, which point to the presence of more exclusive and excluding economies of mobility.

Spiritualized walking has dominated recent popular and academic discourses about the pilgrimage to Compostela. Not only car and bus drivers but even cyclists are sidelined in this foregrounding of a certain form of ethical journeying, as the body in effortful motion is represented as the purest and most virtuous means of movement. Such stories are eloquently crafted by those who may already possess a powerful voice in other spheres of life. Shifting analytical focus from pilgrims to administrators reveals a further negotiation between what is foregrounded and what is obscured along the Way. The interview with Paco forms part of Pablo Alonso González's examination of how authorities use the Camino to reverse the depopulation of rural areas of Northern Spain (2018, 969). Since the early 2000s, the government in Castilla y León, the region where Alonso González carried out his fieldwork, has come to define the pathway less as an intangible, common good and more as a material, measurable asset that can be deployed to direct flows of pilgrims toward hotels, shelters and restaurants (977–78). Other systems of finance have also come into play. European Union rural development funds have supported such regional regeneration, reinforcing the return of former inhabitants who had left to seek better lives in urban centers but who now wish to restore houses or build second residences in their family villages. Old homes have become new assets for people who have become mobile citizens. Given these changes, less entrepreneurial villagers remain ambivalent toward the active presence of the Camino in the local economy, given its displacement of other systems of value (ibid., 971).[34] The attitude of Paco toward the Camino becomes understandable as he is sidelined by a path that runs through his community but has been restored for others to use. Equally ironically, it turns out that some outsiders—experts in the search for the "truly" authentic—have become wise to the mass production of heritage. Indeed, the book that David produces about his trip advertises itself as following "age-old trails through France rather than the commercialized Spanish route."[35]

This remolding of the Camino has made its mark on the landscape and economy of northern Spain. Frey (1998, 14) refers to the "reanimation" of the pilgrimage, while Alonso González (2018) calls his essay "The Camino Is Alive."[36] Such regeneration is sparked by the powerful conjunction of two apparently separate economies of mobility. The desire to explore spaces of becoming on the part of individual pilgrims resonates with the strategies of various levels of government to encourage visits to neglected geographical regions. Both constituencies support a vision of large swaths of rural landscape being laid open to travelers. Frey (1998, 14) notes, for instance, that one of the reasons for the promotion of the Camino by the EU is its embodiment of the notion of a "borderless Europe" where the Eurocitizen is "supposed to move freely" (ibid., 69). Indeed, José Chemin (2016, 25) argues that the heritagized pilgrimage addresses the cultural conundrum of an increasingly multicultural continent, using the Way of St. James "to naturalise the idea of Europe as an evolutionary consequence of history" (34). What is being promoted in this rebranding of the route is not just Europe per se but also a frame of transnational governance that enables apparent flows of bodies to occur.

In this perspective, pilgrimage produces the very opposite of an enclave, emphasizing the "breaking down of political and social borders on a pan-European scale" (Frey 1998, 14). It supposedly promotes an image of frictionless motion in relation to traversing regions and nations; a material infrastructure that facilitates free movement through the countryside. Yet in practice, participation in the Camino is revealed as an act of privilege, entailing progression through a politically and economically gated path (Peña 2011; Vásquez 2008). The likes of David and Alison, or the pilgrims referred to by Anthony (2018) who self-consciously resist hypermobility, generally do so from a position of being able to access swift travel in other parts of their lives. Some pilgrims are undoubtedly aware of their good fortune and of the existence of other, very different trajectories of movement that can also be traced around the continent. Here are the words of another David, a Fordham University history professor who reflects on his journey to Compostela, writing in May 2016:[37]

> I mark the actual beginning . . . neither in New York nor Spain, but in Munich, Germany. Strange as that seems, the Way of St. James (*Jakosbsweg*) goes through Germany and Munich's St. James Square (*Sankt Jakobs Platz*). In that square, the city and the Jewish community of Munich in 2006 dedicated the new synagogue Ohel Jakob (Jakob's Tent) to replace the temple deliberately destroyed in the Pogrom of November 9, 1938, known to some as 'the Night of Broken Glass' (*Kristallnacht*). . . .
>
> The synagogue stands now in the center of the square and next to the Catholic Church of St. James (*Sankt Jakob*), also rebuilt after being destroyed by American and British bombs in World War II. The two buildings remind us of our good fortune—our luck–in being able to choose, freely, to walk along the Way. For much of human history, peoples have been forced to wander and migrate—to undertake forced pilgrimages to unknown lands and unwanted fates. Whether of Africans ripped from their homes and shipped across the Atlantic in the seventeenth century, or Jews hauled in train cars to work and death camps in the twentieth, migration and wandering have been a common part of human experience and misery.
>
> Today, a new forced migration has brought wave upon wave of unwilling pilgrims to Europe, to Germany, and yes, to Munich, where their final reception, though a credit to the city at least for now, remains uncertain.

This narrative connects the Camino to a ramifying set of spatial and historical contexts. The close juxtaposition of different regimes of movement, from refugeehood to migration to pilgrimage, points to the troubled historical circumstances that spurred European unification in the postwar period. It also indicates the political challenges of the present in a Germany—and a Europe—where the reception given to refugees is uncertain once more. Unlike travelers on the Camino, the latter do not have the luxury of celebrating chronic movement over final arrival; they search not so much for becoming as for permission to remain.

Some narratives go further in using pilgrimage to think of those seeking refuge. A North American woman reflects ruefully on an online Camino forum from 2018 that she has "bragged" of trekking a thousand kilometers even as a caravan of people fleeing poverty and violence in Central America has been attempting to cover the three thousand kilometers to the United States border.[38] Despite complaints from others that the discussion is becoming too political, one of her interlocutors notes that when she undertook the Camino in 2014, she took one hundred kilograms of clothing and blankets as donations to a refugee organization. As with the *Suspended* exhibition at Canterbury, these clothes may act as proxies of humans, but in this case, they function not as relics but as gifts, retaining their original use-value while establishing material links between different experiences in an era of hypermobility.

Thus, walking the Camino does not preclude the possibility of cultivating broader perspectives. Nonetheless, trekking along the Way makes a virtue out of focusing in an enclaved manner on reflexive embodiment, biographical connection, and proximate landscape. A self-consciously grounded point of view is framed by a heritage infrastructure that is wasteful of time and space but enables uninterrupted motion on the part of the walker. Such walking offers a ritualized means to translate lives marked by rapid transport into exemplars of virtuous toil, and it focuses attention on embodied, porous wayfaring in ways that many participants find powerful. The escape being enacted is more ethically complex than might first appear, however. It enshrines a restless search for becoming as central ideals in an era when fluidity of existence is made to seem desirable among those who can afford to embrace process as a means to progress. In so doing, it reinforces rather than resists dominant economic paradigms that favor mobile capital and flexible labor, alongside a constant working to better the self. What seems like pure escape looks, from another angle, deeply entangled with mainstream norms in its economic and ideological implications.

Bearing the ethical ambiguities of enclaving in mind, it is time to shift orientation toward an alternative and complementary view of the rhythms and articulations formed—or reformulated—by pilgrimage. I move to examine cases where agency over movement is less clearly defined or available, yet where people are anxious to connect with, rather than escape from, societal structures.

Only Connect: Entraining

The verb *to entrain* is rarely used in common parlance, but it has useful associations. Merriam-Webster defines it as the power to draw "along" or "after oneself," together with notions of influencing temporal phases and rhythms.[39] The term *entrainment* was deployed by geographers Don Parkes and Nigel Thrift (1979; see also Blue 2017) to highlight how different cycles of human activity move toward synchronization. In their words, "certain rhythmic events perform the role of pacemakers because through their reliable periodicity . . . they pace either a single behaviour or a constellation of behaviours" (Parkes and Thrift 1979, 360)—as, for instance, an industrial plant may entrain local neighborhood life into its patterns of operation through the way it influences the daily routines of large numbers of people. Where numerous rhythms are juxtaposed, relations between different cadences may eventually be resolved in favor of a single, common tempo (362), but they may also remain frictional and awkward (Byron 2020; Edensor 2016; cf. Tsing 2005).

Such synchronization is reminiscent of David Downie's account of his gradual reengagement with "natural" rhythms on the Camino, but while Downie's experience remains embedded within privileged zones of travel, I use the notion of entrainment to consider contexts marked by very different forms of striving, where pilgrimage plays an active and politicized role in linking different forms of mobility and rhythm. Such connections may involve synchronization, but they are as likely to entail temporal relationships that are awkward and stuttering yet socially and ritually consequential. Entrainment resonates with my depiction of pilgrimage as a form of seduction (cf. Di Giovine and Picard [2015]), but rather than considering individual travelers drawn however unwillingly into the ritual orbits of shrines, I now refer to situations where whole pilgrimage complexes are created that actively seek the possibility of becoming entangled with wider institutions and socio-spatial arrangements. For the mobile, often vulnerable groups on whom I focus, entraining asserts temporal links and historical lineages where they might not have existed or been acknowledged before.

I begin to illustrate my argument by reanalyzing a number of ethnographic cases that connect with the Camino in complex and indirect ways. The routes to Compostela draw on a largely European history of Spanish Catholicism that runs from the medieval period to the current day, culminating in forms of devotion that shade into varieties of spirituality, heritage, and self-cultivation. Rather different experiences of mobility are discernible among Spanish-speaking communities of the New World, whose past is rooted in European forms of colonialism and whose present often blends economic migration with refugeehood. The three cases I consider involve Latinx populations—people of broadly Latin American heritage living in the United States—who are engaged in chronic negotiations over borders, political agency, and civic identity within their adopted country.

My first example goes back to the work of Thomas Tweed, but not to the arguments of *Crossing and Dwelling* (Tweed 2006). Rather, I refer to *Our Lady of the Exile* (1997), which provides a detailed analysis of the diasporic religion of Cuban exiles embodied in a shrine in Miami dedicated to their patroness, Our Lady of Charity.[40] Dedicated in 1973, by the 1990s, the shrine had grown into the sixth largest Catholic pilgrimage site in the United States, attracting hundreds of thousands of pilgrims each year—all the more impressive because in their homeland Cubans had not been particularly devout by Latin American standards (Rey and Stepick 2013, 24). The shrine is located in Florida but is ritually and architecturally oriented toward an island situated two hundred miles to the south. On her feast day, thousands come to observe the Virgin processing to the altar (130). By standing in front of their patroness's image, these pilgrims are positioned in a line that points directly toward Cuba (101). Furthermore, under Our Lady's altar are placed earth, stone, and sand from the island's traditional provinces, cast with water originally brought by fifteen refugees who died while trying to make their way to the United States. Cuban exiles therefore both map and inscribe the landscape and history of the homeland on to a new and urban environment, constituting a form of "geopiety" (87) through "transtemporal" and "translocative" symbols that convey people imaginatively to a place of memory and desire. As microcosm of the island, the shrine even provides a way of making new citizens: to be brought to it as a child is seen as a way of becoming Cuban (1997, 119).

Tweed offers a finely layered account of a sacred location while tracing the interrelated forms of mobility that animate its construction and use: the involuntary, unpredictable, risky movements of exile that brought the first refugees and migrants; the much more orchestrated and regular visits to the shrine at significant parts of the year; the procession of the Virgin, who is carried at a stately pace. As history is turned into ritual, different cadences are entrained with, but not reduced to, each other. The shrine becomes a catalyst for controlled, liturgical movement while serving as a permanent reminder of a foundational event of chaotic displacement, involving the terrors of refugeehood.[41] It is no mere enclave, separated from wider contexts of history or economy. What ultimately unites the actions Tweed describes is the ritualized emphasis on a horizontal rather than vertical plane (1997, 97). Participants are oriented outward and across social realms, but they combine spatial breadth with temporal depth as they express what it means to be identified with multiple homes.

Our Lady of Exile presents pilgrimage as being situated both at the center of a community and within a transnational field of action where politics, ritual, and history are not easily separated. Similar complexity is manifested in Elaine Peña's (2011) ethnography of pious devotions performed by Latinx Catholics in honor of the Virgin of Guadalupe. The disparate locations explored by Peña tell a powerful story of multi-sited connectedness (17): the famous shrine in Mexico City, founded in 1531; its replica in Des Plaines, Illinois, established in 2001; but also a vulnerable sidewalk shrine produced in 2001 by Mexican nationals in the Rogers Park area of Chicago's North Side. Each venue provides possibilities for the public presencing of both the Virgin and her followers, and I highlight just two dimensions of Peña's rich analysis. First, her conception of the pilgrimage field extends far beyond that of home and shrine, or even multiple homes and shrine. In considering "the institutional and noninstitutional production of sacred spaces among ethnoreligious communities between the Midwest and central/western Mexico" (ibid.), she lays out connectivities among multiple spaces, traditions, embodied practices and forms of devotional labor. Second, Peña exposes the risky, performative politics of the trajectories and temporalities of sacred movement enacted through pilgrimage. The shrine of Guadalupe in Mexico City now operates at a spectacular scale, commemorating an ancient tradition as people move toward a well-established center. By contrast, the sidewalk shrine asserts—entrains—a novel and contestable association between specific community and public space, pitched into the busy life of a multiethnic neighborhood of Chicago. It is based around an apparition of the Virgin granted to a possibly undocumented migrant Mexican woman and is focused on the tenuous trace of a sacred image on a tree.[42] Fragile as such an articulation of the divine is, it catalyzes impressive gatherings of people whose immigration and economic statuses deny them the opportunity to visit familiar Guadalupan shrines in Mexico; movement in one direction is juxtaposed with *lack* of the possibility of movement in another, reminiscent of the Cuban case. Peña shows how an emergent (counter-)public is mobilized through devotional and other performative acts oriented around the site. These actions also become performances of memory, as people reenact rituals learned from previous generations.

The Virgin in Rogers Park manifests the inchoate qualities of a proto-pilgrimage site that occupies municipal land, reaching out toward a proximate urban realm rather than a remote desert or mountain. If much discussion of pilgrimage is about alignment in space and time—about the joy of realizing that one's footsteps trace the steps of others who have gone before—here a path to a new center is being created, however tentatively.[43] The links with Catholic tradition and varieties of belonging are forged through aspirational if potentially frictional articulations of ritual, which face in various directions: global Marian imagery, Mexican landscapes of devotion, and the civic arena of a multicultural and iconic American city. This public and "tactical" (de Certeau 1984) expression of faith succeeds in attracting attention. But coming into visibility carries risks. Achieving public presence attracts disapproval from Catholic authorities, distrust from neighbors, and in all likelihood unwelcome surveillance from both police and immigration authorities.[44]

The shrine in Mexico City that forms part of the pilgrimage field explored by Peña receives more visitors than any other Catholic sanctuary in the world—some 20 million people in 2006 (Ruiz-Navarro 2010, 243). As a "Mexican National Symbol" (Wolf 1958), the Virgin of Guadalupe on the Hill of Tepeyac has taken on further resonances in an age of migration and hyper-mediation. In an analysis that complements Peña's, Patricia Ruiz-Navarro shows how the shrine conveys an empowering, transnational identity for Mexicans based abroad (238), becoming an object of intense devotion for people based in the United States. Such symbolism is activated through an annual event that highlights movement *from* rather than *to* the site. The Antorcha Guadalupana is a relay run that conveys a torch from the shrine in Mexico City to St. Patrick's Cathedral in New York City and is linked to a march/procession in New York intended to promote social justice for immigrants, including those without legal status. Staged over two months and concluding on December 12, the Feast Day of the Virgin, it commemorates migrants who have died attempting to cross the border to the United States. The first run across the national border occurred in 2002, and one of the coordinators of the event is the Asociación Tepeyac, a community-based organization located in New York that offers legal and human rights advice to undocumented immigrants. The event concludes with a spectacular occupation of the interior of St. Patrick's Cathedral through dance, prayer, and song. If the Virgin's appearance in Roger's Park in Chicago is powerful but informal, the Guadalupano torch run bridges the gap between official and unofficial institutions. It entrains different forms of movement, expressed literally, metaphorically, and virtually: conventional pilgrimage melded with the urgency of negotiating borders.

Tweed's and Peña's interlocutors construct pilgrimage itineraries that acknowledge the political and economic realities of blocked mobility, and consequently, they look very different from the cosmopolitan, freer-flowing qualities of the Camino. Meanwhile, the Antorcha Guadalupana both highlights and challenges a national boundary; the run from Mexico City to New York draws a cartographic line between two defined and official points on the map and then publicly enacts a journey between those points (cf. Ingold 2007). Based around urgent running conjoined with a public procession, the Antorcha demonstrates what is at stake politically, economically, and legally—as well as spiritually—in rendering a national border ritually permeable through coordinated efforts of humans in motion.

Despite their differences, these three cases provide variations on similar themes: spirituality and citizenship; ambiguities of belonging;

appeal to urban publics; reflections on the past combined with aspirations for the future. Rather than offering slowed-down, enclaved, processual technologies of the becoming self, they promote rhythmically complex, outwardly oriented feats of communal and devotional labor, which sometimes shade into protest. Instead of contrasting "moving" and "dwelling," they experiment with temporal entrainments between the two—for instance, as chaotic flight becomes stately procession, with the solemn cadence of the latter expressing not chronic becoming so much as ritualized control. Their contestations are aimed not at others within a shrine but in the direction of external institutions and spaces.[45] As pilgrimage complexes that negotiate diasporic identities on American soil, they place not only Catholic but also ethnically marked forms of worship into public contexts historically dominated by Protestant assumptions (Fessenden 2007). In line with my analysis in the previous chapter, they use spiritually and geographically charged narrative to locate themselves strategically in—and across—landscapes of both biblical and political significance.

Pilgrimage cannot be thought of as a sui generis act in any of these cases but becomes a confluence of different forms of movement, pace, and aspirational senses of belonging. A productive way of thinking through the tensions and intersections between the forms of mobility and immobility thus encompassed is to juxtapose them with recent discussions around the contemporary politics of waiting. The latter often entails "an imposed form of sanctioning used to slow down movement" of migrants and refugees (Bandak and Janeja 2019, 7; see Peña 2017; Hage 2009)—across borders, away from transit camps, sometimes toward citizenship. As Bandak and Janeja point out, displaced peoples tend to cultivate agentive dispositions that challenge mere acceptance of marginality (7). While many among the Latinx populations I describe have already achieved relatively settled positions in their new country, they still find themselves suspended between states of belonging, so that pilgrimage—among many other things—provides a conduit for action in the present, drawing on forms of legitimation that go beyond the laws of any single state. It may also force waiting onto *others*—as when the slow march of Mexican Americans in New York enables the labor of carrying an image of Our Lady to stop traffic, ensuring that *her* pace takes precedence over that of the city; Mary can now afford to proceed slowly (cf. Bandak 2014, 254).

These examples also point to a broader phenomenon: the growing contemporary resonance of Marian imagery as pilgrimage adapts to conditions of modernity that include but go far beyond debates over secularization. In a volume called *Moved by Mary* (2009), Anna-Karina Hermkens, Willy Jansen, and Catrien Notermans trace the increasingly globalized deployment of Marian pilgrimages in struggles for political empowerment:

> By repetitive performative acts, by selecting or duplicating her image, carrying it around, gazing at it, or narrating about it, presence is communicated and invested in Mary, enabling her to operate, to move and mobilize people. This communicating presence is both profane and sacral. It takes place between the living, between the living and the dead, and between the living and Mary. (8)

Such presence is activated through the creation of "cogent connections" (ibid.)—expressions of compelling relations between human and divine worlds—but also through horizontal diffusions of Marian imagery that move across political and economic boundaries. Referring to the worldwide distribution of devotion to Our Lady of Fátima in Portugal, they note (7): "Through the transnational use of her image and the rituals related to her . . . people become interconnected. They are, as it were, 'enchained' . . . as each image or devotional act not only stands for Mary but also connects devotees of Mary globally."

Sketched out here is an expansive terrain of Catholic devotion that draws on incremental accumulations of mobilities and mediations. It looks very different from Pentecostal representations of easy fluidity of movement but shares the evangelical aspiration to reach into the world to create new pathways rather than retrace old ones (cf. Pasura and Erdal 2016).[46] A striking example of such innovation is provided by Hermkens (2012) as she examines "journeys of violence and peace" in documenting Marian pilgrimages across Bougainville, Papua New Guinea. These journeys are staged in the aftermath of the brutal war between supporters and opponents of Bougainville independence. A year after a priest's house containing a statue of Mary is burned down, the same figure is found intact by a young girl, earning it the moniker "The Miracle Statue." Hermkens notes that although a chapel was eventually built for it, in 1997 and 2005 the statue was carried across mountainous terrain to visit various villages. The 1997 walkabout took place during a key period in post-conflict negotiations and was initiated with a mass before moving between settlements, accompanied by prayers and talks aimed at promoting peace through the good name of "Mama Maria." In this account, we see both traversing and transgressing of boundaries coming to the fore. The centerpiece of activity is not a specific place but rather the delineation of a moral landscape that recalls already existing sacred locations in Bougainville (stones, trees, mountaintops, rivers) while promoting a message of Christian reconciliation pitched against tribal divisions. Such movement enacts the wishes of women in particular—mothers, wives, and sisters of soldiers—as they assert a novel and dominant place in ritual action. The result is a dramatic commingling of human and divine agency (cf. Mitchell 2007); the miraculous statue lends legitimacy to the journey, but it is humans who take responsibility for bearing her across the landscape, distributing Marian presence as they move from spot to spot.

In its more creative, politically risky manifestations, pilgrimage as entraining practice deploys ritualized travel to sketch out landscapes of sovereignty that coexist uneasily with those of other territorial authorities. Away from Christian examples, Lokesh Ohri (2020) examines ritual processions of divine kings (locally understood as pilgrimages) across the former kingdom of Mahasu in the western Himalayas. Like Hermkens, Ohri shows how traces of memory are recovered and bound together through mobile ritual to challenge the exclusive legitimacy of currently prevailing political powers, which are depicted as lacking historical depth. The processions reinvoke semi-divine rulers whose past powers to govern have been successively replaced by the Gurkhas, the British, and finally the Indian state yet retain salience for local populations. Contemporary cultural autonomy is enacted through the ritualized movement of a palanquin containing the image of a king. It crisscrosses the region, borne over rough and possibly snowy terrain by devotees who walk barefooted. This effortful, marked motion sketches out an expansive realm of authority that is not fully coterminous with "the modern concept of territory as a space where the external borders must be marked to describe it" (ibid., 55; cf. Yang 2004). Here, then, the point is to traverse such terrain *without* becoming entrained in its modernist rhythms. Assertion of the continued legitimacy of divine kingship is vulnerable to suppression yet demonstrates the possibility for older markers of identity to exist away from the cartographic gaze or regulating rhythms of national government.[47]

Victims of Capitalism?

An irony of this chapter is that it has presented not only economically pressed migrants but also voluntary trekkers as "victims" of economic liberalization and accompanying forms of space-time compression (Harvey 1989). Middle-class complaints about the pressures of hyper-mobility have been juxtaposed with ritualized responses to the risky journeys taken by much less privileged populations. The link between these different economies and experiences of mobility has been pilgrimage: a heterogenous practice articulated in ways that are embedded within, and address, contemporary challenges in the organization of time, space, and movement. My locating pilgrimage within a political economy approach thus encourages appreciation of wider "geometries of power" (Amit and Salazar 2020, 4) within which sacralized traveling and placemaking operate, where such factors as pace, access to infrastructure, and visibility are subjected to liturgical as well as more broadly political regimes of governance.

Enclaving creates a sense of distance from other forms of spatiality and mobility, with such separation cultivating a focus on grounded movement coupled with lack of attention to wider context. I have examined its implications by focusing on a reanalysis of the Camino, but enclaving takes many other social and spatial forms, including the closely guarded experiences of the Israeli students described by Feldman or certain focused experiences of the Hajj. While enclaving may encourage communitas-type experiences, numerous varieties of sociality, both formal and informal, are cultivated under its aegis. Entraining, by contrast, makes explicit connections with other realms of society; its contestations and entanglements are directed less toward others at a particular shrine (pace Eade and Sallnow 1991) and more toward authorities and institutions existing elsewhere. In such cases, pilgrimage provides a legitimating idiom through which a public—or a counter-public—may be formed, appealing to issues that go far beyond the purely religious or spiritual. Pilgrimage becomes a medium through which to enact such a public through face-to-face interaction (cf. Warner 2002; Rao forthcoming)—to make it present within spatial domains that are visible to, and occupied by, others.

Both stances are sustained through embodied and administrative labor. Their articulations and claims are far from inevitable, but my aim is to systematize understandings of dynamic ways in which pilgrimage practices are embedded within ramifying and often interrelated manifestations of movement. In the cases highlighted in this chapter, whether the emphasis has been on enclaving or entraining, pilgrimage makes mobility a marked theme for attention and ritualization.

One risk of my approach is that it may look like a return to functionalism—pilgrimage existing in order to achieve these 'beneficial' ends. Such an interpretation would be far too determinist. To talk of the motivations and consequences of social actions is not to claim that these are the sole or primary reasons for such actions to exist. I also emphasize the ideological ambiguities of what is intended and achieved. Walkers who escape into the Camino still inscribe dominant values of mobility, responsibilization, and flexibility into their life trajectories. In addressing questions of peripherality, the Latinx examples of Marian devotion that I describe contain complex stances toward authority, including some that demand public recognition within society at large, but in doing so, they may entrain themselves further to an economic and political system that continues to restrict opportunity. As a mobile and multiscalar symbol, Mary travels widely in such neoliberal contexts, but she does not necessarily offer a critique of current conditions and structures. She equally readily offers hope of advancement *within* the current political and economic dispensation.[48] At its farthest reach, within and beyond Christian examples, pilgrimage contributes to global fields of activity, linking sites but also populations as they move across variegated landscapes, impelled by multiple imperatives. In doing so, it operates via articulations—both acknowledged and not acknowledged by participants—with wider economies of mobility. In the final chapter, I want finally to bring together the several ways that pilgrimage activities lead us to, but also around and far beyond, shrines themselves.

Conclusion

Restoring the Powers: Summary and Reflections

Pilgrimage is a beguiling topic. Scholars have written with great eloquence of its most striking features—intense experiences entailed in seeking bonds of unmediated fellowship, strong emotions roused by competing over sacred resources, and stern challenges faced in arduous journeys of self-discovery alongside encountering the divine. The argument of this book has been that these portrayals have proved analytically productive but highly partial. They have aroused interest in the field but have restricted scholarly awareness of pilgrimage as a social and cultural force. By shifting attention to less spectacular dimensions of pilgrimage, it is possible to uncover other presences, other powers: lateral actions and penumbral spaces produced in and around shrines; narratives and social exchanges performed far from spiritual centers; politically loaded intersections of ritual rhythms and acts of civic engagement.

For the potential of the field to be fulfilled, its dimensions must continue to be enlarged spatially, methodologically, and theoretically. Throughout this volume, we have reflected on excellent work that has already contributed to such expansion. But there is much left to do. I propose here an agenda that aims, however paradoxically, to increase awareness of pilgrimage as a social force by encouraging attentiveness not only to ritual and institutional cores but also to backgrounds, overflows, and "dynamic interfaces" (Marsden and Retsikas 2013, 4). Viewed this way, pilgrimage goes beyond the liminal to incorporate the lateral and the loose. It leaves traces in ritual, material, and narrative forms that extend beyond any given sacred center, becoming both more pervasive and more routine than is usually supposed. It invokes bodily dispositions that are inchoate and fragmented as well as conscious and disciplined.[1] Expanding the pilgrimage field entails researching formal processions made to St. Cuthbert's Feretory in Durham Cathedral, but also the actions of two young boys as they light candles in the long shadows cast by the saint's tomb, uncertain whether they are commemorating divine worship, past birthday parties, or a beloved grandmother. Similarly, the Hajj may be examined by entering the sacred precincts at Mecca, but also by listening to popular pilgrimage songs that seep into the everyday lives of Moroccan citizens, lending savor to regular family gatherings and mundane morning rituals (Al-Ajarma 2020, 260). As ethnographic awareness of the field becomes more supple, pilgrims no longer take center stage by default. Administrators, guides, local inhabitants, families and friends of travelers, and numerous other interlinked institutions demand equal or more attention, depending on the analytical focus.

Extension of ethnographic and analytical frames enhances rather than dilutes appreciation of pilgrimage's potential as topic of study. The aim of this book has not been to ignore its established and formal dimensions, but to uncover ongoing articulations with multiple other spaces, times, and socialities—articulations that should not be regarded as adjuncts to pilgrimage proper, but recognized as among its vital components. Pilgrimage presences that disseminate from shrines are not necessarily etiolated by such travel. Reconstituted, they suffuse social worlds in ways that extend their effects beyond dramas of liminality, contestation, and ordeal and may act recursively to influence shrines through the habits of returning pilgrims. They are also likely to contribute to a wide array of theoretical conversations beyond the obviously religious, and we have discussed debates around migration, the circulation and transduction of cultural forms, and the creation of urban publics.

Like other interdisciplinary fields, pilgrimage studies involves the "collaborative confection" of a topic of research capable of being perceived through numerous "epistemic vantage points" (Palmié 2013, 8). However, limits should also be set. Coherent scholarly conversations require common theoretical, linguistic, and methodological ground. In this book, we have blended comparative ethnography with considerations of past and present social scientific theory, and the argument has placed gradually increasing emphasis on the formation of ramifying social and semiotic connections.[2] Firm boundaries delineating a fixed image of pilgrimage are loosened as the sui generis fellowship of chapter 3 morphs into the lateralities and penumbras of chapter 6 and then the modes of ritualized entraining described in chapter 8. The theoretical scope has expanded correspondingly, departing from classic tropes of communitas and contestation to incorporate themes of frictional engagement, mediated presence, and political economies of mobility. Meanwhile, in methodological terms, my call for greater flexibility in tracing pilgrimage-related activities encourages greater appreciation of the politics of attention surrounding the construction of knowledge about pilgrimage. One obvious area where such politics are salient is the gendered character of much pilgrimage activity, especially as it relates to ritual expressions of authority. Hillary Kaell's (2012, 2014) ethnography of American evangelical visitors to the Holy Land provides just one example; male pastors preach in public, sanctified spots, but lay women tend to carry out the less spectacular but socially weighty labor of purchasing and distributing souvenirs back home. Penumbral spaces and lateral actions are likely to reward detailed analysis through a lens of gender, given that they are connected to questions of authority, agency, and visibility.

The expanded perspective offered here also reflects significant ethnographic shifts in the contemporary practice of pilgrimage, given that most shrines are generally much harder to separate from everyday contexts than they would have been even during the 1970s, when Victor and Edith Turner were writing *Image and Pilgrimage* (1978). Chapter 7 drew on the work of Nadia Caidi and Suzan Beazley and Laia Colomer Marquez (2018) on "holy selfies" to show how pilgrims to Mecca appeal simultaneously and synchronously to dispersed audiences as they tour the holy city (similar points are made by Suzanne van der Beek [2018] for the Camino and John Shultz [2009] for Shikoku). Marjo Buitelaar, Manja Stephan-Emmrich, and Viola Thimm (2021) argue that the Hajj pilgrimage is increasingly routinized as it is subject to repeat visits but also that its identity as a place of sacred ritual begins to shift as Wi-Fi access allows pilgrims to remain in touch with family and friends even as they circumambulate the Kaaba (see also Davis and Jurgenson 2018).

In sketching out these theoretical, methodological, and ethnographic moves, I have ranged widely while drawing on certain recurring examples: Walsingham, the Camino, Mecca, Shikoku, the multireligious terrain of Israel-Palestine, and the complex pilgrimage landscape of eastern India. These sites are not equivalent in scale, history, shape, or definition, nor do they cover all varieties of pilgrimage, given that they remain mostly oriented around larger, well-established ritual centers associated with world religions. They do permit comparative reflections across religious traditions, indicating how pilgrimage might be regarded as a polythetic category, constituted not only by space, ritual, narrative, and movement, but also by culturally specific processes of defining and maintaining links among these features.

I have extended comparison by making regular reference to a field of research that lies beyond the normal range of pilgrimage studies. Like pilgrimage, Pentecostalism is a popular religious and cultural phenomenon that makes mobility a central theme of much of its practice. However, the fates of these institutions as topics of scholarly conversation have diverged. Pentecostalism is often depicted as an aggressively missionizing movement that adapts well to both modernity and globalization (cf. Coleman and Vásquez 2017; Robbins 2009). Its study prompts discussion of how a "religion made to travel" (Dempster, Klaus, and Petersen, 1999) spiritualizes space-time compression and makes a virtue out of both universalism and disembedding identity from place. Pilgrimage, by contrast, is associated with preserving tradition, slowing experience of time, and claiming uniqueness for local, sacred locations. We have seen, however, that stark contrasts are misleading. Through resisting the temptations of "singularism," scholars can look further than individual shrines and acknowledge the vibrant and ongoing articulation of proliferating pilgrimage landscapes that operate transregionally or transnationally.[3] Established sites give birth to fractal offshoots—smaller or newer shrines recursively patterned on already existing models. Successful pilgrimage paradigms such as the Camino are strategically adopted and adapted by practitioners in different cultural and religious contexts. Some pilgrims travel promiscuously across sites and religious traditions in creating globetrotting itineraries of personal spiritual significance. Pilgrimage as instrument of mobility is enmeshed not only with tourism but also with heterogeneous processes of economic circulation, refugeehood, and contested spatial governance.[4]

Tracking the dynamic formation of pilgrimage landscapes beyond single shrines is often done most effectively by subsequent comparative analysis. In chapter 8, we juxtaposed ethnographic work published by Elaine Peña (2011) and Patricia Ruiz-Navarro (2010) to explore the multilayered significance of spaces and mobilities formed in relation to the shrine of Our Lady of Guadalupe. A composite field emerged, taking in Mexico City, New York City, Des Plaines, and Chicago, and incorporating numerous forms of movement—processional, athletic, sacrificial, migratory—as well as sacred locations ranging from an enormous ancient shrine to an image scarcely visible on a tree. Other ethnographies oriented around Guadalupe would produce differently configured terrains, but the point is that such a ramifying, multiscalar, multi-sited approach has been surprisingly rare in pilgrimage studies. More implicit conjunctions can be brought to light in relation to other, less overtly connected sites. For instance, in chapter 7, we drew on works by Jackie Feldman (2002), Vida Bajc (2007), and Hillary Kaell (2014) to examine how journeys of Israeli youth to Poland and of American Christians to the Holy Land ostensibly occupied separate cultural and religious landscapes yet belonged to a common geopolitical universe reliant on specific interpretations of Judeo-Christian histories, both ancient and modern.

Pilgrimage's entanglements with transnationalism reach beyond the physical journeys of pilgrims or the formation of diasporic landscapes to encompass broader cartographies of ideological association between sites. Unlike Pentecostalism, however, pilgrimage does not usually constitute a self-consciously globalizing institution. Its travelers tend not to perceive the world per se as their prime context of operation and orientation. Instead, study of pilgrimage is exceptionally well equipped to examine co-occurrences of diverse experiences of location, mobility, and rhythm, as space-time compression and decompression are smoothly or frictionally conjoined within the totality of a given journey. From this perspective, the now standard scholarly focus on the Camino as enclave (seen from the point of view of the pilgrim) should be complemented by showing how it maintains complex ritual engagements with the city of Santiago de Compostela, travel industries, ecclesiastical constructions of movement and place, national and transnational conceptions of heritage, contested rights to mobility and citizenship, and dissemination of the Camino paradigm of slowed-down mobility to other parts of the world. Sketching out such larger frames generates greater awareness of the openness or gatedness of different regions of the world to traveling populations, reflecting how pilgrimage contributes to what Manuel Vásquez (2008, 167) calls the "global logic of risk management."[5] It also alerts the researcher to novel ethnographic and theoretical juxtapositions. For instance, Pentecostal notions of unfettered flow and the Camino's championing of effortful becoming may seem worlds apart geographically and culturally, but when juxtaposed, they appear united in a key respect: both downplay the significance of the political and economic infrastructures that make their respective enactments of mobility possible.

One pilgrimage more obviously linked to global frameworks is the Hajj, reliant as it is on a conception of belonging reflected in the worldwide Muslim community of the *umma*. Habitual orientation to Mecca is enabled through the *qibla*, the prayer niche that reminds dispersed Muslims of their location in relation to the sacred city.[6] Robert Bianchi (2013) highlights the significance of contemporary Muslim pilgrimage to Islamic globalization through stressing its contributions to transnational forms of modernization. He juxtaposes such pilgrimage with "capitalist economic development, political and religious democratization, and growing assertiveness in world diplomacy" (1), presenting all these activities as inherently connected. As prime "hallmark of Islamic globalization" (3), the Hajj is a revealing index of demographic, institutional, social, and economic shifts in the Islamic world, attracting increasing proportions of women, the young, urbanites, and university graduates. Buitelaar, Stephan-Emmrich, and Thimm (2021) take such analysis a stage further by arguing that its rapid globalization is accompanied by a feminization of transnational mobility, bringing Mecca increasingly within reach of women from a variety of social backgrounds. The overall message seems clear: while the Hajj can profitably be understood through the analytical lens of globalization, work on globalization is equally enriched through studying the Hajj.

This expansive view of pilgrimage speaks powerfully to another key question concerning the place of religion in modernity, one that already occupied the Turners in the 1970s: its engagement with ostensibly secular realms, at least as the secular has been perceived through Euro-American lenses. Again, comparison with contemporary Pentecostalism is suggestive, given that the latter's readiness to engage public spheres and popular culture bolsters its scholarly reputation as a religious force. Pentecostalism's unabashed proselytizing and rhetorical promotion of unrelenting religious commitment look very different from an academic image of pilgrimage that focuses on periodic visits to sacred and distant enclaves. To be sure, successful sites may be appropriated for civil religious or nationalist purposes, but in this book, we have seen how pilgrimage presences also work their semiotic seductions more subtly, and more widely, than generally realized. Memories, narratives, and ritual engagements operate far away from the public formalities of holy shrines, becoming bound up with multistranded, cross-generational social encounters—as a Muslim child living in Turkey learns to yearn for Mecca by listening to bed-time Hajj stories told by a parent; as an English couple sit at their kitchen table and discuss an annual family pilgrimage that is uncomfortably reminiscent of their discarded religious identities; or as Japanese seniors keep a watchful eye on local children by setting up mini-journeys around shrines in their shared neighborhood.[7] In these examples, pilgrimage rituals, discourses, and sensibilities are expressed through diffuse media and (re)animated in everyday places, freed from "arthritic" ritual tendencies (cf. Bloch 1974) while demonstrating an "elastic" tendency "to absorb and be absorbed by other cultural forms and representations" (Gemzöe 2016, 128). To adapt Richard Fenn's words (1982), these cases illustrate ritualized, performative interventions into daily life that become "eventful." They do not represent clear expressions of creed or spiritual devotion, which is precisely the point: they are embedded within already existing obligations of kinship, sociality, and care. In showing how pilgrimage sensibilities can work through numerous institutions—not merely the obviously religious ones—they recall an important point made by Ian Reader, explored in chapter 8, that pilgrimages may "operate not only in the marketplace but through it" (2015, 8). Viewed in this way, the market is not an enemy of pilgrimage: it is an important medium for its operation.

In tracing pilgrimage's engagements with varieties of secularity or non-religion, I drew on my own ethnographic work in England to examine ritualized performances within and around shrines. While sacred centers such as Walsingham create impressive ceremonial reference points for the already committed, their liturgies can be off-putting to those whom Grace Davie describes as occupying "the middle ground in the religious life of both Britain and Europe . . . the very large number of people (around 50% of the population) who are neither involved in organised religion, nor consciously opposed to it" (2010, 261). Whether strategically or more haphazardly, shrines may prompt the emergence of seductive, loosely articulated areas of pilgrimage-related activity that accommodate casual, passing, or ambivalent visitors in ways generally neglected in the literature. I deploy a socio-spatial theoretical vocabulary to encourage precision in describing the emergent, evanescent, events and performances characteristic of such heterogeneous zones.[8] *Adjacencies* refers to the close juxtaposition of otherwise distinct behavioral, ethical, and semiotic frames, as when a casual visitor observes the actions of a pious pilgrim, or vice versa. Such occasions may result in mimetic behavior on the part of the inexperienced visitor, who is tempted to try out a prayer or procession; simultaneously, the pious pilgrim is likely to become aware of being turned into an object of attention, developing a reflexivity typical of ritual in semipublic realms of famous sites (cf. Hughes-Freeland 1998). *Porosities* describe social and cultural interpenetrations between shrines and their surroundings, and as Katherine Rousseau (2016) points out, they enable the close interaction of heterogeneous constituencies and engagements. My fieldwork within English cathedrals provides striking illustrations of the ethical and aesthetic tensions roused around the policing of porosity. Heated discussions occur as to how closely a gift shop should be located to an altar or whether setting up a cathedral museum depicting the history of pilgrimage detracts from the authenticity of the real experience, available at a shrine just a few yards away (Coleman 2018b). If nothing else, these debates indicate that the limits of sanctity often operate through gradual diffusion rather than rigid boundaries. Complementing such themes, *penumbras* portray zones of loosely articulated ritual framing whose character is influenced by perceived proximity to a shrine. I use the metaphor of a shadow cast by an object to convey the sense of an area of ritualization that gradually loses definition as it diffuses across a given terrain, eventually becoming indistinguishable from the outside world. Finally, *lateral* behaviors indicate not a space but a quality of behavior that indexes degree of separation from ritual intensity and commitment—well suited to taking advantage of the material affordances provided by penumbras, porosities, and adjacencies.[9]

The terms that make up this analytical lexicon have a horizontal orientation.[10] They shift ethnographic attention sideways, encouraging observation of encounters taking place between and across different behavioral and ethical frames. The fact that they retain a degree of proximity to shrines suggests their salience to long-standing questions surrounding the embeddedness of art and ritual in contexts of original production. In the 1930s, Walter Benjamin (1968) famously examined the ways in which the compound reproduction of an aesthetic form threatens to sever its links to the specific location and performance that provide it with its unique quality, or aura. As Benjamin Lee (2001, xii) has summarized the point, "The authentic token now becomes a token of a type that is no longer appreciated by an audience tethered to an act of ritual performance, but to a dispersed reception made up of individualized acts of appreciation. The uniqueness and permanence associated with traditional artworks are replaced in modernity with transitoriness and reproducibility." In adapting Benjamin's frame to pilgrimage centers, we might consider how even a replicated site can create an aura as it acquires its own ritual constituency and history of miracle working or as a multiply circulated paradigm such as the Camino becomes reembedded in new landscapes.[11] What is particularly interesting is how penumbral space generally combines its centrifugal quality with continued attachment to the exceptional qualities and presences of shrines: context remains important. I can express the point concretely by drawing on one of my fieldwork examples. As a mixed group of Anglican and Roman Catholic students performs the stations of the cross in a lane outside Walsingham, they trace not only distance from, but also proximity to, the site. Ritual links to the putative "original" are not severed; they are bodily rearticulated.[12] A question for the future is whether penumbral space and time can be presenced anew through virtual means, recultivating an auratic sense of proximity to a shrine within spaces that are geographically remote from it.

Although Davie and I are both interested in unattached or ambivalent constituencies, we approach ritual from different standpoints. Davie's (2007b) description of worship vicariously performed by an active minority on behalf of a passive majority places emphasis on liturgies that are publicly and expertly performed. My aim instead is to uncover performances carried out at pilgrimage sites by members of a majority whose agency and stance appear more multifaceted. Though lateral types of behavior occur under many circumstances, pilgrimage sites provide particularly rich resources for their enactment, given that shrines often contain substantial, shifting constituencies alongside numerous opportunities for adjacency, all combined with relative lack of direct surveillance by authorities. These elements constitute diffuse ethical and spatial infrastructures that seduce rather than funnel visitors into ritual participation. At their most effective, they contain dispositional traps (Gell 1996) aided by generic forms of "ritual syntax" (Albera 2019a) that bridge the large and ill-defined gap between indifference and engagement while permitting the exercise of relative ethical freedom (Laidlaw 2013). At Walsingham, such infrastructures will likely include an empty shrine and a leafy lane, a candle stand or holy well, possibly even a semiformal procession that encourages the liturgically uninitiated to participate, including those with no particular desire to *be* initiated.[13] Such elements gain further seductive powers when, through their lateral qualities, they are enacted on a fuzzy behavioral terrain where everyday comportment articulates positively with liturgical etiquette; here I think not only of the boys and their birthday candles in Durham Cathedral but also, for instance, of Paul as he joins a family procession toward the Roman Catholic shrine at Walsingham that also recalls both his childhood and the feeling of a walk along a country lane.[14] Both occasions may seem ritually inconsequential, but they build on powerful and intimate ties of kinship, memory, and habitual action, spanning some of the disjunctions described (and lamented) by Martyn Percy (2013, 125) between episodic and dispositional engagements in religious institutions. My point here is not only about resonances between worship and everyday life. I am also highlighting a realm of performative engagement that goes beyond sterile contrasts between secular and sacred forms of pilgrimage or debates over what is or is not authentic ritual action.

Despite our different emphases, Davie and I agree on a fundamental methodological point: we are both uncovering phenomena that are "subtle, many-layered, shifting, and constantly evolving" (Davie 2010, 264) and not readily susceptible to binary assessment. My lexicon is meant to sharpen ethnographic attention, not to prompt positivist assertions about presence or absence of belief or other forms of religious conviction. It describes not a fixed pilgrimage repertoire but certain dimensions of action that will manifest in different forms and intensities according to circumstance. Above all, I stress that the pilgrimage performances I describe are often ritually inchoate but socially significant.

In other work on the supposedly marginal role of religion in modernity, especially as it is manifested in public contexts, Matthew Engelke (2012) has referred to "ambient" expressions of faith, which inhabit the background of everyday consciousness while acting as potential semiotic bridges to more sharply defined forms of religious devotion (see also Oliphant 2021). My description of the penumbral inhabits broadly the same realm of ritual indeterminacy, with the exception that it describes contexts where participants become involved in performance, however tenuously.

Much of this discussion about semidetached ritual engagement emerges from fieldwork deeply rooted in English Christian contexts, but it encourages comparison and contrast with other pilgrimage landscapes. Walsingham points to wider trends within Europe, and possibly beyond. The relative tolerance of behavioral fluidity at and around the site has counterparts in studies of Christian pilgrimage elsewhere, reflecting a growing tendency to understand pilgrimage "as a context-dependent kaleidoscope of elements rather than a denominationally discrete institution or all-embracing model" (Rock 2006, 194). Similarly, the disjunction between participation in pilgrimage and lack of other institutional engagements with religion is increasingly common around Europe, though its implications differ. In her analysis of religious trends in contemporary Russia, Jeanne Kormina (2018, 144) highlights the development of a "nomadic religious regime" comprising those who prefer to undertake pilgrimages rather than engaging in "a regular religious life" in local parishes. Although this nomadic stance seems more intentional and strategic than that displayed by most of my interlocutors at Walsingham, it raises similar structural questions concerning ritual engagements that flourish without obvious rootedness in congregational life, and without the chains of attachment to parochial place that Danielle Hervieu-Léger (2000) highlights for the history of French Catholicism.

Intriguing comparative questions emerge when I apply my framework to very different pilgrimage contexts. Ann Gold's *Fruitful Journeys* (1988) provides a useful reference point given that it presents a social and cultural landscape very remote from that prevalent in Europe and North America, one where the lukewarm qualities of much English religion and the hostilities of European secularism have little in common with

Rajasthani village life. Gold's ethnography shows how local pilgrimage activities are embedded within many areas of existence—labor, kinship, health, death, land. She also describes a long trip by villagers to the temple of Lord Jagdish at Puri that includes—in my terms—decidedly lateral as well as liminoid behaviors in a penumbral zone. On the first day of their visit, the Rajasthani pilgrims dutifully attend the temple, but on the second, they convene at the nearby seashore, where their loose behavior—frolicking in the waves—provides a striking response to the affordances of the coastal landscape. Shrine and beach provide complementary opportunities for varieties of ritualized engagement. These pilgrims are in a very different position to religiously unaligned visitors to Walsingham, whose ambivalences over religion are expressed through distance from conventional shrine worship; rather, they feel that their formal obligations have been completed by the time they decide to go to—and into—the sea.[15] Gold uncovers the sheer variety of pilgrimage's spatial and semiotic presences in the lives of her interlocutors—in domestic shrines, the local landscape, and distant destinations, both foregrounded and backgrounded in people's attention.

The overall dimensions of the expanded field that I am constructing can now be summarized. Pilgrimage is often located in ritual cores, but such cores are commonly porous and connected with wider fields of social and ritual relations, including penumbral spaces, lateral behaviors, and ritualized traces of pilgrimage that permeate everyday life. Much pilgrimage is routinized, and action in penumbral zones is creative without necessarily making a permanent mark on the sacralized landscape.[16] On the other hand, newer complexes may be generated that draw on the models and legitimacy of more venerable examples. Furthermore, pilgrimages are prone to enact ritual entrainments that intersect with and even interrupt civic space and time.

Although I am drawing attention to sometimes neglected dimensions of pilgrimage, I do not insist that research must always make it the center of analytical attention. It is also possible to learn much about pilgrimage by making it a smaller part of a larger analytical picture. Nor do I recommend that every study invoke the totality of the field presented here: there is always room for self-consciously parochial approaches, focused on particular places, disciplines, and analytical questions. My intention is not hubristically to suggest an agenda that must be repeated in every study. It is to widen the range of places and behaviors where pilgrimage presences, powers, and effects are acknowledged to exist.

My argument might seem like a sustained attempt to tarnish the Turnerian image of pilgrimage, but I intend, rather, to give it much more scope and nuance. The image has many more dimensions than is usually acknowledged, as revealed by examining the intellectual roots of the Turners' position. Some influences are well known, such as van Gennep's grand vision of ritual, commitment to Catholicism, engagement with academic circles in the United States, and the anti-structural events of the 1960s. Less discussed by pilgrimage scholars but equally vital are the attempts of a postwar, postcolonial social anthropology to grapple with issues of order and disorder: the causes and mitigation of conflict; the influence of social process in ethnographic fields whose stability could not be assumed. While subsequent debates over contestation would open up new ways of thinking about pilgrimage (Eade and Sallnow 1991), the Turners themselves had long been involved in thinking through the consequences of conflict for social groups. At the same time, placing communitas temporarily in the background of any reading of their work helps to highlight other dimensions of their approach: the structured comparisons between sites; the early recognition of the material affordances of shrines; the conceptualization of pilgrimage as a wider system or culture. Victor and Edith's attempt to characterize pilgrimage as going beyond "a single circumscribed social field" (Turner and Turner 1978, xxiv) had its flaws, but it anticipated theoretical perspectives about the global that would become vitally important to the social sciences in the subsequent decades.[17]

Admittedly, when the Turners refer to "Christian culture," their scope remains limited. Much of the time, they make Roman Catholic pilgrimage stand for Christianity and Christianity stand for problematically universal values of fellowship and ritual creativity. Donald Weber (1995, 530) notes how Victor's popularity within American cultural studies began to wane in the 1980s as the more consensual, teleological dimensions of the theoretical apparatus of liminality and anti-structure became apparent. From the perspective of scholars studying industrial, plural, urban settings, liminality privileges the return of initiates to dominant social structures without recognizing the unresolved status of chronically marginal social actors. In this sense, the work lacks a "recognition of culture as political contestation" (532).[18] Citing Renato Rosaldo (1990), Weber argues that the borders defining liminality may themselves be porous zones that house multiple identities and ongoing ambiguities.[19]

In this book, I have drawn on the work of the sociologist Stuart Hall to provide an ongoing foil to such Turnerian representations of identity and marginality. Hall (1932–2014) was a rough contemporary of the Turners, and like them, he drew on a wide range of influences in work that analyzed the dynamics of social movements, intersections between literature and the social sciences, and popular culture (e.g., Hall 2019).[20] Victor and Edith moved to the United States from the United Kingdom, while Hall's education took him from Jamaica to 1950s England, where he would stay to become an important academic and public commentator on the country's shift from imperial power to increasingly diverse, diasporic society. The Turnerian view of transformation tended to find its most productive analytical soil in anti-structural enclaves, but Hall drew on Gramsci and Althusser as he strove to adapt a Marxist framework to non-determinist diagnoses of social change. Whereas *Image and Pilgrimage* edged toward the rhetorical construction of a single Christian culture, Hall developed a plural and influential vision of cultural studies that recalled his own experience of "migranthood" (Hall 1987, 44; see Clarke 2015; Morley and Chen 1996).

Hall was interested in liminality and the work of Victor Turner (Hall 1969), though he did not specialize in the study of religion.[21] His lack of direct engagement with pilgrimage forces me to look beyond the usual theoretical tropes in characterizing pilgrimage as a cultural phenomenon. I do not adopt Hall's position wholesale, but his discussion of articulation is valuable in its exploration of the ongoing and always fragile work that lies behind the making of social, economic, and cultural connections. As Lawrence Grossberg puts it in his extended reflections on Hall's ideas, "Articulation is the production of identity on top of differences, of unities out of fragments, of structures across practices. Articulation links this practice to that effect, this text to that meaning, this meaning to that reality, this experience to those politics. And these links are themselves articulated into larger structures" (1986, 54).[22] In line with currently commonplace metaphors of assemblage, Hall's perspective highlights the significance of chronic emergence in the making and remaking of institutions and socio-spatial formations, but he emphasizes two important further dimensions. One is continued emphasis on the material workings of power in the creation and articulation of culture. The other is the argument that articulation refers simultaneously to expression and connection, the ways in which the two become both conjoined and co-constitutive.

Applied to pilgrimage, Hall's approach highlights the importance of seeing how different elements of a given tradition of religious travel are linked together at any given moment, but it also suggests how actions associated with pilgrimages may be made and remade at the very points where they articulate with other institutions and practices. Thus, while chapters 3, 4, and 5 of this book explored centripetal tropes in the theorization of cultures of pilgrimage, the rest of the volume invoked the formative powers of articulation as we examined pilgrimage as a centrifugal phenomenon, animated through connections across frameworks of cultural difference and reconstituted through media extending beyond conventional worship.[23] I have sought, then, to demonstrate the benefits of dwelling in the midst of an enlarged ethnographic and theoretical landscape that presents pilgrimage not as hedged around with boundaries but rather as a "boundary object" (Star 2010) with powerful capacities to enable the conjunction of groups, ethical frames, and institutions. Pilgrimage spreads across time, space, and scale. In doing so, it turns the ongoing labor of making, remaking, and denying connections—temporal, spatial, ideological—into a deeply ritualized part of its practice. The challenge for scholars is to follow these connections still further in exploring and expanding the possibilities and powers of the field.

ACKNOWLEDGMENTS

Walking along pilgrimage paths is hard but rewarding work, and so is writing. I have many people to thank for helping me along the journey that this book traces, only some of whom can be mentioned here. A constant conversation partner has been John Eade; indeed, I feel that we have been talking about pilgrimage ever since he first wrote to me some time in the last millennium, using an ancient technology (pen and paper). Another scholarly companion, always ready to chat or share a reference that she has conjured up from somewhere, is Evgenia Mesaritou. At the University of Toronto, I have learned much from fellow participants in our Pilgrimage Forum, and I would especially like to thank Nadia Caidi, Jill Caskey, and Shayne Dahl. Students on my Pilgrimage as Idea and Practice course have often been an inspiration, and I learned much from Amin Mansouri when we taught it together. Fellow cathedral enthusiasts, with whom I have shared both fieldsites and numerous cups of tea, include Marion Bowman, Grace Davie, Dee Dyas, Louise Hampson, John Jenkins, and Tiina Sepp. Many scholars of pilgrimage have been inspiring to me in person as well as on the page, and here I mention Kholoud Al-Ajarma, Dionigi Albera, Matthew Anderson, Ellen Badone, Vida Bajc, Kathryn Barush, Glenn Bowman, Marjo Buitelaar, Jill Caskey, Douglas Davies, Michael Di Giovine, Jill Dubisch, Jaś Elsner, Anna Fedele, Jackie Feldman, Victoria Fomina, Connie Gagliardi, David Geary, Lena Gemzöe, René Gothóni Alana Harris, Angie Heo, Anna-Karina Hermkens, Hillary Kaell, Mario Katić, Jeanne Kormina, Jens Kreinath, Ashley Lebner, Marc Loustau, Hannah Lunde, Nimrod Luz, Peter Margry, Ksenia Medvedeva, Jonathan Miles-Watson, Hildi Mitchell, Jon Mitchell, Anna Niedźwiedź, Yigal Nizri, Daniel Olsen, Filippo Osella, Elaine Peña, Ian Reader, Robert Orsi, Stella Rock, John Shultz, Matan Shapiro, Nurit Stadler, Michael Stausberg, Sara Terreault, Thomas Tweed, Meaghan Weatherdon, Deana Weibel, Emrah Yildiz, Donna Young, Mahshid Zandi, and Laurel Zwissler.

I was honored to benefit from Edith Turner's remarkable generosity of spirit and mind on a number of occasions. Both Candace Lukasik and Joey Youssef proved very helpful interpreters of Coptic Christianity, and Martyn Percy and Martin Warner helped educate me in the ways of Anglicanism. Over the years—even when we haven't been talking about pilgrimage—I have learned much from Andreas Bandak, Jon Bialecki, James Bielo, Ruy Blanes, Fenella Cannell, Michael Carrithers, Peter Collins, Abby Day, Matthew Engelke, David Garbin, Rosalind Hackett, Sondra Hausner, Sue Hyatt, Becky Johnson, Matthew Johnson, Cleonardo Mauricio Junior, Webb Keane, Ann Kingsolver, Kim Knibbe, Tammy Kohn, Pamela Klassen, Gareth Millington, Xavier Moyet, Valentina Napolitano, Joel Robbins, Ramon Sarró, Bob Simpson, Alana Souza, Anna Strhan, Matthew Tomlinson, Devaka Premawardhana, and Joe Webster. Kyle Byron both appears in the bibliography and helped me put the bibliography into some kind of order. Jennifer Hammer has been the best kind of editor—constructive, patient, positive. She also supplied two excellent referees, whom I thank here for their hard work and sage advice.

Producing a book is often a family effort. I discussed this project with my parents, John and Rochelle, and am full of sadness that my mother did not live to see its publication. I have to thank Eli, Gabriel, and Talia for putting up with an occasionally distracted dad. During my writing of this book, Leslie became a prize-winning author of fiction, and she helped me immensely by reading and editing the entire text. She also kept asking, "So is the book done yet?" I guess it is now.

NOTES

INTRODUCTION

1 The Cathedral is one of the oldest Christian buildings in the country.

2 See the project website, www.pilgrimageandcathedrals.ac.uk/. Also see Coleman and Bowman (2019).

3 See the project website, www.canterbury-cathedral.org/learning/heritage-lottery-funding-the-canterbury-journey/. Also see Coleman (2018).

4 See the exhibition website, www.arabelladorman.com/suspended/. The exhibition was also staged in St. James's Church Piccadilly. Notably, Canterbury Cathedral suspended its normal entry fee for those wishing to see the exhibition, a privilege also granted to those wishing to pray rather than sightsee.

5 See Frankie Boyle, "David Cameron Used 'Swarm' Instead of 'Plague' In Case It Implied That God Had Sent the Migrants," *Guardian*, August 3, 2015, www.theguardian.com.

6 Brexit refers to the result of the 2016 United Kingdom referendum that mandated departure from the European Union.

7 On the juxtaposition of power with pilgrimage, see also the subtitle of a volume edited by Hermkens, Jansen, and Notermans (2008): "The Power of Pilgrimage in the Modern World."

8 Pesach (Passover), the oldest, celebrates deliverance from enslavement in Egypt; Sukkot (literaly, "tabernacles") commemorates the forty years spent by the Jews in the wilderness; Shavuot (literaly, "weeks") was originally a harvest festival that also marked the giving of the Ten Commandments to Moses on Mount Sinai.

9 On the wider significance of questions of seduction in relation to pilgrimage, see Di Giovine and Picard (2015).

10 Most obviously, see Hobsbawm and Ranger (1983).

11 Daniel Olsen and Dallen Timothy (2006b, 1) argue that religion has long been considered a vital motivation for undertaking journeys and is "usually considered the oldest form of non-economic travel." They add that around 240 million people a year go on pilgrimages, the majority being Christians, Muslims, and Hindus (see also Preston 2020).

12 Frey (2017) observes that in 1996, 23,218 pilgrims reached Compostela (65 percent men and 35 percent women), whereas in 2015, the figure was 262,516 (53 percent men and 47 percent women).

13 See the Shikoku "Facts and Details" website, factsanddetails.com/japan/cat25/sub171/entry-6583.html.

14 I capitalize Hajj, in line with my descriptions of other pilgrimages, such as the Camino.

15 See Geeta Pandey, "Kumbh Mela: How to Plan a Festival for 100m People," *BBC Online News*, January 14, 2019, www.bbc.com/news/world-asia-india-46834335.

16 All this occurred in an English county that had voted forcefully in favor of Brexit, a political act designed precisely to prevent the free movement of people into the United Kingdom.

17 Compare Tweed (2006).

18 See the Merriam-Webster definition at www.merriam-webster.com/dictionary/articulation. A similar point was made by the cultural theorist Stuart Hall in an interview (Grossberg 1986), as I shall discuss in chapter 4.

19 Arguably, one of the reasons Dorman's exhibition finds an awkward and yet not inappropriate place within Canterbury Cathedral lies in the affinities between her work and certain contemporary Anglican emphases on immanence, a sense of divinity dwelling within the world.

20 Note that they use the allied term *systematicity* to refer to "the types of connections and disconnections that people of Muslim background make in order to evince and eclipse 'the religious' as being a more or less central dimension of their lives" (Marsden and Retsikas 2013, 2). Much of their broader inspiration comes from the philosophers Deleuze and Guattari (1980), who emphasize the dynamic and ongoing formation of categories and connections that make up social life, as well as the French sociologist of science Bruno Latour's (1993) understanding of the social as a network of human and non-human elements, formed by successive processes of assembly and disassembly.

21 Ian Reader (2007) argues that the contemporary growth of pilgrimages involves increasing numbers of sites that are not associated with any specific religious traditions. In a later work (Reader 2015), he refers to "the growth of what are described as either secular or nonreligious pilgrimages," as actions of visitors resonate with those evident in religious shrines, such as public enactment of grief at the Vietnam Veterans Memorial in Washington DC (12–13).

22 See Takaki Tominaga, "Shikoku's 'Path Less Traveled' Is Busier Than Ever," *Japan Times*, May 21, 2016, www.japantimes.co.jp.

23 There are different semiotic ideologies at play in this example. Webb Keane refers to such ideologies as containing "basic assumptions about what signs are and how they function in the world," including questions surrounding the workings of human and divine language, intention, and agency more generally (2003, 419).

24 See also Stella Rock, "Russia's New Saints and the Challenges of Memory," August 9, 2011, *Open Democracy*, www.opendemocracy.net.

25 In Marcus's terms, maintaining a constant awareness of the "elsewhere" that constitute a given fieldwork site, as well as following the flows of people, ideas, goods and so on across sites. See also Coleman and von Hellermann 2011.

26 See, for example, Coleman (2000); Coleman and Maier (2016).

27 Clearly, Pentecostalism is limited as a comparative tool by its embeddedness within Christianity, but in other respects, this dimension encourages the analyst to question assumptions concerning the homogeneity and integrity of any single world religion.

28 Compare Carole Cusack and Justin Digance's argument that in many parts of the contemporary world, supposedly transcendent experiences occur in places outside traditional religious territories (2008, 229).

29 The more general project here refers to what William Cavanaugh (2008) refers to as "Mobility and Identity in a Global Age." He juxtaposes such figures as the "Migrant, Tourist, Pilgrim, Monk" in his title, noting that "images of mobility dominate literature on globalization" (340). While acknowledging the value of Cavanaugh's figures, I question assumptions that the global is automatically synonymous with the mobile. It may also involve key points of immobility (see chapter 8).

30 I borrow the useful notion of seduction in relation to pilgrimage from Di Giovine and Picard (2015).

31 For an important study challenging triumphalist accounts of Pentecostalism, see Premawardhana (2018).

32 *Field* was a term much used by Victor Turner, the single most influential theorist of pilgrimage in anthropological circles, and in chapter 3, I make the case that his work has often been read very selectively, in a way that has failed to appreciate his potentially very broad understanding of the field of pilgrimage studies.

33 I focus particularly but not exclusively on Anglophone scholarship. See Eade and Albera (2017) for a useful account of how Anglophone and other literatures on pilgrimage do—and do not—relate to each other.

1. PILGRIMAGE

1 See also Coleman and Hackett (2015, 39).

2 Following Robert Baird (1991).

3 Even what constitutes an acceptable definition may change over time. The scholar of pilgrimage Aghehananda Bharati notes that the pilgrimage entry in the *Encyclopedia of Religion and Ethics* from the early part of the twentieth century contains no overarching introduction and leaps straight into describing specific pilgrimages—Muslim, Christian, Buddhist, and so on (Bharati 1991, 26). In contrast, the new *Encyclopedia of Religion* (1987) contains numerous generalizations, including many that Bharati finds dubious.

4 As anthropologist Stephan Palmié remarks in discussing the study of Afro-Cuban religion, it becomes important to avoid "the kind of Aristotelian nominalism that suggests that if there is a name for something, then that something must (somehow) exist" (2013, 3).

5 Glenn Bowman observes: "As people's cultures are re-formed by events and encounters, so too are the objects of desire they seek to find in the sites to which they go on pilgrimage" (2014, 155).

6 Morinis's useful typology of pilgrimages indicates the variety of journeys that might be possible: devotional (aimed at encounter with a divinity); initiatory (aimed at transforming participants); instrumental (aimed at achieving worldly goals); normative (part of the ritual calendar); obligatory (required as a form of penance or through the strictures of faith); and wandering (having no predetermined goal) (Morinis 1992, 10–13; also discussed in Frey 1998, 262).

7 Ronald Grimes puts the point succinctly: "We religion scholars write religion into being as surely as anthropologists write culture into being" (2000, 20).

8 Though historically, some pilgrimages have lacked a specific destination, such as early Irish ascetic monks who wandered constantly, with no physical goal.

9 For a useful working definition, see Ian Reader's observation that pilgrimage incorporates three main elements: travel/movement, veneration, and a special place or places, often associated with sacred figures or founders (2015, 40).

10 Kathryn Rountree illustrates the politics of *ignoring* such distinctions in her account of how neo-pagans collapse dichotomies between "spiritual rapture and bodily pleasure," challenging old spirit/body splits in Western discourse (2006b, 100).

11 Luz and Collins-Kreiner place their remarks in the context of "the state's attempts to consecrate the land as part of ongoing conflict with Palestinians as well as religious resurgence and radicalisation within Israeli-Jewish society" (2015, 130).

12 See Stadler's (2020) important study of the revival of rituals at female saints' shrines in Israel-Palestine, which she links to the assertion of rights to land.

13 Eade and Albera note that the words *pilgrim* and *pilgrimage* derive from the Latin (2107, 7ff). Terms such as *peregrinus, peregrinatio, peregrinitas, peregrinor*, and *peregrines* have a common root: *per ager*, meaning across the fields, used during the Roman period to refer to aliens or those traveling abroad. By 1694, The *Dictionary of the Académie* lists *pellerin* as someone who makes a journey to a place of worship. While Italian and English see the emergence of the terms *pellegrinaggio* and *pilgrimage*, German has retained both *Pilgerfahrt* and *Wallfahrt*.

14 The Hindu pilgrimage Kumbh Mela, which can literally be translated as "the festival of the sacred pitcher," refers to a pot (*kumbha*) said to have contained an elixir of immortality, drops of which fell on the four earthly sites where the festival is staged.

15 See Reader and Swanson (1997). Shultz (2009, 9) comments that *henro* combines *hen*, meaning "widely" or "generally," with *ro*, meaning "route" or "road." He also refers to a more general term that may be used to refer to pilgrimage, *junrei*, implying "going around and worshiping."

16 The word is broadly similar in Arabic and Persian.

17 A cliché, and also a crude characterization; see, Neville (1987), Peacock and Tyson (1989), and Coleman (2004) for challenges to this assumption. I document the lack of interaction between Coptic studies and pilgrimage studies in Coleman (2019).

18 Reader (2017) also observes that Anglophone studies of pilgrimage have largely been based in anthropology (and to some extent history), whereas German, Hun-

garian, and Japanese traditions of study have included other fields, such as folk studies (184).

19 Reader also remarks that Retief Müller's discussion of flows of people, goods, and services to and around sites in southern Africa would have been helpful to his 2014 book, though he was unaware of Müller's work at the time (2017, 191).

20 Though one of these (Bhardwaj 1991) is on Hindu migrants from India and their translation of pilgrimage practices to the United States.

21 Though see, for example, Ranger (1987) and Nthoi (2006).

22 Discussed further in chapter 8.

23 Further dimensions of du Plooy's argument are expressed in her fascinating if brief discussion of the notion of "evolving pilgrimage" in African contexts (2017, 133), with local debts and obligations apparently "entrapping" pilgrims into developing particular relationships with a journey, a landscape, and each other.

24 There are a few studies examining Pentecostal forms of pilgrimage, which tend to emphasize the particularities of understanding of place, space, and time among such believers (Coleman 2004; Fortuny and de Mola 2018).

25 It is notable that in their overviews of the topic separated by some twenty-two years, both Jill Dubisch (1995, 34) and Ian Reader (2017, 192) spend some time speculating whether pilgrimage exists as a unitary category.

26 Drawing on Strathern (2004).

27 This point echoes the geographer Doreen Massey's view of places as intrinsically elusive and as "the coming together of the previously unrelated, a constellation of processes rather than a thing. . . . Not capturable as a slice through time in the sense of an essential section. Not intrinsically coherent" (2005, 141).

28 For a succinct discussion of the emergence of a powerful Muslim focus of pilgrimage activity away from Mecca, see Michael Di Giovine and Jaeyeon Choe's description of Arbaeën—the Shia pilgrimage to Karbala in Iraq commemorating the martyrdom of Hussein (grandson of Muhammad) and now one of the largest pilgrimages in the world (2019, 12). Despite its size, it is precisely not a pan-Islamic pilgrimage but "one that memorializes the period in which religio-political divisions in the Middle Eastern world were solidified" (ibid.). Sophia Rose Arjana (2017) also provides an excellent analysis of the full range of Muslim pilgrimage.

29 Luz draws on Dawut (2009).

30 As Chris Hann (2007) has noted, there are times when we might wish to remake our fields of study by cutting across them in new ways. For instance, a project attempting to understand the maintenance of community relations in a given region might both observe behavior at holy places and deploy analytical categories that have little to do with studies of pilgrimage as such.

31 See chapter 6, as well as Jason Danely's (2017) discussion of how pilgrimage constantly exceeds its immediate context (drawing on Coleman [2002]; discussed in Reader [2017, 193]).

32 My phrasing of the title of this section echoes Malcolm Ruel's survey of belief, English literature, and anthropological epistemology in his reflections on "looking

through categories and not just at them" (1997, 230). Ruel mediates between English scholar F. R. Leavis and anthropologist E. E. Evans-Pritchard in considering
the relationship between objectivist and humanist accounts of culture.

33 Tweed notes that among the inspirations for his imagery of flow are Deleuze
and Guattari's "hydraulic model" for the "ambulant sciences" and Bruno Latour's
actor-network theory, with its imagery of circulating fluids (Tweed 2006, 59).

34 We might re-describe such times as periods of dis- and rearticulation. Note also
that Durkheim was influenced by William Robertson Smith's *Religion of the
Semites* (1889), which described the role of pilgrimage and associated hospitality
in creating the bonds that underlay ancient Jewish life.

35 Fedele and Isnart (2015, 175) count just three explicit mentions in *The Elementary
Forms*. In their view, Durkheim's main aim is to link going on pilgrimage to a
more general cult of ancestors, and to an evolutionist genealogy expressing the
continuity of his totemic explanatory scheme.

36 See Hertz (2017). Pilgrimage did form a recurring subject for folklore studies in
Europe in the nineteenth and early twentieth centuries, though what marked out
Hertz's study was its theoretical and ethnological contribution to the Durkheimian sociological project. Fedele and Isnart (2015) observe that even though France
was one of the earliest European centers for the social scientific study of religion,
pilgrimage attracted relatively little direct attention before the second half of the
twentieth century (171). They see opposition between clerical and more spontaneous forms of devotion as one of the "interconnected red lines" running through
French traditions of pilgrimage studies (172).

37 In reflecting on Hertz's paper, Alexander Riley (forthcoming) places more emphasis on how the celebration of St. Besse also departs from a purely Durkheimian
vision in its depiction of conflict. Riley notes, "The cult of Saint Besse turns out
on inspection to be several cults, and the contours of local versions of the cultic
legend and the rites attached to it are rooted in the social structures and cultural
histories of those places. Different sets of beliefs and rites inform the veneration
of Besse in the valley and in the mountains, and struggle over which is the authentic saint is a constant throughout the cult's history" (ibid.). This interpretation
sees Hertz's work as anticipating that of Eade and Sallnow (1991) on contestation,
discussed in chapter 4.

38 The writing of the *Golden Bough* interrupted Frazer's translation of *Description of
Greece* by a Greek writer of the second century CE called Pausanias. Pausanias's
work was a combination of guidebook and pilgrimage account, tracing temples,
shrines, and ritual practices in the Peloponnese and central Greece (see Alcock,
Cherry, and Elsner 2001).

39 Fedele and Isnart (2015) note that Hertz's study made little impact when it first
appeared (176). In Anglophone contexts, its dissemination was aided by its translation into English in 1997 (MacClancy and Parkin 1997).

40 Alexander Riley notes that Czarnowski's work (e.g., 1919) was an important source
for James Joyce in writing *Finnegan's Wake*.

41 Quoted in Niedźwiedź (2015, 79).

42 Helmut Eberhart reports that in Germany, in the immediate post–Second World War years, "research on pilgrimage was largely pushed into the background because the focus was primarily on technological change and 'progress'" (2015, 114). Interest from folklorists, ethnologists, and other social scientists revived as it became clear from the 1980s and 1990s that increasing numbers of people in German-speaking countries were going on pilgrimage.

43 *Post-secular* refers here to the persistence or efflorescence of religious and spiritual engagement, despite predictions that with modernity must come secularization. Post-secular spirituality tends to imply non-institutionalized forms of practice and may also be linked to notions of the postmodern.

2. CONSTRUCTING THE FIELD

1 The notion of single-village fieldwork was itself always something of a myth, evidenced, for instance, by the spatial complexities revealed in Bronislaw Malinowski's *Argonauts of the Western Pacific* (1922) or E. Evans-Pritchard's *The Nuer* (1940).

2 Kaell acknowledges that other authors, such as Nancy Frey (1998, 2004, for the Camino de Santiago) and Anna Fedele (2012, for alternative Catholic pilgrimage in France) have posed follow-up questions to pilgrims after they have returned home (Kaell 2014, 209). A fascinating approach to considering such mobilities is discussed by Buitelaar et al. (2021), where they reflect on increasingly "flow-form" conceptions of movement, in which temporal and spatial boundaries are viewed as fluid and porous and mobility does not imply clear-cut transitions from one stage or territory to another but more continual and gradual change, or a moving back and forth between "here" and "there." Away from purely Christian examples, Nadia Caidi's (2019) account of the Hajj presents pilgrimage site and home as extensions of each other.

3 In its location of pilgrimage practices within an ethnography of the everyday, Kholoud A. M. Al-Ajarma's (2020) "Mecca in Morocco" provides a vivid counterpart to Gold's work, written over thirty years later.

4 Buitelaar et al. (2021) provide an excellent example of duplication: the ways in which *ziyara* practices at local saint shrines may be staged during the Hajj season and treated as "Hajj of the poor," substituting the pilgrimage for those who do not have the means to go to Mecca.

5 Typologies of pilgrimage can provide useful insights into wider classificatory assumptions contained within religious traditions. Thus, Yueh-po Huang summarizes Joseph Kitagawa's (1987) division of Japanese pilgrimage into three categories: "pilgrimages to sacred mountains; pilgrimages based on faith in a specific divinity who is the image of worship of several linked sites; and pilgrimages based on visits to a number of sites associated with charismatic holy figures" (Huang 2017, 285–86).

6 Ronan Foley has explored the role of Irish holy wells as small-scale sites that speak to wider geographies and yet, because of their size, bring ritual and everyday action very close to each other (2013, 45–46).

7 Shrines that are shared across religious boundaries are common and bring their own methodological challenges. Laksana provides an extended analysis of the intersections of Muslim and Catholic traditions in south central Java, showing how they "coalesce and illuminate each other" (2014, 192). Indeed, the pilgrimage tradition as a whole has become "a privileged milieu in which a distinctively hybrid religio-cultural identity formation and negotiation is forged among Javanese Muslims and Catholics" (195).

8 The argument is that pilgrimage systems can be seen as constantly evolving at different scales, constituted through spatial geometries that involve the interaction (rather than the mere opposition) of the centripetal and the centrifugal, the inner and the outer, the sacred and profane, order and chaos (cf. Bajc, Coleman, and Eade 2007).

9 The ambition of his analysis is reminiscent of anthropologist Stanley Tambiah's (1976) use of the Hindu and Buddhist mandala pattern as the basis of his depiction of Southeast Asian "galactic polities" as organized into concentric circles of ever decreasing control. This model is adapted by Michael Di Giovine (in press) in his analysis of the diffusion of the cult of Padre Pio within and beyond Italy.

10 Paolo Apolito's early study, *The Internet and the Madonna* (2005), argued that the internet gave new life to Catholic worship by broadcasting an eclectic mix of modern technology and Marian visions, enabling new forms of religious charisma to become widely diffused (see also Hill-Smith 2011).

11 Such "singularism" may represent the parochialism of anthropology in particular, as well as past limitations of scholarship that focuses on Christianity. Huang (2017, 286) notes how Reader and Swanson (1997) differentiate between single-site and multiple-site pilgrimage in their analysis of Japanese traditions. Thus "linear" pilgrimage, focused on one shrine, contrasts with "circuit" pilgrimage, involving a number of sites linked together, with each site granted equal importance. Note, however, that what I and Loustau and DeConinck are describing also covers the possibility of pilgrims weaving together sites that do not normally form part of a conjoined system.

12 Olsen and Timothy note that in Europe visits to religious sites have been increasing while regular church attendance declines (2006b, 3).

13 They note that the word *palimpsest* derives from a Greek compound word that means scraped clean and ready to be used again. The same metaphor is used by Stephen Platten in his discussion of contemporary cathedrals, where he notes that "most church buildings are palimpsests, where successive historical periods have added the story of their own particular local communities" (2017, 11). The palimpsest is also invoked by Rousseau (2016, 253), inspired by J. Z. Smith's (1987) use of the image to describe the Emperor Constantine's building program in Palestine as creating a new order for Christianity, placed over other myths, histories, and physical constructions. See also Kinnard's (2014) drawing on Andreas Huyssen (2003) to reflect on how in Indian sites such as Ayodhya, one can discern "a kind of palimpsest quality that in part constitutes the sacrality of places, in which sto-

ries and myths and histories and building materials are layered one upon another" (Kinnard 2014, 34).

14 These points resonate with Dubisch's list of different ways to study pilgrimage. She mentions examining it as experienced by people who journey from home to site, focusing on a site, and taking a macro-level look at systems of pilgrimage within particular religious traditions (1995, 40).

15 Compare Morinis (1992).

16 See also Andreas Nordin's comment, in the context of a paper concerning pilgrimage and cognition, that it is not helpful to focus on only one aspect of pilgrimage and then offer this as a magic-bullet explanation for all manifestations (2016, 5). He suggests the utility of fractionating pilgrimage into its constituent parts.

17 Compare Christoph Bergmann and Jürgen Schaflechner's (2019) discussion of ritualized journeying in South Asia. Following Catherine Bell (1992, 74), they avoid essentialized definitions of such travel in order to "scrutinize the strategies of ritualization through which actors create, assemble, and rearticulate certain modes of displacement such as to differentiate them from their everyday forms of locomotion," resulting in "a polythetic . . . perspective, [leaving it] open to empirical scrutiny whether a ritual journey features . . . certain characteristics and functions" (Bergmann and Schaflechner 2019, 2).

18 I use the term *sacralized* here to indicate that continuous work is required to maintain the special qualities of a space, but I do not imply that what a given person or group regards as sacred must entail divine intervention.

19 See my discussion of figure and ground in chapter 1.

20 This point about the lack of attention paid to Obeyesekere's work within pilgrimage studies has been made by Albera (2019a).

21 In her re-analysis of Lourdes, Alana Harris (2013) shifts the conventional frame of the pilgrimage field into the notion of the *therapeutic landscape*, a well-known term within medical anthropology and sociology.

22 For an earlier discussion of politics and gender relations, focused on Himalayan pilgrimage, see William Sax (1991). Filippo and Caroline Osella (2003) examine expressions of masculinity during the Sabarimala pilgrimage in Kerala.

23 See also, for example, Rountree (2002) and Zwissler (2011). In addition, some writing has combined some of the themes I am raising, such as the analyses of intersections between gender and healing provided by Lena Gemzöe (2005) and Susan Sered (2005). For wide-ranging work on Muslim women pilgrims, see Buitelaar et al. (2021). For reflections on Marianism at Walsingham see Coleman (2009a).

24 Certain features of pilgrimage also appear well suited to exploration of current emergent research areas. Evolutionary approaches to the study of pilgrimages are beginning to ask what social benefits might be derived from such apparently "costly" behaviors (e.g., Chvaja and Řezníček 2019). Another obvious focus revolves around subject-object relations inherent in interactions with shrines, a

potential link between ethnographic and art historical methodologies (cf. Hazard 2013).

25 In common with one of the meanings of *definition*, articulation retains the possibility of coming in and out of focus, of sometimes being sharply demarcated and on other occasions becoming fuzzier in outline (cf. Bandak 2012). To such a shape-shifting quality, it adds the possibility of making links of greater or lesser degrees of strength and distinctiveness with other institutions and activities. Compare also Bialecki's Deleuzian discussion of the refusal of the anthropology of Christianity to define its object, leading him to suggest that "we should take the object of anthropology to be Christianity in its virtual form, as a multiplicity which is predicated on and produces difference" (Bialecki 2012, 298).

3. A TROPE MADE TO TRAVEL

1 A piece by Marjorie Snipes (2018) is called "'*Communitas* Keeps Revealing Itself': The Unfinished Business of *Communitas*." See also the special issue from 2011 focusing on the theme "Pilgrimage: Communitas and Contestation, Unity and Difference" (Di Giovine 2011).

2 Thomas Tweed describes tropes as "orienting metaphors" (2006, 29). This sense of providing direction is inherent in the very etymology of the word, given that the Greek *tropos* derives from *trepein*, to turn.

3 For a useful summary, see Park and Bucholtz (2009).

4 This shift from African ethnography takes on extra significance in the light of the general failure of pilgrimage studies to address African case studies.

5 Di Giovine's (2011) excellent introduction to his special issue is an exception. See also Edith Turner's (2006) memoir *Heart of Lightness*.

6 Stephen Glazier notes that the couple favored the names Vic and Edie (2018, 35).

7 Edith did not receive a university education and was never formally trained in anthropology.

8 Timothy Larsen notes that even the Turners' marriage involved an act of defiance, though one that later became ironic, having chosen a secular ceremony at a registry office in Oxford, in contrast to their later enmeshment in Roman Catholic ritual (2014, 174).

9 Frankenberg is referring in particular to a famous piece by Gluckman (1958) nicknamed "The Bridge Paper" by the latter's students—an apt image, given the Turners' interest in pilgrimage as a crossing of boundaries.

10 Though Gluckman was not opposed to the study of ritual per se. Larsen remarks that the original plan for Victor's PhD had involved carrying out a study of the economic life of the Mambwe in what is now Zambia, but at the last minute, Gluckman telegraphed to the couple, "Suggest you change to Ndembu tribe Northwestern Providence much malaria yellow fever plenty of ritual" (quoted in Larsen 2014, 179; from E. Turner 1992, 2). For further reflections on Gluckman's influence on the Turnersa see the interview with Edith conducted by George Mentore (Mentore 2009).

11 Reflecting on Victor's discussions with Gluckman and the relationship between the rite of passage model and Marxism, Edith noted, "We saw the idea of the inevitability of change embedded in Marxism too. So when Vic came to study rites of passage, he thought about the dialectic, and he thought about change in the context of a new station of life" (E. Turner 2009, ii).

12 Despite the clear connections between Turnerian and Durkheimian understandings of the workings of ritual, Victor denounced what he saw as the latter's attempt to explain away religious phenomena through naturalistic frames of analysis (Larsen 2014, 189).

13 Glazier remarks that Manchester colleagues were vexed when Victor accepted a professorship in the United States but even more agitated when the Turners announced their conversion to Catholicism (2018, 37).

14 See Deflem (1991, 7). The book had not been available in English until 1960. Riley (forthcoming) notes that van Gennep studied for some years under Mauss, who supervised van Gennep's 1904 thesis on taboo and totemism in Madagascar. Nonetheless, van Gennep was critical of what he saw as the unreliable ethnographic evidence underlying the claims of *The Elementary Forms.*

15 See also Max Gluckman's (1962) edited *Essays on the Ritual of Social Relations,* which was dedicated to the memory of van Gennep.

16 Van Gennep himself perhaps represented a transitional or mediating figure for the Turnerian vision of pilgrimage; he worked on the cusp between earlier folkloric and later ethnographic methods of studying religion.

17 Thus Turner: "The neophyte in liminality must be a tabula rasa, a blank slate, on which is inscribed the knowledge and wisdom of the group, in those respects that pertain to the new status" (V. Turner 1969, 103).

18 Later, the critical theorist Homi Bhabha (2004) would link the apparent fluidity of the notion of liminality to discussions of African postcolonial identity (see Kalua 2009, 23).

19 Clifford Geertz memorably calls Victor "British-formed, American re-formed" (1983, 172). Nelson Graburn (2011) mentions the significance of Victor's period of leave (1961–62) in the very "unstructured" Center for the Advanced Studies in the Behavioral Sciences in Palo Alto, California.

20 Edith adds that Victor gained a sense of communitas when working in the British Army during World War II, as a conscientious objector loading food on to railroad wagons (E. Turner 2012, 6).

21 Most famously in *Leviathan* (1651), taken from the Latin: *Bellum omnium contra omnes.*

22 Larsen remarks that Victor was indeed criticized for ignoring the dark side of communitas (2014, 207).

23 Another important influence for Victor Turner in linking notions of flow to an anthropology of experience was the German thinker Wilhelm Dilthey (see, e.g., Turner and Bruner [1986]).

24 Bruce Kapferer argues that Turnerian liminality is the site of mutually counteracting forces or principles. He sees the idea as reliant as much on Nietzsche's well-known Apollonian-Dionysian contest as on van Gennep (Kapferer 2015, 10).

25 The notion also recalls the idea of the cosmic center, or axis mundi, promoted by Mircea Eliade, a Romanian scholar of religion who moved to the United States in the 1950s, settling in Chicago.

26 In the late 1970s, the pair moved to the University of Virginia, where they stayed for the rest of their careers.

27 The book represented a further methodological shift from the Ndembu years. As Edith recalled, "For the pilgrimage work, we did do 'traditional fieldwork' in the sense that we went on pilgrimages ourselves. But a lot of it was textual analysis. We looked a lot at writing by devotees. . . . And then of course the experience of going on the pilgrimages as Catholics was personal as well as observational" (Engelke 2008, 287). At the same time, Edith makes a connection between this approach to pilgrimage and the writing about ritual from a decade earlier, suggesting that it "strikes me as being . . . more a continuation of the latter chapters in the *Ritual Process*" (ibid.).

28 Compare their perspective with Avril Maddrell and Richard Scriven's more recent depiction of Lough Derg's "Celtic nature" as being "(re)created and reinforced in the inherent balance between the structural elements, such as clerical governance, liturgy, customs and the built environment, and the mobilities through which the pilgrimage is (re)produced anew by each pilgrim" (2016, 11–12).

29 As Laurel Zwissler astutely points out, the Turners acknowledge certain forms of difference within the study of communitas—for instance, as conflicts cement bonds among pilgrims against religious authorities (2011, 335).

30 The sense of a wider pilgrimage landscape is picked up again when the Turners use geographer Surinder Bhardwaj's (1973) analysis of Hindu shrines to consider the catchment areas of Christian shrines as existing at scales ranging from inter-village to international levels (Turner and Turner 1978, 238–39).

31 Compare this claim with Ingvild Flaskerud and Richard Natvig's balanced assessment of potential parallels between communitas and the establishment of a sense of a global Muslim community, or *umma*, aided by the hajj, "Communitas is always temporary, whereas the sense of being part of an *umma* can be long-standing. However, the spontaneous sensation of existential communitas, experienced by some pilgrims during hajj, may enhance the feeling of being part of the *umma*" (2018, 17).

32 For Nimrod Luz, the Turnerian model has also contributed to a reluctance among scholars of Islam to engage in studies of non-Hajj pilgrimage (2020, drawing on Boivin [2017]). The sense that the Hajj is both liminal and forms a paradigm for a whole religion is expressed well in the title of the edited British Museum volume *Hajj: Journey to the Heart of Islam* (Porter et al. 2012).

33 As Pnina Werbner notes of the theory, Turner's study of "sacred peripherality" emphasized the tendency for pilgrimage centers to embody "an alternative ethical

order, one uncircumscribed by territorially defined relations of power and authority" (2003, 17).

34 Jacob Kinnard notes of communitas that "certainly this essentially utopian vision of humanity is not without attraction; indeed, there is something quite seductive about it." Part of the seduction, in his terms, is that the Turners say relatively little about the structural context that helps to produce it, so that they present a "peculiarly agentless formation of a . . . group identity" (2014, 6).

35 Appendix A is termed "Notes on Processual Symbolic Analysis," and B is a chronology of the Lough Derg pilgrimage.

36 *Limen* is Latin for threshold. *Communitas* in Latin refers to an unstructured community in which people are equal.

37 It is perhaps ironic that the Turners celebrated the ritual democratization of Vatican II yet constructed a Latinate vocabulary to describe anti-structural creativity.

38 In Larsen's view, communitas is equivalent to Eden, Pentecost, and the heavenly kingdom of God in the Turnerian schema (2014, 192). He adds that a Catholic might also think of "the hyperliminal moment of the Eucharist elevation when bread is transubstantiated into Host whose consumption converts parishioners of diverse social structural attributes into the single Mystical Body of the Church, and a moment of pure existential communitas is realised" (193–94).

39 In much of his work, Gluckman also was concerned to divorce understanding of ritual from an automatic association with the sacred.

40 It is worth considering this processual approach in the light of Hodges's remarks (2008, 400) that, as globalization has become implicated in anthropological analysis, the sense that social experience is fluid has become a dominant paradigm. See also Kapferer's (2006, 135) linking of Gluckman's situational ideas to Deleuze and Guattari's (1980) emphasis on continual becoming. Kapferer (2019, 1) also compares Turnerian liminality to Deleuze and Guattari's descriptions of the virtual. He sees Victor Turner as moving beyond a Hegelian dialectic of structure/anti-structure into conceptualizing communitas as capable of creating new assemblages of relations, meaning, and value.

41 Dean MacCannell's *The Tourist* (1976) is a well-known exploration of the structure of modern mass leisure that explores the quest for an authenticity missing from everyday lives. Graburn's (1977) influential essay "Tourism: The Sacred Journey" equates pilgrimage and tourism by showing similarities in their structure.

42 Katherine Rousseau (2016, 40) documents the Turnerian view that normative and ideological communitas "rob existential communitas of its potency and purity." Flaskerud and Natvig note, "Existential communitas . . . is best developed theoretically and has become the most influential" (2018, 17).

43 If Cannell's argument seems abstract, we might consider how the history of colonialization has often involved European missionaries condemning local "pagans" for being in thrall to materialism and idolatry. In contemporary contexts, those Christians who receive the most skepticism are often those blending spiritual and material concerns, as in the Health and Wealth Gospel (Coleman 2015b).

44 Hillary Kaell (2014, 100–1) notes of post-Vatican II Roman Catholic pilgrims to the Holy Land that they may see themselves as Jesus centered and scripture focused in a way not always appreciated by scholars who have emphasized differences from Protestant evangelicalism. See also Orsi's (2005) reflections on the ritual effects of Vatican II.

45 She was writing at a time when Catholic charismatic renewal was emerging.

46 Contrast this antinomianism with Mary Douglas's emphasis on hierarchy, structure, and order, though Douglas was also interested in developing a symbolic anthropology in which the powers and dangers of thresholds came to the fore (e.g., Douglas 1966, 1970; see also Larsen 2014, 193). A contrast with E. E. Evans-Pritchard's generally more implicit brand of Catholicism is also evident.

47 As Eade notes (2000a, xii), Bowman's argument is highly apt here, to the effect that the Turners separated interpretation from what Bowman calls "the constraints of history and society" while presenting communitas as "a transhistorical and omnipresent archetypal form" (Bowman 1985, 3). Albera (2019a) contrasts the prominence and influence of their theory with the obscurity of French writer Romain Roussell, author of a general cultural theory of pilgrimage—*Pèlerinages à travers les siècles* (1954). As an autodidact, Roussell lacked the powerful institutional backing that Victor regularly enjoyed (notwithstanding Victor's self-positioning as an outsider) and wrote in French rather than English. Roussell also emphasized the tendency for shrines to encourage different religions to converge on the same site, while the Turners played down the cultural, social, and spatial complexities involved in the sharing of shrines.

48 Thus, Victor Turner: "Communitas strains towards universalism and openness" (1974, 202).

49 Thus Tsing: "Liberal universals mix and meld with the universals of science, world religions (especially Christianity and Islam), and emancipatory philosophies including Marxism and feminism" (2005, 9).

50 Writing in a volume devoted to pilgrims and sacred sites in China, Susan Naquin and Chün-fang Yü observe of Victor Turner that "whether they agree with his theory or not, most researchers have felt the need to address his ideas" (1992, 7).

51 Discussing the relevance of communitas to North African Jewish pilgrimage, Oren Kosansky notes that it proves useful in describing how "quotidian social hierarchies of gender, age, and wealth recede" during *hillulot* (celebrations of the anniversary of a Jewish holy man, or *ṣaddiq*). (2002, 365–66). However, he adds that social hierarchies may also be enacted and reproduced on such occasions.

52 Buitelaar et al. (2021) note of Muslim female pilgrims that "various axes of differentiation such as class, gender, ethnicity and nationality intertwine in pilgrimage practices in particular ways." The intersectional quality of such analysis contrasts with the Turnerian stripping away of social statuses.

53 Although the Turners could not have predicted the impact of social media on pilgrimage, we should also reflect on the ways in which use of such media challenges

the possibility of being set apart from mundane space and time. See discussion in chapter 7.

54 As in most other commentaries, the distinction between the liminal and the liminoid is conflated in Weber's argument. In fact, the latter contains social critique in the original Turnerian model.

55 Pnina Werbner, married to Richard Werbner and also a distinguished anthropologist, is a niece of Max Gluckman.

56 For a distinguished historian's critique of the Turnerian framework as reflecting the Christianity "of a particular class, gender and historical period" see Caroline Walker Bynum (1992, 28).

57 Michael Agnew (2019, 37) notes that as scholars move away from Turnerian depictions of sacred centers as being "out there," such sites begin to be described as second homes for visitors who returned regularly to the same shrine.

58 Also quoted in Badone and Roseman (2004, 4).

59 For Jha, writing primarily from the perspective of pilgrimage in India, meaning is also irrelevant to ritual, including those belonging to pilgrimage: "A pilgrimage is emically successful when it has been properly performed, not when the chants and prayers used by pandits and other functionaries have been understood" (1990, 24). This emphasis on performance rather than meaning and experience suggests that Jha is describing a fundamentally different semiotic ideology to that assumed by the Turners, maintaining very different assumptions as to the interrelations of language, materiality, and personhood. Jha's remark anticipates some of Humphrey and Laidlaw's (1994) important discussion of ritual as "archetypal action."

60 Compare such a verdict with Clifford Geertz's critique of the earlier social drama model. Geertz remarks that the model provides "a form for all seasons" and that "this hospitableness in the face of cases is at once the major strength of the ritual theory version of the drama analogy and its most prominent weakness. It can expose some of the profoundest features of social process, but at the expense of making vividly disparate matters look drably homogeneous" (1983, 173).

61 The Turners could not have foreseen in the late 1970s the ways in which social media have collapsed sharp distinctions between planning, making, and reflecting on trips. Nancy Frey concludes that under current circumstances of diffused knowledge and experience pilgrimages can often "be more reaffirming rather than transformative" (2017, 25).

62 What Margry means by falsification might imply that no communitas has been located in a given shrine (as suggested by Messerschmidt and Sharma) or rather that it is not the only form of sociality to be observed.

63 All scholarly tropes shift over time, but when they block alternative perspectives, they become like Thomas Kuhn's (1962) famous notion of "normal science," where established paradigms discourage the questioning of long-established assumptions.

64 Katherine Rousseau notes, "Many studies of pilgrimage continue to use the Turners as interlocutors" (2016, 24). Stella Rock remarks in a summary of pilgrimage research: "The general direction of travel in pilgrimage studies has been away from the universalizing, structuralist approach of the Turners, whose seminal study of Christian pilgrimage nevertheless remains the starting point for much anglophone study and research" (2006, 195).

65 Suzanne van der Beek (2018, 19) summarizes the ritual scholar Catherine Bell's (2002, 16–17) characterization of Victor Turner's general approach as a practice of decontextualization, designed to reveal the universality of "the ritual process."

66 A useful contrast is provided by Buitelaar et al.'s depiction of visits to saints' tombs carried out by urban women in Morocco, Turkey, or Iran: a regular Friday outing rather than an exceptional event (2021).

67 Michael Di Giovine and David Picard define seduction "as a particular social process in which an actor deliberately, strategically . . . leads his or her subject to an unintended, incorrect, or opposite course of action by cultivating in this subject a strong desire or 'fascination' . . . that runs contrary to the target's pre-existing dispositions, motives, interests, needs, or ideas of well-being" (2015, 2). I retain their sense of a diversion from an expected or anticipated direction, though I leave open the question of Turners' strategic use of communitas as a generic yet fascinating term.

68 Jonathan Miles-Watson and Sukanya B. Miles-Watson (2011, 327) refer to other studies of pilgrimage in the Himalayas (Sax 1991; van der Veer, 1988) that see communitas as providing too simplistic a model for understanding motivations for pilgrimage.

69 Even Mark MacWilliams's survey of "Virtual Pilgrimages on the Internet" devotes a section to discussing whether such activities can "offer [an] . . . experience of communitas" (McWilliams 2002, 326).

70 There are honorable exceptions to this tendency. Emily Porth (2005) argues for the importance of specifically normative communitas at a Canadian Catholic shrine.

71 The terms *primitive* and *modern* are no longer part of the anthropological lexicon, given their misleading evolutionary assumptions. Note that the potential for more imaginative adaptations of communitas exists, even if it has not been fully realized. An interesting example is provided by Kiran Shinde's (2011) attempt to focus on socio-spatial arrangements rather than experiential perspectives in generating communitas.

72 The mutually reinforcing dimensions of the Turnerian center and communitas can be discerned in the way both point to experiences of maximum intensity that are untied to mundane geographical moorings.

73 Or as Huang shows in his own work on Taiwanese pilgrims going to Tenri, people may not see themselves as leaving everyday life so much as establishing significant continuities with it: connectivity trumps communitas (2017, 301).

74 See also Coleman (2014).

4. FRICTIONAL ENERGIES

1 Sallnow's central concern is with "the articulation of individuals and communities through the cults of translocal and regional shrines" (1987, 1). In his assessment of the Manchester School, Werbner explains his development of the concept of the regional cult as an attempt to "crystallize our theoretical interest in sacred places and the changing flows around them and across communities," while contextualizing "cult change in a dialectical relation with a wider social field having its own changing values and its own changing distribution of power and resources" (1984, 172).

2 Dubisch (1995, 43) points out that even when ordinary social relationships are suspended or muted during pilgrimage, this process does not necessarily lead to communitas. She cites Sallnow's argument (1981) that in Andean pilgrimage, a new supralocal arena of competition may be created under such circumstances.

3 *Schism and Continuity* acknowledged the inevitability of conflict over the course of tribal life, but by the time of *Image and Pilgrimage,* the Turners were likely to interpret conflict as a disruption of idealized Christian relations of mutual harmony.

4 In his later work Sallnow notes, "Pilgrimage intensifies the bonds of kinship and neighbourhood" (Sallnow 1987, 3). In his description of traveling with a pilgrim band, Sallnow states of the leader of his group, called Manuel, "The office of master is necessarily paradoxical. In one sense he is primus inter pares . . . yet in another sense he exercises an autocratic authority within the group, precisely in the interest of maintaining absolute equality among its members. It was this contradiction that made Manuel the focus of anger and resentment in the closing stages of the pilgrimage, when emotional thresholds had been lowered by days of intemperance, and individual jealousies and insecurities began to surface" (1987, 200).

5 I am grateful to John Eade for his stimulating comments on an initial version of this chapter. In a personal communication, Eade noted that he and Sallnow met when Sallnow was assigned to assess the validity of social anthropology courses designed by Eade for the Roehampton Institute (as it was then). Eade invited Sallnow to the 1989 conference that would lead to the edited volume of 1991.

6 Literally, "stretcher bearer."

7 As Eade and I discussed in a personal communication, it is interesting to compare the Turners' positive attitudes to Vatican II to that of Mary Douglas, another Catholic anthropologist writing about Christianity (and, like Eade, a student of Evans-Pritchard). Douglas's focus on questions of symbolic and social order tended to see the liturgical reforms of the period as based on false premises concerning the bases of cohesion within bounded, hierarchical systems of human organization (1970; see also Fardon 2013).

8 Though Eade (2019) does refer to the intensity of ritual experience evident at Lourdes rather than in regular congregational life.

9 The ethnographic complexity caught in this passage by Eade and in Sallnow's monograph is omitted in the generic contestation model, in part because the model does not provide a sophisticated enough analytical vocabulary to comprehend variations in contestatory behavior.

10 For Glenn Bowman, the new volume provided a kind of "Oedipal rectification" of the Turnerian paradigm (1988, 21).

11 Thus, what the Turners might have depicted as a dominant symbol was emptied of particular significance and made into a passive receptacle of meaning.

12 Though note Barkan and Barkey's suggestion that what constitutes centrality may itself be up for debate (2014, 14).

13 The argument recalls the Norwegian anthropologist Fredrik Barth's famous work, *Ethnic Groups and Boundaries* (1969), which analyzed what Barth saw as the organization of cultural difference.

14 In a post-9/11 world where nationalisms are growing across Europe and Asia, we might witness an increasing trend of shrines tending to cater to increasingly exclusive religious constituencies. In July 2020, Turkish president Recep Tayyip Erdoğan prompted a Turkish court to reconvert the Hagia Sophia in Istanbul from a museum and UNESCO World Heritage site into a mosque.

15 This dissimilarity in style may reflect the need to incorporate a variety of positionalities within the ethnography; writing about plurality is more likely to disrupt the possibility of adopting an integrated authorial voice.

16 Though in reality, the material affordances of sites set limits on the ways in which ritual engagements may be enacted. Materiality per se is not examined in the volume, although authors provide useful descriptions of the spatial dynamics of shrines.

17 Reader (2005, 250) provides a critique of analyses of pilgrimage that focus on transient activities at shrines.

18 Though Roderick Stirrat's (1991) contribution to the book, on Sinhala Catholic pilgrimage, provides a striking case study of holy figures as moving, sacred centers.

19 Eade speculates whether questions of exchange and the gift might also have proved useful coordinates to pursue (personal communication).

20 Coleman and Eade (2004) suggest that modulations of movement should also be considered a key component of pilgrimage. Compare with my discussion of a polythetic definition of pilgrimage in chapter 2.

21 Nthoi's book is called *Contesting Sacred Space*.

22 Di Giovine quotes, for instance, Clift and Clift (1996), Vukonić (1996), Swatos and Tomasi (2002), and Olsen and Timothy (2006). Relevant works are Morinis (1992), Reader and Walter (1993), Dubisch and Winkelman (2005), and Margry (2008).

23 Di Giovine (2011, 252) reiterates the point that Victor Turner acknowledged the presence of contestation in pilgrimage, even if he chose to downplay it.

24 Di Giovine (2011, 249) notes that fostering communitas meets the idealistic objectives of some stakeholder groups who view tourism as an instrument for creating

cross-cultural communication and education. See also Antón Pazos's (2016) edited volume on pilgrimages and peacemaking.

25 Kaell provides a variation on this point in her ethnography of American Christians visiting the Holy Land. She notes that pilgrims strive to avoid open disagreements, though this ethic may reflect not only the experience of being on pilgrimage but also broader Golden Rule assumptions of doing unto others as you would have them do unto you that facilitate interaction among middle-class believers (2014, 58–59).

26 *Darshan*, a Sanskrit term meaning "viewing," refers to the blessing entailed in the reciprocal viewing of a deity, religious leader, or sacred figure by the Hindu worshiper.

27 For important work on this topic, which includes activities ranging from ritual to urban planning, see Luz and Stadler (2018).

28 This is a classic anthropological point, engaged by Gluckman but made most famously in E. E. Evans-Pritchard's (1940) characterization of the African Nuer as organized through a basic principle of segmentary opposition. The Nuer were not pilgrims, but they were mobile, reliant on pastoral nomadism for subsistence. In relation to my observation, Eade remarked that it is useful to consider the interactions between contestation and collaboration in the broad shift from structural to post-structural contexts of operation (personal communication). Evans-Pritchard was concerned to study the establishment of social, cultural, and political order in the absence of the state but still within what he understood to be the broad framework of tribal relationships. Much work on pilgrimage deals with less obviously bounded fields, as we traced in the Turners' shift from their focus on the Ndembu to more global social movements (chapter 3).

29 Ma Tsu, born in 906 CE, was said to have lived a virtuous life devoted to Buddhist self-cultivation. She was also famed as a swimmer and predictor of weather before becoming a goddess of the sea with the power to protect sailors and fisherfolk. According to myth, she achieved apotheosis in Mei-chou, an island off the coast that houses another important temple to the goddess.

30 Terence Turner argues further that behind the iconic structure of the rite of passage, there exist certain "higher-level principles" forming the "transcendental ground" of the ritual system, which nonetheless contributes to social production and reproduction (Sangren 1993, 562; T. Turner 1977, 65).

31 Compare Henri Lefebvre's (2004) distinctions among the proper synchronization of rhythms (eurhythmia), the state when several rhythms coexist without conflict (polyrhythmia), and the problematic desynchronization of rhythms (arrhythmia).

32 Though as Mario Katić has pointed out (personal communication), a significant difference between Bowman's and Hayden's work involves the former's focus on contemporary relations and the latter's examination of relations over longer time periods.

33 Bowman's argument shows why it is important to pay attention to the shifting social and semiotic framings of visitors' movements, activities, and identities at and around shrines themselves.

34 Eade pointed to Hall's general emphasis on "identification rather than identity, since the latter suggests fixity and closure whereas identification implies process and change" (personal communication).

35 We might also think of Donald Weber's (1995) discussion (see chapter 3) of how the model of the liminal became replaced in American cultural theory by a notion of the border. As a theoretical metaphor, articulation works more readily through borders than through claims of establishing set apart, hermetically sealed space and time.

5. THE CENTER CANNOT HOLD

1 The poem's expression of the chaotic aftermath of conflict has proved highly resonant, famously in the title of Chinua Achebe's novel of encounter between precolonial Nigeria and Western Christianity, *Things Fall Apart* (1958). Victor Turner quoted Yeats in a late essay called "Morality and Liminality" (1993, 161), drawing on Yeats's reference in his poem *Byzantium* to "the winding path" that may lead away from death.

2 Translatable into English as road, path, or way.

3 While the word *trope* derives from the Greek word *tropos*, meaning "turning" or "way," the Camino entails a turning of attention away from center to path.

4 Former professor of modern languages and founder of the William and Mary Institute for Pilgrimage Studies.

5 Michael Sallnow passed away tragically early in 1990.

6 Contestation was inherently flexible, not only because of its underdetermination but also because of its explicit concession that any cultural or social material might be brought to a shrine.

7 Though *Image and Pilgrimage* had itself focused on shrines in France, Ireland, and England, as well as in Mexico.

8 Also known as the *Liber Sancti Jacobi* (Book of Saint James), associated with Pope Callixtus II. This codex reinforced the recognition of the authenticity of the apostle's relics by the papacy in Rome, as well as providing a guide for the pilgrimage to Santiago.

9 See Santos and Cabrera (2014).

10 This is not to say that the church does not attempt to reclaim the religious dimensions of the pilgrimage. Frey remarks that in 1993, the Spanish Diocesan Commission acknowledged that the traditional pilgrimage was made on foot but that the essential element of the contemporary pilgrimage was to make it in a spirit of faith, irrespective of mode of transport (1998, 126).

11 Fedele notes that some of the pilgrims she studied felt that "they were activating through their journey a route of pilgrimage related to Mary Magdalene and the Sacred Feminine" (2012, 249). Furthermore, "This new feminine route linking places related to Mary Magdalene appeared complementary to the route leading to Santiago which the pilgrims described as mainly masculine, related to a male saint and attracting mainly male pilgrims eager to test and display their capacity for physical strength and endurance" (250).

12 Mats Nilsson and Mekonnen Tesfahuney isolate three major episodes as lying behind the growth of pilgrimages to Santiago de Compostela: (1) the recognition of the city as a world heritage site by UNESCO in 1985; (2) the official visit by Pope Johannes Paulus II in 1989; (3) the declaration of "Il Camino" as the nine-hundred-kilometer pilgrim trail to Santiago de Compostela, verified by a stamped certificate or Compostela, issued by the local Catholic Church to those who travel at least one hundred kilometers on foot (2016, 22).

13 As an anonymous reviewer of this volume has pointed out, we might also think of the impact of journeying to a shrine via water, as occurs, for instance, in relation to the Fjord Pilgrim Route in Norway, which Lisbeth Mikaelsson and Torunn Selberg (2020) describe as "Caminoization at sea." Interestingly, this route retains the idea of slow, effortful movement, as walking is complemented by sailing and paddling (548). A more general point is that the Camino points to wider questions of how walking contributes to discussions of how tourism might be linked to sustainability (cf. Kato and Prograno 2017).

14 See Zwimmer's discussion of the blurring between religious and non-religious spheres in contemporary European pilgrimage, not least as "social and religious communities no longer constitute closed groups, and as communication is globalised," and as diasporas become "open to a multitude of references and identities, weakening their reliance on old centres and traditions" (2018, 366). Zwimmer also quotes the Pilgrim's Reception Office in Santiago as registering over 277,000 arriving pilgrims in 2016, of which 44 percent declared themselves as having a "religious" motivation, 48 percent a "religious-cultural" motivation, and 8 percent a "purely cultural" motivation (369).

15 Frey notes, "Part of the Camino's enormous appeal as a symbol is its flexibility to accommodate various interpretations of its spaces and encounters yet still retain its basic structure" (1998, 220).

16 See the discussion in chapter 3.

17 As I write (March 2019), Michelle Obama's book *Becoming* (2018) lies on top of the New York Times non-fiction best-seller list.

18 Nilsson and Tesfahuney refer to the post-secular tourist's "topos-disloyalty" and tendency to appropriate meanings and senses of place to personal ends (2018, 169). Cusack and Digance observe that transcendent experiences may now occur in places far outside traditional religious territory: for them, the experience of the sacred in the everyday is made possible by a decoupling of the sacred from religion (2008, 229).

19 The name derives from the Latin *finis terrae* or "land's end."

20 Margry (2008, 25) points to similar "transit pilgrimages" such as many occurring in and around Glastonbury in the United Kingdom, as well as motorcycle pilgrimages undertaken by Vietnam veterans across the United States (Dubisch 2004). See also David Zwimmer's (2018) parallels between the deinstitutionalization evident on the Camino and the veneration of Mary at Mariastein in Switzerland.

21 In its conjunction of localizing and globalizing tendencies, it contains elements of so-called glocalization. See also Alonso González's comment that "the Camino can be interpreted as much as a local reality as a 'global form' (Collier and Lakoff 2005), a dynamic flow of people with great potential for reterritorialization" (2018, 971).

22 When I first became aware of these processes some years ago, I referred to them as Compostelaization, but Bowman and Sepp's term—*Caminoization*—is more apt, because it highlights the power of the imagery and practice of the pathway rather than the shrine.

23 We might consider here the etymological link between the Latin word *credo*, "I believe," and the term *credential*.

24 The opening lines of Sánchez y Sánchez and Hesp's book claim, "Over the last twenty years, the success of the Camino de Santiago has not been lost on others. St. Olav Ways in Norway, the Via Francigena to Rome, and the Camino Salvado in Western Australia are just a few of the sites that have been improving their respective footpaths in order to mirror the success found on the Camino de Santiago" (2016, 1).

25 See Coleman and Bowman (2019).

26 Pilgrims may even have their rosaries blessed in this Anglican context (Bowman and Sepp 2019, 88).

27 See Emily McFarlan Miller, "Episcopalian Pilgrims Bring Spain's Camino de Santiago to the Appalachian Trail," *Religion News Service*, June 28, 2019, www.religionnews.com.

28 As part of the creation of the Path of the Sun in São Paulo State, an image was brought from Santiago itself. Steil had assumed that its placement in a forest garden in the town of Águas de São Pedro would provide a sacred focus for travelers at the end of the journey. However, he was assured by the path's creator, the local council, and even the local priest that it was much more to do with establishing St. James as the patron saint of the town. For the pilgrimage itself, a single altar or ritual center was not needed.

29 A nineteenth-century abbot, Dom Rosendo Salvado, transported olive trees to Australia and eucalyptus trees to Galicia (Genoni 2016, 172). The exemplarity of the Camino appears to be mediated here and in Steil's examples by what Sir James Frazer (1890) would have called both "sympathy" and "contagion"—both the cultivation of *resemblance* to the Spanish pilgrimage and the effects of literal *contact* with the latter, via pilgrims or material objects.

30 Antón Pazos (2014) refers to the replication of this "Jacobean model" on Shikoku. He remarks ruefully on what he sees as a significant contrast, however: "The Shikoku pilgrimage has the advantage that the pilgrim must visit the temples. The Way of St James can be done with no obligation to visit anything, from beginning to end" (2).

31 Eck (1983) notes that Kashi, the most ancient name for the city, means "the city of light." She adds, "One will hear that Kashi is supreme among India's *tirthas*,

but in the Hindu world this does not mean what the Westerner might imagine. It does not mean that Kashi is unique, *the* most holy of *tirthas*. Singularity is not especially prized as a cultural value in India. Fitting in is more important in this interdependent world than standing out" (39).

32 In this sense, we should not overemphasize the influence of Camino as a trope. It is more a symptom of wider social, political, and economic forces than it is an independent force for the transformation of pilgrimage.

33 Emphasis on the significance of the path is nothing new. Fuller (1992, 213; see Karve 1988) discusses the multiple processions of pilgrims that converge on Pandharpur, a town in southern Maharashtra containing the principal temple of the god Vithoba, but where arrival is less important than the journey. These Hindu pilgrims "draw attention to their exceptional state, which reflects partial, temporary renunciation of the mundane world" (Fuller 1992, 213), though a renunciation with rather different cultural associations to the post-secular orientation of many Camino pilgrims.

34 Some walking groups, meanwhile, may be organized by a parish and focus explicitly on theological issues related to spiritual development (Frey 1998, 32).

35 Though some pieces emphasize the political economy of tourism rather more. See, for example, Chemin (2016) and Steil (2018).

36 In their academic representation, such Pentecostals do not fit very well with Edith Turner's (2011, xix) optimistic depiction of Pentecostalism as a popular movement that could express freedom from religious hierarchy.

37 When Kyung-Mi Im and JuSung Jun (2015) carried out a study of Camino travelers, they found that at least three of their eight informants were linked to academic occupations.

38 In his discussion of the renewal of pilgrimage to Santiago de Compostela, Rubén Lois-González (2013, 9) argues that much important analysis is still provided by writing in romance languages, most notably Galician and Spanish.

39 Although Frey does address this issue more than many authors working in Western contexts.

6. PILGRIMAGE PENUMBRAS

1 Laterality and the lateral appear to derive from the Latin *lateralis*, belonging to the side. Note that I am using the term in a different sense to that deployed in studies of cognition and physiology, where laterality refers to the human preference to favor one side of the body over another in performing certain tasks, as exhibited in right- or left-handedness.

2 Clearly, the Turners are presenting a vision of the path in close proximity to the shrine, as opposed to the more diffuse and geographically stretched ritual ecology of the Camino.

3 See www.dictionary.com.

4 See "A surrounding or adjoining region in which something exists in a lesser degree," from the Merriam-Webster definition at www.merriam-webster.com/dic-

tionary/. The word derives from the Latin *paene*, "almost," and *umbra*, "shadow." As a term, the *penumbra* also usefully mediates between understandings of clearly marked, unambiguous sacred place and "more open, fluid, and dynamic" space (Sing 2019, 14).

5 I am grateful to Devaka Premawardana and Marc Loustau for referring me to Jackson's book. See also Premawardana's reference to Jackson's work and discussion of religious eclecticism and improvisation as a "situational, shape-shifting mode of existence" (2018, 18).

6 I agree with João Pina-Cabral and Frances Pine's assertion that looking at the margins of religion is less about a perverse focus on "odd" behavior and more about appreciating how religion, among many other things, often "inhabits the margins of other socio-cultural areas" (2008, 3) (cf. Bandak 2012; Marsden and Retsikas 2013).

7 Arguably, all ritual events and spaces are prone to creating penumbras. However, larger pilgrimage sites will tend to involve more varied and anonymous, and less ritually expert, participants than sites of habitual worship by stable constituencies of worshipers.

8 Such as the COVID-19 pandemic prevailing at the time of writing in 2020.

9 Semi-*de*tached also implies semi-attached.

10 They recall broader debates concerning the location of religious engagement in supposedly secularizing contexts, such as those surrounding "implicit religion" (e.g., Bailey 1997). Note that my argument touches on examples of pilgrimage already encountered in this book, such as the spiritually ambivalent pilgrims who make their way along the contemporary Camino. Frey's (1998) ethnography implies that such people might be good candidates to occupy penumbral spaces existing in relation to Compostela, spaces that have a different ritual identity to the cathedral or even the Camino itself. Discussing "the ambivalence of arrival" (143), she refers to ways in which her interlocutors go to the cathedral seeking closure but find more satisfaction in rejecting both the pious congregations and the more obviously touristic crowds who fill the ecclesiastical space. They may travel on to Finisterre in the coastal region situated west of the shrine to construct their own rites of purification (170). In quite penumbral imagery, Frey refers to how "in Santiago pilgrims are at the point of intensification found before the grains fly out into the undirected open space on the other side of the perpetual goal" (165).

11 See also, for example, Loustau and DeConinck (2019); Eade and Katic (2014, 11).

12 The word *porosity* stems from the Greek word *poros*, which means "passage" or "ford." One reason for increased use of porosity metaphors in the literature may be the influence of the philosopher Charles Taylor's (2007) well-known discussion of the contrast between the modern, buffered self that is separated from others and the porous self that is more open to external influences, including worlds of spirits and wider cosmic forces. (See also Charles Taylor, "Buffered and Porous Selves," *The Immanent Frame*, September 2, 2008, tif.ssrc.org/2008/09/02/buff-

ered-and-porous-selves/.) Porosity is also commonly associated with posthuman-ist challenges to boundaries between human, animal, and technological realms of existence (Haraway 1991).

13 In this sense, laterality comes close to what Magnus Marsden and Retsikas (2013, 12), in their exploration of the unstable ways in which religious dispositions may be constituted over time, call a form of articulation (14)—a means through which apparently distinct strands of social life may become mutually enmeshed.

14 Compare Coleman (2009).

15 Compare de Certeau (1984, 101): "The long poem of walking manipulates spatial organizations, no matter how panoptic they may be: it is neither foreign to them (it can take place only within them) nor in conformity with them (it does not receive its identity from them). It creates shadows and ambiguities within them. It inserts its multitudinous references and citations into them (social models, cultural mores, personal factors)."

16 See the project website www.pilgrimageandcathedrals.ac.uk/about. York is both a cathedral and a minster.

17 Such centers correspond well with the growing field of interrituality, defined by Jens Kreinath (2017, 260) as the study of relationships facilitated through ritu-als that members of different religious communities use as they cross religious boundaries through mutual coordination and implication.

18 In its apparent liturgical staidness, Walsingham contrasts with Glastonbury, an English site more associated with alternative forms of spirituality (e.g., Bowman 2008).

19 See Matthew Davies, "Walsingham Voted the UK's Favourite Spiritual Place," *Anglican Communion News Service*, August 12, 2003, www.anglicannews.org.

20 See Harriet Sherwood, "Church of England Attendance Falls below 1m for First Time," *Guardian*, January 12, 2016, www.theguardian.com. On the relationship between parishes and pilgrimage in Europe, see Eade (2016).

21 See Alliance of Religions and Conservation report, www.arcworld.org.

22 Interview September 11, 1995.

23 Anglo-Catholicism is a branch of Anglicanism that emphasizes its Catholic heritage. It has often been associated with the nineteenth-century Oxford move-ment as well as opposition to more evangelical branches of the Church. Anglo-Catholics are sometimes call High Anglicans.

24 In 1894, the ruin was bought by Charlotte Pearson Boyd, restored, and given back to the Roman Catholic Church, though it was not treated as a national shrine until the 1930s.

25 Interview September 7, 1995.

26 In his strategic decision to overlook certain actions of visitors in and around Walsingham, Warner engages in what Erving Goffman (1971) called "civil inat-tention," the capacity to avoid direct focus on the actions of others, especially valuable in contexts of mixed and frequently anonymous interaction.

27 Interviewed September 7, 1995.

28 Elsewhere (Coleman 2009b), I have used a metaphor of ritual risk to refer to such engagements at Walsingham.

29 See Dan Grimmer, "Thousands of Tamil Worshippers Make Pilgrimage to Walsingham," *Eastern Daily Press*, July 9, 2017, www.edp24.co.uk.

30 Interviewed September 1995.

31 John Eade and Nurit Stadler are further developing a "more-than-representational" approach to pilgrimage (personal communication), drawing on geographers as well as the work of anthropologist Tim Ingold (e.g., 2004). For an early discussion of this approach in relation to pilgrimage, see Kiyomi Doi (2011). See also Stadler (2020, 160) on the palimpsest as expressive of multiple claims on land in Israel-Palestine.

32 Though see, for example, Francis and Muskett (2015); Coleman and Bowman (2019).

33 Theos and the Grubb Institute (2012).

34 For details of the project "Pilgrimage and England's Cathedrals," see www.pilgrimageandcathedrals.ac.uk/. Participant observation (2015–17) was combined with over one hundred interviews with cathedral staff and visitors, and 502 questionnaires spread across the four sites.

35 Interviewed May 13, 2015.

36 Durham Cathedral contains the graves of two saints, Cuthbert and Bede.

37 Oliver (2017, 36), invoking Charles Taylor, speculates that visitors to a cathedral may be brought into an environment in which the self can become more porous.

38 Compare Rousseau's description of ritual at Chartres : "No one directs all this activity. There are no signs telling people where they can walk and where they cannot. Apart from observable displays of devotion—kneeling in prayer, touching the column beneath the statue with evident emotion—there is no way to know which people consider themselves tourists, or cultural visitors, or pilgrims, or devotees, or some combination of all these things. Everyone moves and interacts simultaneously, choosing one spot over another—even overlooking the most renowned relic in the cathedral's history" (2016, 75).

39 What looks like low-key, "ritual browsing" (cf. Coleman and Elsner 1998, 46) may also be interpreted as precisely the kind of context where connections are made with what the Church has to offer, and where the stakes of liturgical and congregational commitment are low.

40 See also Coleman (2019, 399–400).

41 Interviewed November 27, 2014.

42 Interviewed May 27, 2015.

43 Compare Jörg Schneider's analysis of candle use in German Protestant churches and his assertion that what had been a Roman Catholic practice now expresses liturgical openness through a mixing of public and private forms of piety. "Private Candles in German Protestant Churches," *Reverberations*, 2015, http://forums.ssrc.org/ndsp/2015/10/19/private-candles-in-german-protestant-churches/. See also Zimmer (2018).

44 July 31, 2016.

45 If such ritual engagement lies somewhere between established disposition and novel action, it also emerges from an unclear meeting point between habituated response and ethical reflection (cf. Laidlaw 2013, 179). For a fascinating analysis of gendered performances of pilgrimage in relation to ritual repertoires, see Baker (2010).

46 See also Coleman (2018a, 396).

47 Compare Ilana Gershon's discussion of the ethnographic challenge of observing how social orders are kept both "distinct and porous (enough) to allow people, objects, forms, and ideas to circulate across them in appropriate ways" (2019, 404).

48 There are exceptions, such as the Walsingham Way, leading from the East Anglian Cathedral city of Ely along the fifty-mile route to Walsingham. See, for instance Lawrence Lew, "Walking the Walsingham Way," *Godzdogz*, July 25, 2007, www.english.op.org.

49 Though Bloch accepts that other ethnographic contexts may indeed contain more mixed orientations to ritual.

50 The flexibility of ritual orientation I am describing here parallels the ways in which Albera (2019a) takes up Michael Carrithers's (2000) notion of polytropy in discussing practical, multidirectional expressions of religious engagement. For Carrithers, writing of South Asia, puja offerings (applied widely to objects, persons, and relationships) express the polytropic idea most obviously, whereas Albera locates it in the "interreligious porosities" that he observes in multireligious contexts of the Mediterranean.

51 Cohen is also drawing on an older analytical vocabulary of distinguishing between so-called great and little traditions of religious practice (see Redfield 1956).

52 There is a distant echo here of the role of Finesterre for the Camino: a place associated with nature that concludes and partially subverts the more official dimensions of a journey. Walsingham, too, has seashores within a few miles of its altars and shrines, to which pilgrims may repair after their visits. Although attitudes to the natural world vary hugely between the lives of the travelers across these sites in India and Europe, certain affordances of the shoreline are present in all: not merely the sense of an edge, or the constant movement of the water, but also the beach as a place remote from architectural and ritual prompts provided by shrines.

7. TELLING TALES

1 A significant form of discourse missing from this chapter, and generally overlooked in anthropologies of pilgrimage, is the language of administration and bureaucracy, which is often vital to the maintenance of sites (Coleman 2019).

2 In this sense, their conjoining of shrines resonates with Marc Loustau and Kate DeConinck's (2019) critique of "singularism" in pilgrimage studies, discussed in chapter 2.

3 See the translation at https://corpus.quran.com/translation. jsp?chapter=22&verse=27.

4 The Sanskrit term *kali yuga* refers to fourth and last world age in the eternally repeting four-yuga cycle, characterized by conflict (the present age falls within the *kali yuga*).

5 Feldman data were derived from the Israel's Education Ministry's pre-visit instruction course as well as six trips taken between 1992 and 1997 as part of ministry-organized delegations to Poland, "of which five were with state secular schools and the last with a National Religious group" (2002, 85). He adds that over one hundred thousand Israeli youngsters have visited the death camps in Poland since the mid-1980s.

6 For instance, an encounter with a local inhabitant who turns out to be welcoming.

7 Similarly, Marc Loustau draws on Merleau-Ponty's *Phénomènologie de la perception* (1945) to reflect on how narration immerses the subject in "and establishes a pattern, cycle, momentum, or thrust that tends toward completion" (Loustau 2019, 120).

8 A direct encounter between text and landscape is evident in one of the earliest Christian pilgrimages recorded, that of Egeria, who travels to the Holy Land in the early 380s (Leyerle 1996). Egeria reads the appropriate biblical passage at every holy place.

9 Compare Bowman (1991) and Hummel and Hummel (1995) on Protestant experiences of the Holy Land.

10 A feature of the performance is the preparatory work carried out by the pastor. Group members have several meetings prior to the trip where they go through scripture readings, prayers, and the studying of maps.

11 Writing of tourism, Dean MacCannell (1976) refers not just to guides or guidebooks but also to onsite markers such as placards and brochures that help constitute the atmosphere of a site and orient visitors.

12 Though of course, guidebooks to Walsingham exist, such as Warner (1996). On pilgrimage guiding see Mesaritou, Coleman, and Eade (2016).

13 Luhrmann (2004, 519) reports that the most important phrase used in this evangelical culture is "to walk with God." Compare Paul's account of walking with his family, discussed later in this chapter.

14 Many scholars have pointed to the political implications of the panoramic gaze, for example, in the context of nineteenth-century Euro-American imperialism (Kaell 2014, 86; compare Coleman 2002b).

15 For an example of how a guide can also subtly unsettle the religious assumptions of visitors, see Feldman (2020).

16 Van der Beek (2018, 225) draws on Mikhail Bakhtin to explore the multivoiced quality of the Camino. She notes how Bakhtin describes literature "as a dialogue between different parties, in which every individual narrative is only one part in a chain of narratives" (226).

17 See Nancy Frey, "Pilgrimage in the Internet Age," *Walking to Presence*, January 28, 2017, walkingtopresence.com.

18 Such an emphasis may be evident in what van der Beek calls institutional narratives—those aimed at a wide audience or readership, and disseminated by publishing houses, broadcasting networks, or Hollywood studios (2018, 42–43). Famous examples are by Hape Kerkeling (*Ich bin dan mall weg* [I'm off then], 2006), Shirley MacLaine (*The Camino: A Journey of the Spirit*, 2001), and Cees Nooteboom (*De omweg naar Santiago* [Roads to Santiago], 1992). Films include Emilio Estevez's *The Way* (2010) and the documentary *Walking the Camino* (2014) by Lydia Smith.

19 My translation.

20 Shultz (2009, 14) counts at least eighty book-length memoirs written in the decade before he wrote his PhD.

21 *The Prayer of 88* (Akimoto 2004; see also discussion in Baffelli, Reader, and Staemmler 2009, 108; Shultz 2011).

22 Point-of-view shots are common in pilgrims' blogs. Van der Beek (2018, 89) refers to the "almost canonical" depiction of the Camino showing the road stretching in front of the walker and leading into the far distance.

23 This depiction of the Hajj as diffused discourse in Turkey is echoed later by Kholoud Al-Ajarmi's (2020) ethnography of "Mecca in Morocco."

24 Robert Bianchi notes, "Because debates about the Hajj never take a day off, the pilgrimage remains at the forefront of popular imaginations year round. In this sense, today's Hajj never stops. It no longer occupies a special season on the margins of everyday life. Instead, it embodies everyday life" (2013, 22).

25 Caidi interviews twelve younger Muslims who have different cultural backgrounds.

26 Buitelaar (2020) refers to processes of "rearticulating the conventions of Hajj storytelling" in her study of second-generation, Moroccan-Dutch female pilgrims. Buitelaar's interlocutors produce narratives acutely conscious of the multiple audiences and life-worlds that they face on an everyday basis as they negotiate public debates over the compatibility or otherwise of being both Muslim and Dutch (3).

27 Badone (2014, 16), drawing on Frey's work, refers to the ways in which the Camino can become an organizing metaphor in the lives of pilgrims, many of whom—like those who walk the *henro* on Shikoku—repeat the route multiple times.

28 The word is derived from the French *souvenir*, "remember," which itself comes from the Latin *subvenire*, "occur to the mind." The classic work on souvenirs is Susan Stewart's *On Longing* (1992).

29 While Bloch implies that the ritual participant comes back to society with their identity refixed, Kaell shows how the persona of American Christian pilgrims to the Holy Land continues to evolve through the operation of ongoing narrative,

material, and ritual exchanges. Kenney's ethnography lies somewhere in between these more fixed and more fluid alternatives.

30 An example of medieval virtual pilgrimage mediated through art is provided by Marie-Louise Ehrenschwendtner's (2009) work on the enclosed community of St. Katharine's Convent in Augsburg. See also Rock's discussion of the history of traveling mentally to holy places (2006, 198).

31 For van der Beek, some online pilgrimages challenge the assumption that movement is an essential component of pilgrimage, given that "in a cyberpilgrimage . . . the importance of the journey is rather different from that in a terrestrial pilgrimage. We cannot think about the distance of online sites in terms of the amount of kilometers between them. Rather, online places are divided by a number of clicks of the mouse" (2018, 177–78).

32 See also Anastasia Karaflogka's (2002, 284–85) distinction between religion *on* cyberspace (i.e., basic information uploaded by any organization) and religion *in* cyberspace—"a religious, spiritual or metaphysical expression which is created and exists exclusively in cyberspace" (285).

33 See Ori Schwarz's (2010) discussion of the use of cellphone videos as a means of extending women's distanciated participation in male-only Orthodox Jewish ritual. A similar point is made by Gabi Abramac (2020) in her discussion of use of digital technologies among Hasidic communities in New York.

34 https://vimeo.com/27156797. A twist on this theme of creating a sense of close proximity to a site even when it is electronically mediated is provided by Oren Golan and Michele Martini (2018) in their discussion of how a Franciscan media center takes advantage of its mandate to produce and distribute Holy Land–related communications. They argue that such mediated videos constitute "soft" forms of authoritative religious texts, placing holy sites and traditional clergy at the core of viewers' perspective, with webmasters as intermediaries (12).

35 See Shemaiah Gonzalez, "My Virtual Camino: Celebrating the Feast of St. James in My Own Backyard," *Busted Halo*, July 19, 2017, www.bustedhalo.com.

36 Concerns over the links between religious mobility and plague have a long history. See, for example, Nükhet Varlik's *Plague and Contagion in the Islamic Mediterranean* (2017).

37 Interview September 7, 1995.

38 Interview August 2, 1994.

39 See Ingold and Vergunst's (2008, 8) discussion of de Certeau's (1984, 134) analogy between narrative and walking. Bloch's characterization of formal ritual as articulation is also relevant: "Ritual is a kind of tunnel into which one plunges, and where, since there is no possibility of turning either to right or left, the only thing to do is to follow; but the reason why this direction has been taken is only misleadingly explained in terms of a conscious choice between equally possible directions. Units in ritual do not follow each other logically, but sequentially" (Bloch 1974, 76).

40　Matthew Tomlinson refers to patterned sequences that are meant to generate ritual efficacy as "performative paths" (2014, 38).

41　Loustau (2019) provides an excellent example of a family story cycle that bears comparison with mine. He shows how a devout mother and skeptical daughter construct contrasting but tightly intermeshed tales of their respective experiences of the Romanian pilgrimage site of Csíksomlyó. During his conversation with the mother, Loustau finds her substituting a story about Lourdes for one relating to the Romanian site, indicating the potential for narrative transposition between different sites.

8. ENCLAVING AND ENTRAINING

1　For a useful discussion, see Badone and Roseman (2004).

2　Much work in tourism management studies has assessed the broad economic impact of travel to sacred sites (e.g., Raj and Griffin 2015), but generally speaking, ethnographers have not considered wider political and economic processes in equally systematic ways.

3　On the politics, economics, and infrastructure of sacred placemaking, see Mart Bax (1995) on Medjugorje (Croatia) and James Lochtefeld (2010) on Hardwar (India).

4　Reader also refers (2015, 16) to Suzanne Kaufman's (2005) study of Lourdes, which traces ways in which commercialization has been a significant factor in Lourdes's emergence as a shrine.

5　Reinforcing Yadav's perspective, Shadia Taha (2019) examines commercial forms of pilgrimage management that construct pilgrims as consumers as well as worshipers. Significant work locating Muslim pilgrimage in the context of globalization and politics includes Bianchi (2013), McLoughlin (2009), Mols and Buitelaar (2015).

6　See Coleman and Eade (2018) for case studies on pilgrimage and political economy.

7　See Tish Sanghera, "Hajjonomics: The Business of Getting India's Pilgrims to Mecca," *Aljazeera*, August 9, 2019, www.aljazeera.com. On "Meccanomics," see Nasr (2010).

8　See Holly Ellyatt, "Tourism to Replace Oil Economy in Saudi Arabia," CNBC, October 2, 2015, www.cnbc.com. The assumption of the reliability of such income is challenged by events such as the COVID-19 pandemic.

9　See the Makkah Clock Royal Tower Fairmont Hotel website, www.fairmont.com.

10　A more general issue relates to the emergence of Muslim forms of tourism (e.g., Jafari and Scott 2014), as well as the extent to which an increasingly variegated constituency of pilgrims to Mecca is choosing to combine trips with other forms of recreation. For a discussion of links between heritage, tourism, and pilgrimage in the making of Iranian state politics, see Zandi (2020). For a vivid study of intersection between trade, leisure, contraband, and Muslim pilgrimage see Emrah

Yildiz, "Fugitive Markets and Arrested Mobilities: Gaziantep's Iranian Bazaar," *Jadaliyya*, 2013, www.jadaliyya.com.

11 Andreas Bandak and Manpreet Janeja (2018, 13) draw on Reinhart Koselleck (2004) in reflecting on the ways in which modernity is often characterized as involving both the acceleration and the secularization of time, as prophecy is supposedly replaced by prognostication and rational planning. The juxtaposition of a spectacular clock tower with the central space of the Hajj suggests a striking commingling of temporalities.

12 A significant area of political economy not explored here involves the intersections between secular and ritual economies of exchange relating to pilgrimage. Two excellent studies are Oren Kosansky's (2002) discussion of connections between tourism, charity, and profit in Moroccan Jewish pilgrimage and Erin Kenny's (2007) documenting of Muslims making gifts of religious commodities in Guinea.

13 Saudi authorities wish to encourage pilgrims to Mecca but still operate a quota system that regulates the number of citizens who can come from individual countries each year. Such measures have become even more visible as I write in spring 2020, when the effects of a global pandemic (COVID-19) are causing administrators at Mecca and elsewhere to consider the postponement of gatherings of large numbers of people at sacred sites.

14 For early insights into the intersections between tourism, migration, and ritual in the Mediterranean, see Boissevain (1992) and (1996).

15 Gatherings involved meetings with friends and relatives but also encouraged contacts with business associates from other tribes, while reaffirming the right to use territorial resources.

16 Nimrod Luz (2020) discusses the ambiguities over the uses of the Anglophone terms *pilgrimage* and *tourism* in relation to Muslim practices, alongside the problem of focusing on the Hajj as the default example of Muslim pilgrimage, given that most of the religious travel carried out by Muslims is to other places.

17 Such tendencies run athwart more recent attempts to focus on forms of personal piety within Islam (see Dogra 2019).

18 Compare with Paul Basu's (2004) discussion of "root" and "route" metaphors in relation to genealogy-related tourism and pilgrimage.

19 See Katherine Rousseau's (2016, 42) discussion of the dynamics and instabilities of sacred centers.

20 It also resonates with Thomas Tweed's (2006) *Crossing and Dwelling*, which presents religion as made up of the interaction between two orienting spatial metaphors of traversing boundaries and finding a home. Orvar Löfgren argues (2008) that some versions of the "nomadic turn" risk assuming almost effortless flux at the expense of emphasizing the cultural mediations of mobility. Tweed's approach is more subtle, but I share Manuel Vásquez's (2011, 151) concern that metaphors of flow "tend to overstate pervasiveness of porous boundaries and movement." Following Ronen Shamir (2005), he argues that "not every flow [is] created equal"

given that mobility regimes operate through forms of selective osmosis and paradigms of suspicion, not least in a post 9/11 world (208, 167). To that, we can now
add a post-COVID world.

21 Commenting on Deleuze and Guattari's *Nomadology* (1986), David Heller (2000,
7) remarks that the figure of the nomad is often presented as male.

22 See Ismail Alatas's study of Indonesian pilgrimage to Yemen, which see it as "as a
poetic project that . . . hinges on the construction of multiple chronotopes that are
juxtaposed, compared, contrasted, and assembled into meaningful alignments"
(2016, 607).

23 For an interesting account of links between rhythm and ritual see Kreinath and
Shapiro (2019).

24 See chapter 7.

25 For a piece linking slow tourism, heritage and sustainable development in Japan,
see Kato and Progano (2017).

26 See Elatia Harris, "The Accidental Pilgrim: David Downie on Extreme Questing,"
3 Quarks Daily, April 8, 2013, www.3quarksdaily.com.

27 It illustrates "meta-movement": a "combination of mobility itself with a degree of
reflexivity as to its meaning, form and function" (Coleman and Eade, 2004,18).

28 Matt Hodges (2008) observes that analytical frames since the heydays of both
functionalism and structuralism have adopted a processual vocabulary of tempo,
rhythm and flow, as fluidity has become a root metaphor for inquiry (401). The
"mobility turn" contains a sense of the processual still more encompassing than
that available to Gluckman and the Turners.

29 Compare Kathryn Rountree's (2006) phenomenological analysis of contemporary
pagans' experience of place.

30 Tim Ingold and Jo Vergunst remark that "just as word follows word along a line of
text, so print follows print along a track" (2008, 8). See also de Certeau on writing
as itinerant practice (1984, 134).

31 Social commentators such as Simmel and Benjamin saw in the figure of the
insouciant, strolling (male) flaneur a symptom of the semidetached social
relations characteristic of the anonymous metropolis. The currently popular
practice of psychogeography was inspired by writers such as Benjamin and Guy
Debord.

32 Although it encompasses travelers of many different religions, the Camino in-
scribes a Christian-inflected route into the heart of Europe. An alternative route is
developing called the Sultan's Trail, instituted by a Muslim who has himself been
on the Camino, moving from Vienna to Istanbul and celebrating the history of
the Ottoman Empire. See the trail website at www.sultanstrail.net/.

33 Gemzöe (2014a) traces influences of the Camino in Sweden but also emphasizes
the relevance of local factors, such as Swedish levels of secularization and the
Nordic tradition of *friluftsliv*, or open-air recreation.

34 Sharon Roseman (2015) vividly documents Galician ambivalence to the Camino
as source of low income and insecure employment. A further issue here, worthy

of separate discussion, relates to pilgrimage and sustainability—not only eco-nomic, but also environmental (e.g., Stronza 2001).

35 See the Amazon entry at www.amazon.ca/Paris-Pyrenees-Skeptic-Pilgrim-Walks/dp/1605985562.

36 Though Alonso González's view is a skeptical one, suggesting that regional administrators fetishize the presence of sheer numbers of travelers as a means of extracting measurable value from the routes.

37 Author given as "David," "Many Ways, One Goal," *Mapping the Camino*, May 24, 2016, mappingthecamino.wordpress.com.

38 See Jill Gat, "Pondering the Experiences of Refugees," *Camino Guides*, November 12, 2018, www.caminodesantiago.me.

39 See the Merriam-Webster definition at www.merriam-webster.com/dictionary/entrain. The term was originally associated with the seventeenth-century Dutch physicist Christian Huygens, famous for the development of pendulum clocks.

40 I use the ethnographic present in my description of the work.

41 Tweed's analysis of Cubans in Miami bears comparison with Terry Rey and Alex Stepick's (2013) work on Haitian migrants to South Florida. In both cases, reli-gious devotion and identification with a distant homeland are conjoined in what Rey and Terry call "nostalgic visualizations" (101).

42 The shrine in Guadalupe (according to legend) originally involved a vision granted to a peasant, Juan Diego, in the mid-sixteenth century.

43 For a fine account of the role played by apparitions of the Virgin Mary as part of negotiating Christian-Muslim mediations and differences in urban space in Cairo, see Angie Heo (2018). Jason Danely (2017) describes a different kind of occupation of the street in his discussion of grassroots neighborhood-watch-type pilgrimages created by older adults in Kyoto, Japan. He sees such pilgrimage as enabling seniors to inhabit spaces of civic social engagement while contesting their relative invisibility in contemporary Japan.

44 For work on the politics of visibility, see Jörgen Hellman's (2017) discussion of how local pilgrims relate to ancestors at Mount Sunda, Indonesia, while attempt-ing to avoid the gaze of nationalist and Muslim forms of governance.

45 Each case also involves the production or extension of newly sacralized space within diaspora. They contrast with the phenomenon of migrant populations accommodating themselves to already existing pilgrimage landscapes (e.g., Eade and Garbin 2007).

46 Compare Joel Robbins's (2009) application of Randall Collins's (2005) notions of interaction ritual chains, rhythmic synchronization of bodily action, and emo-tional entrainment to Pentecostals.

47 Ohri's fieldwork shows how ritualized movement can simultaneously act as politi-cal statement, remolder of landscape, and embodiment of a relationship with the past. These points emerge powerfully in contexts where walking is both identity-marker and explicit tool of socialization. Meaghan Weatherdon (2020) raises such themes in her account of "the Journey of Nishiiyuu," an event initiated on

January 16, 2013, as six young Cree men, inspired by the Idle No More movement in Canada, left their homes in northern Quebec to embark on a 1,600-kilometer expedition by foot to the nation's capital, Ottawa.

48 In *Image and Pilgrimage* (1978), the Turners note that the image of the Virgin remains vulnerable to being subverted by political structure into becoming a symbol of nationalism (Turner and Turner 1978, 171). We might think of the image of Mary as the queen of the Polish nation, which presents her as morally superior to more liberal parts of the European Union (De Busser and Niedźwiedź 2009, 13).

CONCLUSION

1 In these conclusions, I draw on ethnographic examples already cited in the book.

2 As such theory has developed primarily though not exclusively through Anglophone scholarship.

3 See Loustau and DeConinck (2019).

4 For a parallel discussion of Roman Catholicism as an "encompassing" institution, see Mayblin (2017, 511).

5 Such risk management takes on new implications in the context of the spread of viruses such as COVID-19.

6 Arrival at the city itself rather than the character of the journey is prioritized, at least compared with the stylizations of mobility inherent in Pentecostal flow and Camino-esque becoming.

7 On such Japanese pilgrimage, see Danely (2017).

8 Compare Anderson and McFarlane (2011).

9 Generally speaking, contestation is too strong a term to describe their relations with the spaces and etiquettes of orthodoxy, though there may be tactical dimensions to their relative social obscurity (de Certeau 1984).

10 They emphasize neither concentration at a center nor assertions of vertical ties to a transcendent realm, though they acknowledge linkages with both. Compare with the spatial imagery of Ursula Goodenough's discussion of "Vertical and Horizontal Transcendence" (2001).

11 Benjamin, like Sir James Frazer before him (see chapter 1), found inspiration in the early Greek traveler Pausanias. We might also note here Benjamin's interest in the notion of porosity as a way of conceptualizing the shifting, ambiguous, material and social connections enabled by city spaces. For a recent discussion see Haenni (2020).

12 In the context of his adaptation of Benjamin's work, Greg Urban might call such reflexive ritual action "meta-cultural" (2001, 3), as the latter is "culture that is about culture" (ibid.), which is subject to "lateral dissemination" (67) through a form of replication that is also a transformation (cf. Tauschek 2011).

13 In the language of actor network theory, these syntactical elements encourage shifting alliances to emerge between human and non-human actants, aggregating and disaggregating within extended pilgrimage spaces in ways that challenge fixed

assumptions as to the location of religious authority or social agency (cf. Latour 1993; Hatfield 2010, 12).

14 Discussed in chapter 7.

15 The beaches local to Walsingham also regularly host ritualized overspills from the village, where visitors often decide to carry out personalized rituals.

16 The creative and imaginative dimensions of the penumbra might also be compared here with the geographer Edward Soja's notion of the thirdspace (1996), also drawn on by Arjana (2017) in her discussion of Muslim pilgrimage sites as sites for the intersection of the social, the political, and the imaginary.

17 Eric Wolf, who published an important piece on the Virgin of Guadalupe in 1958, was also a major contributor to world systems and globalization theory (Wolf 2000).

18 Presumably unknowingly echoing Eade and Sallnow (1991).

19 We must remember that Turnerian distinctions between the liminal and the liminoid, fragile as they were, tended to be lost in others' interpretation of their work, and sometimes in their own.

20 Victor's dates were 1920–83; Edith's were 1921–2016.

21 See Hall (1985) for a piece where he does address religion. Ken Thompson notes that Hall saw African-Jamaican religion "as a constant process of breaks, interruptions, and reorganization, in which the religious formation is reordered, rearranged, dislocated, and repositioned, so as to provide a new religious language and practices within which to articulate new historical realities . . . we often find a double movement in which new collective subjects are formed in the same process by which the group articulates itself" (2016, 386).

22 In certain respects, Hall's position on articulation anticipates Ilana Gershon's discussion of how anthropological fields are increasingly understood to consist of multiple, contingent, porous, and interconnected social orders (2019, 404).

23 This last theme provides a bridge between Hall's work and Anna Tsing's (2012) perspective on globalization, where "frictional" relations need not imply irredeemable conflict but rather "many other kinds of difference-based interactions, including alliance, borrowing, merging, translation, and accommodation" (1).

BIBLIOGRAPHY

Abramac, Gabi. 2020. "The Social Practices and Linguistic Spaces of Shababniks in Brooklyn." In *Off the Derech: Leaving Orthodox Judaism*, edited by Ezra Cappell and Jessica Lang, 335–60. Albany: State University of New York Press.

Adler, Judith. 2002. "The Holy Man as Traveller and as Travel Attraction." In *From Medieval Pilgrimage to Religious Tourism*, edited by William Swatos and Luigi Tomasi, 25–50. Westport, CT: Praeger.

Agnew, Michael. 2019. "'This Is a Glimpse of Paradise': Encountering Lourdes through Serial and Multisited Pilgrimage." *Journal of Global Catholicism* 3, no. 1: 26–62.

Akimoto, Kaito. 2004. *88 no inori: Shikoku arukihenro 1400 kiro no tahi.* Tokyo: Tokyo Shoseki.

Alatas, Ismail. 2016. "The Poetics of Pilgrimage: Assembling Contemporary Indonesian Pilgrimage to Ḥaḍramawt, Yemen." *Comparative Studies in Society and History* 58, no. 3: 607–35.

Albera, Dionigi. 2019a. "Digressions on Polytropy: An Exploration of Religious Eclecticism in Eurasia." *Entangled Religions* 9: 139–64.

———. 2019b. "Pilgrims at Shared Shrines: An Epistemological Challenge for Pilgrimage Studies?" Paper delivered September 5, 2019, to the "Approaching Pilgrimage: Methodological Issues Involved in Researching Routes, Sites and Practices" Conference, Pilgrimage Studies Network of European Association of Social Anthropologists, University of Zadar.

Alcock, Susan, John Cherry, and Jaś Elsner, eds. 2001. *Pausanias: Travel and Memory in Roman Greece.* New York: Oxford University Press.

Alonso González, Pablo. 2018. "'The Camino Is Alive': Minor Logics and Commodification in the Camino de Santiago." *Anthropological Quarterly* 91, no. 3: 969–1000.

Amit, Vered, and Noel Salazar. 2020 "Why and How Does the Pacing of Mobilities Matter?" In *Pacing Mobilities: Timing, Intensity, Tempo and Duration of Human Movements*, edited by Vered Amit and Noel Salazar, 1–17. Oxford: Berghahn.

Anderson, Ben, and Colin McFarlane. 2011. "Assemblage and Geography." *Area* 43, no. 2: 124–27.

Anthony, Cara. 2018. "Walking as Resistance to Hypermobility: The Camino de Santiago Pilgrimage." *Spiritus: A Journal of Christian Spirituality* 18, no. 1: 1–13.

Apolito, Paolo. 2005. *The Internet and the Madonna.* Chicago: University of Chicago Press.

Arjana, Sophia Rose. 2017. *Pilgrimage in Islam: Traditional and Modern Practices.* London: Oneworld.

Asad, Talal. 1993. *Genealogies of Religion: Discipline and Reasons of Power in Christianity and Islam*. Baltimore, MD: John Hopkins University Press.

Badone, Ellen. 2014. "Conventional and Unconventional Pilgrimages: Conceptualizing Sacred Travel in the Twenty-First Century." In *Redefining Pilgrimage: New Perspectives on Historical and Contemporary Pilgrimages*, edited by Antón Pazos, 7–31. Farnham: Ashgate.

Badone, Ellen, and Sharon Roseman. 2004. "Approaches to the Anthropology of Pilgrimage and Tourism." In *Intersecting Journeys: The Anthropology of Pilgrimage and Tourism*, edited by Ellen Badone and Sharon Roseman, 1–23. Urbana: University of Illinois Press.

———. 2014. "Conventional and Unconventional Pilgrimages: Conceptualizing Sacred Travel in the Twenty-First Century." In *Redefining Pilgrimage: New Perspectives on Historical and Contemporary Pilgrimages*, edited by Antón Pazos, 7–23. Farnham: Ashgate.

Baffelli, Erica, Ian Reader, and Birgit Staemmler, eds. 2009. *Japanese Religions on the Internet*. London: Routledge.

Bailey, Edward. 1997. *Implicit Religion in Contemporary Society*. Kampen: Kok Pharos.

Baird, Robert. 1991. *Category Formation and the History of Religions*. Berlin: Mouton de Gruyter.

Bajc, Vida. 2006. "Christian Pilgrimage Groups in Jerusalem: Framing the Experience through Linear Meta-Framing." *Journeys* 7, no. 2: 101–28.

———. 2007. "Creating Ritual through Narrative, Place and Performance in Evangelical Protestant Pilgrimage in the Holy Land." *Mobilities* 2, no. 3: 395–412.

Bajc, Vida, Simon Coleman, and John Eade. 2007. "Introduction: Mobility and Centring in Pilgrimage." *Mobilities* 2, no. 3: 321–29.

Baker, Vanessa. 2010. "Women's Pilgrimage as Repertoiric Performance: Creating Gender and Spiritual Identity through Ritual." PhD diss., Bowling Green State University.

Bálint, Sándor. 1936. "People of Szeged on Pilgrimage to Radna." *Ethnographia* 46: 317–18.

Bandak, Andreas. 2012. "Problems of Belief: Tonalities of Immediacy among Christians of Damascus." *Ethnos* 77, no. 4: 535–55.

Bandak, Andreas, and Manpreet Janeja. 2018. "Introduction: Worth the Wait." In *Ethnographies of Waiting: Doubt, Hope and Uncertainty*, edited by Manpreet Janeja and Andreas Bandak, 1–39. London: Bloomsbury.

Bandak, Andreas, and Jonas Jørgensen. 2012. "Foregrounds and Backgrounds—Ventures in the Anthropology of Christianity." *Ethnos* 77, no. 4: 447–58.

Barkan, Elazar, and Karen Barkey. 2014. Introduction to *Choreographies of Shared Sacred Sites: Religion, Politics, and Conflict Resolution*, edited by Elazar Barkan and Karen Barkey, 1–31. New York: Columbia University Press.

Barna, Gábor. 2015. "Pilgrimages in Hungary: Ethnological and Anthropological Approaches." In *International Perspectives on Pilgrimage Studies: Itineraries, Gaps and Obstacles*, edited by Dionigi Albera and John Eade, 95–113. London: Routledge.

Barth, Fredrik. 1969. *Ethnic Groups and Boundaries: The Social Organization of Culture Difference*. Oslo: Universitetsforlaget.

Bartholomew, Craig, and Robert Llewelyn. 2003. Introduction to *Explorations in a Christian Theology of Pilgrimage*, edited by Craig Bartholomew and Fred Hughes, xii–xvi. London: Routledge.

Barush, Kathryn. 2016. *Art and the Sacred Journey in Britain, 1790–1850*. London: Routledge.

Basu, Paul. 2004. "Route Metaphors of 'Roots-Tourism' in the Scottish Highland Diaspora." In *Reframing Pilgrimage: Cultures in Motion*, edited by Simon Coleman and John Eade, 150–74. London: Routledge.

Bauman, Richard. 1986. *Story, Performance, and Event: Contextual Studies of Oral Narrative*. Cambridge, UK: Cambridge University Press.

Bauman, Zygmunt. 1996. "From Pilgrim to Tourist." In *Questions of Cultural Identity*, edited by Stuart Hall and Paul Du Gay, 18–36. Los Angeles: Sage.

———. 2000. *Liquid Modernity*. Cambridge, UK: Polity.

Bax, Mart. 1995. *Medjugorje: Religion, Politics, and Violence in Rural Bosnia*. Amsterdam: VU Uitgeverij.

Bell, Catherine. 1992. *Ritual Theory, Ritual Practice* Oxford: Oxford University Press.

———. 2002. "Ritual Tensions: Tribal and Catholic." *Studia Liturgica* 32: 15–28.

Benjamin, Walter. 1968. *The Work of Art in the Age of Mechanical Reproduction*. In *Illuminations*, edited by Hannah Arendt, 214–18. London: Fontana.

Berger, John. 1984. *And Our Faces, My Heart, Brief as Photos*. New York: Vintage.

Bergmann, Christoph, and Jürgen Schaflechner. 2019. "Introduction: Constellations and Contestations of Mobility and Space in South Asian Ritual Journeys." In *Ritual Journeys in South Asia: Constellations and Contestations of Mobility and Space*, edited by Christoph Bergmann and Jürgen Schaflechner, 1–10. London: Routledge.

Bhabha, Homi. 2004. *The Location of Culture*. New York: Routledge.

Bharati, Aghehananda. 1991. "Grammatical and Notational Models of Indian Pilgrimage." In *Social Anthropology of Pilgrimage*, edited by Makhan Jha, 19–29. New Delhi: Inter-India.

Bhardwaj, Surinder. 1973. *Hindu Places of Pilgrimage in India*. Berkeley: University of California Press.

———. 1991. "Hindu Pilgrimage in America." In *Social Anthropology of Pilgrimage*, edited by Makhan Jha, 81–98. Delhi: Inter-India Publication.

———. 1999. "Circulation and Circumambulation in Tirtha Yatra." Paper presented at Pilgrimage and Complexity, Delhi. Retrieved from www.colorado.edu/Conferences/pilgrimage/papers/Bhardwaj.html.

Bhardwaj, Surinder, and Gisbert Rinschede. 1998. *Pilgrimage in World Religions*. Berlin: Dietrich Reimer Verlag.

Bialecki, Jon. 2012. "Virtual Christianity in an Age of Nominalist Anthropology." *Anthropological Theory* 12, no. 3: 295–319.

Bianchi, Robert. 2013. *Islamic Globalization: Pilgrimage, Capitalism, Democracy, and Diplomacy*. New Jersey: World Scientific.

Bingenheimer, Marcus. 2017. "Pilgrimage in China." In *New Pathways in Pilgrimage Studies: Global Perspectives*, edited by Dionigi Albera and John Eade, 18–35. New York: Routledge.

Bloch, Maurice. 1974. "Symbols, Song, Dance and Features of Articulation: Is Religion an Extreme Form of Traditional Authority?" *European Journal of Sociology* 15, no. 1: 55–81.

———. 1991. *Prey into Hunter: The Politics of Religious Experience*. Cambridge, UK: Cambridge University Press.

Blue, Stanley. 2017. "Institutional Rhythms: Combining Practice Theory and Rhythm-analysis to Conceptualise Processes of Institutionalization." *Time & Society* 28, no. 3: 922–50.

Boissevain, Jeremy, ed. 1992. *Revitalizing European Rituals*. London: Routledge.

———. 1996. Introduction to *Coping with Tourists: European Reactions to Mass Tourism*, edited by Jeremy Boissevain, 1–26. Oxford: Berghahn.

Bowler, Kate. 2016. *Blessed: A History of the American Prosperity Gospel*. New York: Oxford University Press.

Bowman, Glenn. 1985. "Theoretical Itineraries towards an Anthropology of Pilgrimage." In *Dimensions of Pilgrimage: An Anthropological Appraisal*, edited by Makhan Jha, 1–9. New Delhi: Inter-India Publications.

———. 1988. "Pilgrimage Conference." *Anthropology Today* 4, no. 6: 20–23.

———. 1991. "Christian Ideology and the Image of a Holy Land." In *Contesting the Sacred: The Anthropology of Christian Culture*, edited by John Eade and Michael J. Sallnow, 98–121. London: Routledge.

———. 1993. "Nationalizing the Sacred: Shrines and Shifting Identities in the Israeli-Occupied Territories." *Man* 28, no. 3: 431–60.

———. 2012. "Sharing the *Sacra*." In *Sharing the Sacra: The Politics and Pragmatics of Intercommunal Relations around Holy Places*," edited by Glenn Bowman, 1–9. Oxford: Berghahan.

———. 2014. "Concluding Thoughts." In *Pilgrimage, Politics and Place Making in Eastern Europe: Crossing the Borders*, edited by John Eade and Mario Katić, 153–58. Farnham: Ashgate.

———. 2016. "Grounds for Sharing—Occasions for Conflict: An Inquiry into the Social Foundations of Cohabitation and Antagonism." In *Post-Ottoman Coexistence: Sharing Space in the Shadow of Conflict*, edited by Rebecca Bryant, 258–75. Oxford: Berghahn.

Bowman, Marion. 2008. "Going with the Flow: Contemporary Pilgrimage in Glaston-bury." In *Shrines and Pilgrimage in the Modern World: New Itineraries into the Sacred*, edited by Peter Jan Margry, 241–80. Amsterdam: Amsterdam University Press.

Bowman, Marion, and Tiina Sepp. 2019. "Caminoisation and Cathedrals: Replication, the Heritagisation of Religion, and the Spiritualisation of Heritage." *Religion* 49, no. 1: 74–98.

Bremborg, Anna Maria. 2013. "Creating Sacred Space by Walking in Silence: Pilgrimage in a Late Modern Lutheran Context." *Social Compass* 60, no. 4: 544–60.

Buber, Martin. 1923. *Ich und Du*. Leipzig: Insel-Verlag.

Bunyan, John. 1678. *The Pilgrim's Progress from This World, to That Which Is to Come*. London: Nathaniel Ponder.

Buitelaar, Marjo. 2015. "The Hajj and the Anthropological Study of Pilgrimage." In *Hajj: Global Interactions through Pilgrimage*, 9–25. Edited by Luitgard Mols and Marjo Buitelaar. Leiden: Sidestone Press.

———. 2018. "Moved by Mecca: The Meanings of the Hajj for Present-Day Dutch Muslims." In *Muslim Pilgrimage in Europe*, edited by Ingvild Flaskerud and Richard J. Natvig, 29–42. London: Routledge.

———. 2020. "Rearticulating the Conventions of Hajj Storytelling: Second Generation Moroccan-Dutch Female Pilgrims' Multi-Voiced Narratives about the Pilgrimage to Mecca." *Religions* 11, no. 7: 373. doi:10.3390/rel11070373.

Buitelaar, Marjo, Manja Stephan-Emmrich, and Viola Thimm. 2021. *Muslim Pilgrimage through the Lens of Women's New Mobilities*. New York: Routledge.

Bynum, Caroline Walker. 1992. *Fragmentation and Redemption: Essays on Gender and the Human Body in Medieval Religion*. New York: Zone.

Byron, Kyle. 2020. "Weapons for Witnessing: American Street Preaching and the Rhythms of War." *Religion and Society* 11, no. 1: 61–74.

Caidi, Nadia. 2019. "Pilgrimage to Hajj: An Informational Journey." *The International Journal of Information, Diversity, and Inclusion* 3, no. 1: 44–74.

Caidi, Nadia, Susan Beazley, and Laia Colomer Marquez. 2018. "Holy Selfies: Performing Pilgrimage in the Age of Social Media." *The International Journal of Information, Diversity, and Inclusion* 2, no. 1/2: 8–31.

Cannell, Fenella. 2006. "Introduction: The Anthropology of Christianity." In *The Anthropology of Christianity*, edited by Fenella Cannell, 1–45. Durham, NC: Duke University Press.

Carrithers, Michael. 2000. "On Polytropy: Or the Natural Condition of Spiritual Cosmopolitanism in India: The Digambar Jain Case." *Modern Asian Studies* 34, no. 4: 831–61.

Cavanaugh, William. 2008. "Migrant, Tourist, Pilgrim, Monk: Mobility and Identity in a Global Age." *Theological Studies* 69: 340–56.

Cazaux, François. 2011. "To Be a Pilgrim: A Contested Identity on Saint James' Way." *Tourism* 59, no 3: 353–67.

Chemin, José. 2016. "Re-inventing Europe: The Case of the Camino de Santiago de Compostela as European Heritage and the Political and Economic Discourses of Cultural Unity." *International Journal of Tourism Anthropology* 5, no. 1/2: 24–46.

Chvaja, Radim, and Dan Řezníček. 2019. "An Integrative Framework of Commitment Displays in Religious Systems." *Human Ethology* 34: 41–52.

Clarke, John. 2015. "Stuart Hall and the Theory and Practice of Articulation." *Discourse: Studies in the Cultural Politics of Education* 36, no. 2: 275–86.

Clifford, James. 1997. *Routes: Travel and Translation in the Late Twentieth Century*. Cambridge, MA: Harvard University Press.

Clift, Jean, and Wallace Clift. 1996. *The Archteype of Pilgrimage: Outer Action with Inner Meaning*. Mahwah: Paulist Press.

Coelho, Paulo. 1986. *The Pilgrimage*. New York: Harper One.

Cohen, Erik. 1992. "Pilgrimage Centers: Concentric and Excentric." *Annals of Tourism Research* 19, no. 1: 33–50.

Coleman, Simon. 2000. *The Globalisation of Charismatic Christianity*. Cambridge, UK: Cambridge University Press.

———. 2002a. "Do You Believe in Pilgrimage?: From Communitas to Contestation and Beyond." *Anthropological Theory* 2, no. 3: 355–68.

———. 2002b. "From the Sublime to the Meticulous: Art, Anthropology and Victorian Pilgrimage to Palestine." *History and Anthropology* 13, no. 4: 275–90.

———. 2006a. "Studying 'Global' Pentecostalism: Tensions, Representations and Opportunities." *PentecoStudies* 5, no. 1: 1–17.

———. 2006b. "The Multi-Sited Ethnographer." In *Critical Journeys: The Making of Anthropologists*, edited by Maya Unnithan and Geert de Neve, 31–46. Aldershot: Ashgate.

———. 2009a. "Mary on the Margins? The Modulation of Marian Imagery in Place, Memory and Performance." In *Moved by Mary: The Power of Pilgrimages in the Modern World*, edited by Anna-Karina Hermkens, Willy Jansen, and Catrien Notermans, 17–32. Surrey: Ashgate.

———. 2009b. "On Mirrors, Masks and Traps: Ambiguity, Risk and 'Lateral' Participation in Ritual." *Journal of Ritual Studies* 23, no. 2: 43–52.

———. 2011. "Accidental Pilgrims: Passions and Ambiguities of Travel to Christian Shrines in Europe." *Brown Journal of World Affairs* 22, no. 1: 71–81.

———. 2014. "Pilgrimage as Trope for an Anthropology of Christianity." *Current Anthropology* 55: 281–91.

———. 2015a. "Anthropological Tropes and 'Historical Tricksters': Pilgrimage as an 'Example' of Persuasion." *Journal of the Royal Anthropological Institute* 21, no. 1: 144–61.

———. 2015b. "Borderlands Ethics, Ethnography, and 'Repugnant' Christianity." *Hau* 5, no. 2: 275–300.

———. 2018a. "From Excess to Encompassment: Repetition, Recantation, and the Trashing of Time in Swedish Christianities." *History and Anthropology* 30: 170–89.

———. 2018b. "From the Liminal to the Lateral: Urban Religion in English Cathedrals." *Tourism Geographies* 29, no. 3: 384–404.

———. 2018c. "On Praying in an Old Country: Ritual, Heritage, and Powers of Adjacency in English Cathedrals." *Religion* 49, no. 1: 120–41.

———. 2018d. "What of Effervescence? Durkheim in the Cathedral." *Durkheimian Studies/Etudes Durkheimiennes* 23: 57–75.

———. 2019. "The Anthropology of Christian Pilgrimage: The Broadening Out of a Field." *Journal of the Canadian Society for Coptic Studies* 11: 25–38.

Coleman, Simon, and Marion Bowman. 2019. "Religion in Cathedrals: Pilgrimage, Place, Heritage, and the Politics of Replication." *Religion* 49, no. 1: 1–23.

Coleman, Simon, and John Eade, eds. 2004. *Reframing Pilgrimage: Cultures in Motion*. London: Routledge.

———. 2018. *Pilgrimage and Political Economy: Translating the Sacred*. Oxford: Berghahn.

Coleman, Simon, and John Elsner. 1995. *Pilgrimage Past and Present: Sacred Travel and Sacred Space in the World Religions*. Cambridge, MA: Harvard University Press.

———. 1998. "Performing Pilgrimage: Walsingham and the Ritual Construction of Irony." In *Ritual, Performance, Media*, edited by F. Hughes-Freeland, 46–65. London: Routledge.

———. 2002a. "Pilgrim Voices: Authoring Christian Pilgrimage." In *Pilgrim Voices: Narrative and Authorship in Christian Pilgrimage*, edited by Simon Coleman and John Elsner, 1–17. New York: Berghahn.

———. 2002b. *Pilgrim Voices: Narrative and Authorship in Christian Pilgrimage*. New York: Berghahn.

Coleman, Simon, and Rosalind Hackett. 2015. Introduction to *The Anthropology of Global Pentecostalism and Evangelicalism*, edited by Simon Coleman and Rosalind Hackett, 1–37. New York: New York University Press.

Coleman, Simon, and Tamara Kohn, eds. 2007. *The Discipline of Leisure*. Oxford: Berghahn, 2007.

Coleman, Simon, and Katrin Maier. 2013. "Redeeming the City: Creating and Traversing 'London-Lagos.'" *Religion* 43, no. 3: 353–64.

———. 2016. "In, of, and beyond Diaspora? Mapping, Migration, and the Production of Space among Nigerian Pentecostals." *Diaspora* 19, no. 1: 9–31.

Coleman, Simon, and Pauline von Hellermann, eds. 2011. *Multi-Sited Ethnography: Problems and Possibilities in the Translocation of Research Methods*. London: Routledge.

Collier, Stephen J., and Andrew Lakoff. 2005. "On Regimes of Living." In *Global Assemblages*, edited by Stephen J. Collier and Aihwa Ong, 22–39. Malden, MA: Wiley-Blackwell.

Collins, Randall. 2005. *Interaction Ritual Chains*. Princeton, NJ: Princeton University Press.

Collins-Kreiner, Noga. 2010. "Researching Pilgrimage: Continuity and Transformation." *Annals of Tourism Research* 37, no. 2: 440–56.

Collins-Kriener, Noga, Shmueli, Deborah and Michal Ben-Gal. 2013. "Pilgrimage Sites in the Holy Land: Pathways to Harmony and Understanding or Sources of Confrontation?" In *Pilgrims and Pilgrimages as Peacemakers in Christianity, Judaism and Islam*, edited by Antón Pazos, 177–200. Farnham: Ashgate.

Corten, André, and Ruth Marshall-Fratani, eds. 2001. *Between Babel and Pentecost: Transnational Pentecostalism in Africa and Latin America*. London: Hurst.

Couroucli, Maria. 2012. "Cthonian Spirits and Shared Shrines: The Dynamics of Place among Christians and Muslims in Anatolia." In *Sharing the Sacra: The Politics and Pragmatics of Intercommunal Relations around Holy Places*," edited by Glenn Bowman, 44–60. Oxford: Berghahan.

Crumrine, Ross, and Alan Morinis, eds. 1991. *Pilgrimage in Latin America*. New York: Greenwood.

Csordas, Thomas. 1993. "Somatic Modes of Attention." *Cultural Anthropology* 8, no. 2: 135–56.

Curteyne, Alice. 1944. *Lough Der: St Patrick's Purgatory*. London: Burns, Oates and Washbourne.

Curtis, Simon. 2016. "English Cathedrals: Events and Spiritual Capital." *International Journal of Religious Tourism and Pilgrimage* 4: 1–11.

Cusack, Carole, and Justine Digance. 2008. "'Shopping for a Self': Pilgrimage, Identity-Formation, and Retail Therapy." In *Victor Turner and Contemporary Cultural Performance*, edited by Graham St. John, 227–41. Oxford: Berghahn.

Czarnowski, Stefan. 1919. *Le Culte des héros et ses conditions sociales: Saint Patrick, Héros National de l'Irlande*. Paris: Alcan.

———.1938. *Kultura*. Warszawa: "Wiedza i Życie."

Dahl, Shayne. 2019. "Mountains of Time: Historical Consciousness and Sacred Mountains in Japan." PhD diss., University of Toronto.

Dahlberg, Andrea. 1991. "The Body as a Principle of Holism: Three Pilgrimages to Lourdes." In *Contesting the Sacred: The Anthropology of Christian Culture*, edited by John Eade and Michael J. Sallnow, 30–50. London: Routledge.

Danely, Jason. 2017. "A Watchful Presence: Aesthetics of Well-Being in a Japanese Pilgrimage." *Ethnos* 82, no. 1: 165–92.

David, Hans Jürgen. 2019. "In Fear of the Past: The Pilgrimage to Badrinath in Perspective." In *Ritual Journeys in South Asia: Constellations and Contestations of Mobility and Space*, edited by Christoph Bergmann and Jürgen Schaflechner, 11–28. New York: Routledge.

Davidson, Linda Kay. 2014. "Reformulations of the Pilgrimages to Santiago de Compostela." In *Redefining Pilgrimage: New Perspectives on Historical and Contemporary Pilgrimages*, edited by Antón Pazos, 159–81. Farnham: Ashgate.

Davie, Grace. 2007a. *The Sociology of Religion*. London: Sage.

———. 2007b. "Vicarious Religion: A Methodological Challenge." In *Everyday Religion: Observing Modern Religious Lives*, edited by Nancy Ammerman, 21–35. Oxford: Oxford University Press.

———. 2010. "Vicarious Religion: A Response." *Journal of Contemporary Religion* 25, no. 2: 261–66.

———. 2012. "A Short Afterword: Thinking Spatially about Religion." *Culture and Religion* 13: 485–89.

Davis, Jenny, and Nathan Jurgenson. 2018. "Context Collapse: Theorizing Context Collusions and Collisions." *Information, Communication and Society* 17, no. 4: 476–85.

Dawut, Rahilä. 2009. "Shrine Pilgrimage among the Uighurs." *Silk Road* 6, no. 2: 56–67.

De Busser, Cathelijne, and Anna Niedzwiedz. 2009. "Mary in Poland: A Polish Master Symbol." In *Moved by Mary: The Power of Pilgrimage in the Modern World*, edited by Anna-Karina Hermkens, Willy Jansen, and Catrien Notermans, 87–100. Farnham: Ashgate.

de Certeau, Michel. 1984. *The Practice of Everyday Life*. Berkeley: University of California Press.

DeConinck, Kate. 2019. "Traversing Mass Tragedies: Material Religion between the 9/11 and Newtown Memorials." *Journal of Global Catholicism* 3, no. 1: 126–53.

Deflem, Mathieu. 1991. "Ritual, Anti-structure, and Religion: A Discussion of Victor Turner's Processual Symbolic Analysis." *Journal for the Scientific Study of Religion* 30, no. 1: 1–25.

Delaney, Carol. 1990. "The Hajj: Sacred and Secular." *American Ethnologist* 17, no. 3: 513–30.

Deleuze, Gilles, and Félix Guattari. 1980. *A Thousand Plateaus: Capitalism and Schizophrenia*. Minneapolis: University of Minnesota Press.

———. 1986. *Nomadology: The War Machine*. Los Angeles: Semiotext(e).

Della Dora, Veronica. 2016. "Infrasecular Geographies: Making, Unmaking, and Remaking Sacred Space." *Progress in Human Geography* 42: 1–28.

Dempster, Murray, Byron Klaus, and Douglas Petersen, eds. 1999. *The Globalization of Pentecostalism: A Religion Made to Travel*. Oxford: Regnum.

Di Giovine, Michael. 2011. "Pilgrimage: Communitas and Contestation, Unity and Difference—An Introduction." *Tourism Review* 59, no. 3: 247–69.

———. 2012. "Padre Pio for Sale: Souvenirs, Relics, or Identity Markers?" *International Journal of Tourism Anthropology* 2, no. 2: 108–27.

———. 2013. "Apologia Pro Turismo: Breaking Inter- and Intra-disciplinary Boundaries in the Anthropological Study of Tourism and Pilgrimage." *Journal of Tourism Challenges and Trends* 6, no. 2: 63–94.

———. 2016. "A Higher Purpose: Sacred Journeys as Spaces for Peace." In *Pilgrims and Pilgrimages as Peacemakers in Christianity, Judaism and Islam*, edited by Antón M. Pazos, 11–28. New York: Routledge.

———. In press. "Galactic Shrines and the Catholic Cult of St. Padre Pio of Pietrelcina." *In Landscapes of Christianity: Destination, Temporality, Transformation*, edited by James Bielo and Amos Ron. London: Bloomsbury.

Di Giovine, Michael, and Jaeyeon Choe. 2019. "Geographies of Religion and Spirituality: Pilgrimage beyond the 'Officially' Sacred." *Tourism Geographies* 21, no. 3: 361–83.

Di Giovine, Michael, and David Picard, eds. 2015. *The Seductions of Pilgrimage: Sacred Journeys Afar and Astray in the Western Religious Tradition*. Farnham: Ashgate.

Dogra, Sufyan Abid. 2019. "Living a Piety-Led Life beyond Muharram: Becoming or Being a South Asian Shia Muslim in the UK." *Contemporary Islam* 13: 307–24.

Doi, Kiyomi. 2011. "Onto Emerging Ground: Anticlimactic Movement on the Camino de Santiago de Compostela." *Tourism* 59, no. 3: 271–85.

Dott, Brian R. 2004. *Identity Reflections: Pilgrimages to Mount Tai in Late Imperial China*. Cambridge, MA: Harvard University Press.

Douglas, Mary. 1966. *Purity and Danger: An Analysis of Concepts of Pollution and Taboo*. London: Routledge.

———. 1970. *Natural Symbols: Explorations in Cosmology*. London: Cresset.

———. 1993. *In the Wilderness: The Doctrine of Defilement in the Book of Numbers*. Oxford: Oxford University Press.

Downie, David. 2013. *Paris to the Pyrenees: A Skeptic Pilgrim Walks the Way of Saint James*. New York: Pegasus.

Du Plooy, Shirley. 2017. "South(ern) African Journeys of Reverence." In *New Pathways in Pilgrimage Studies: Global Perspectives*, edited by Dionigi Albera and John Eade, 124–41. New York: Routledge.

Dubisch, Jill. 1972. "The Open Community: Migration from a Greek Island Village." PhD diss., University of Chicago.

———. 1995. *In a Different Place: Pilgrimage, Gender, and Politics at a Greek Island Shrine*. Princeton, NJ: Princeton University Press.

———. 2004. "'Heartland of America': Memory, Motion and the (Re-)Construction of History on a Motorcycle Pilgrimage." In *Reframing Pilgrimage: Cultures in Motion*, edited by Simon Coleman and John Eade, 105–32. London: Routledge.

Dubisch, Jill, and Mark Winkelman, eds. 2005. "Introduction: The Anthropology of Pilgrimage." In *Pilgrimage and Healing*, edited by Jill Dubisch and Michael Winkelman, ix–xxxvi. Tucson: University of Arizona Press.

Dubuisson, Eva-Marie, and Anna Genina. 2011. "Claiming an Ancestral Homeland: Kazakh Pilgrimage and Migration in Inner Asia." *Central Asian Survey* 30, no. 3/4: 469–85.

Duncan, James, and Derek Gregory. 1999. *Writes of Passage: Reading Travel Writing*. New York: Routledge.

Durkheim, Émile. (1912) 1961. *The Elementary Forms of the Religious Life*. New York: Collier.

Dwyer, Claire. 2016. "Why Does Religion Matter for Cultural Geographers?" *Social & Cultural Geography* 17, no. 6: 758–62.

Dyas, Dee, and John Jenkins. 2020. Introduction to *Pilgrimage and Cathedrals: Past Present, and Future*, edited by Dee Dyas and John Jenkins, 1–26. London: Palgrave Macmillan.

Eade, John. 1991. "Order and Power at Lourdes: Lay Helpers and the Organization of a Pilgrimage Shrine." In *Contesting the Sacred: The Anthropology of Christian Pilgrimage*, edited by John Eade and Michael Sallnow, 51–76. London: Routledge.

———. 2000a. Introduction to the Illinois paperback edition of *Contesting the Sacred: The Anthropology of Christian Pilgrimage*, edited by John Eade and Michael Sallnow, ix–xxvii. Urbana: University of Illinois Press.

———. 2011. "The Expanding Field of Pilgrimage Studies: Beyond Binaries." *Tourism* 59, no. 3: 387–89.

———. 2016. "Parish and Pilgrimage in a Changing Europe." In *Migration, Transnationalism and Catholicism Global Perspectives*, edited by Dominic Pasura and Marta Bivand Erdal, 75–92. London: Palgrave Macmillan.

———. 2019. "Exploring Pilgrimage: Reflections of an Academic Traveller." doi:10.13140/RG.2.2.31920.00001.

Eade, John, and Dionigi Albera. 2017. "Pilgrimage Studies in Global Perspective." In *New Pathways in Pilgrimage Studies: Global Perspectives*, edited by Dionigi Albera and John Eade, 1–17. London: Routledge.

Eade, John, and David Garbin. 2007. "Reinterpreting the Relationship between Centre and Periphery: Pilgrimage and Sacred Spatialisation among Polish and Congolese Communities in Britain." Mobilities 2, no. 3: 413–24.

Eade, John, and Mario Katić. 2014. "Introduction: Crossing the Borders." In *Pilgrimage, Politics and Place Making in Eastern Europe: Crossing the Borders*, edited by John Eade and Mario Katić, 1–12. Farnham: Ashgate.

Eade, John, and Michael J. Sallnow, eds. 1991. *Contesting the Sacred: The Anthropology of Christian Culture*. London: Routledge.

Eberhart, Helmut. 2015. "From Religious Folklore Studies to Research of Popular Religiosity: Pilgrimage Studies in German-Speaking Europe." In *International Perspectives on Pilgrimage Studies: Itineraries, Gaps and Obstacles*, edited by Dionigi Albera and John Eade, 1–22. London: Routledge.

Eck, Diana L. 1983. *Banaras: City of Light*. London: Routledge.

Edensor, Timothy. 2000. "Staging Tourism: Tourists as Performers." *Annals of Tourism Research* 27, no. 2: 322–44.

———. 2016. *Geographies of Rhythm: Nature, Place, Mobilities and Bodies*. London: Routledge.

Egan, Keith. 2010. "Walking Back to Happiness? Modern Pilgrimage and the Expression of Suffering on Spain's Camino de Santiago." *Journeys* 11, no. 1: 107–32.

Ehrenschwendtner, Marie-Luise. 2009. "Virtual Pilgrimages? Enclosure and the Practice of Piety at St. Katherine's Convent, Augsburg." *Journal of Ecclesiastical History* 60, no. 1: 45–73.

Eickelman, Dale F., and James Piscatori, eds. 1990a. *Muslim Travellers: Pilgrimage, Migration, and the Religious Imagination*. London: Routledge.

———. 1990b. "Social Theory in the Study of Muslim Societies." In *Muslim Travellers: Pilgrimage, Migration, and the Religious Imagination*, edited by Dale F. Eickelman and James Piscatori, 3–25. London: Routledge.

Eliade, Mircea. 1987. *Encyclopedia of Religion*. New York: Macmillian.

Engelke, Matthew. 2004. "'The Endless Conversation': Fieldwork, Writing, and the Marriage of Victor and Edith Turner." In *Significant Others: Interpersonal and Professional Commitments in Anthropology*, edited by Richard Handler, 6–50. Madison: University of Wisconsin Press.

———. 2007. *A Problem of Presence: Beyond Scripture in an African Church*. Berkeley: University of California Press.

———. 2008. "An Interview with Edith Turner." In *Victor Turner and Contemporary Cultural Performance*, edited by Graham St. John, 275–96. Oxford: Berghahn.

———. 2012. "Angels in Swindon: Public Religion and Ambient Faith in England." *American Ethnologist* 39, no. 1: 155–70.

Esposito, John, ed. 2004. *The Islamic World: Past and Present*. New York, Oxford University Press.

Evans-Pritchard, Edward E. 1940. *The Nuer: A Description of the Modes of Livelihood and Political Institutions of a Nilotic People*. Oxford: Clarendon.

Evens, T. M. S., and Don Handelman. 2006. "The Ethnographic Praxis of the Theory of Practice." In *The Manchester School: Practice and Ethnographic Praxis in Anthropology*, edited by T. M. S. Evens and Don Handelman, 1–11. Oxford: Berghahn.

Faist, Thomas. 2013. "The Mobility Turn: A New Paradigm for the Social Sciences?" *Ethnic and Racial Studies* 36, no. 1: 1637–46.

Fardon, Richard. 2013. "Introduction: Drawn from Life: Mary Douglas's Personal Method." In *A Very Personal Method: Anthropological Essays Drawn from Life*, edited by Richard Fardon, 1–12. London: Sage.

Fedele, Anna. 2013. *Looking for Mary Magdalene: Alternative Pilgrimage and Ritual Creativity at Catholic Shrines in France*. New York: Oxford University Press.

Fedele, Anna, and Cyril Isnard. 2015. "From Cryptic to Critique: Early and Contemporary French Contributions to the Study of Pilgrimage." In *International Perspectives on Pilgrimage Studies: Itineraries, Gaps and Obstacles*, edited by Dionigi Albera and John Eade, 171–92. London Routledge.

Feldhaus, Anne. 2003. *Connected Places: Region, Pilgrimage, and Geographical Imagination in India*. New York: Palgrave Macmillan.

Feldman, Jackie. 2002. "Marking the Boundaries of the Enclave: Defining the Israeli Experience through the Poland Experience." *Israel Studies* 7, no. 2: 84–114.

———. 2020. "How Can You Know the Bible and Not Believe in Our Lord? Guiding Pilgrims across the Jewish–Christian Divide." *Religions* 11, no. 6: 294. https://doi.org/10.3390/rel11060294.

Fenn, Richard. 1982. *Liturgies and Trials: The Secularization of Religious Language*. New York: Pilgrim.

Flaskerud, Ingvild. 2018. "Mediating Pilgrimage: Pilgrimage Remembered and Desired in a Norwegian Home Community." In *Muslim Pilgrimage in Europe*, edited by Ingvild Flaskerud and Richard Natvig, 43–57. London: Routledge.

Flaskerud, Ingvild, and Richard Natvig. 2018. Introduction to *Muslim Pilgrimage in Europe*, edited by Ingvild Flaskerud and Richard Natvig, 1–28. London: Routledge.

Foley, Ronan. 2013. "Small Health Pilgrimages: Place and Practice at the Holy Well." *Culture and Religion* 14, no. 1: 44–62.

Fortuny, Patricia, and de Mola, Loret. 2018. "A Pentecsotal Shrine in Mexico: Ethnography of Migration and Pilgrimage." In *Pilgrimage and Political Economy: Translating the Sacred*, edited by Simon Coleman and John Eade, 136–54. Oxford: Berghahn.

Francis, Leslie, and Judith Muskett. 2015. "Shaping Cathedral Studies: A Scientific Approach." In *Anglican Cathedrals in Modern Life: The Science of Cathedral Studies*, edited by Leslie Francis, 1–28. New York: Palgrave Macmillan.

Franck, Karen, and Quentin Stevens, eds. 2007a. *Loose Space: Possibility and Diversity in Urban Life*. New York: Routledge.

———. 2007b. "Tying Down Loose Space." In *Loose Space: Possibility and Diversity in Urban Life*, edited by Karen Franck and Quentin Stevens, 1–33. London: Routledge.

Frankenberg, Ronald. 2006. "A Bridge over Troubled Waters, or What a Difference a Day Makes: From the Drama of Production to the Production of Drama." In *The

Manchester School: Practice and Ethnographic Praxis in Anthropology, edited by T. M. S. Evens and Don Handelman, 202–20. Oxford: Berghahn.

Frazer, James. 1890. *The Golden Bough: A Study in Comparative Religion*. London: Macmillan.

———. 1951. *The Golden Bough: A Study in Magic and Religion*. Abr. ed. New York: The Macmillan Company.

Frey, Nancy. 1998. *Pilgrim Stories: On and off the Road to Santiago, Journeys along an Ancient Way in Modern Spain*. Berkeley: University of California Press.

———. 2004. "Stories of Return: Pilgrimage and Its Aftermaths." In *Intersecting Journeys: The Anthropology of Pilgrimage and Tourism*, edited by Ellen Badone and Sharon R. Roseman, 89–109. Chicago: University of Illinois Press.

———. 2017. "The Smart Camino: Pilgrimage in the Internet Age." www.walkingtopresence.com.

Fuller, Christopher J. 1992. *The Camphor Flame: Popular Hinduism and Society in India*. Princeton, NJ: Princeton University Press.

Gauthier, François, Tuomas Martikainen, and Linda Woodhead. 2013. "Introduction: Religion in Consumer Society." *Social Compass* 58, no. 3: 291–301.

Geary, David. 2018. "Transnational Courting through Shakyamuni Buddha: Japanese Pilgrimage and Geographical Dowries in North India." In *Pilgrimage and Political Economy: Translating the Sacred*, edited by Simon Coleman and John Eade, 40–58. Oxford: Berghahn.

Geertz, Clifford. 1973. *The Interpretation of Cultures*. New York: Basic Books.

———. 1983. *Local Knowledge: Further Essays in Interpretive Anthropology*. New York: Basic Books.

Gell, Alfred. 1996. "Vogel's Net: Traps as Artworks and Artworks as Traps." *Journal of Material Culture* 1, no. 1: 15–38.

Gemzöe, Lena. 2005. "The Feminisation of Healing in Pilgrimage to Fátima." In *Pilgrimage and Healing*, edited by Jill Dubisch and Michael Winkelman, 25–48. Tucson: University of Arizona Press.

———. 2014a. "Every Minute out There: Creating Ritual among Swedish Pilgrims on Their Way to Compostela." *Journal of Ritual Studies* 28, no. 2: 65–75.

———. 2014b. "I Skrivande Pilgrimers Fotspår." In *Fiktion och Verklighet: Mångvetenskapliga Möten*, 123–45. Gothenburg: Makadam.

———. 2016. "Working the Way to Santiago de Compostela: Masculinities and Spiritualities of Capitalism." In *Contemporary Encounters in Gender and Religion: European Perspectives*, edited by Lena Gemzöe, Marja-Liisa Keinänen, and Avril Maddrell, 77–101. London: Palgrave Macmillan.

Genoni, Paul. 2016. "The Australian Way: Transnational Flows and the 21st-Century Camino." In *The Camino de Santiago in the 21st Century: Interdisciplinary Perspectives and Global Views*, edited by Samuel Sánchez y Sánchez and Annie Hesp, 172–93. London: Routledge.

Gershon, Ilana. 2019. "Porous Social Orders." *American Ethnologist* 46, no. 4: 404–16.

Glazier, Stephen D. 2018. "From Dissection to Discernment: Edie Turner, Victor Turner, and Jonathan Edwards on the Ontological Status of Spirits." In *The Intellectual Legacy of Victor and Edith Turner*, edited by Frank Salamone and Marjorie Snipes, 35–53. Lanham, MD: Lexington.

Gluckman, Max. (1940) 1958. *Analysis of a Social Situation in Modern Zululand*. Manchester: Manchester University Press for the Rhodes-Livingstone Institute.

———, ed. 1962. *Essays on the Ritual of Social Relations*. Manchester: Manchester University Press.

Golan, Oren, and Michele Martini. 2018. "Digital Pilgrimage: Exploring Catholic Monastic Webcasts." *Communication Review* 21, no. 1: 24–45.

Gold, Ann. 1988. *Fruitful Journeys: The Ways of Rajasthani Pilgrims*. Berkeley: University of California Press.

Gomes, Carlos, Nieves Losada, and Xerardo Pereiro. 2019. "Motivations of Pilgrims on the Portuguese Inner Way to Santiago de Compostela." *International Journal of Religious Tourism and Pilgrimage* 7, no. 2: 31–40.

Goodman, Percival, and Paul Goodman. 1947. *Communitas: Means of Livelihood and Ways of Life*. Chicago: University of Chicago Press.Goodenough, Ursula. 2001. "Vertical and Horizontal Transcendence." *Zygon* 36: 21–31.

Gothóni, René. 1991. "The Progress of Pilgrimage on the Holy Mountain of Athos." *Social Anthropology of Pilgrimage*, edited by Makhan Jha, 292–309. New Delhi: Inter-India.

Graburn, Nelson. 1977. "Tourism: The Sacred Journey." In *Hosts and Guests: The Anthropology of Tourism*, edited by Valene Smith, 17–32. Philadelphia: University of Pennsylvania Press.

———. 2011. "Binaries and Boundaries." *Tourism* 59, no. 3: 391–98.

Greenia, George. 2016. Foreword to *The Camino de Santiago in the 21st Century: Interdisciplinary Perspectives and Global Views*, edited by Samuela Sanchéz y Sanchéz and Annie Hesp, ix–xi. New York: Routledge.

Gregory, Derek. 1999. "Scripting Egypt Orientalism and the Cultures of Travel." In *Writes of Passage: Reading Travel Writing*, edited by James Duncan and Derek Gregory, 114–50. London: Routledge.

Grimes, Ronald. 2000. *Deeply into the Bone: Re-inventing the Rites of Passage*. Berkeley: University of California Press.

Grossberg, Lawrence. 1986. "On Postmodernism and Articulation: An Interview with Stuart Hall." *Journal of Communication Inquiry* 10, no. 2: 45–60.

Hage, Ghassan. 2009. "Waiting Out the Crisis: On Stuckedness and Governmentality." In *Waiting*, edited by Ghassan Hage, 97–106. Carlton: Melbourne University Press.

Hall, Stuart. 1969. "The Hippies, an American Moment." In *Student Power*, edited by J. Nagel, 170–202. London: Merlin.

———. 1985. "Religious Ideologies and Social Movements in Jamaica." In *Religion and Ideology*, edited by Robert Bocock and Ken Thompson, 269–97. Manchester: Manchester University Press.

———. 1987. "Minimal Selves." In *The Real Me: Postmodernism and the Question of Identity*, ICA Documents 6, 44–46. London: Institute of Contemporary Arts.

———. 2019. *Essential Essays. Vol. 1.* Durham, NC: Duke University Press.

Hammoudi, Abdellah. 2005. *A Season in Mecca: Narrative of a Pilgrimage.* New York: Hill and Wang.

Hann, Chris. 2007. "The Anthropology of Christianity Per Se." *European Journal of Sociology* 48, no. 3: 383–410.

Hann, Chris, and Hermann Goltz. 2010. "Introduction: The Other Christianity?" In *Eastern Christians in Anthropological Perspective*, edited by Chris Hann and Hermann Goltz, 1–29. Berkeley: University of California Press, 2010.

Haraway, Donna. 1991. *Simians, Cyborgs, and Women: The Reinvention of Nature.* New York: Routledge.

Harding, Susan. 1991. "Representing Fundamentalism: The Problem of the Repugnant Cultural Other." *Social Research* 58, no. 2: 373–93.

Harris, Alana. 2013. "Lourdes and Holistic Spirituality: Contemporary Catholicism, the Therapeutic and Religious Thermalism." *Culture and Religion* 14, no. 1: 23–43.

Hastrup, Kirsten. 2013. "Scales of Attention in Fieldwork: Global Connections and Local Concerns in the Arctic." *Ethnography* 14, no. 2: 145–64.

Hatfield, Donald J. W. 2010. *Taiwanese Pilgrimage to China: Ritual, Complicity, Community.* New York: Palgrave Macmillan.

Hazard, Sonia. 2013. "The Material Turn in the Study of Religion." *Religion and Society* 4, no. 1: 58–78.

Heelas, Paul. 1996. *The New Age Movement: Religion, Culture and Society in the Age of Postmodernity.* Oxford: Blackwell.

Helland, Christopher. 2002. "Surfing for Salvation." *Religion* 32, no 4: 293–302.

Hellman, Jörgen. 2017. "Living Together with Ancestors: Cultural Heritage and Sacred Places on West Java." *International Journal of Religious Tourism and Pilgrimage* 5, no. 1: 78–88.

Heo, Angie. 2018. *The Political Lives of Saints: Christian-Muslim Mediation in Egypt.* Berkeley: University of California Press.

Hermkens, Anna-Karina, Willy Jansen, and Catrien Notermans, eds. 2009. "Introduction: The Power of Marian Pilgrimage." In *Moved by Mary: The Power of Pilgrimage in the Modern World*, edited by Anna-Karina Hermkens, Willy Jansen, and Catrien Notermans, 1–13. Farnham: Ashgate.

Herrero, Nieves, and Sharon Roseman, eds. 2015. *The Tourism Imaginary and Pilgrimage to the Edges of the World.* Bristol: Channel View.

Hertz, Robert. 2017. "Excerpt from 'St Besse: A Study of an Alpine Cult.'" In *The Anthropology of Catholicism*, edited by Kristen Norget, Valentina Napolitano, and Maya Mayblin, 33–42. Berkeley: University of California Press.

Hervieu-Léger, Danièle. 2000. *Religion as a Chain of Memory.* New Brunswick, NJ: Rutgers University Press.

Herzfeld, Michael. 2001. *Anthropology: Theoretical Practice in Culture and Society.* Oxford: Wiley.

Higgins, Leighanne, and Kathy Hamilton. 2020. "Pilgrimage, Material Objects and Spontaneous Communitas." *Annals of Tourism Research* 81: 1–11.

Hill-Smith, Connie. 2009. "Cyberpilgrimage: A Study of Authenticity, Presence, and Meaning in Online Pilgrimage Experiences." *Journal of Religion and Popular Culture* 21, no. 2: 6.

———. 2011. "Cyberpilgrimage: The (Virtual) Reality of Online Pilgrimage Experience." *Religion Compass* 5, no. 6: 236–46.

Hirsch, Eric, and Michael O'Hanlon, eds. 1995. *The Anthropology of Landscape: Perspectives on Place and Space*. Oxford: Oxford University Press.

Hobbes, Thomas. 1651. *Leviathan: Or the Matter, Forme and Power of a Commonwealth Ecclesiasticall and Civil*. London: Andrew Crooke.

Hobsbawm, Eric, and Terence Ranger, eds. 1983. *The Invention of Tradition*. Cambridge, UK: Cambridge University Press.

Hodges, Matt. 2008. "Rethinking Time's Arrow: Bergson, Deleuze and the Anthropology of Time." *Anthropological Theory* 8, no. 4: 399–429.

Huang, Yueh-po. 2017. "Pilgrimage, Modernity, Tourism, and Nostalgia: Tenrikyō's Ojibagaeri in Post-colonial Taiwan." *Japanese Journal of Religious Studies* 44, no. 2: 281–307.

Huber, Toni. 2008. *The Holy Land Reborn: Pilgrimage and the Tibetan Reinvention of Buddhist India*. Chicago: University of Chicago Press.

Hughes-Freeland, Felicia, ed. 1998. *Ritual, Performance, Media*. London: Routledge.

Hummel, Thomas, and Ruth Hummel. 1995. *Patterns of the Sacred: English Protestant and Russian Orthodox Pilgrims of the Nineteenth Century*. London: Scorpion Cavendish.

Humphrey, Caroline, and James Laidlaw. 1994. *The Archetypal Actions of Ritual: A Theory of Ritual Illustrated by the Jain Rite of Worship*. Oxford: Clarendon.

Huyssen, Andreas. 2003. *Present Pasts: Urban Palimpsests and the Politics of Memory*. Stanford, CA: Stanford University Press.

Im, Kyung-Mi, and JuSung Jun. 2015. "The Meaning of Learning on the Camino de Santiago Pilgrimage." *Australian Journal of Adult Learning* 55, no. 2: 329–49.

Ingold, Tim. 2004. "Culture on the Ground: The World Perceived through the Feet." *Journal of Material Culture* 9, no. 3: 315–40.

———. 2007. *Lines: A Brief History*. London: Routledge.

Ingold, Tim, and Jo Lee Vergunst. 2008. *Ways of Walking: Ethnography and Practice on Foot*. Burlington: Ashgate.

Jackson, Michael. 2009. *The Palm at the End of the Mind: Relatedness, Religiosity, and the Real*. Durham, NC: Duke University Press.

Jafari, Jafar, and Noel Scott. 2014. "Muslim World and Its Tourisms." *Annals of Tourism Research* 44: 1–19.

Jha, Makhan, ed. 1991. *Social Anthropology of Pilgrimage*. Delhi: Inter-India Publication.

Kaell, Hillary. 2012. "Of Gifts and Grandchildren: American Holy Land Souvenirs." *Journal of Material Culture* 17, no. 2: 133–51.

———. 2014. *Walking Where Jesus Walked: American Christians and Holy Land Pilgrimage*. New York: New York University Press.

Kalinock, Sabine. 2006. "Going on Pilgrimage Online: The Representation of Shia Rituals on the Internet." *Online: Heidelberg Journal of Religions on the Internet* 2, no. 1: 6–23.

Kalua, Fetson. 2009. "Homi Bhabha's Third Space and African Identity." *Journal of African Cultural Studies* 21, no. 1: 23–32.

Kamau, Lucy Jayne. 2002. "Liminality, Communitas, Charisma, and Community." *Intentional Community: An Anthropological Perspective*, edited by Susan Love Brown, 17–40. Albany: State University of New York Press.

Kapferer, Bruce. 2006. "Situations, Crisis, and the Anthropology of the Concrete: The Contribution of Max Gluckman." In *The Manchester School: Practice and Ethnographic Praxis in Anthropology*, edited by T. M. S. Evens and Don Handelman, 118–55. Oxford: Berghahn.

———. 2015. Introduction to *In the Event—Toward an Anthropology of Generic Moments*, edited by Lotte Meinert and Bruce Kapferer, 1–28. Oxford: Berghahn.

———. 2019. "Crisis and Communitas: Victor Turner and Social Process." *Anthropology Today* 35, no. 5: 1–2.

Karaflocka, Anastasia. 2002. "Religious Discourse and Cyberspace." *Religion* 32: 279–92.

Karić, Dženita. 2018a. *Multiple Paths to the Holy: Continuity and Change in Bosnian Hajj Literature*. PhD diss., University of London.

———. 2018b. "Online Bosnian Hajj Narratives." In *Muslim Pilgrimage in Europe*, edited by Ingvild Flaskerud and Richard J. Natvig, 58–69. London: Routledge.

Karve, Irawati. (1951) 1988. "'On the Road': A Maharashtrian Pilgrimage." In *The Experience of Hinduism: Essays on Religion in Maharashtra*, edited by Eleanor Zelliot and Maxine Berntsen, 69–75. Albany: State University of New York Press.

Kato, Kumi, and Ricardo Nicolas Progano. 2017. "Spiritual (Walking) Tourism as a Foundation for Sustainable Destination Development: Kumano-Kodo Pilgrimage, Wakayama, Japan." *Tourism Management Perspectives* 24: 243–51.

Kaufman, Suzanne. 2005. *Consuming Visions: Mass Culture and the Lourdes Shrine*. Ithaca, NY: Cornell University Press.

Keane, Webb. 2003. "Semiotics and the Social Analysis of Material Things." *Language & Communication* 23, no. 3: 409–25.

———. 2006. "Epilogue: Anxious Transcendence." In *The Anthropology of Christianity*, edited by Fenella Cannell, 308–23. Durham, NC: Duke University Press.

———. 2013. "On Spirit Writing: Materialities of Language and the Religious Work of Transduction." *Journal of the Royal Anthropological Institute* 9, no. 1: 1–17.

Kenny, Erin. 2007. "Gifting Mecca: Importing Spiritual Capital to West Africa." *Mobilities* 2, no. 3: 363–81.

Kerkeling, Hape. 2006. *Ich bin dan mall weg* [I'm off then]. München: Malik.

Kinnard, Jacob N. 2014. *Places in Motion: The Fluid Identities of Temples, Images, and Pilgrims*. New York: Oxford.

Kirkpatrick, Julie. 2010. *The Camino Letters*. Millbrook, ON: Pyxis.

Kirsch, Thomas. 2008. *Spirits and Letters: Reading, Writing and Charisma in African Christianity*. Oxford: Berghahn.

Kitagawa, J. M. 1987. *On Understanding Japanese Religion*. Princeton, NJ: Princeton University Press.

Klungel, Janine. 2009. "Family Pilgrimages to the Sea in Guadeloupe: Matrifocality under Pressure." In *Moved by Mary: The Power of Pilgrimage in the Modern World*, edited by Anna-Karina Hermkens, Willy Jansen, and Catrien Notermans, 165–79. Farnham: Ashgate.

Kormina, Jeanne. 2018. "Inhabiting Orthodox Russia: Religious Nomadism and the Puzzle of Belonging." In *Praying with the Senses: Contemporary Orthodox Christian Spirituality in Practice*, edited by Sonja Luerhmann, 143–62. Bloomington: Indiana University Press.

Kosansky, Oren. 2002. "Tourism, Charity, and Profit: The Movement of Money in Moroccan Jewish Pilgrimage." *Cultural Anthropology* 17, no. 3: 359–400.

Koselleck, Reinhardt. 2004. *Futures Past: On the Semantics of Historical Time*. New York: Columbia University Press.

Kreinath, Jens. 2017. "Inter-rituality as a New Approach for Studying Interreligious Relations and Ritual Dynamics at Shared Pilgrimage Sites in Hatay, Turkey." *Interreligious Studies and Intercultural Theology* 1, no. 2: 257–84.

Kreinath, Jens, and Matan Shapiro. 2019. "Introductory Note on Play and Ritual: Rhythm, Pulsation, and Fractal Dynamics." *Anthropological Theory* 20, no. 2: 190–92.

Kuhn, Thomas. 1962. *The Structure of Scientific Revolutions*. Chicago: University of Chicago Press.

Laidlaw, James. 2013. "Ethics." In *A Companion to the Anthropology of Religion*, edited by Janice Boddy and Michael Lambek, 171–88. Oxford: Wiley Blackwell.

Laksana, Albertus Bagus. 2014. *Muslim and Catholic Pilgrimage Practices: Explorations through Java*. Farnham: Ashgate.

Lambek, Michael. 2013. "What Is 'Religion' for Anthropology? And What Has Anthropology Brought to 'Religion'?" In *A Companion to the Anthropology of Religion*, edited by Janice Boddy and Michael Lambek, 1–32. Oxford: Wiley-Blackwell.

Latour, Bruno. 1993. *We Have Never Been Modern*. Cambridge, MA: Harvard University Press.

Lee, Benjamin. 2001. Foreword to *Metaculture: How Culture Moves through the World*, edited by Greg Urban, ix–xvii. Minneapolis: University of Minnesota Press.

Leyerle, Blake. 1996. "Landscape as Cartography in Early Christian Pilgrimage Narratives." *Journal of the American Academy of Religion* 64, no. 1: 119–43.

Lochtefeld, James. 2010. *God's Gateway: Identity and Meaning in a Hindu Pilgrimage Place*. Oxford: Oxford University Press.

Löfgren, Orvar. 2008. "Motion and Emotion: Learning to Be a Railway Traveller." *Mobilities* 3, no. 3: 331–51.

Lois-González, Rubén C. 2013. "The Camino de Santiago and its Contemporary Renewal: Pilgrims, Tourists and Territorial Identities." *Culture and Religion* 14, no. 1: 8–22.

Loseries-Leick, Andrea. 1998. "On the Sacredness of Mount Kailasa in the Indian and Tibetan Sources." In *Pilgrimage in Tibet*, edited by Alex McKay, 143–64. Richmond, VA: Curzon.

Loustau, Marc. 2019. "Substituting Stories: Narrative Arcs and Pilgrimage Material Culture between Lourdes and Csíksomlyo." *Journal of Global Catholicism* 3, no. 1: 101–25.

Loustau, Marc, and Kate DeConinck. 2019. "Editor's Introduction." *Journal of Global Catholicism* 3, no. 1: 13–25.

Luhrmann, Tanya. 2004. "Metakinesis: How God Becomes Intimate in Contemporary U.S. Christianity." *American Anthropologist* 106, no. 3: 518–28.

Luz, Nimrod. 2020. "Pilgrimage and Religious Tourism in Islam." *Annals of Tourism Research* 82. doi.org/10.1016/j.annals.2020.102915.

Luz, Nimrod, and Noga Collins-Kreiner. 2015. "Exploring Jewish Pilgrimage in Israel." In *International Perspectives on Pilgrimage Studies: Itineraries, Gaps and Obstacles*, edited by Dionigi Albera and John Eade, 134–51. London Routledge.

Luz, Nimrod, and Nurit Stadler. 2018. "Urban Planning, Religious Voices and Ethnicity in the Contested City of Acre: The Lababidi Mosque Explored." In *Urban Geopolitics. Rethinking Planning in Contested Cities*, edited by Jonathan Rokem and Camilo Bonano, 138–51. London: Routledge.

Lyotard, Jean-François. 1979. *The Postmodern Condition: A Report on Knowledge*. Minneapolis: University of Minnesota Press.

MacCannell, Dean. 1976. *The Tourist: A New Theory of the Leisure Class*. New York: Schocken.

MacClancy, Jeremy, and Robert Parkin. 1997. "Revitalization or Continuity in European Ritual? The Case of San Bessu." *Journal of the Royal Anthropological Institute* 3: 61–78.

Macfarlane, Robert. 2012. *The Old Ways: A Journey on Foot*. London: Penguin.

MacLaine, Shirley. 2001. *The Camino: A Journey of the Spirit*. New York: Pocket.

MacWilliams, Mark. 2002. "Virtual Pilgrimages on the Internet." *Religion* 32, no. 4: 315–35.

———. 2004. "Virtual Pilgrimage to Ireland's Croagh Patrick." In *Religion Online: Finding Faith on the Internet*, edited by Lorne Dawson and Douglas Cowan, 223–38. New York: Routledge.

Maddrell, Avril, and Richard Scriven. 2016. "Celtic Pilgrimage, Past and Present: From Historical Geography to Contemporary Embodied Practices." *Social & Cultural Geography* 17, no. 2: 300–21.

Malinowski, Bronislaw. 1922. *Argonauts of the Western Pacific: An Account of Native Enterprise and Adventure in the Archipelagoes of Melanesian New Guinea*. London: Routledge.

Marcus, George. 1995. "Ethnography in/of the World System: The Emergence of Multi-Sited Ethnography." *Annual Review of Anthropology* 24: 95–117.

Margry, Peter. 2008. "Secular Pilgrimage: A Contradiction in Terms?" In *Shrines and Pilgrimage in the Modern World: New Itineraries into the Sacred*, edited by Peter Margry, 13–46. Amsterdam: Amsterdam University Press.

Marsden, Magnus, and Kostas Retsikas. 2013. "Un-expecting Muslims: Islam, Anthropology, Ethnography." In *Articulating Islam: Anthropological Approaches to Muslim Worlds*, edited by Magnus Marsden and Kostas Retsikas, 1–31. Dordrecht: Springer.

Martin, Wallace. 1986. *Recent Theories of Narrative*. Ithaca, NY: Cornell University Press.

Marx, Emanuel. 2013. *Bedouin of Mount Sinai: An Anthropological Study of Their Political Economy*. Oxford: Berghahn.

Massey, Doreen. 1993. "Power-Geometry and a Progressive Sense of Place." In *Mapping the Futures*, edited by Jon Bird, Barry Curtis, Tim Putnam, George Robertson, and Lisa Tickner, 59–69. London: Routledge.

———. 2005. *For Space*. London: Sage.

Masuzawa, Tomoko. 2005. *The Invention of World Religions: Or, How European Universalism Was Preserved in the Language of Pluralism*. Chicago: University of Chicago Press.

Mayblin, Maya. 2017. "The Lapsed and the Laity: Discipline and Lenience in the Study of Religion." *Journal of the Royal Anthropological Institute* 23, no. 3: 503–22.

McDougall, Debra. 2009. "Rethinking Christianity and Anthropology: A Review Article." *Anthropological Forum* 19, no. 2: 185–94.

McLoughlin, Seán. 2009. "Contesting Muslim Pilgrimage: British-Pakistani Identities, Sacred Journeys to Makkah and Madinah and the Global Postmodern." In *Pakistani Diasporas: Culture, Conflict and Change*, edited by Virinder Kalra, 233–65. Oxford: Oxford University Press.

Meneley, Anne. 2019. "Walk This Way: Fitbit and Other Kinds of Walking in Palestine." *Cultural Anthropology* 34, no. 1: 130–54.

Mentore, George. 2009. "Interview with Edith Turner." *Revista de Antropología Iberoamericana* 4, no. 3: i–xviii.

Merleau-Ponty, Maurice. 1945. *Phénomènologie de la perception*. Paris: Gallimard.

Mesaritou, Evgenia. 2009. "The Dialectics of the Sacred: Institutionalization, Power and Transformation of Padre Pio's Charisma at the Shrine of Santa Maria delle Grazie." PhD diss., University of Cambridge.

Mesaritou, Evgenia, and Simon Coleman. 2018. "On Distinction and Devotion: Shifting Boundaries between Pilgrimage and Tourism." *Groniek* 215: 179–92.

Mesaritou, Evgenia, Simon Coleman, and John Eade. 2016. "Introduction: Guiding the Pilgrim." *Tourism Studies* 16, no. 1: 3–22.

Messerschmidt, Don, and Jyoti Sharma. 1981. "Hindu Pilgrimage in the Nepal Himalayas." *Current Anthropology* 22, no. 5: 571–72.

Meyer, Birgit. 2004. "Christianity in Africa: From African Independent to Pentecostal-Charismatic Churches." *Annual Review of Anthropology* 33: 447–74.

Meyer, Birgit, and Peter Pels, eds. 2003. *Magic and Modernity: Interfaces of Revelation and Concealment*. Stanford, CA: Stanford University Press.

Mikaelsson, Lisbeth. 2018. "Nidaros Cathedral: A Recreated Pilgrim Church." *Religion* 49, no. 1: 99–119.

Mikaelsson, Lisbeth, and Torunn Selberg. 2020. "Caminoization at Sea: The Fjord Pilgrim Route in Norway." *Numen* 67: 537–56.

Miles-Watson, Jonathan, and Sukanya Miles-Watson. 2011. "Conflicts and Connections in the Landscape of the Manimahesh Pilgrimage." *Tourism* 59, no. 3: 319–33.

Mitchell, Hildi. 2002. "Postcards from the Edge of History: Narrative and the Sacralization of Mormon Historical Sites." In *Pilgrim Voices: Narrative and Authorship in Christian Pilgrimage*, edited by Simon Coleman and John Elsner, 133–58. Oxford: Berghahn.

Mitchell, Jon. 2007. "Ritual Structure and Ritual Agency: 'Rebounding Violence' and Maltese Festa." *Social Anthropology* 12, no. 1: 57–75.

Mitchell, Timothy. 1988. *Colonising Egypt*. Berkeley: University of California Press.

Mols, Luitgaard, and Marjo Buitelaar, eds. 2015. *Hajj: Global Interactions through Pilgrimage*. Leiden: Sidestone.

Moore, Sally F., and Barbara Myerhoff, eds. 1977. *Secular Ritual*. Amsterdam: Van Gorcum.

Morgan, David. 2005. *The Sacred Gaze: Religious Visual Culture in Theory and Practice*. Berkeley: University of California Press.

Morinis, Alan. 1984. *Pilgrimage in the Indian Tradition: A Case Study of West Bengal*. Oxford: Oxford University Press.

———. 1992. "The Territory of the Anthropology of Pilgrimage." In *Sacred Journeys: The Anthropology of Pilgrimage*, edited by Alan Morinis, 1–27. Westport, CT: Greenwood.

Morinis, Alan, and N. Ross Crumrine. 1991. "La Peregrinación: The Latin American Pilgrimage." In *Pilgrimage in Latin America*, edited by N. Ross Crumrine and Alan Morinis, 1–17. New York: Greenwood.

Morley, David, and Kuan-Hsing Chen. 1996. Introduction to *Critical Dialogues in Cultural* Studies, edited by Stuart Hall, 1–22. London: Routledge.

Muskett, Judith A. 2016. "Mobilizing Cathedral Metaphors: The Case of 'Sacred Space, Common Ground.'" *Practical Theology* 9, no. 4: 275–86.

Müller, Retief. 2011. *African Pilgrimage: Ritual Travel in South Africa's Christianity of Zion*. London: Routledge.

Naquin, Susan, and Chün-fang Yü. 1992. *Pilgrims and Sacred Sites in China*. Berkeley: University of California Press.

Nasr, Vali. 2010. *Meccanomics: The March of the New Muslim Middle Class*. Oxford: Oneworld.

Needham, Rodney. 1975. "Polythetic Classification: Convergence and Consequences." *Man* 10, no. 3: 349–69.

Neville, Gwen Kennedy. 1987. *Kinship and Pilgrimage: Rituals of Reunion in American Protestant Culture*. Oxford: Oxford University Press.

Niedźwiedź, Anna. 2015. "Old and New Paths of Polish Pilgrimages." In *Pilgrimage Studies: Itineraries, Gaps and Obstacles*, edited by John Eade and Dionigi Albera, 69–94. London: Routledge.

Nilsson, Mats, and Mekonnen Tesfahuney. 2016. "Performing the 'Post-secular' in Santiago de Compostela." *Annals of Tourism Research* 57, 18–30.

Nooteboom, Cees. 1992. *De omweg naar Santiago* [Roads to Santiago]. Amsterdam: Atlas.

Nordin, Andreas. 2016. "Cognition and Transfer of Contagious Substance in Hindu Himalayan Pilgrim Journeys." *Open Theology* 2: 3–22.

Norget, Kristin, Valentina Napolitano, and Maya Mayblin, eds. 2018. *The Anthropology of Catholicism: A Reader*. Berkeley: University of California Press.

Nthoi, Leslie. 2006. *Contesting Sacred Space: A Pilgrimage Study of the Mwali Cult of Southern Africa*. London: Africa World.

Obama, Michelle. 2018. *Becoming*. New York: Crown.

Obeyesekere, Gananath. 1981. *Medusa's Hair: An Essay on Personal Symbols and Religious Experience*. Chicago: University of Chicago Press.

Olaveson, Tim. 2001. "Collective Effervescence and Communitas: Models of Ritual and Society in Emile Durkheim and Victory Turner." *Dialectical Anthropology* 26, no. 2: 89–124.

Oliphant, Elayne. 2021. *The Privilege of Being Banal: Art, Secularism, and Catholicism in Paris*. Chicago: University of Chicago Press.

Oliver, Simon. 2017. "The Cathedral and Rooted Growth." In *Holy Ground: Cathedrals in the Twenty-First Century*, edited by Stephen Platten, 23–40. Durham, NC: Sacristy.

Olsen, Daniel. 2008. "Contesting Identity, Space and Sacred Site Management at Temple Square in Salt Lake City, Utah." PhD diss., University of Waterloo.

Olsen, Daniel, and Dallen J. Timothy, eds. 2006a. *Tourism, Religion and Spiritual Journeys*. New York: Routledge.

———. 2006b. "Tourism and Religious Journeys." In *Tourism, Religion and Spiritual Journeys*, edited by Dallen J. Timothy and Daniel H. Olsen, 1–21. New York: Routledge.

Oram, Elizabeth. 2002. "In the Footsteps of the Saints: The Monastery of St. Antony, Pilgrimage, and Modern Coptic Identity." In *Monastic Visions: Wall Paintings in the Monastery of St. Antony at the Red Sea*, edited by Elizabeth Bolman, 203–16. New Haven, CT: Yale University Press.

Orsi, Robert. 2005. *Between Heaven and Earth: The Religious Worlds People Make and the Scholars Who Study Them*. Princeton, NJ: Princeton University Press.

———. 2009. "Abundant History: Marian Apparitions as Alternative Modernity." In *Moved by Mary: The Power of Pilgrimage in the Modern World*, edited by Anna-Karina Hermkens, Willy Jansen, and Catrien Notermans, 215–25. Farnham: Ashgate.

Osella, Filippo, and Caroline Osella. 2003. "'Ayyappan Saranam': Masculinity and the Sabarimala Pilgrimage in Kerala." *Journal of the Royal Anthropological Institute* 9, no. 4: 729–54.

Österlund-Pötzsch, Susanne. 2010. "Pedestrian Art: The Tourist Gait as Tactic and Performance." *Ethnologia Europaea* 40, no. 2: 14–28.

Owen, Suzanne. 2011. "The World Religions Paradigm: Time for a Change." *Arts and Humanities in Higher Education* 10, no. 3: 253–68.

Palmié, Stephan. 2013. *The Cooking of History: How Not to Study "Afro"-"Cuban" "Religion."* Chicago: University of Chicago Press.

Park, Joseph Sung-Yul, and Mary Bucholtz. 2009. "Public Transcripts: Entextualization and Linguistic Representation in Institutional Contexts." *Text & Talk* 29, no. 5: 485–502.

Parker, John, and Hilary Stansworth. 2015. *Explaining Social Life: A Guide to Using Social Theory.* New York: Macmillan.

Parkes, Don, and Nigel Thrift. 1979. "Time Spacemakers and Entrainment." *Transactions of the Institute of British Geographers* 4, no. 3: 353–72.

Pasura, Dominic, and Marta Bivand Erdal, eds. 2016. *Migration, Transnationalism and Catholicism Global Perspectives.* London: Palgrave Macmillan.

Pazos, Antón, ed. 2013. *Pilgrims and Pilgrimages as Peacemakers in Christianity, Judaism and Islam.* London: Routledge.

———. 2014. Introduction to *Redefining Pilgrimage: New Perspectives on Historical and Contemporary Pilgrimages*, edited by Antón Pazos, 1–6. Farnham: Ashgate.

Peacock, James. 2018. "Talking about the Weather: Radical Critical Empathy and the Reality of Communitas." In *The Intellectual Legacy of Victor and Edith Turner*, edited by Frank Salamone and Marjorie Snipes, vii–xv. Lanham, MD: Lexington.

Peacock, James, and Ruel Tyson. 1989. *Pilgrims of Paradox: Calvinism and Experience among the Primitive Baptists of the Blue Ridge.* Chapel Hill: University of North Carolina Press.

Peña, Elaine. 2011. *Performing Piety: Making Space Sacred with the Virgin of Guadalupe* Berkeley: University of California Press.

———. 2017. "Time to Pray: Devotional Rhythms and Space Sacralization Processes at the Mexico–US Border." *Material Religion* 13, no. 4: 461–81.

Percy, Martyn. 2013. *Anglicanism: Confidence, Commitment and Communion.* Farnham: Ashgate.

Peters, F. E. 1994. *The Hajj: The Muslim Pilgrimage to Mecca and the Holy Places.* Princeton, NJ: Princeton University Press.

Pina-Cabral, João, and Frances Pine. 2008. "On the Margins: An Introduction." In *On the Margins of Religion*, edited by Frances Pine and João Pina-Cabral, 1–10. Oxford: Berghahn.

Piraino, Francesco. 2018. "Pilgrimages in Western European Sufism." In *Muslim Pilgrimage in Europe*, edited by Ingvild Flaskerud and Richard J. Natvig, 157–69. London: Routledge.

Platten, Stephen. 2017. *Holy Ground: Cathedrals in the Twenty-First Century.* Durham, NC: Sacristy.

Porter, Jennifer. 2004. "Pilgrimage and the IDIC Ethic: Exploring Star Trek Convention Attendance as Pilgrimage." In *Intersecting Journeys: The Anthropology of Pilgrim-*

age and Tourism, edited by Ellen Badone and Sharon Roseman, 160–79. Chicago: University of Illinois Press.

Porter, Venetia, Abdel Haleem, Karen Armstrong, Robert Irwin, Hugh Kennedy, and Ziauddin Sardar. 2012. *Hajj: Journey to the Heart of Islam*. London: British Museum Press.

Porth, Emily. 2005. "Healing through the Holy Spirit: Contesting Catholicisms and Communitas at a Canadian Catholic Shrine." Master's thesis, McMaster University.

Premawardhana, Devaka. 2018. *Faith in Flux: Pentecostalism and Mobility in Rural Mozambique*. Philadelphia: University of Pennsylvania Press.

Pritchard, Elizabeth. 2015. "Pilgrimages and Publics: The Case of Taizé." *Anthropological Theory* 15, no. 1: 68–91.

Raj, Razaq, and Kevin Griffin. 2015. *Religious Tourism and Pilgrimage Management*. Wallingford: CABI.

Ranger, Terence. 1987. "Taking Hold of the Land: Holy Places and Pilgrimages in Twentieth-Century Zimbabwe." *Past and Present* 117, no. 1: 158–90.

Rao, Ursula. Forthcoming. "Religion and the Public Sphere." In *Oxford Handbook of the Anthropology of Religion*, edited by Simon Coleman and Joel Robbins. Oxford: Oxford University Press.

Rapport, Nigel, and Andrew Dawson. 1998a. "The Topic and the Book." In *Migrants of Identity: Perceptions of Home in a World of Movement*, edited by Nigel Rapport and Andrew Dawson, 3–18. Oxford: Berg.

———. 1998b. "Home and Movement: A Polemic." In *Migrants of Identity: Perceptions of Home in a World of Movement*, edited by Nigel Rapport and Andrew Dawson, 19–38. Oxford: Berg.

Rasch, Nicole. 2016. "The Camino de Santiago as Global Narrative: Literary Representations and Identity Creation." In *The Camino de Santiago in the 21st Century; Interdisciplinary Perspectives and Global Views*, edited by Samuel Sánchez y Sánchez and Annie Hesp, 194–211. London: Routledge.

Reader, Ian. 2005. *Making Pilgrimage, Meaning and Practice in Shikoku*. Honolulu: University of Hawai'i Press.

———. 2007. "Pilgrimage Growth in the Modern World: Meanings and Implications." *Religion* 37, no. 3: 210–29.

———. 2011. "The Shikoku Pilgrimage Online." In *Japanese Religions on the Internet: Innovation, Representation and Authority*, edited by Erica Baffelli, Ian Reader, and Birgit Staemmler, 80–100. New York: Routledge.

———. 2013. *Pilgrimage in the Marketplace*. London: Routledge.

———. 2015. *Pilgrimage: A Very Short Introduction*. Oxford: Oxford University Press.

———. 2017. "Breaking Barriers, Eroding Hegemony: Reflections on the Importance of Multilingual Studies of Pilgrimage beyond the Anglophone World." In *New Pathways in Pilgrimage Studies: Global Perspectives*, edited by Dionigi Albera and John Eade, 181–98. London: Routledge.

Reader, Ian, and Paul Swanson. 1997. "Editor's Introduction: Pilgrimage in the Japanese Pilgrimage Tradition." *Japanese Journal of Religious Studies* 24, no. 3/4: 225–70.

Reader, Ian, and Tony Walter, eds. 1993. *Pilgrimage in Popular Culture*. London: Macmillan.

Redfield, Robert. 1956. *The Little Community*. Chicago: University of Chicago Press.

Reinhardt, Bruno. 2014. "Soaking in Tapes: The Haptic Voice of Global Pentecostal Pedagogy in Ghana." *Journal of the Royal Anthropological Institute* 20, no. 2: 315–36.

Riley, Alexander. Forthcoming. "The French Tradition." In *Handbook of the Anthropology of Religion*, edited by Simon Coleman and Joel Robbins. Oxford: Oxford University Press.

Robbins, Joel. 2003. "What Is a Christian?: Notes Toward an Anthropology of Christianity." *Religion* 33, no. 3: 191–99.

———. 2004. "The Globalization of Pentecostal and Charismatic Christianity." *Annual Review of Anthropology* 33: 117–43.

———. 2006. "Anthropology and Theology: An Awkward Relationship?" *Anthropological Quarterly* 79, no. 2: 285–94.

———. 2007. "Continuity Thinking and the Problem of Christian Culture: Belief, Time, and the Anthropology of Christianity." *Current Anthropology* 48, no. 1: 5–38.

———. 2009. "Pentecostal Networks and the Spirit of Globalization: On the Social Productivity of Ritual Forms." *Social Analysis* 53, no. 1: 55–66.

———. 2014. "The Anthropology of Christianity: Unity, Diversity, New Directions." *Current Anthropology* 55, no. 10: 157–71.

Rock, Stella. 2006. "Pilgrimage." In *The Bloomsbury Handbook to Studying Christians*, edited by George D. Chryssides and Stephen E. Gregg, 195–99. London: Bloomsbury Academic.

———. 2014. "Rebuilding the Chain: Tradition, Continuity and Processions of the Cross in Post-Soviet Russia." In *Orthodox Paradoxes: Heterogeneities and Complexities in Contemporary Russian Orthodoxy*, edited by Katya Tolstaya, 275–301. Leiden: Brill.

Rosaldo, Renato. 1990. "Response to Geertz." *New Literary History* 21: 337–41.

Roseman, Sharon. 2004. "Santiago de Compostela in the Year 2000, from Religious Centre to European City of Culture." In *Intersecting Journeys: The Anthropology of Pilgrimage and Tourism*, edited by Ellen Badone and Sharon R. Roseman, 171–208. Champaign: University of Illinois Press.

———. 2015. "Turigriños Go Home." *Via*, 8. https://doi.org/10.4000/viatourism.1579.

Ross, Deborah. 2011. Introduction to *Image and Pilgrimage in Christian Culture*, edited by Victor Turner and Edith Turner, xxix–lvii. New York: Columbia University Press.

Rountree, Kathryn. 2002. "Goddess Pilgrims as Tourists: Inscribing the Body through Sacred Travel." *Sociology of Religion* 63, no. 4: 475–96.

———. 2006a. *Performing the Divine: Neo-pagan Pilgrimages and Embodiment at Sacred Sites*. New York: Routledge.

———. 2006b. "Performing the Divine: Neo-pagan Pilgrimages and Embodiment at Sacred Sites." *Body & Society* 12, no. 4: 95–115.

Rousseau, Katherine. 2016. "Pilgrimage, Spatial Interaction, and Memory at Three Marian Sites." PhD diss., University of Denver.

Ruel, Malcolm. 1997. *Belief, Ritual and the Securing of Life: Reflective Essays on a Bantu Religion.* Leiden: Brill.

Ruiz-Navarro, Patricia. 2010. "New Guadalupanos: Mexican Immigrants, a Grassroots Organization and a Pilgrimage to New York." In *Gender Religion and Migration: Pathways of Integration*, edited by Glenda Tibe Bonifacio and Vivienne S. M. Angeles, 237–55. Lanham, MD: Lexington.

Saayman, Andrea, Melville Saayman, and Agyapong Gyekye. 2014. "Perspectives on the Regional Economic Value of a Pilgrimage." *International Journal of Tourism Research* 16, no. 4: 407–41.

Sallnow, Michael. 1981. "Communitas Reconsidered: The Sociology of Andean Pilgrimage." *Man* 16, no. 2: 163–82.

Sánchez y Sánchez, Samuel, and Annie Hesp. 2016. *The Camino de Santiago in the 21st Century: Interdisciplinary Perspectives and Global Views.* London: Routledge.

Sangren, Steven. 1987. *History and Magical Power in a Chinese Community.* Stanford, CA: Stanford University Press.

———. 1993. "Power and Transcendence in the Ma Tsu Pilgrimages of Taiwan." *American Ethnologist* 20, no. 3: 564–82.

Santos, Xose, and Laura Pena Cabrera. 2014. "Management of Tourist Flows: The Cathedral of Santiago de Compostela." *Pasos* 12, no. 4: 719–35.

Sax, William. 1991. *Mountain Goddess: Gender and Politics in a Himalayan Pilgrimage.* Oxford: Oxford University Press.

Schwarz, Ori. 2010. "Praying with a Camera-Phone: Mediation and Transformation in Jewish Rituals." *Culture and Religion* 11, no. 3: 177–94.

Scriven, Richard, and Eoin O'Mahony. 2020. "(Re)Inscribing Meaning: Embodied Religious-spiritual Practices at Croagh Patrick and Our Lady's Island, Ireland." *International Journal of Religious Tourism and Pilgrimage* 8, no. 4: 1–13.

Sered, Susan. 1992. *Women as Ritual Experts: The Religious Lives of Elderly Jewish Women in Jerusalem.* New York: Oxford University Press.

———. 2005. "Exile, Illness, and Gender in Israeli Pilgrimage Narratives." In *Pilgrimage and Healing*, edited by Jill Dubisch and Michael Winkelman, 69–90. Tucson: University of Arizona Press.

Shamir, Ronen. 2005. "No Borders? Notes on Globalisation as a Mobility Regime." *Sociological Theory* 23, no. 2: 197–217.

Shehadeh, Raja. 2007. *Palestinian Walks.* London: Profile.

Sherry, John, and Roberts Kozinets. 2007. "Comedy of the Commons: Nomadic Spirituality and the Burning Man Festival." *Research in Consumer Behavior* 11: 119–47.

Shinde, Kiran. 2011. "Placing Communitas: Spatiality and Ritual Performances in Indian Religious Tourism." *Tourism* 59, no. 3: 335–52.

Shultz, John. 2009. "Characters on a Page, Characters on a Pilgrimage: Contemporary Memoirs of the Shikoku *Henro*." PhD diss., University of Manchester.

Sing, Manfred. 2019. "Introduction: (How) Do We Share the Sacred?" *Entangled Religions* 9: 3–33.

Singh, Vikash. 2013. "Work, Performance, and the Social Ethic of Global Capitalism: Understanding Religious Practice in Contemporary India." *Sociological Forum* 28, no. 2: 283–307.

Sjödin, Agneta. 2006. *En kvinnas resa*. Oslo: Bazar.

Slavin, Sean. 2003. "Walking as Spiritual Practice: The Pilgrimage to Santiago de Compostela." *Body & Society* 9, no. 3: 1–18.

Smith, Alison. 2018. "Walking Meditation: Being Present and Being Pilgrim on the Camino de Santiago." *Religions* 9, no. 3: 82.

Smith, J. Z. 1987. *To Take Place: Toward Theory in Ritual*. Chicago: University of Chicago Press.

Smith, William Robertson. 1889. *Lectures on the Religion of the Semites*. New York: D. Appleton.

Snipes, Marjorie M. 2018. "'*Communitas* Keeps Revealing Itself': The Unfinished Business of *Communitas*." In *The Intellectual Legacy of Victor and Edith Turner*, edited by Frank Salamone and Marjorie Snipes, 15–32. Lanham, MD: Lexington.

Soja, Edward. 1996. *Thirdspace: Journeys to Los Angeles and Other Real-and-Imagined Places*. Oxford: Wiley-Blackwell.

Solnit, Rebecca. 2002. *Wanderlust: A History of Walking*. New York: Viking.

Spiegel, Andrew. 2011. "Categorical Difference versus Continuum: Rethinking Turner's Liminal-Liminoid Distinction." *Anthropology Southern Africa* 34, no. 1/2: 11–20.

Spivak, Gayatri. 1999. *A Critique of Postcolonial Reason: Towards a History of the Vanishing Present*. Cambridge, MA: Harvard University Press.

Stadler, Nurit. 2020. *Voices of the Ritual: Devotion to Female Saints and Shrines in the Holy Land*. Oxford: Oxford University Press.

Star, Susan Leigh. 2010. "This Is Not a Boundary Object: Reflections on the Origin of a Concept." *Science, Technology & Human Values* 35, no. 5: 601–17.

Stark, Rodney, and Roger Finke. 2000. *Acts of Faith: Explaining the Human Side of Religion*. Berkeley: University of California Press.

Stark, Werner. 1968. "The Place of Catholicism in Max Weber's Sociology of Religion." *Sociological Analysis* 29, no. 4: 202–10.

Stausberg, Michael. 2011. *Religion and Tourism: Crossroads, Destinations and Encounters*. London: Routledge.

Steil, Carlos. 2018. "The Paths of Saint James in Brazil: Body, Spirituality and Market." In *Pilgrimage and Political Economy: Translating the Sacred*, edited by Simon Coleman and John Eade, 155–72. Oxford: Berghahn.

Stewart, Susan. 1992. *On Longing: Narratives of the Miniature, the Gigantic, the Souvenir, the Collection*. Baltimore, MD: Johns Hopkins University Press.

Stirrat, Roderick. 1991. "Place and Person in Sinhala Catholic Pilgrimage." In *Contesting the Sacred: The Anthropology of Christian Pilgrimage*, edited by John Eade and Michael Sallnow, 122–36. London: Routledge.

Strathern, Marilyn. 2004. *Partial Connections*. Walnut Creek, CA: Altamir.

Stromberg, Peter. 1993. *Language and Self-Transformation: A Study of the Christian Conversion Narrative*. Cambridge, UK: Cambridge University Press.

Stronza, Amanda. 2001. "Anthropology of Tourism: Forging New Ground for Ecotourism and Other Alternatives." *Annual Review of Anthropology* 30, 261–83.

Swatos, William, and Luigi Tomasi, eds. 2002. *From Medieval Pilgrimage to Religious Tourism: The Social and Cultural Economics of Piety*. London: Praeger.

Taha, Shadia. 2019. "Sacred Journeys: A Lucrative Revenue Stream." *Journeys* 20, no. 1: 7–30.

Tambiah, Stanley. 1976. "The Galactic Polity in Southeast Asia." In *Anthropology and the Climate of Opinion*, edited by S. A. Freed, 69–97. New York: New York Academy of Sciences.

Tauschek, Markus. 2011. "Reflections on the Metacultural Nature of Intangible Cultural Heritage." *Journal of Ethnology and Folkloristics* 5, no. 2, 49–64.

Taylor, Charles. 1989. *Sources of the Self: The Making of the Modern Identity*. Cambridge, MA: Harvard University Press.

———. 2007. *A Secular Age*. Cambridge, MA: Harvard University Press.

Theos and the Grubb Institute. 2012. *Spiritual Capital: The Present and Future of English Cathedrals*. London: Theos and the Grubb Institute.

Thompson, Ken. 2016. "Stuart Hall at the Open University." *Critical Studies in Media Communication* 33, no. 5: 385–87.

Tomlinson, Matt. 2014. *Ritual Textuality: Pattern and Motion in Performance*. Oxford: Oxford University Press.

Tomlinson, Matt, and Matthew Engelke. 2006. "Meaning, Anthropology, Christianity." In *The Limits of Meaning: Case Studies in the Anthropology of Christianity*, edited by Matthew Engelke and Matt Tomlinson, 1–37. New York: Berghahn.

Tsing, Anna. 2005. *Friction: An Ethnography of Global Connection*. Princeton, NJ: Princeton University Press.

———. 2012. "Frictions." In *The Wiley-Blackwell Encyclopedia of Globalization, edited by George Ritzer, 1–3*. Oxford: Blackwell.

Turner, Edith. 1992. "Prologue: Exploring the Trail." In *Blazing the Trail: Way Marks in the Exploration of Symbols*, edited by Edith Turner, ix–xxi. Tucson: University of Arizona Press.

———. 1993. "The Reality of Spirits: A Tabooed or Permitted Field of Study?" *Anthropology of Consciousness* 4, no. 1: 9–12.

———. 2006. *Heart of Lightness: The Life Story of an Anthropologist*. Oxford: Berghahn.

———. 2011. Preface to the paperback edition of *Image and Pilgrimage in Christian Culture*, by Victor Turner and Edith Turner, xiii–xxi. New York: Columbia University Press.

———. 2012. *Communitas: The Anthropology of Collective Joy*. New York: Palgrave Macmillan.

Turner, Victor. 1957. *Schism and Continuity in an African Society*. Manchester: Manchester University Press.

———. 1964. "Betwixt and Between: The Liminal Period in Rites de Passage." In *Symposium on New Approaches to the Study of Religion: Proceedings of the 1964 Annual Spring Meeting of the American Ethnological Society*, edited by June Helm, 4–20. Seattle, WA: American Ethnological Society.

———. 1967. *The Forest of Symbols*. Ithaca, NY: Cornell University Press.

———. 1969. *The Ritual Process: Structure and Anti-structure*. Ithaca, NY: Cornell University Press.

———. 1973. "The Center out There: Pilgrim's Goal." *History of Religions* 12, no. 3: 191–230.

———. 1974. *From Ritual to Theatre: The Human Seriousness of Play*. New York: PAJ.

———. 1993. "Morality and Liminality." *Blazing the Trail: Way Marks in the Exploration of Symbols*, edited by Edith Turner, 132–62. Tucson: University of Arizona Press.

Turner, Victor, and Edward Bruner, eds. 1986. *The Anthropology of Experience*. Urbana: University of Illinois Press.

Turner, Victor, and Edith Turner. 1978. *Image and Pilgrimage in Christian Culture*. New York: Columbia University Press.

Tweed, Thomas. 1997. *Our Lady of the Exile: Diasporic Religion at a Cuban Catholic Shrine in Miami*. New York: Oxford University Press.

———. 2006. *Crossing and Dwelling: A Theory of Religion*. Cambridge, MA: Harvard University Press.

Urban, Greg. 2011. *Metaculture: How Culture Moves through the World*. Minneapolis: University of Minnesota Press.

Urry, John. 1990. *The Tourist Gaze: Leisure and Travel in Contemporary Societies*. London: Sage.

———. 2000. *Sociology beyond Societies: Mobilities for the Twenty-First Century*. London: Routledge.

Vadakkiniyil, Dinesan. 2019. "Mahishi's Rage: Communitas and Protest at Sabarimala, Kerala." *Anthropology Today* 35, no. 5: 16–20.

van der Beek, Suzanne. 2018. "Pilgrim Narratives in Dialogue." PhD diss., Tilburg University.

van der Veer, Peter. 1988. *Gods on Earth: The Management of Religious Experience and Identity in a North Indian Pilgrimage Centre*. London: LSE Monographs.

van Gennep, Arnold. 1960. *The Rites of Passage*. London: Routledge.

Varlik, Nükhet. 2017. *Plague and Contagion in the Islamic Mediterranean*. Kalamazoo, MI: Arc Humanities.

Vásquez, Manuel. 2008. "Studying Religion in Motion: A Networks Approach." *Method and Theory in the Study of Religion* 20, no. 2: 151–84.

———. 2011. *More Than Belief: A Materialist Theory of Religion*. Oxford: Oxford University Press.

Vukonić, Boris. 1996. *Tourism and Religion*. Oxford: Pergamon Press.

Wagner, Roy. 1981. *The Invention of Culture*. Chicago: University of Chicago Press.

Wallace, Anne. 1993. *Walking, Literature and English Culture*. Oxford: Clarendon.

Warner, Martin. 1996. *Walsingham: An Ever-Circling Year*. Oxford: Oxford University Press.

Warner, Michael. 2002. *Publics and Counterpublics*. New York: Zone.

Weatherdon, Meaghan. 2020. "The Rise of Nishiyuu: Walking the Land for Self-Determination." PhD diss., University of Toronto.

Weber, Donald. 1995. "From Limen to Border: A Meditation on the Legacy of Victor Turner for American Cultural Studies." *American Quarterly* 47, no. 3: 525–36.

Werbner, Pnina. 2003. *Pilgrims of Love: The Anthropology of a Global Sufi Cult*. London: Hurst.

Werbner, Richard, ed. 1977. *Regional Cults*. London: Academic Press.

———. 1984. "The Manchester School in South-Central Africa." *Annual Review of Anthropology* 13: 157–85.

Williams, Alan. 1996. Foreword to *Walsingham: An Ever-Circling Year*, by Martin Warner, vii–x. Oxford: Oxford University Press.

Wolf, Eric. 1958. "The Virgin of Guadalupe: A Mexican National Symbol." *The Journal of American Folklore* 71, no. 279: 34–39.

———. 2000. "Pathways of Power: Building an Anthropology of the Modern World." Berkeley: University of California Press.

Woodhead, Linda. 2012. Introduction to *Religion and Change in Modern Britain*, edited by Linda Woodhead and Rebecca Catto, 1–33. London: Routledge.

Yadav, Smita. 2019. "Introduction: Heritage Tourism and Neoliberal Pilgrimages." *Journeys* 20, no. 1: 1–6.

Yamba, C. Bawa. 1995. *Permanent Pilgrims: The Role of Pilgrimage in the Lives of West African Muslims in Sudan*. Edinburgh: Edinburgh University Press.

Yang, Mayfair. 2004. "Goddess across the Taiwan State: Matrifocal Ritual Space, Nation-State, and Satellite Television Footprints." *Public Culture* 16, no. 2: 209–38.

Zandi, Mahshid. 2020. "'Welcome to Divinity College': Subjectificatiion in Pilgrimage to the Iran-Iraq Battlefields in Contemporary Iran." *Journeys* 21, no. 1: 85–104.

Zapponi, Elena. 2011. *Marcher vers Compostelle: Ethnographie d'une Pratique Pèlerine*. Paris: L'Harmattan.

———. 2015. "Italian Studies on Pilgrimage: Beyond Folklore towards a National Anthropological Tradition and the International Circulation of Ideas." In *International Perspectives on Pilgrimage Studies: Itineraries, Gaps and Obstacles*, edited by Dionigi Albera and John Eade, 152–70. London: Routledge.

Zimmer, David. 2018. "Between Art Tourism and 'Protestant Pilgrimage': Individual Journeys to Artworks in Two Churches of Reformed Denomination Near Bern, Switzerland." *Culture and Religion* 19, no. 4: 361–75.

Zwissler, Laurel. 2011. "Pagan Pilgrimage: New Religious Movements Research on Sacred Travel within Pagan and New Age Communities." *Religion Compass* 5, no. 7: 326–42.

INDEX

Abrahamic faiths, 27
abstraction, 69–76
academic representations, 31
"The Accidental Pilgrim" (Harris, E.),
 217–18
Achebe, Chinua, 274n1
actor network theory, 289n13
Acts of Faith (Stark and Finke), 22
adjacency, 11, 151–52, 162–63, 201, 209,
 244–46
Africa, 31–32, 58–59, 259n19, 273n28,
 274n1, 290n21. *See also specific topics*
Agnew, Michael, 142
Albera, Dionigi, 26, 68–70, 104–5, 258n13,
 268n47, 281n50
ambiguous sanctuaries, 104–5
ambulant sciences, 260n33
American Anthropological Association,
 84
analytical perspectives, 12–16, 29–30, 33–
 34, 72–73
Anglicanism, 157–58, 200, 279n23
Anglicans, 147, 158, 199, 279n23
Anglo-Catholicism, 279n23
Anglophone anthropology, 53, 257n33
Anthony, Cara, 219
anthropology: Africa in, 273n28; Anglophone, 53, 257n33; articulation
 in, 290n22; Christianity in, 73–74; of
 communitas, 63–69; of consciousness,
 77; contestation in, 93–96; Eade for, 26;
 entextualization in, 84–86; fieldwork
 in, 40–41; globalization for, 267n40;
 groups in, 59; from Israel, 177–78;

laterality for, 164–65; for Needham, 51;
 of Pentecostalism, 97; pilgrimage in,
 270n71; process, 61; of religion, 21–26;
 rite-of-passage model in, 143–44;
 scholarship for, 29–30, 257n32; singularism for, 262n11; spaces in, 141
antinomianism, 268n46
anti-structure, 69–71, 70–71, 74, 79–80, 120
Apolito, Paolo, 262n10
Appalachian Camino, 125
archaeological sites, 25–26
architecture, 11
Aristotle, 177
Armenian Orthodox Christians, 196
Articulating Islam (Marsden and Retsikas), 8
articulation: analytical perspectives of,
 15–16; in anthropology, 290n22; approaches for, 108–9; of connectivity,
 13; definitions of, 7–8, 50–53, 264n25;
 disarticulation and, 8–9; in England,
 109–10; extended, 188–93; friction and,
 107–12; of Hajj, 283n26; for Hall, 135;
 hidden, 96–100; internal, 79; for Judaism, 260n34; of laterality, 11, 279n13;
 of liminality, 11, 250–51; of penumbra,
 139–45, 155–56; of pilgrimage, 206–7; in
 rituals, 107–8, 165–66, 284n39
Arunta tribe, 38–39
Asia, 263n17
Asociación Tepeyac, 230
assassinations, 39–40
Australia, 126
Austria, 25

authenticity traps, 130–31
autobiographical narratives, 188–89
awkward engagement, 111, 142

Badone, Ellen, 78–79, 283n27
Bálint, Sándor, 41
Barna, Gábor, 41
Bauman, Zygmunt, 37–38, 214
Becket, Thomas, 1–2
van der Beek, Suzanne, 185–87
belief, 259n32
belonging, 230–31
Benjamin, Walter, 245
Between Babel and Pentecost (Corten and
    Marshall-Fratani), 36
"Betwixt and Between" (Turner, V.), 62
Bhabha, Homi, 265n18
Bharati, Aghehananda, 257n3
Bhardwaj, Surinder, 32, 46–47, 50, 259n20
Bianchi, Robert, 167–68, 208, 242, 283n24
Bingenheimer, Marcus, 26
Bloch, Maurice, 103–4, 107, 165–66, 201,
    218, 243, 281n49, 283n29, 284n39
borders, 274n35
Bosnia, 193–94
Bowman, Glenn, 95, 105–6, 121, 257n5,
    268n47
Brazil, 125–26, 276n28
Bremborg, Anna Davidson, 221
Buber, Martin, 64–65
Buddhism: Buddha, 3; Christianity com-
    pared to, 126; Hinduism and, 51–52,
    262n8; in Japan, 188; mobility for, 210;
    self-cultivation in, 273n29; Shikoku
    for, 4, 126, 188; shrines in, 31; in Tai-
    wan, 102; in Thailand, 77
Buitelaar, Marjo, 127–28, 190, 239, 242,
    261n2, 261n4, 268n52, 270n66, 283n26
Burning Man ceremony, 82
Buyskykh, Iuliia, 106–7

Caidi, Nadia, 189–90
Cameron, David, 2

Camino: *Caminoization*, 276n22;
    economies of, 287n34; for Europe,
    216–17, 222–25; Hajj compared to,
    127–28; history of, 113–22, 276n24;
    hypermobility at, 219–20; narratives
    from, 185–87, 282n16; Pentecostalism
    related to, 289n6; psychology of, 217–
    18, 226–27, 278n10; for religion, 168,
    245, 287n32; scholarship on, 129–34,
    187–88; Shikoku compared to, 10,
    283n27; for social sciences, 133–35;
    spaces in, 221–22; spirituality from,
    218–19; in Sweden, 287n33; tourism
    at, 122–29, 241–42; in United States,
    194–95; Walsingham compared to,
    281n52
Camino de Santiago, 115–16
"The Camino is Alive" (González), 223
The Camino Letters (Kirkpatrick), 114
candles, 160–62, 280n43
Cannell, Fenella, 73–74, 267n43
Canterbury Cathedral, 1–2, 6–7, 210–11,
    256n19
Canterbury Tales (Chaucer), 3, 124
cathedrals, 156–60, 163–65
Catholicism: Anglo-Catholicism, 279n23;
    Christianity compared to, 199–200;
    communitas for, 267n38; hierarchies
    in, 48; Islam and, 262n7; in Mexico,
    228–30; pilgrimage in, 228–30; Protes-
    tantism and, 191–92, 231; Reformation
    for, 118, 146–47; scholarship on, 130;
    Second Vatican Council, 74; in Spain,
    116, 227; Vatican II for, 63, 89, 91, 116,
    267n37, 268n44; worship in, 74–75. *See
    also* Roman Catholics
Cavanaugh, William, 38
Certeau, Michel de, 95, 107, 279n15,
    284n39
charisma, 70
Charlemagne, 115–16
Chaucer, Geoffrey, 3, 124
China, 82–83

ABOUT THE AUTHOR

Simon Coleman is Chancellor Jackman Professor at the Department for the Study of Religion, University of Toronto. He is former President of the Society of the Anthropology of Religion, American Anthropological Association, and is Coeditor of the journal *Religion and Society*. Among his books are *Pilgrimage Past and Present in the World Religions* (Harvard University Press, 1995) and the edited volume *Pilgrimage and Political Economy* (Berghahn, 2018).